83 MINUTES

83 MINUTES

THE DOCTOR, THE DAMAGE, AND THE SHOCKING DEATH OF MICHAEL JACKSON

MATT RICHARDS & MARK LANGTHORNE

THOMAS DUNNE BOOKS
St. Martin's Press
New York

THOMAS DUNNE BOOKS.
An imprint of St. Martin's Press.

83 MINUTES. Copyright © 2015 by Matt Richards and Mark Langthorne. All rights reserved. Printed in the United States of America. For information, address St. Martin's Press, 175 Fifth Avenue, New York, N.Y. 10010.

www.thomasdunnebooks.com
www.stmartins.com

Designed by Blink Publishing

Library of Congress Cataloging-in-Publication Data

Names: Richards, Matt, 1967– author. | Langthorne, Mark, author.
Title: 83 minutes : the doctor, the damage, and the shocking death of
    Michael Jackson / Matt Richards and Mark Langthorne.
Other titles: Eighty-three minutes
Description: First U.S. edition. | New York : Thomas Dunne Books, 2016.
Identifiers: LCCN 2016005229| ISBN 9781250108920 (hardcover) |
    ISBN 9781250108937 (e-book)
Subjects: LCSH: Jackson, Michael, 1958–2009. | Jackson, Michael, 1958–2009—
    Death and burial. | African American rock musicians—Biography. |
    Rock musicians—United States—Biography. | African American singers—
    Biography. | Singers—United States—Biography. | Rock musicians—
    United States—Death.
Classification: LCC ML420.J175 R53 2016 | DDC 782.42166092—dc23
LC record available at http://lccn.loc.gov/2016005229

Our books may be purchased in bulk for promotional, educational, or business use. Please contact your local bookseller or the Macmillan Corporate and Premium Sales Department at 1-800-221-7945, extension 5442, or by e-mail at MacmillanSpecialMarkets@macmillan.com.

First published in Great Britain by Blink Publishing, an imprint of the Bonnier Publishing Group

First U.S. Edition: June 2016

10   9   8   7   6   5   4   3   2   1

For Lucy and Tom
– Matt

For Marc and Roland
– Mark

1

*Never say goodbye because goodbye means going
away and going away means forgetting.*
J.M. Barrie, *Peter Pan*

T hursday, 25 June 2009. In time zones around the world, the
news was dominated by one headline: 'Michael Jackson, the
"King of Pop", is dead.'

Earlier that day, at 13:14 Pacific Standard Time (PST), an
ambulance had arrived at the Ronald Reagan UCLA Medical
Center in Los Angeles. Anxious to shield the identity of the patient
it was carrying from the gathering press, the vehicle reversed up
to the doors of the Emergency Room (ER) and a towel was placed
over the face of the casualty. The ambulance was returning from a
911 emergency call placed at 12:21 PST, some 53 minutes earlier.
Alberto Alvarez had made the call from a mansion in nearby
Carolwood Drive.

This mansion, in the prestigious area of Holmby Hills, was
being rented for $100,000 per month by a man who was once the
biggest pop star in the world and who remained one of the most
famous and fascinating figures on the planet: Michael Jackson.

Jackson was in Los Angeles to rehearse and prepare for his

upcoming and eagerly anticipated 'This Is It' comeback tour, which consisted of 50 sold-out shows in the UK at London's O2 Arena and which was scheduled to begin in just 13 days time.

Jackson's rented property was only four minutes from UCLA. The 911 call was frantic with audible commotion in the background, including the angry voice of someone speaking in an undistinguishable foreign language:

911 Operator: Paramedic 33, what is the nature of your emergency?

Alvarez: Yes, sir, I need an ambulance as soon as possible.

911 Operator: Okay, sir, what is your address?

Alvarez: Los Angeles, California, 90077.

911 Operator: Is it Carolwood?

Alvarez: Carolwood Drive, yes [barely audible]

911 Operator: Okay, sir, what's the phone number you're calling from and [barely audible] and what exactly happened?

Alvarez: Sir, we have a gentleman here that needs help and he's not breathing, he's not breathing and we need to – we're trying to pump him but he's not…

911 Operator: Okay, how old is he?

Alvarez: He's fifty years old, sir.

911 Operator: Fifty? Okay, he's unconscious and he's not breathing?

Alvarez: Yes, he's not breathing, sir.

911 Operator: Okay, and he's not conscious either?

Alvarez: No, he's not conscious, sir.[1]

Neither the 911 operator, nor the team of paramedics dispatched from Fire Station 71 in Bel Air to this emergency call were aware that the 'gentleman' who was unconscious and not breathing was none other than Michael Jackson.

They didn't even initially recognise Jackson when they arrived at his beside at 12:26 (PST). Paramedic Richard Senneff, who testified at the 2011 trial into Jackson's death, said: 'And the patient, he appeared to me to be pale and underweight. I was thinking along the lines of this is a hospice patient.'[2]

For the next 31 minutes, Senneff and his team of paramedics worked tirelessly on Jackson's body to save his life. It appeared a futile task. All the evidence in front of them suggested that Jackson had gone into arrest long before they had arrived, but one man present in the room convinced the paramedics to continue. 'It had just happened', he said of the patient's arrest. This man was Dr Conrad Murray, Jackson's personal physician.

Regardless of his assurances, Paramedic Senneff wasn't convinced. 'There is a lot of little variables. But all I can tell you is it was my gut feeling at the time this did not just happen', Senneff said at the 2011 trial.

Nevertheless, Senneff and his team continued though, despite their best efforts, they could not revive the 'King of Pop'. Throughout the procedure, Richard Senneff was in contact with UCLA, whose doctors and nurses were relaying to him standard orders for the procedure via mobile phone.

At 12:57 (PST), Senneff and his team were advised over the mobile phone by Dr Richelle Cooper at UCLA that all attempts were futile, they had done all they could, and permission was given to pronounce the patient dead.

Dr Murray, however, was determined not to accept this pronunciation of death and, inspecting the patient himself, declared that he had felt a femoral pulse in Jackson's neck. Paramedic Senneff checked the same area. He felt nothing, but Murray implored the paramedics to continue, demanding that Jackson be transferred to UCLA for further care.

Richard Senneff discussed the situation with UCLA, relaying

the conversation he had had with Dr Murray and explaining that the patient's personal physician wasn't comfortable with the decision to stop treatment at that point. UCLA replied by asking if Dr Murray was willing to assume complete control of the call and, if so, whether he was also willing to accompany the patient in the ambulance to the hospital. Dr Murray responded categorically that he *would* assume control. In his statement to police, Dr Murray would later say:

> I mean I love Mr. Jackson. He was my friend. And he opened up to me in different ways. And I wanted to help him as much as I can. You know, he was a single parent. You don't always hear that from a man. But he would state that, you know, he was a single parent of three. And I – I always thought of his children, you know, as I would think about mine. So I wanted to give him the best chance.[3]

With the paramedics now having relinquished authority, Jackson was placed on a gurney and put in the ambulance at 13:07 (PST). It was now over 40 minutes since the paramedics had first arrived at the scene.

As the ambulance slowly reversed out into the street, a bus carrying 13 tourists on a guided tour of the homes of Hollywood stars saw the drama unfold. 'This is Michael Jackson's estate everyone,' the tour guide announced, 'so we'll find out later in the news what happened.'[4]

By this stage, the broadcasters, bloggers, paparazzi and the internet outlets were aware that something was happening with Michael Jackson, and the ambulance was followed by an increasing number of cars, motorcycles and helicopters as it made its way to UCLA.

Seven minutes later, the ambulance backed up to the UCLA Medical Center door. A crowd had already begun to gather and hospital security had yet to be deployed. Dr Murray asked, before Jackson was taken off the ambulance, whether a towel or something could be put over Michael's face. When this was done, the back doors of the ambulance were opened and the gurney carrying the body of Michael Jackson was rolled through the security corridor and right into the ER where Dr Richelle Cooper and her team of 14 staff were ready to go to work.

Dr Murray had also made his way into the ER and immediately came face-to-face with Dr Cooper who, just under 20 minutes earlier, had been prepared, according to LA County EMS[5] Protocols, to pronounce Michael Jackson dead.

The first thing Dr Cooper wanted to know from Dr Murray, as Jackson was being placed on monitors, was Murray's interpretation of what had happened. He simply told her that the patient had not been ill but had been working long hours, that Jackson had had trouble sleeping and was dehydrated.[6]

Dr Cooper asked about any narcotics Dr Murray might have given the patient and he stated that he had given Jackson 2mg of Lorazepam, a drug generally used to treat anxiety disorders, at some point during the morning and then later given him another 2mg of the same drug before he witnessed the patient arrest.[7]

She continued to ask Dr Murray about any other drug administration, drug use or history of drug use in the patient. Murray told her that Jackson was also taking Flomax (used for urinary problems in someone who has a large prostate) and Valium (used, like Lorazepam, as a sedative).[8]

Following this brief exchange, Dr Murray could only watch on as Dr Cooper and her team did everything possible to revive the stricken Jackson.

Dr Cooper later testified:

> There was a report by Dr Murray that he had felt a
> faint pulse separate, which conflicted with the report
> of the paramedics that there wasn't a pulse. When the
> patient arrived, I made the decision we will attempt to
> resuscitate to confirm.

Dr Cooper and her team resumed CPR on Jackson, administered more medications, including initial IV fluids (based on the reported dehydration) and ventilated the patient – but everyone in the room was aware they were fighting a losing battle.

There was a small glimmer of hope at 13:21 (PST) when one of the medical team thought they found a weak femoral pulse in Jackson but, despite more medication being administered, there was no return to what Dr Cooper described as '…spontaneous circulation'.[9]

Another member of the medical team at UCLA, Cardiology Fellow Dr Thao Nguyen, also spoke to Dr Murray to enquire about the medication he might have already administered to Jackson. Dr Murray said he had given Jackson 4mg of Ativan (a trademarked name for Lorazepam) and then continued to say he '…later found the patient not breathing'.[10] Dr Nguyen asked Dr Murray for any recollection of time, such as when he found the patient not breathing or when he had found Jackson in relation to the 911 call, but Dr Murray simply responded that he '…had no concept of time'.[11]

While the ER medical team continued their efforts to revive Jackson, elsewhere in the hospital friends and family of the singer were arriving, among them Jackson's mother, Katherine, his three children (Prince, Paris and Blanket) and his brother Jermaine. As they all gathered they had to pass the room where the medical team were working frantically on Jackson. 'Outside the room we heard them working on him. We thought he was alive' said one of those gathered, Jackson's ex-manager Frank Dileo.[12]

Meanwhile, Dr Murray was continuing to watch events unfolding in the ER, as the medical staff made one last effort to save Jackson by inserting an intra-aortic balloon pump: a mechanical device that helps the heart pump blood that is often used for drug-induced cardiovascular failure and increases the oxygen supply direct to the heart muscle. However, as Dr Thao Nguyen stated in her testimony at the 2011 trial, such a procedure is a '…last ditch effort', and was not generally used on a patient without a pulse, but the procedure was implemented in this instance '…per request of Murray not to give up easily'.[13]

Dr Nguyen also stated that '…before inserting the balloon pump, there was an understanding made with Dr Murray that if this method or measure should fail to revive the patient, or resuscitate the patient successfully, we will call it quits.'[14]

The balloon pump was successfully inserted into Jackson but it failed to revive him and, at 14:26 (PST), the singer was pronounced dead.

While this drama was unfolding inside UCLA Medical Center, outside the hospital walls various media outlets were drawing their own conclusions. The USA celebrity website, TMZ.com, was the first to post news of Michael Jackson being unwell and stated that the singer had been taken to a hospital in Los Angeles after suffering a heart attack. There was no confirmation from reliable sources however, and the hospital itself was prevented from making statements owing to patient confidentiality. Even Michael Jackson's father, Joe, was unable to shed any light on the events taking place.

But it wasn't long before the *Los Angeles Times* claimed it had verified the news that Jackson was not breathing when paramedics arrived at his Carolwood mansion. And the news all Jackson fans had been dreading arrived just minutes later when TMZ.com, despite no formal confirmation, published a story, which began: 'We've just learned Michael Jackson has died. He was 50.'

Given TMZ.com's reputation for showbiz scoops, many began to believe that this story was accurate and news channels across the planet began reporting Jackson's death, even though it was still unconfirmed.

Eventually, the Los Angeles Coroner's Office announced that Jackson had been pronounced dead at 14:26 local time and almost four hours later Michael's brother, Jermaine, delivered a carefully worded statement to a gathering of media in the UCLA Medical Center's conference room. In it he said:

> This is hard. My brother, the legendary King of Pop, Michael Jackson, passed away on Thursday, June 25th, 2009, at 2:26pm. It is believed he suffered cardiac arrest in his home. However, the cause of death is unknown until the results of the autopsy are known.

Over the next two months Michael Jackson's body underwent two autopsies, and samples of hair were taken from his corpse for further possible toxicological investigation. The results of these autopsies opened a window to the world on the shocking and tragic life of Michael Jackson. A life that had become, in his later years, swamped and consumed by paranoia, deceit, drug abuse, greed and manipulation. They painted a painful and brutal portrait of an entertainer in the midst of a storm that was always destined to blow itself out in tragic circumstances. They also raised many questions about what really happened to Michael Jackson. And, ultimately, who was responsible for his death.

To find the answers to *these* questions, we need to ask just how did Michael Jackson get to that fateful day in June 2009?

2

He had ecstasies innumerable that other children
can never know; but he was looking through the window at the
one joy from which he must be forever barred.
J.M. Barrie, *Peter Pan*

In the autumn of 2007 Michael Jackson was living in a 1.7-acre compound hidden in the centre of Las Vegas. The property, named Hacienda Palomino, at 2710 Palomino Lane, was owned by the real estate mogul and philanthropist Aner Iglesias and was being leased by Jackson from Iglesias for $7,000 per month.

The house, which was brought over brick-by-brick from Mexico in 1952,[1] featured 12 bedrooms, recording studio facilities, a guest house, lifts leading to the master bedroom and three kitchens, as well as a fountain and a sculpture of a crescent moon being hugged by a pair of nude cherubs. It also included a chapel adorned with musical insignia and guarded by a statue of Saint Francis, the patron saint of animals. The name of the chapel was Neverland Chapel. Beneath the complex was a labyrinthine subterranean vault where, rumour has it, Michael Jackson housed his collection of art, which was insured for $600 million.[2]

Hacienda Palomino, now also called Thriller Villa by some,

is located in a neighbourhood of Las Vegas whose inhabitants are a virtual who's who of the entertainment world, and it's just a few miles away from the glittering lights of the Strip. In 2007, though, Jackson was a million miles away from the heady days of his super-stardom in the early 1980s – a period of global success that saw him dominate pop music and popular culture throughout the world.

The intervening years from 1984 to 2007 had seen Jackson beset by a number of financial problems and personal scandals. Injuries sustained on the set of a Pepsi commercial, as well as a serious back injury suffered during a live show in Germany in 1999, had taken their toll and, as a result, the singer had found himself increasingly dependent on prescription medicines and he had developed a chronic addiction to them over the years.

To make matters worse, his spending seemed out of control and unsustainable. Despite making a fortune from *Thriller* and subsequent albums, such as *Bad* and *Dangerous* (which between them sold over 110 million copies globally) Jackson owed $30 million by 1993. Just five years later that debt had grown to $140 million.

In the last couple of years of his life, Jackson was still earning around $25 million annually, a sum derived mainly from song royalties and revenue from his joint share in the Sony/ATV catalogue[3] (he had purchased this for $49.5 million in 1985 and the catalogue included every song by The Beatles as well as Elvis Presley hits such as 'Hound Dog' and 'Jailhouse Rock', amongst others). However, Jackson was spending up to two and half times his annual income – and had been doing so for over a decade. By 2007 Jackson's total debts were approaching a staggering half-a-billion dollars. He had countless lawsuits filed against him for unpaid fees or contracts that had been reneged upon. And he was effectively homeless.

It was a spectacular financial fall from grace, and one that had seemed so unlikely a quarter of a century before when, on 30 November 1982, an album was released to the world that went on to become a worldwide phenomenon: *Thriller*. A follow-up to Jackson's critically acclaimed and commercially successful 1979 album *Off The Wall*,[4] *Thriller* wasn't simply an album – it was a work that dominated global media from 1982 to 1984 and made Michael Jackson, quite possibly, the most famous man on the planet.

Recorded over seven months at Westlake Recording Studios in Los Angeles in 1982 at a cost of $750,000, it shipped over 50 million copies worldwide, becoming the biggest-selling album of all time, shifting 500,000 copies per week at its peak. Seven singles were released from the album, including 'Billie Jean', 'Beat It', 'Wanna Be Startin' Somethin'' and the title track 'Thriller'. For their $750,000 investment, CBS made around $60,000,000 from *Thriller*. They cleverly exploited the birth of MTV and spent lavishly on music videos for 'Beat It' and 'Billie Jean' as well as splashing out a reputed $1 million overall on the 14-minute video for 'Thriller'.[5]

Rolling Stone magazine said of Jackson at this time,

> No single artist – indeed, no movement or force – has eclipsed what Michael Jackson accomplished in the first years of his adult solo career. Jackson changed the balance in the pop world in a way that nobody has since. He forced rock & roll and the mainstream press to acknowledge that the biggest pop star in the world could be young and black, and in doing so he broke down more barriers than anybody.[6]

It wasn't only CBS who did well out of the album. Jackson, himself, was reported to have been on an average 42 per cent of the wholesale price of each record sold. This meant that he received just over $2 for every one of the 29 million albums sold in the USA alone.[7] In addition, Jackson made over $15 million from foreign sales and received further income from the royalties for the four songs he composed for the album.[8]

Thriller emerged at exactly the right time, despite the USA being in the midst of a recession. Just a few months earlier in 1982, *Newsweek* had published the article, 'Is Rock On The Rocks',[9] recalling the '...good old days' when artists such as Elvis Presley and The Beatles were worldwide pop music figures, before going on to predict that '...in today's fragmented music marketplace, no rock star can hope to have that kind of impact'. The record industry was in the doldrums, worldwide sales had dropped, there was no excitement in the pop scene and MTV was in its infancy. Michael Jackson's *Thriller* changed all that. It didn't simply knock on the door – it smashed the door down and destroyed the walls around it. Michael Jackson, aged just 24, was now not only the most successful and popular entertainer on the planet, he was also one of the wealthiest.

But success and wealth bring their own set of problems, and Jackson quickly found himself surrounded by hangers-on and advisors, who were keener to look after their own prospects than those of Michael Jackson.

While *Thriller* was being recorded, Jackson was still living at home with his parents. In a rare British interview, he told *Smash Hits'* Mark Ellen,[10] 'I still live with my folks. I'd die of loneliness if I moved out'.[11] In fact, he was living with his family in the five-bedroom, six-bathroom mock Tudor Hayvenhurst mansion in Encino, California, which had been the nerve centre of the Jackson family since his father, Joe, bought it in 1971 for $250,000. Ironically, in a forewarning of what was to come, it was Michael who bought the house from his father when Joe Jackson faced financial difficulties of his own in the early 1980s following some bad investments.[12]

Born in Arkansas in 1928, Joseph 'Joe' Jackson was the eldest of five children. When his own parents divorced, Joe went with his father to Oakland in California while his mother took his brothers and sisters to live in Chicago. Eventually, Joe joined them in Indiana, and it was here that he met Katherine Scruse.[13] Joe was already married, but once divorced began going out with Katherine. In November 1949 the two of them married and within a year had relocated to Gary, Indiana where they moved into a three-bedroom house at 2300 Jackson Street. By May 1966, the house was bursting at the seams with Joe and Katherine sharing the cramped accommodation with their nine children.[14]

During the day, Joe worked as a crane operator, but he had his own musical ambitions and was the guitarist in a four-piece rhythm and blues band called The Falcons, which played in the local bars and clubs. The extra cash Joe made from these gigs enabled him to supplement the family income. The Falcons would cover songs by artists such as Chuck Berry, Little Richard and Otis Redding. The fact that the band would rehearse at weekends in the living room of the Jackson house in Gary meant that Michael was exposed to music and performance from a young age. In his 1988 autobiography, *Moonwalk*, Michael Jackson recalls, 'Music was what we did for entertainment and those times helped keep us together and kind of encouraged my father to be a family-oriented man.'

When Joe's dreams of commercial success for The Falcons foundered, he turned his attention to living out his dreams through the talents of his sons and began working with his three eldest boys, Sigmund (now nicknamed Jackie), Tariano (now known as Tito) and Jermaine. They were known as The Jackson Brothers. Before long, Marlon and Michael had joined the group, and the boys were entering talent contests under the new name of The Jackson Five.

Twice a day, before school and after school, every day of the week, Joe would ensure the brothers rehearsed, but his method of encouragement often bordered on the brutal. Any shortfall in performance or any mistake, however small, would result in Joe smacking the children with his belt, hurling them against walls or even locking them in closets.[15] Michael seemed to suffer more than his brothers as, despite his age and size, he would attempt to fight back, sometimes taking off his shoes and hurling them at his father.

In spite of, or perhaps because of, his brutality towards his sons, they soon began to win talent contest after talent contest, first around their hometown of Gary, Indiana and then further afield in Chicago. In order to pay for all their travelling and accommodation, Joe fixed The Jackson Five up with a booking as a regular act at Mr Lucky's, a notorious Gary nightspot. Here they would perform five sets a night, six nights a week to increasingly appreciative audiences, all the while honing their techniques and repertoire, and it was this constant routine of rehearsals and performance that led them to win a prestigious amateur talent show at The Regal Theatre in Chicago.[16] Soon, in August 1967, they would also win the Superdog Contest, America's most prestigious and competitive talent contest held at the fabled Apollo Theatre in Harlem, which led to them getting their first recording contract with Gordon Keith who ran a company called Steeltown Records in Gary, Indiana. It was shortly afterwards that The Jackson Five released their first single 'Big Boy', which, despite having what Michael Jackson would refer to as a 'mean bass line', was instantly forgettable.

Buoyed by having recorded a single,[17] The Jackson Five continued their relentless schedule, constantly pushed onwards by their father. By 1968 they were gaining quite a reputation and the Motown singer, Gladys Knight, managed to persuade some of Motown's wheelers and dealers to watch them perform in Chicago. But the Motown executives failed to share her enthusiasm for the boys and it took another Motown artist, Bobby Taylor, of Bobby Taylor and the Vancouvers, to champion The Jackson Five before Motown would sit up and take notice.[18] Taylor managed to convince Ralph Seltzer, head of Motown's creative department, to allow the boys an audition in Detroit. However, that same day The Jackson Five were scheduled to appear on *The David Frost Show* in New York. Without consulting Katherine, Joe decided to cancel this TV appearance and head for Detroit, and the Hitsville USA studio, with the boys.

Disappointed as they were to discover upon arrival in Detroit that Berry Gordy, the legendary head of Motown, was actually over 2,000 miles away in Los Angeles, The Jackson Five nevertheless performed James Brown's 'I Got The Feeling' followed by 'Tobacco Road' before finishing with their version of a Motown song, Smokey Robinson's 'Who's Loving You?'. The eight Motown staff members who watched the audition somewhat unenthusiastically didn't applaud or say anything. Ralph Seltzer had filmed the audition and promised that he would make sure that Berry Gordy watched the film.

He kept his promise and within two days, Berry Gordy had viewed the footage of the boys performing enthusiastically and, impressed with what he saw, decided to sign them up. In July 1968, Joe Jackson, without having any independent advice and without reading it properly, signed a contract between Motown and The Jackson Five for an initial year.[19]

Despite the group signing as The Jackson Five, Berry Gordy quickly identified Michael as being the star attraction even though he was only nine years old. When the boys made their public debut as a Motown act in August 1968, with Diana Ross amongst the audience, they were announced as, 'The Jackson Five, featuring sensational eight-year-old Michael Jackson.'[20] A month later, Gordy installed Michael in Diana Ross's house while the other brothers stayed in sleazy hotels in Los Angeles. He reasoned, and hoped, that with the imminent release of the first The Jackson Five single, the already successful Diana Ross would become a mother figure to Jackson and help Michael adapt to superstardom. While Michael was given this special attention, his brothers suffered the indignity of staying in hotels populated by whores and drug dealers. And with Jackson securing the favouritism of Motown's legendary owner, the rift between him and his siblings grew larger still, on course to explode later in all of their lives.

The first Motown single that The Jackson Five were set to release was initially an instrumental track called 'I Want To Be Free' and was intended for Gladys Knight & The Pips. After the lyrics had been written and an exhausting recording session completed, what was then Motown's most expensive single to date was released in October 1969 under the new title of 'I Want You Back' with Michael performing the main vocal. It had also been decided, without Joe Jackson's input, that the group would now be called The Jackson 5.[21] The single was an enormous success. It reached Number 1 in the US *Billboard* Hot 100 Chart and Number 2 in the UK singles chart, selling over 6 million copies worldwide and being voted number 121 of the '500 Greatest Songs of All Time' by *Rolling Stone* magazine.[22] But its biggest impact was introducing the world to Michael Jackson.

The next three singles by The Jackson 5: 'ABC', 'The Love You Save' and 'I'll Be There', all reached the top of the Hot 100, and they became the first recording act in history to have their first four singles all reach Number 1. America was overcome with

Jacksonmania, and it wasn't only restricted to the USA. Their music was a hit worldwide and they soon replaced The Supremes as Motown's biggest-selling group.

Towards the end of 1969, the entire Jackson family moved into a house leased for them in Los Angeles by Berry Gordy, and Michael moved out from Diana Ross's home to join the rest of his family at 1601 Queens Road.[23] By now, The Jackson 5 were becoming regulars on national TV shows and had starting touring throughout the USA to packed out audiences at venues such as Madison Square Garden and the Los Angeles Forum.[24] It was after one of these tours, in May 1971, that Joe Jackson purchased the Hayvenhurst estate although they still kept their small house in Gary, Indiana, and the street upon which it stood, Jackson Street, had now been proudly renamed Jackson 5 Boulevard.

In 1971, the decision was taken to allow Michael to release a solo single, while also remaining a member of The Jackson 5. It was Berry Gordy's idea to take this route and make Michael one of the first acts to 'step outside' a group, although Joe saw it simply as an opportunity to make more money. The song chosen for Michael's first solo release was 'Got To Be There' and it was released in October 1971. It broke into the Top 5 in both the USA and the UK, and sold over 1.5 million copies. His next solo single, 'Rockin' Robin', reached Number 2 on the US *Billboard* Hot 100 and Number 3 in the UK charts. The other members of The Jackson 5 suddenly realised that Michael could achieve success without them. To reinforce this, in 1972 Michael's next solo single was his first record to go to Number 1 as a solo artist. 'Ben' was originally written for Donny Osmond but Michael ended up recording the song when Osmond was unavailable owing to his touring schedule. Written by Don Black and Walter Scharf for the film of the same name, 'Ben' was used over the closing credits of the film and, as well as selling over 1.7 million copies and winning a Golden Globe for Best Song, it was also nominated for an Academy Award for Best Original Song in 1973.[25]

In 1972, after the release and subsequent success of 'Ben', The Jackson 5 embarked on an international tour, which was to begin in England. On this tour, Randy performed with the group for the first time, although he was very much in the background, playing bongos. From England, they hopped across to France, The Netherlands, Belgium, Germany and Switzerland before flying to China, Japan, Australia, New Zealand and then Africa.

Despite the mobs of cheering fans at airports and outside hotels, the decline of The Jackson 5 had already begun. In fact, they were only to have one more chart-topping single, 'Mama's Pearl'. With record sales dwindling, Motown decided to switch their focus towards acts such as Marvin Gaye and Stevie Wonder, leaving Joe Jackson fuming.

However, Joe had other things on his mind. His wife, Katherine, had filed for divorce in January 1973 when she discovered that one of his mistresses was pregnant. Motown, upon hearing of the scandal, were worried about the implications it might have on the wholesome public image of The Jackson 5 as a loving family. They felt that the whole episode could turn into a PR nightmare at a time when the group was already suffering poor record sales. Motown officials and executives were in constant contact with Katherine attempting to persuade her to reconcile with her husband. Michael, however, had already confided to Diana Ross that he was convinced the marriage was over but, after deliberation, Katherine surprised everyone, and delighted the Motown officials, by halting divorce proceedings and moving back into the Hayvenhurst house.[26]

With his marriage seemingly restored, Joe could now concentrate once more on the faltering career of The Jackson 5. Their 1973 album, *Skywriter*, was their least successful album selling only

2.8 million copies worldwide, and failing to even chart in the UK, but Joe was convinced his boys had a future. When Motown postponed the release of one of Michael's singles in 1974 after the disappointing sales of his two previous albums,[27] Joe began to look elsewhere for a record deal. He was to find it at CBS Records. Not only was he looking for more money, more promotion and more control; the boys themselves were eager to compose their own songs for future releases. Motown had categorically told them this was not going to happen and, despite beginning to write individually, none of the Jacksons' original compositions had made it onto any record so far, not even the B-sides.

As well as a $750,000 signing-on bonus, a $500,000 'recording fund' and a guarantee of $350,000 per album, CBS Records were also offering the Jacksons a royalty rate of 27 per cent per record sold, ten times the 2.7 per cent that they were currently receiving from Motown. In addition, there was also some artistic freedom promised, with the boys allowed to choose up to three songs for each album and have their own compositions considered for inclusion.

However, there was a stumbling block that Joe Jackson had failed to consider; Jermaine had fallen in love with, and married, Hazel Gordy, the daughter of the boss of Motown, and, when presented with the new CBS contract, Jermaine refused to sign it. He then called Berry Gordy, his new father-in-law, and explained what was happening and that he was determined to stay with Motown regardless of what his brothers did.

In the meantime, The Jackson 5 still had performances to fulfil. One of them was at the Westbury Music Fair in New York and, although the tension within the family was now at breaking point, Jermaine acted in a professional manner. But, as he was about to take the stage he received a phone call from Berry Gordy. Gordy let it be known to him that he had to decide which family was most important to him, his or the Jacksons. Jermaine completely understood the ramifications of making the wrong decision at this point in his life and so, 30 minutes before the group were due to go on stage, he packed his suitcase, got into a limousine and went to the airport with Hazel from where they flew back to Los Angeles. Distraught, the remaining members of The Jackson 5 took to the stage, with Marlon filling in Jermaine's lines.

Jermaine's departure hit Michael hard. Throughout his career, Jermaine had been the person standing next to Michael on stage, and now he was no longer there. Michael felt that his father, Joe, had handled the situation poorly, not only in the way Jermaine had been forced to make the decision to leave, but also with the way his own career, and that of the Jacksons, were going.

Michael had good cause to be concerned. Berry Gordy wasn't going to let Joe Jackson get away with the split from Motown lightly. In June 1975, Gordy notified Joe that Motown owned the name The Jackson 5 and there was nothing Joe could do about it – he had signed the original contract without reading it in 1968 and there was a clause in it stating that Motown owned all rights to the name. Not stopping there, Gordy also sued Joe Jackson, The Jackson 5 and CBS for $5 million, and suggested he would release, on various compilations, up to 295 songs The Jackson 5 had recorded for Motown and that remained unreleased in their archives.

Michael Jackson would later say the brothers were relieved that they had finally cut ties with Motown, but at the time it must have seemed a terrible misjudgement: they were being sued by Berry Gordy, they also owed another $500,000 for recordings the public hadn't heard, they couldn't use The Jackson 5 name and they would have to wait eight more months, until their contract with Motown ran out, before they could record for CBS.

To fill the gap and to keep them in the public eye, Michael joined his brothers, augmented in performance now by their three sisters, in a new TV series called *The Jacksons* on CBS. A summer variety series, it was the first time a black family had hosted a TV show, but Michael was less than enthusiastic. There already existed an animated *Jackson 5ive* series and Michael felt the new TV series was '…a dumb move' and said later that '…[he] hated every minute of it'.[28] So, it seems, did the viewers as it was cancelled after less than a year.

By now, though, they were back in the recording studio under their new name, The Jacksons. Their first album for CBS was, imaginatively, titled *The Jacksons*. It wasn't a huge hit upon release in 1976, reaching Number 36 in the US *Billboard* Pop Albums. The album did, however, include Michael's first recorded composition, 'Blues Away', a song about a man coming out of depression, which was also the B-side of the single, 'Show You The Way To Go'.[29]

The next album from The Jacksons was a major disappointment. *Goin' Places* was released in October 1977 and only reached Number 63 in the USA and Number 45 in the UK, where it lasted just one week on the charts.[30] Unbeknown to Joe, or any of the boys, CBS had already decided to drop The Jacksons from the label given their slump in fortunes and their apparent decline in popularity.

Bobby Colomby, an executive at CBS, was given the task of getting the label out of their deal with The Jacksons using a $100,000 pay-off to soften the blow. However, Colomby personally liked the band and managed to persuade his bosses to give them one more album to prove themselves. Part of his bargaining was that the group would be more creatively involved so that, if the album proved to be an unmitigated disaster, the only people to blame would be The Jacksons themselves.

Michael was now 19 years old. The Jacksons had failed to set the world on fire and he was no longer the cute kid who reached Number 1 with 'Ben'. Unconvinced that his father, Joe, was the ideal man to take his career forward, let alone that of The Jacksons,

Michael decided to take some time out, away from his family and his father and throw his creative energies into a project elsewhere.

The project that landed on his doorstep was a film, *The Wiz*. An all-black musical interpretation of *The Wonderful Wizard of Oz*, it was actually being made by Berry Gordy's Motown Productions and was to be filmed in New York for three months from October 1977. The Head of Motown Productions, Rob Cohen, wanted Michael to play the role of the Scarecrow and when he mentioned it to the film's leading lady, she wholeheartedly agreed. It helped that the leading lady was none other than Diana Ross. She, in turn, mentioned it to Michael but he was, at first, reluctant. Not because of any doubt over his abilities, but for fear that bad blood might still exist between Berry Gordy and any representative of the Jackson family following their split from Motown two years previously. Diana laid Michael's fears to rest and following an audition with the film's director Sidney Lumet,[31] Michael was offered the part.

Michael was thrilled to land a part in the $24 million film, but his father, Joe, was less than enthusiastic. He was concerned that any solo work by Michael, in whatever creative environment, might overshadow his siblings and create an artistic rift. Joe warned Michael that it would be a big mistake to accept the role, but there was little Joe could do. Michael had loved the stage production of *The Wiz* and he now had a chance to star in the film adaptation of it alongside Diana Ross. There was no way he would turn this chance down so, in July 1977, Michael moved to New York to begin rehearsals and settled into a $2,500 per month apartment in Manhattan with his sister, La Toya.

The film began shooting on 3 October 1977 at New York's Astoria Studios[32] and Michael threw himself into the role. He was a huge fan of Charlie Chaplin and borrowed from some of the mannerisms of Chaplin's characters to bring the Scarecrow to life. Despite Jackson's efforts, the film was a massive flop,[33] with

Motown losing some $10 million on the production. However, Michael did receive some rave reviews for his performance with critics praising his acting talent.[34]

In spite of the film's failure, Michael thoroughly enjoyed the experience. It gave him a new creative avenue for a while and allowed him to distance himself from his family – and most importantly from his father. It also gave him a newfound confidence in himself as an artist. Furthermore, around this time, Jackson met someone who would later have a massive impact on his professional and personal life: Quincy Jones, who had been hired to compose the score for *The Wiz*.

Following his adventure making *The Wiz* in New York, Michael returned to join his brothers at the Hayvenhurst mansion to begin work on the next album from The Jacksons. Given a reprieve by CBS, much depended on the success of this album which was to be titled *Destiny*. For the first time, the brothers were allowed to compose and produce their own material[35] and they wrote much of this new material in their homemade recording studio at Hayvenhurst.

Recording the album within two months alongside an arsenal of veteran and up-and-coming LA session musicians, *Destiny* was released on 15 December 1978 and re-established The Jacksons as a major group. The first single from the album, 'Blame It On The Boogie',[36] didn't perform well in the USA, only reaching Number 54 on the *Billboard* Hot 100, but it did make the Top 10 in the UK. The most successful song on the album, though, was 'Shake Your Body (Down to the Ground)'. Written by Michael with his brother Randy, this disco/funk track peaked at Number 7 on the *Billboard* Hot 100 chart and Number 4 in the UK chart.[37] It sold over 2 million copies in the USA and proved that The Jacksons could write hits themselves when given the opportunity. The success of the singles helped *Destiny* shift over a million copies in the USA alone and it was The Jacksons' biggest album success.

But Michael, by now 21 years old, was still desperate to replicate, and even surpass, The Jacksons' success with his solo career. He was becoming concerned that his brothers were riding on his coat tails. He had assumed most of the lead vocals on the *Destiny* album, was the focal point in most of the group's live performances and had been responsible for writing the biggest hit from the last album.[38] He remained anxious about the role his father, Joe, was having in directing his career and began wondering, in fact, if Joe was stalling his progress rather than progressing it.

Part of the deal with CBS was that Michael would have the opportunity to record solo albums but, as far as CBS were concerned, albums by The Jacksons were consistently out-selling any of Michael's solo work. What Michael desperately needed was a breakthrough album as a solo artist, an album that was significantly different from anything that The Jacksons had recorded, and to achieve that he needed help. Fortunately, he had met just the man to help him while working on *The Wiz* – producer Quincy Jones.

Born in Chicago in 1933, Quincy Jones was inspired by Ray Charles into following his own musical career. After winning a scholarship to Seattle University, where Clint Eastwood was also studying music, Jones joined Lionel Hampton's band as a trumpeter. It was while touring with Hampton that Jones showed an aptitude for arranging songs and this led to him working with artists such as Sarah Vaughan, Count Basie, Duke Ellington and, his idol, Ray Charles. It was in the 1960s that Jones rose to prominence when he became Vice-President of Mercury Records and also composed the music for *The Pawnbroker*.[39] This success saw Jones move to Los Angeles where he was in demand as a composer for film and TV, as well as continuing to arrange songs for artists such as Ella Fitzgerald and Frank Sinatra. He also began producing and in 1975 founded his own production company,

Qwest Productions, through which he produced albums for Frank Sinatra amongst others, as well as the soundtrack for *The Wiz*.

It was while working on *The Wiz* that Michael had asked Jones to recommend some producers for his next solo album. Jones gave him some suggestions for potential producers, talked to him at length about people in the business and pop music in general, and also offered to do whatever he could to help, if Michael needed it. Michael liked what he heard from Jones and in December 1978, shortly after the *Destiny* album had been released, Michael started work on his fifth solo album, with Quincy Jones assuming the role of producer, in Los Angeles.

Originally intended to be titled *Girlfriend*, after the title of the Paul McCartney song that was to be featured on the album, the album would eventually be called *Off The Wall*. Throughout the recording process Michael was as driven as any artist Quincy Jones had previously worked with and the two of them developed a close friendship. Three of Michael's own compositions were to be included on the album: 'Don't Stop 'Til You Get Enough', 'Working Day And Night' and 'Get on the Floor'.[40] Other songs were written by artists as diverse as Stevie Wonder, Carole Bayer Sager, Tom Bahler and, of course, Paul McCartney. One of the other songwriters on the album was Rod Temperton, who would go on to have a long working relationship with Jackson. Temperton was the keyboard player for the British band Heatwave and also their chief songwriter. Quincy Jones had been attracted to some of the songs he had previously written, such as 'Boogie Nights', 'Always and Forever' and 'The Groove Line', and asked him to come up with some songs for *Off The Wall*. Temperton's songs eventually included on the album were 'Rock With You', 'Off The Wall' and 'Burn This Disco Out'.

Michael later reflected that making the album was one of the most difficult periods of his life. His combined hard work and quest for success and perfection left him lonely and isolated, but in terms of musicality, it provided the desired results. Released in the summer of 1979, *Off The Wall* was an enormous success that caught everybody off-guard. The first single released, Michael's own composition, 'Don't Stop 'Til You Get Enough', was his first single to reach Number 1 in the USA in seven years, and was Number 1 in another seven countries, as well as peaking at Number 3 in the UK. It sold over 2.5 million copies and won Michael a Grammy for Best Male R&B Vocal Performance. The album's follow-up single, Temperton's 'Off The Wall' was also a Top 10 hit in both the USA and the UK. This was followed by 'Rock With You', which stormed to the top of the charts in the USA and was another Top 10 hit in the UK. The final release, 'She's Out of My Life', reached the Top 10 in America and Number 3 in the UK. With the success of these four singles, the album became the first ever by a solo artist to generate four USA Top 10 hits.

Off The Wall was a huge hit, both critically and commercially, and Michael, at 21, became a millionaire seemingly at the top of his game. Yet relations with his father remained tense, both personally and professionally, and Michael was becoming increasingly eager to find someone new to represent him in the entertainment industry.

First, however, he had to get back into the studio with his brothers to record their next album. Titled *Triumph*, it was the first album by any of the Jackson groups that was made up entirely of compositions by the brothers. Michael had a hand in six of the nine tracks on the album, including all four singles released: 'Can You Feel It', 'Lovely One', 'Walk Right Now' and 'This Place Hotel'[41] which Michael thought, up to that point, was the most ambitious song he had composed.[42] The singles from *Triumph* performed reasonably well in both the UK and USA charts, but none of them reached Number 1, unlike Michael's previous solo effort, and they sold considerably less.

Now that he was the dominant force in the Jackson family, Michael continued to seek new representation. He found it in the form of John Branca, who was in his early thirties and had a background in corporate tax law and music industry negotiations. Branca's pedigree was certainly good, a product of UCLA and an entertainment lawyer at 27 years old, he had worked with artists such as Neil Diamond, The Beach Boys and Bob Dylan, and Berry Gordy referred to him as '…the Smokey Robinson of deal making'. What's more, Branca loved music, especially rock music.

Shortly after he had hired him, Branca renegotiated Michael's CBS contract and raised his royalty rate to an astonishing 37 per cent. In addition, Branca reached an agreement with CBS and The Jacksons' legal advisors that Michael was free to leave The Jacksons at any time without his brothers' recording deal with CBS being in jeopardy. Initially, Joe Jackson was accepting of the deal. In his mind, The Jacksons were bigger than any one of the brothers individually and the group would continue successfully with or without Michael.

To begin with, that seemed to be the case; the *Triumph* tour, which began in Memphis on 9 July 1981, was hugely successful in its own right, culminating at the Los Angeles Forum with a four-night sell-out run. The show combined the best elements of the *Destiny* and *Triumph* albums with Michael also showcasing his hits from *Off The Wall*, which generally got the best reception from the audiences. This solo-based adulation during the performances coupled with the time Michael spent negotiating his own deals with his lawyer at rehearsals began to widen the rift that had been slowly growing between him and his brothers. A rift that would, over subsequent decades, prove irreparable and isolate Michael even more from the family unit.

Indeed, at this point it began to cause issues at home, which for all of them was still the Hayvenhurst estate. But, in February

1981, presumably no longer too concerned about dying '...of loneliness', as he had once told the British press, Michael actually bought a property for himself in Los Angeles upon the advice of John Branca. Branca was keen for Jackson to establish some form of independence, so encouraged him to buy a three-bedroom condominium for $210,000 a few blocks away from Hayvenhurst. As it turned out, Jackson couldn't bear living away from his mother so he remained in the family mansion, with his new house being used by other family members as a sanctuary during times of difficulty.

One of those family members going through difficult times was Joe Jackson. He had significantly overstretched himself in the previous few years in a doomed attempt to show to Berry Gordy that he could be a successful music mogul in his own right. Now, desperate for cash to get out of the predicament that he found himself in, Joe sold 75 per cent of the stake in the Hayvenhurst estate to Michael. Katherine retained the other 25 per cent so, in effect, Joe was now homeless and dependent on the goodwill of Michael to let him remain in the house.[43]

On 14 April 1982, Michael resumed his partnership with Quincy Jones and began work on his next solo album at Westlake Studios in Los Angeles. It would be his sixth solo album and he reassembled many of the musicians and songwriters who had worked on *Off The Wall*, including Rod Temperton. By April 1982 Michael had sold 6 million copies of *Off The Wall* in the USA alone and 20 million copies worldwide, but he had ambitions to make an even bigger album. He was determined that his new album would be the biggest-selling album of all time.

From an initial 700 proposed songs and demos, Michael and Quincy Jones selected nine that would make up the album and began working on them. For Michael, being the perfectionist that he was, the recording of the album was intense and demanding but

Quincy Jones had full confidence in what they were producing. Speaking to Alex Haley for a *Playboy* interview in 1990, Quincy Jones said:

> All the brilliance that had been building inside Michael Jackson for twenty-five years just erupted. It's like he was suddenly transformed from this gifted young man into a dangerous, predatory animal. I'd known Michael since he was twelve years old, but it was like seeing and hearing him for the first time. I was electrified, and so was everybody else involved in the project. That energy was contagious, and we had it cranked so high one night that the speakers in the studio actually overloaded and burst into flames. First time I ever saw anything like that in forty years in the business.

Originally, this new album was going to be titled *Starlight*, and Michael had written four of the nine songs to be recorded and included on it: 'Beat It', 'Wanna Be Startin' Somethin'', 'This Girl Is Mine' and 'Billie Jean'.[44] These songs, along with the other five, were recorded over eight weeks. All the while, the record company were hassling the production team to deliver, warning them of an impending deadline.

One night, Rod Temperton, who had already written 'Baby Be Mine' and 'The Lady In My Life' for the album, was trying to come up for a catchy title for the album to replace *Starlight*.[45] He wrote down between 200 and 300 prospective titles and arrived at *Midnight Man*. Waking up the next morning, something in his head was telling him another title, and this one stuck. It was *Thriller*.

When the sessions for the album were complete, everyone gathered with a mixture of excitement and apprehension to hear the results. They were all devastated, the final mix just didn't sound good and Michael fled from the studio in tears. Returning later, he demanded that the album not be released. Everybody's hard work and dreams seemed shattered by the reaction to the album, especially Michael's. They needed to rescue the huge investment in the project. There was a solution – the whole album would have to be painstakingly remixed, and that's what happened. When Michael returned to the studio with John Branca a month later to hear the remixes, he was aptly thrilled with what he heard. Those around him, though, warned him not to expect too much with regards to potential sales. The USA was in the middle of a recession and record sales were at a 20-year low. Nobody wanted to get Michael's hopes up and they encouraged him to expect sales in the region of 2 million and not to even hope of replicating the success of *Off The Wall*.

So when it came, the stratospheric reception to *Thriller* caught everyone by surprise and single-handedly transformed the record industry. Selling half a million copies a week at its peak, the album was a musical and cultural phenomenon. Globally, Michael was now a superstar, the biggest star on the planet. Within a year, it had sold nearly 22 million copies worldwide and had already become the biggest-selling solo album ever. In February 1984, it would overtake the Bee Gees' *Saturday Night Fever* and become the biggest-selling album of all time. It spawned seven US *Billboard* 100 Top 10 hits, two of which went to Number 1.[46] The album won a record-breaking eight Grammy Awards in 1984 including Album of the Year and eight American Music Awards. The videos that accompanied some of the singles, especially 'Billie Jean', were lauded for their style and innovation, and the groundbreaking 14-minute video for the 'Thriller' single was an international event in its own right when it was first released and broadcast.

Although the exact figures aren't known, it is estimated that

Michael Jackson made between $92 million and $220 million from the *Thriller* album, thanks to the generous royalty payment John Branca had secured for him. With such success and wealth, it was inevitable that the vultures came circling. Unsurprisingly, Michael's father, Joe, was keen to stay on the scene, putting out the idea for a reunion of all his sons as part of a Jacksons' worldwide tour to capitalise on Michael's global success. It fell on deaf ears and Joe was shocked to receive a letter from John Branca in June 1983 informing him that he, Joe, no longer represented Michael.

Undeterred, Joe could still exert some influence in other ways and reasoned to himself that, given Michael's huge success with *Thriller*, what could be better than to record a new album with The Jacksons, followed by a tour? Even more appealing, he thought, would be the inclusion of Jermaine in the line-up. This could be the answer to all of Joe's financial problems. Michael was totally against the idea, but after a heart-to-heart with his mother, he capitulated, and reluctantly agreed to record the new album, albeit with minimal input, and to grudgingly take part in the subsequent tour.

The album, *Victory*, was the first, and only, album to feature all six Jackson brothers together as a group. Jermaine's solo career at Motown had stalled[47] and Berry Gordy released him from his contract so he could participate in this new Jackson project. Recorded between November 1983 and May 1984, the album sold over 7 million copies worldwide and reached Number 4 on the US *Billboard* 200. Michael wrote two songs for the album: 'Be Not Always'[48] and 'State of Shock',[49] the latter a duet with Mick Jagger and the biggest single success from the album, reaching Number 3 in the USA and Number 14 in the UK.[50] The *Victory* tour[51] that followed, promoted by legendary boxing promoter Don King, took in the USA and Canada, and grossed around $75 million making it, then, the highest grossing tour in history.[52]

Before they could tour though, a sponsor was needed to fund it. Don King had an idea that Pepsi would undertake the sponsorship and they agreed, paying a fee of $5 million up front. Michael was less than enthusiastic about Pepsi coming on-board. He didn't drink Pepsi, he didn't believe in the Pepsi brand, didn't want to appear in a Pepsi commercial and, once all the various expenses and deductions had been taken out and the $5 million split between the rest of the family, Michael would only receive $700,000 – peanuts to a man who was now phenomenally wealthy. For the rest of the group, this was money they couldn't turn down so, one by one, they all cajoled and coerced Michael into agreeing to the deal against his wishes.

On 27 January 1984, Michael arrived at the Shrine Auditorium in Los Angeles to film the Pepsi commercial that was part of the sponsorship deal. A crowd of 3,000 people was assembled to create the atmosphere of a live concert performance. But despite apparently endorsing the product to the public, behind the scenes Michael had stipulated that the only close-up of him was to strictly last for no more than four seconds.

Following five performances during the day to cater for various camera angles and technical requirements, the sixth performance began at 6:30pm. The song they were performing was 'You're A Whole New Generation' and as Michael descended the stairs a magnesium flash bomb went off less than 2 ft away from him. Within seconds, Michael's hair was on fire. People ran onto the stage as Michael pulled his jacket over his head before he fell down in searing pain. He was rushed in an ambulance to Cedars-Sinai Medical Center and treated for third degree burns to his scalp. While in the hospital, he was offered painkillers. Initially he refused, having never taken narcotics of any kind before, but with the pain so intense, he finally accepted and took the painkillers Percocet and Darvocet.[53] The drugs eased the pain, but they were also the catalyst for a tragic chain of events. Before his accident, Michael was, beyond doubt, the King of Pop and was sitting on top of the entertainment world. But this serious injury, and his subsequent exposure to prescription medicine, sent the singer off on a downward spiral of chronic pain and prescription narcotic abuse.

As far as Michael Jackson was concerned, 27 January 1984 was the beginning of the end.

3

All this has happened before, and it will all happen again.
J.M. Barrie, *Peter Pan*

Following recuperation, and a $1.5 million payout from Pepsi to prevent a lawsuit,[1] Michael began work on the *Victory* tour. Despite being opposed to both the album and the tour in the beginning, Michael enjoyed performing with his brothers again. They played 55 shows over five months and it was a chance for them all, and the audiences, to relive the days of The Jackson 5 and The Jacksons. But as the tour progressed, Michael became increasingly unhappy, being particularly disappointed and frustrated with the staging of 'Billie Jean'. His brothers were less than enamoured with Michael, too. He had taken to travelling alone and was refusing to stay on the same hotel floor as them. The tour closed in Los Angeles on 9 December 1984. Whilst its promoters, along with Joe Jackson, were discussing a European leg of the tour, Michael had made his mind up that there would be no more performances. In a final nod to his distaste for the tour, and not wanting any legacy from it, Michael donated his entire earnings from it – some $5 million – to charity.

Before the tour began, Michael had already started to look for a new manager to work alongside John Branca and had decided upon Frank Dileo, whom Michael believed was responsible for a lot of the *Thriller* success in the way he had promoted the album. Frank Dileo had begun his career at RCA Records while in his twenties and then became Epic's Vice-President of Promotion with huge success. He was an enormous character, both in charisma and physical presence, and was just the man to steer Michael forward with John Branca remaining as his attorney.

It was Dileo and, more prominently, Branca who oversaw Michael's purchase of the ATV Music Publishing Company in 1985. The ATV Music Publishing Company held the rights to over 4,000 songs including 251 songs by The Beatles. During a conversation with Paul McCartney in London, Michael had learnt how profitable investments in such catalogues could be and how Paul himself had tried to buy the ATV catalogue previously, but had baulked at the $20 million asking price. Interested enough to pursue this further, Michael first bought the catalogue of Sly Stone to test the water, and in September 1984 he learned from Branca that the ATV catalogue was available. Not entirely certain of what the ATV catalogue consisted of, it was when Jackson discovered that it contained, amongst others, many of The Beatles' hits, as well as songs by Elvis Presley and Little Richard, that he became adamant he must buy it. From September 1984 to May 1985, Branca worked furiously for Jackson in order to secure the catalogue, but it came at a price – $47.5 million.[2] Paul McCartney had also tried to buy the catalogue during this period, and was hoping to convince Yoko Ono, John Lennon's widow, to provide half of the purchase cost. When she didn't, the door for Jackson was wide open. Few could have seen how lucrative this investment would turn out to be, and Jackson's share in the catalogue virtually single-handedly gave him a financial lifeline later in life. It was a lifeline that prevented him from hitting rock bottom earlier, yet perhaps also one that enabled him to avoid confronting his drug addiction.

In 1987 it had been five years since Michael's last solo album. The years in between had seen the *Victory* album and tour, and also, in 1985, the release of the charity single 'We Are The World', which Michael had co-written with Lionel Richie in aid of African famine relief.[3] Michael had also worked on the 3D film *Captain Eo* in 1986, which was to be shown at Disney theme parks.[4] Jackson was paid $3 million to take the lead role in the short film which was about his character, Captain Eo, going on a mission to bring the inhabitants of a miserable planet light and beauty through music and so transform their evil leader, played by Angelica Huston.[5] Once again, as he did on *The Wiz*, Michael thrived on the medium of film, and took advice about acting from Marlon Brando, who had become a close friend at that time. Michael also performed two new songs in the film: 'Another Part of Me' and 'We Are Here to Change the World'.

'Another Part of Me' was to appear on Michael's next solo album, *Bad*. Recorded from January to July 1987, the album had to follow in the footsteps of Jackson's previous solo album, *Thriller*, which had become the world's biggest-selling album of all time. Once again, he recruited Quincy Jones to act as producer[6] and, between them, they worked to make an album that was as close to perfection as humanly possible.

Michael had written 62 potential songs for the album, which had to be whittled down to 30 songs that would be recorded.[7] Eventually, the album consisted of ten songs,[8] of which Michael composed eight.[9] When it was released at the end of August 1987, it reached Number 1 in 25 countries, and spent six weeks at Number 1 on the US *Billboard* 200,[10] selling over 9 million copies in the USA. It also became Jackson's second-most successful album in the UK, selling almost 4 million copies.

The first five singles released from the album all reached Number 1 in the USA,[11] a feat that topped even *Thriller*. Jackson had wanted to create an album that would appeal to all races and all tastes in music but, despite the commercial success, and critical reception[12] to *Bad*, it just didn't measure up to *Thriller*. How could it? By most standards, *Bad* was an astounding success, but Jackson wasn't satisfied. His ambition had been to sell 100 million copies of the album,[13] yet it had sold *only* 35 million copies worldwide and won just one Grammy Award.[14]

The *Bad* tour that followed saw Jackson walk away with $40 million,[15] and 1988 also saw the release of the film, *Moonwalker*, a film consisting of a number of short films about, and featuring, Jackson. It was during the *Bad* tour that Jackson purchased a property for himself on 5225 Figueroa Mountain Road, Los Olivos, California, from the golf course entrepreneur William Bone. The sprawling 2,700-acre ranch was named Sycamore Ranch but Jackson renamed it Neverland Ranch.[16] The ranch was vital for Jackson as it gave him the isolation he craved, therefore enabling his addictive nature.

Despite the advice of John Branca, who counselled Jackson that it might not be a good business investment, the singer purchased the property for $17 million.[17] He then proceeded to spend another $55 million adding an amusement park, zoo, and private steam railroad to transport passengers up the drive and around the estate.[18] Jackson certainly had the cash, it seemed. In 1988 alone, he earned approximately $125 million.

It was Neverland Ranch, however, that was the scene of the scandal in 1993 that saw the turning point in Michael Jackson's career.

It was when Evan Chandler, father of 13-year-old Jordan Chandler, accused Jackson of sexually abusing his son at Neverland, that Jackson suddenly found himself facing a lawsuit.

His public image was under intense scrutiny and the scandal brewing threatened to tarnish him forever, destroy his career and rob him of his wealth. In many ways it succeeded and he never truly recovered from it, professionally or personally.

Michael had first met Jordan Chandler in Los Angeles in May 1992 in rather bizarre circumstances. Jackson's car had broken down in Beverly Hills and he was standing beside it in frustrated confusion about what to do when an eagle-eyed employee of a car-rental business spotted him and called the owner, David Schwartz. Schwartz was the stepfather of the then 12-year-old Jordan Chandler. He called his wife, June, and told her to bring Jordan to the office where he'd be bringing Michael Jackson. Schwartz had offered Jackson a free rental car if the star would agree to take the boy's phone number and call him.[19] Jackson agreed. He kept his part of the bargain and phoned Jordan.

Jackson didn't limit the communication to just one phone call and continued to speak with Jordan over the phone during the next few weeks. It was during one of these calls that Jackson suggested Jordan visit his apartment in Century City, California. The boy's mother didn't let him visit Jackson at that time as he was preparing for his final seventh grade exams at St Matthew's School in Santa Monica, but, three months later, when Jackson had returned from a major promotional tour, Jordan and his mother and sister, became frequent visitors to Neverland where Jackson showered them with attention and gifts.

The previous year, 1991, Jackson had switched record labels, leaving CBS and joining Sony in one of the most lucrative recording contracts in the history of the entertainment industry, valued at $65 million, with experts suggesting it could eventually rise to $1 billion. He had also released his eighth solo album, *Dangerous*, following 16 months of production. Quincy Jones had been replaced by Teddy Riley in the producer's hot seat, making this the first Jackson album not produced by Jones since 1975. Upon release in November 1991, *Dangerous* became the fastest-selling Michael Jackson album ever in the USA, eventually selling 7 million copies in America alone.[20] However, only one Number 1 single in the US pop charts, 'Black or White', emerged from the album.[21]

A worldwide tour followed, sponsored once more by Pepsi-Cola for a reported $20 million, and again Jackson donated all profits from the 72 concerts to charity. It was during the break between the two legs of this tour, that the Chandlers frequently visited Neverland at Jackson's invitation.[22] Michael showered them with his generosity, including $10,000 shopping trips to Toys 'R' Us.

Jackson also invited Jordan, his mother June and his five-year-old half-sister Lily to Las Vegas in March 1993 where he had a private suite at The Mirage Hotel. One night, June and Lily decided to go to bed early, leaving Michael and Jordan alone. That night, the two of them watched *The Exorcist*[23] together, which scared Jordan so much that he, allegedly, asked to stay in Michael's room.[24] When Jordan's mother ventured into her son's bedroom the following morning and saw that his bed had been undisturbed, she became concerned. June then saw Jordan leaving Michael's bedroom and confronted her son, who reassured her nothing improper had happened. She scolded him against ever doing such a thing again.[25]

The next day, after Jordan had told Jackson about his mother's reaction, Jackson sought out June to discuss the matter with her. He tried to convince her that they had an innocent friendship before breaking down in front of her. The following day, he gave her a $12,000 Cartier bracelet. In April, June took her children to Neverland again for five days and every night from then on, Jordan slept in the same room as Michael.

When word reached Jordan's estranged father, Evan Chandler,

he was less than accepting of the situation. Evan was a wannabe screenwriter who had minor success in Hollywood with the comedy *Robin Hood: Men in Tights*, but he had failed to capitalise on this and by 1993 had fallen behind with alimony payments and was almost $70,000 in debt. When Evan saw an article in the *National Enquirer*, in which Jackson was photographed alongside Jordan with the accompanying article alluding to Jordan being part of Jackson's new, adopted family, Evan decided enough was enough. Even though he was estranged as a father, he still felt threatened that he was being overshadowed as the dominant male figure in his son's life. He made a point of visiting Jordan at home when Michael was there, and felt uneasy enough about Jackson and the situation to ask outright whether Jackson was having sex with Jordan. Calmly, Jackson responded by saying such accusations were preposterous and giggled. Despite Jackson's protestation of innocence, Evan was constantly pressuring Jackson to explain the nature of his relationship with Jordan.

Evan applied to make changes to the custody agreement that he had with June in relation to Jordan in an attempt to stop Jackson seeing more of the boy by preventing Jordan from being anywhere near Jackson. The associated paperwork from Evan suggested he hadn't received a straight answer from Jackson after he had confronted the singer about whether he was having sex with Jordan.

Despite this application, and the damaging material within it, June and Jordan had planned to accompany Michael for five months on the next leg of his *Dangerous* tour. In mid-1993, Dave Schwartz secretly recorded a conversation he had with Evan during which it emerged that Evan suspected Jackson was having sex with Jordan and that he had hired an attorney to investigate the matter in more detail. When Michael heard about this, he didn't think there was much to worry about, but June and Dave felt they should be concerned. They discussed the matter with Jackson's investigator, Anthony Pellicano, and one of Michael's attorneys, Bert Fields. Immediately they sensed an element of extortion and spoke to Jordan independently and alone, who confirmed that no sexual impropriety had taken place between him and Jackson.

An agreement to let Evan have Jordan for a week was agreed between all parties, but, at the last moment, Jackson and June changed plans and whisked Jordan away to Neverland to celebrate his sister's birthday. Evan wasn't informed. Travelling with her son and daughter alongside Jackson in his limousine, June was shocked when the singer responded angrily to a phone call from his attorneys telling him to get Jordan back to his father, where he was supposed to be, immediately. Losing their appetite to go to Neverland following Jackson's outburst, June, her son and daughter, got a cab back to their Los Angeles home. Suddenly suspecting something sinister might actually be going on, June didn't even contest Evan's new custody agreement.

By now, Evan was keen to pursue Jackson and when the LAPD suggested they were already investigating a paedophile claim against Jackson, June began to fear the worst, too.[26] When Michael refused to meet her, on the advice of his lawyer, June became suspicious and sided with Evan in not allowing Jackson access to Jordan. Jackson also refused to meet Evan, for fear of providing him with more ammunition.

A few weeks later, on 2 August 1993, Jordan had a painful tooth removed by Evan, who had given up on his screenwriting career and was now working as a respected dentist in Beverly Hills.[27] During the procedure, Evan used Sodium Amytal to dull the pain his son would feel. Sodium Amytal is otherwise known as a 'truth serum' and while under its influence, Evan claimed Jordan spoke openly about sexual activity with Jackson, saying that the singer had touched his penis.

Two days later, Evan managed to gain a meeting with Michael

Jackson, during which he stated that he believed the singer had acted inappropriately with his son and suggested Jackson undertake a lie detector test. When Jackson, under advice from his lawyer, refused, Evan stormed out of the room. Shortly afterwards, Evan Chandler's attorneys laid their cards on the table – they demanded $20 million from Jackson to avoid a trial.[28]

Jackson was about to begin the next leg of the *Dangerous* tour (the first leg had finished in Japan on New Year's Eve 1992), and his team held a counter press conference, after the allegations were made public, accusing Chandler of trying to extort $20 million from the singer. In the days that followed, two other young boys came forward to confirm they had shared a bed with Jackson but that nothing sexual had occurred.

The first part of 1993 was a tough year for Jackson with the intensity of the allegations growing and growing, and public opinion turning against him. He was concerned it might have a catastrophic effect on ticket sales for the second leg of his tour, beginning in Bangkok on 24 August 1993.

With all of this stress and strife, Jackson began taking painkillers more regularly and in greater quantities, painkillers such as Valium, Xanax and Ativan. He attributed the use of painkillers to the 1984 accident on the set of the Pepsi commercial and continuing surgery he was having on his scalp, although, it seems the truth was that the drugs were recreational, and that he had been dependent on them for some time. Only now he was increasing the quantities.[29]

With the child molestation allegations continuing to dominate his world, Michael lost weight, refused to eat, and had to eventually cancel the remainder of the tour after a show in Mexico City[30] on 11 November 1993, and fly to London with Elizabeth Taylor[31] where he immediately entered a drug rehabilitation clinic.

Meanwhile, back in the USA, having refused to pay the $20

million to the Chandlers, a trial was set for March 1994. Before then, in December 1993, Jackson would have to undergo a humiliating strip search at his ranch,[32] during which detectives would try to establish a connection between Jordan Chandler's description of Jackson's private anatomy and his actual physique.[33] Around this time, Jackson's sister, La Toya, also joined in the ongoing media circus, by speaking out against him. While in Tel Aviv on 8 December 1993, she told reporters at a news conference: 'This has been going on since 1981, and it's not just one child', according to wire service reports. Reuters news agency reported she went on to say that she can no longer 'be a silent collaborator of his crimes against small innocent children. If I remain silent, then that means that I feel the guilt and humiliation that these children are feeling, and I think it's very wrong.'[34] She said that she had seen cheques made out for 'very, very large amounts' to the parents of these children and hinted that she had proof to support the allegation that her brother was a paedophile, and she would reveal it to anyone prepared to listen, but only if they would pay her half-a-million dollars.[35] Newspapers rushed to be the first ones to secure her exclusive story, but it soon became obvious that she had no proof and the newspapers left with their money intact.[36] Despite this, and the anger of her family towards her for encroaching on her brother's tribulations in such a mercenary way, La Toya did appear on a number of documentaries to describe her brother's life and her relationship with him, and made some decent money in the process. But there was no compelling evidence to back up what she said, no smoking gun that confirmed Michael Jackson as a compulsive child molester.

While Jordan Chandler was celebrating his fourteenth birthday on 11 January 1994, documents were filed that day in the Los Angeles Superior Court by the prosecution team as part of evidence against Jackson and also requesting access to his financial records. The details of the case were now in the public domain, and whether people were fans of the singer or not, the case was attracting international attention and opinions were being cast about the guilt or innocence of Michael Jackson.

Within two weeks, with a trial looming, Jackson settled on an out of court agreement that would see him pay a total of more than $20 million to the Chandlers and their attorney despite a lack of evidence and no victims willing to testify against Jackson.[37]

While Jackson himself just wanted to be rid of the case, many around the world saw the fact that he had settled as some confirmation of guilt on his part. As author Lynton Guest wrote,

> Jackson came under intense pressure to settle the case, especially from his management and his record label, Sony, not because they thought he was guilty, but for commercial considerations whatever the outcome of the case might have been. They believed that even if a criminal trial resulted in a not guilty verdict, severe damage would be inflicted on Jackson's career with massive financial consequences for themselves. It must be said that many of them, particularly at Sony, felt Jackson was guilty. What they failed to realize was that a settlement, while not legally an admission of guilt, is nevertheless regarded as such by large sections of the public and most of the media.[38]

Michael Jackson always maintained his innocence but the damage had already been done; within weeks Pepsi-Cola cancelled an endorsement with him, the film projects he had been working on all collapsed without exception and Disneyland stopped showing the 3D film, *Captain Eo*, which heavily featured Jackson.

Throughout the Chandler case, Jackson was without both

Frank Dileo and John Branca. He had fired Dileo around the time he purchased Neverland, primarily on the basis that *Bad* hadn't done as well as *Thriller* and, despite Dileo's best efforts, Jackson felt he perhaps could have done a better job.[39] Of course, it was a no-win situation. How could anybody top *Thriller*? 'We did the best we could. We made the best album and the best videos we could. We don't have anything to be ashamed of,' Frank Dileo recalled of *Bad*.[40] The man tasked with the job of delivering the news of his firing to Dileo was John Branca. And it wasn't long before Branca received a letter from Jackson's new accountant informing him that his services, too, were no longer required by Jackson.[41] Michael had become increasingly insecure with regards to Branca, specifically that he had taken on other clients. One in particular, the British singer Terence Trent D'Arby was perceived by Jackson as competition[42] and another, The Rolling Stones, were embarking on a huge tour that appeared to Jackson to dwarf any tour he had previously done.[43] Despite losing both of these trusted confidantes, Jackson found someone else to lean on during the difficult Chandler period of his life, Lisa Marie Presley. They had met in January 1993 when Presley was pursuing her own singing career having made a rough demo and hoping the input of Jackson, arranged through a mutual friend, might help her hone her skills. Jackson, at that point, wasn't too interested in helping out, but their friendship developed throughout the year against the backdrop of the Chandler scandal.

Lisa Marie was married and had two children with the musician Danny Keough, but Jackson had become besotted with her and plied her with gifts and flowers. In February 1994 he invited her to stay with him at The Mirage Hotel in Las Vegas to see The Temptations, an invitation she accepted, and later that month he asked her to Neverland. In April, Lisa Marie separated from her husband and, 20 days after her divorce came through, she married Michael in the Dominican Republic. It was a week before Lisa Marie told her mother, Priscilla Presley, that she had married Jackson, and it took two months for Jackson and his new wife to announce their marriage to the world. Was this marriage one of true love? Or, was it an attempt to boost Jackson's tarnished image; to prove he was a normal heterosexual man, capable of a fulfilling sexual relationship with a woman who, it was rumoured, had a voracious sexual appetite?

Whatever the reason, just over a year later, the marriage was in trouble. Priscilla Presley was convinced that, indeed, Michael had married her daughter to try to repair his public image, and Lisa Marie had been photographed on holiday in Hawaii with her ex-husband and their children.

Jackson, meanwhile, was hard at work on his new album, the double-album *HIStory*,[44] which was released in June 1995. It was the first album to be released following the accusations of his child molestation and it came out on his own label, MJJ Productions. The album reached Number 1 in the USA, selling over 7 million copies, and also topped the charts in the UK, as well as selling over 6 million copies in Europe.

But despite Sony spending over $30 million promoting the album as well as the $50 million advance Jackson had received for it, only one single – 'You Are Not Alone' – out of five released from it reached Number 1 on the US *Billboard* Top 100.[45] The world tour that accompanied the album was the final solo world tour by Jackson and consisted of 85 concerts in 35 countries attended by over 4.5 million fans and generating over $165 million in gross revenue.[46] As the tour progressed, Jackson's relationship with Presley continued to deteriorate and when Jackson collapsed on 6 December 1995 in New York while rehearsing for a TV special,[47] questions over the state of the marriage began to be asked, particularly when his mother and sister, Janet, managed to visit Michael in hospital before Lisa did and her whereabouts were unknown. More questions were asked when Michael left hospital on 12 December and headed straight to EuroDisney with some cousins but without his wife.[48] In fact, Lisa Marie did visit the hospital but Michael had to be convinced to let her actually visit him, and when she finally saw her husband (in his room decorated with posters of Mickey Mouse and Shirley Temple) a row ensued between the two of them, as she started asking questions about his health and treatment and Michael asked her to leave.[49] Lisa Marie filed for divorce from Jackson, citing irreconcilable differences, in January 1996. The divorce settlement ensured her 10 per cent of royalties from the *HIStory* album, but by that point, another woman, Debbie Rowe, was pregnant with Michael's child.

Debbie Rowe was an assistant to Michael Jackson's dermatologist, Dr Arnold Klein, and the two of them had struck up a friendship over the many years that Jackson had been visiting Klein. The news of the pregnancy emerged in November 1996, as well as the fact that the baby was conceived at the Los Angeles Fertility Institute[50] and that Debbie Rowe would be paid $500,000 by Jackson when she gave birth to the baby.[51] Ten days after the story of the pregnancy was headline news in newspapers worldwide, Jackson married Debbie Rowe. His best man was an 8-year-old boy named Anthony.[52]

From the start of their marriage, Jackson and Rowe lived in separate houses, and the baby was looked after by two nurses and two nannies. Michael and Debbie would divorce amicably in 1999,[53] but their marriage resulted in two children, Prince, born in 1997, and Paris, born a year later.[54]

In 1996, Michael, determined to make it in films, made the little-seen short film, *Michael Jackson's Ghosts*, which was directed by Stan Winston and co-written with Michael by horror-novelist

Stephen King. With Jackson playing five major roles himself, the film was screened out of competition at the 1997 Cannes Film Festival, after which it disappeared without a trace.

Returning to what he did best, Michael released a remix of his *HIStory* album in 1997, *Blood on the Dancefloor: HIStory in the Mix*. On the album, Jackson remixed eight tracks from his previous studio album and performed five new songs. The album sold 6 million copies worldwide, making it the biggest-selling remix album ever released. One of the new songs on the album was a track titled 'Morphine', one of Jackson's darkest songs, full of sadness and anger and a repetitive chorus containing the word, Demerol, which is a narcotic analgesic with effects similar to Morphine. It acts on the central nervous system by tricking the brain into replacing the feeling of pain with a 'high'. Demerol was a drug that Jackson would have become familiar with during his regular visits to his dermatologist, Dr Klein in Beverly Hills. It would have been used as a painkiller during the uncomfortable cosmetic procedures that Jackson was routinely undergoing with Dr Klein and, later, it was rumoured Jackson only underwent cosmetic procedures as they allowed him access to Demerol.

While the album reached Number 1 in the UK, it failed to ignite record buyers' imaginations, only peaking at Number 24 in the US *Billboard* 200 and eventually selling barely 1 million copies in the States. This lack of success, especially in the USA, coupled with the recent controversies, meant that, for Sony, Michael was no longer the priority he thought he was.

Despite this flop, Sony still ended up with costs of anywhere between $30 million and $40 million for Jackson's next album, *Invincible*, as well as spending up to $25 million promoting it. Michael had started recording songs that were included on this album as far back as 1997 but his painstaking perfectionism meant the album wasn't ready for release until October 2001.

He hadn't released a studio album for six years, hadn't toured for almost as long and hadn't secured any commercial endorsements, owing to the whiff of scandal still emanating from the Jordan Chandler affair. All this meant that his income had significantly decreased from its peak less than a decade earlier when Jackson was routinely earning $100 million per year. His annual overheads now were nearly $20 million but his income was considerably less, around $10 million to $12 million, and he was relying on taking out loans against his half of the Sony/ATV catalogue to support his lavish lifestyle. Friends were becoming increasingly concerned about his dependence on prescription painkillers, and Jackson himself was about to discover that his contract with Sony wasn't what he expected it to be.

Before the services of his attorney, John Branca, had been dispensed with unceremoniously in 1990, Branca had overseen Jackson's contract with CBS. The Sony contract had been rewritten, however, without Jackson's knowledge by one of the people that had replaced Branca. Jackson had been under the impression he could get out of the Sony contract in 2000 and that the licence to the masters of albums such as *Thriller* and *Bad* would revert back to him. With these then in his control he could exploit them fully and reap the financial rewards.

What emerged upon closer inspection was that clauses existed that demanded Michael release a new CD for Sony every two years, as well as a Christmas CD and two soundtracks. To make matters worse for Jackson, the original three-album deal had been amended to five albums. There were also massive financial penalties for not completing albums: up to $20 million for each unfinished album. Whatever course of action he took, it appeared Jackson would owe Sony hundreds of millions of dollars even if he managed to get himself out of the contract. But owing to a formula called the 'Dunkirk Clause',[55] if Jackson left Sony, he would inherit the mechanical copyright ownership of his recordings and if Sony attempted themselves to get rid of Jackson, a messy legal case would ensue which would cost them a fortune. As Lynton Guest states in his book, *The Trials of Michael Jackson*, '…those at Sony had to find a way to get rid of Jackson but keep hold of the rights to his recordings.' By keeping control of Jackson's back catalogue, Sony could also keep themselves close to his share of the Sony/ATV catalogue in the hope of eventually gaining full control of that too. They just had to find a convenient way of getting rid of Jackson, whilst making it appear as though he was to blame.[56]

In the end, Jackson found out that the attorney who represented him during the formulation of the deal also represented Sony. It was a classic conflict of interest and enabled Jackson to navigate his way out of the Sony contract on the basis he delivered *Invincible* and a *Greatest Hits* package. But even this backfired, as Sony managed to keep the mechanical rights to Jackson's back catalogue when he failed to deliver the material he was originally contracted for.[57]

There was little motivation for Jackson to put all his effort into *Invincible* in these circumstances, but he finally delivered the album in August 2001 and it was released on 30 October that year. It entered the album charts at Number 1, but only stayed there for one week. Four singles were released from the album, all with just moderate success.[58] The album ended up selling around 10 million copies worldwide, but for an artist of Jackson's stature and reputation, at least in his mind, this was considered a failure.

Shortly after the release of *Invincible*, Jackson performed two shows at Madison Square Garden. His friend, David Gest, produced the shows which celebrated Michael's 30 years as a solo entertainer and contained performances by The Jacksons, along with guest appearances by artists such as Britney Spears, Slash and Kenny Rogers, and, of course, solo performances by Michael himself.[59] Michael was reportedly paid $15 million for the two concerts.[60]

After appearing disoriented during the first concert, David Gest claimed in the documentary, *Michael Jackson: The Life of an Icon*, that Jackson was high on drugs during the shows. Jackson retorted by saying that he simply did not rehearse for the first show.

In 2002, Sony unsurprisingly chose not to renew Jackson's recording contract, which was hardly a tough decision for them to make given the cost of the *Invincible* album, the lack of a tour to promote it, declining sales generally and the fact that Jackson had suggested Sony's then-chairman, Tommy Mottola, was a racist.[61] All of a sudden, Jackson had no record label, although at that point his desire to actually make new music was questionable anyway.

Jackson's unpredictability in 2002 continued when he was photographed dangling his nine-month-old son, Blanket, over the balcony of a hotel in Berlin, then following that event by taking his other two children, Prince and Paris, to visit Berlin Zoo, hiding their faces under hoods and behind masks. But this bizarre behaviour was nothing compared to what was about to happen in February 2003 when a documentary was aired on British television.

Living With Michael Jackson trailed British journalist Martin Bashir from ITV as he spent eight months following Jackson in every aspect of his daily life, including an outrageous shopping spree in a Las Vegas mall where Jackson spent over $1 million in less than an hour on tasteless artefacts. At the heart of the documentary, however, was a relentless investigation of Jackson's constantly changing appearance and his relationships with young boys, including an interview with a 13-year-old cancer survivor named Gavin Arvizo who stated that Jackson had said to him during one of his many visits to Neverland that '…the most loving thing to do is to share your bed with someone, you know?'

Over 50 million people worldwide watched the documentary. Despite Jackson's best efforts at damage limitation – in a video rebuttal he accused Bashir of presenting a distorted picture of the singer's behaviour and conduct – his reputation was in tatters once more.[62]

Jackson's manager at the time, Dieter Wiesner, told *The Sun* that the documentary '…broke him. It killed him. He took a long time to die, but it started that night. Previously the drugs were a crutch, but after that they became a necessity.'[63]

In November 2003, while Jackson was in Las Vegas, Neverland was raided by the police once more as part of an ongoing criminal investigation, and, at a press conference the following day, it was announced that an arrest warrant had been issued for the charge of Jackson molesting a child.[64] If found guilty, Jackson would face 45 years in jail. Jackson went on the offensive and employed a top legal team for the trial, scheduled for February 2005. They discovered that the Arvizo family had a track record of making abuse allegations and, during the trial, when it was alleged by one of Michael Jackson's employees that he had seen the singer fondle child-actor Macaulay Culkin, Jackson's legal team not only discovered the employee had been approached by tabloids to sell the story with a scale of payment increasing according to salaciousness, but also called Culkin to the witness stand where he categorically denied any allegations of abuse against him by Jackson. They also discovered that the dates of the allegations made by Arvizo against Jackson were actually made *after* the Bashir documentary was screened, therefore *after* Arvizo had been recorded on camera saying he and Jackson shared a bed. Put simply, the Arvizo family smelled an opportunity to make money.[65]

The trial lasted for four months, but Jackson was eventually acquitted of all 14 counts in June 2005.[66] With his career now firmly derailed, the singer sought to escape the USA as quickly as possible, maybe forever. His exile began in Bahrain, on 19 June 2005, where Jackson had connections within the tiny Persian Gulf state[67] – he was close friends with Sheikh Abdullah bin Hamad bin Isa Al Khalifa, the second son of the King of Bahrain. Abdullah had loaned Jackson £1.4 million[68] to help pay legal fees after the 2005 child molestation trial.[69]

Sheikh Abdullah considered himself a songwriter and had met Jackson in 2004 when they agreed to work together on some songs to raise money for the victims of the Asian tsunami and Hurricane Katrina. Now, in Bahrain, Sheikh Abdullah spent $300,000 to provide Jackson with a 'motivational guru' and built him a recording studio so they could work together.[70] He had also provided a stately palace and a number of luxury cars for Jackson, his three children and their nanny, Grace Rwaramba.[71] The sheikh also flew out Jackson's hairdresser at his own expense, gave the singer $35,000 to pay utility bills at Neverland,[72] and even paid $350,000 for a European jaunt for Jackson and his entourage.[73]

Whilst in Bahrain, Jackson found himself on the brink of having to default on his $270 million Bank of America loan. The Fortress Investment Group had purchased this loan from the Bank of America in 2003 after Jackson had already missed some payments. With lifestyle expenses far exceeding his income – he was spending about $2 million per month – Jackson's debts were approaching $415 million. He managed to survive by constantly borrowing against his stake in the Sony/ATV catalogue.[74]

On 20 December 2005, Fortress threatened to call in its loan. In order to keep Jackson financially afloat, Sony agreed an extension with Fortress and brought in Citigroup and other potential lenders to arrange a new financing agreement. Citigroup offered Jackson a new loan at an interest rate of 6 per cent when Jackson agreed to give Sony the right to buy half of his 50 per cent stake in The Beatles' catalogue for $250 million – a form of security for

Citigroup if Jackson defaulted again. Fortress then offered the same terms, incredibly, and within four months a deal was in place with Citigroup providing a $25 million re-mortgage on Neverland, most of which Jackson used to buy back a 5 per cent stake in the ATV catalogue held by one of his early advisors, John Branca.[75]

In April 2006, still in Bahrain, Jackson signed a deal with Sheikh Abdullah for a $7 million advance payment, which meant he would write and record new material for an album to be released by Sheikh Abdullah's record company, Two Seas Records. But Jackson reneged on the deal, and in 2006 left Bahrain as quickly as he arrived, leaving Sheikh Abdullah to sue Jackson for the $7 million.[76]

Jackson's next stop was County Westmeath in rural Ireland. He arrived with his family in the summer of 2006 and stayed for the rest of the year in Grouse Lodge, a secluded Georgian estate with its own recording studio that he rented for $150,000 per month. Here, Jackson began working on new music projects with artists such as will.i.am, who flew in from the USA for the sessions. While in Ireland, Jackson started to look at potential houses to buy, but instead of ending up in Ireland, by 2007 Jackson found himself back in the USA, the country he had vowed never to return to following his acquittal at the 2005 trial.

Jackson had secretly flown back to Las Vegas on 22 December 2006. He could no longer escape the financial turmoil he was in by running away. He had severed all ties with his family, except his mother, and the only way he could make some money was to work.[77] And where better for an entertainer to secure a lucrative headline slot than in the hotels that lined the Strip in Las Vegas?

Jackson's Las Vegas residency began in the rented seven-bedroom mansion at 2785 South Monte Cristo Way. Despite having major financial problems, Jackson managed to negotiate a fee of $1 million to rent the property for six months. Soon, word got out that Jackson was living there, and paparazzi were scaling trees to try and get any photo of him and his children from over the 8 ft high security walls.[78]

The paparazzi were unsuccessful in getting photos of Jackson or the children as they were hidden out of sight. One person who did get to see the children in Las Vegas was a local doctor. A doctor who had treated the father of one of Jackson's security guards, he was called out when a bout of influenza struck the Jackson household. His name was Dr Conrad Murray, and he began to visit every six weeks or so to check up on the kids.

Speculation about what Jackson was doing back on American soil was rife. There were all sorts of rumours – he was going to announce a series of 250 concerts at a Las Vegas casino, he would undertake a run of 50 shows at a famous Vegas hotel, there were even rumours that a massive Michael Jackson robot was about to be unleashed in the desert. Another rumour going around was that Jackson was flat-out broke. Those around him simply couldn't believe it. Even his security guards, who would only get intermittent paychecks, refused to believe the King of Pop was on his hands and knees financially.

The reality of the situation was that he could no longer afford the rent in Las Vegas and had so little cash handy that the nanny, Grace Rwaramba, had to fund balloons herself for Paris's tenth birthday party.[79] Any prospect of Jackson performing in Las Vegas seemed to have disappeared when two of the main players in trying to set up concerts for Jackson, promoter, Jack Wishna, and property developer, Steve Wynn, released a statement to the *Las Vegas Review Journal* saying that 'Jackson has given up on trying to relaunch his musical career in Las Vegas and is heading back to Europe.'[80]

But Jackson wasn't returning to Europe. At least, not yet. While his advisors were trying to work out the singer's finances, Jackson took himself off to New York for the summer of 2007 to stay with the family of Frank Cascio, a record producer. It was while in New York that Sheikh Abdullah caught up with him from Bahrain and began legal proceedings to recoup the $7 million he had advanced Jackson for the unproduced record. [81] At roughly the same time, the Fortress Investment Group filed a Notice of Default & Election to Sell with the State of California, which meant foreclosure on Neverland. As it turned out, Jackson owed $23 million on his mortgage on the property and he was given 90 days to settle the account. If he failed to do so, then Neverland would be up for auction. But, behind the scenes, events were unfolding that would offer Jackson another lifeline.

In the spring of 2007, Jackson had met with Randy Phillips, the CEO of AEG Live, an American worldwide sporting and music entertainment producer and promoter. AEG operated the O2 Arena, a 20,000-seat venue on the banks of the Thames in London. Randy Phillips and AEG were on the lookout for a major star to appear at the venue and, despite all the trials and tribulations that had happened to Jackson in the last decade, the thought was that he could still be the key attraction they were looking for. However, at this initial meeting, Jackson seemed distinctly disinterested in the proposal.

He seemed more interested in buying a property in Las Vegas that had caught his attention, a $55 million estate in the Durango neighbourhood owned by the Sultan of Brunei. He even persuaded his two favoured security guards to help him break into it one day so that he could inspect the property and imagine his plans for a future life there. These security guards were amongst the many of Jackson's retinue who were either owed money for previous debts or not being paid for their current work, and they could only wonder how Jackson could possibly think about affording this property.[82]

In the meantime, he was staying at The Palms Casino Resort in Las Vegas, courtesy of its owner, George Maloof, who let Jackson and his family stay in the $20,000-a-night Hugh Hefner Suite for free.[83] While here, he was working in The Palms' studio mixing and recording new material for the *Thriller 25* album, a 25th anniversary edition reissue of his classic 1982 album.[84] However, *Thriller 25* was not going to improve Jackson's finances as Sony informed him they would be keeping all royalties from the album to cover Jackson's half of the administration costs from the Sony/ATV catalogue, which the singer had, once again, fallen behind on.

But this was just a drop in the ocean. A forensic examination of Jackson's financial woes showed that his debts now totalled $331 million.

With Jackson unable to stay at The Palms gratis forever, it was crucial that a new home was found for him and one of Jackson's team, Michael Amir Williams, found the singer a new place to live, the Haciendo Palomino house. Only a few months previously, Michael Amir Williams was hired by Jackson to oversee the archiving of his DVD catalogue. Now, much to the amazement of some of the more established members of Jackson's entourage, Amir Williams, or Brother Michael as he was known within the Nation of Islam, was assuming control of Jackson's life and acting as though he was his manager. His choice of Haciendo Palomino as Jackson's next residence was an odd one; it wasn't in a great neighbourhood in Las Vegas, it was situated right on a busy street, and it was right across the street from an elementary school.

It was at this house that Michael Jackson waited for the arrival of Tom Barrack in the fall of 2007. Tom Barrack was the founder and CEO of Colony Capital, a private international investment firm reported to manage around $35 billion worth of investments. Of Lebanese descent, Barrack is listed by *Forbes* as being the 833rd richest person in the world and was, also, a fan of Michael Jackson.

Jackson's business advisor at the time, Dr Tohme Tohme,[85] was a character who had decided to devote himself to reviving Jackson's flagging career. Dr Tohme Tohme was somewhat of a mystery man, a phrase he dislikes, 'I hate the words "mystery man"' he said in an interview with The Associated Press in July 2009, 'I'm a private man. A lot of people like the media and I don't. I respect the privacy of other people but lately nobody respects mine.'[86] What is known is that, like Tom Barrack, he's of Lebanese descent, is a US citizen raised in Los Angeles and a self-made man in the world of finance. Jermaine Jackson had contacted Tohme Tohme a year earlier to help rescue Neverland from falling into foreclosure. He travelled to Las Vegas to meet with Michael and claimed that the two of them instantly bonded.

Tohme Tohme had heard that Tom Barrack was visiting Las Vegas and had called him to suggest he meet with Jackson, who had a very serious business proposal.[87] Barrack agreed to meet the singer to hear what he had to say and arrived at Hacienda Palomino accompanied by Tohme Tohme. Sitting down, Barrack noticed two sets of financial documents on the coffee table in front of him – one was for Neverland, the other was for the Sony/ATV catalogue. Jackson explained that Neverland was going to foreclose imminently and laid out his financial situation with a sharp and lucid mind. Immediately, without looking at the documents, it was obvious to Barrack that Jackson was facing financial ruin.[88]

Barrack left with the documents, promising to go through everything. What he discovered was the true depth of the financial turmoil Jackson was in. Realistically, Jackson hadn't worked in over a decade, he hadn't toured since 1997 and what income he did have was based predominantly on his Mijac portfolio[89] and the Sony/ATV catalogue. However, this had been refinanced three or four times. His image and likeness earnings had shrunk to just $100,000 per year and, overall, Barrack discovered there was $12 million more going out annually than was coming in[90] and his total debt was now approaching $500 million, with little left to re-mortgage. Yet, seemingly oblivious to his predicament, Jackson kept on spending and spending.

Aware that Jackson was not only about to lose Neverland, but also his entire catalogue, Barrack cut the singer a deal; he would personally write a cheque for $22.5 million to save Neverland and refurbish the ranch with a view to possibly selling it later at a substantial profit.[91]

Despite saving Neverland, Barrack realised he had only scratched the surface of Jackson's financial problems. The singer had ideas such as getting back into films, but Barrack realised the most profitable short-term solution for Jackson to raise substantial sums was a comeback tour.[92] This was something Tohme Tohme had already thought of.

Barrack was frank with Jackson; he told him that it was a straight choice between either a comeback tour or filing for bankruptcy. Tohme Tohme had tried a different approach: using Jackson's children, and the fact that they had never seen him perform as emotional leverage, as well as tempting Jackson with the thought that the money he could make from such a tour might enable him to buy the Sultan of Brunei's house in Durango which he so desperately wanted. Seeing the potential, Jackson initially accepted the idea that he'd have to go back on the road. Tom Barrack, as part of the deal, therefore assumed Jackson's debt on Neverland, and called fellow billionaire Philip Anschutz, the owner of AEG Live, to begin setting up the comeback tour.[93]

The thought was that if Jackson's stature as a performer could be reinvigorated, the value of Neverland would rise, meaning a greater profit if and when sold, and that Jackson could become a resident performer in one of the Las Vegas hotels after the comeback tour.

An intricate cobweb of phone calls and discussions followed, ending with Philip Anschutz encouraging Randy Phillips to meet with Tohme Tohme to investigate what would be needed to secure Jackson performing a series of concerts at the O2 in London.

Unaware that Phillips had already met Jackson to discuss such an event earlier, Tohme Tohme met with Phillips at the Hotel Bel Air to talk about a potential tour. Shortly afterwards, another meeting was held at the MGM Grand in Las Vegas. This time Michael Jackson was present, his youngest son, Blanket, by his side. Also there was Philip Anschutz, Randy Phillips and AEG's co-CEO, Paul Gongaware. Jackson was dressed in a sober black suit and appeared fit and well, and everybody around the table wanted to hear one thing from Jackson: that the King of Pop was ready to make his comeback. As Jackson sipped bottled water, those facing him across the table were cautiously weighing up the situation. They knew Jackson needed the cash, and AEG Live were keen to land the showbiz scoop of the decade for their O2 Arena in London. Philip Anschutz, a devout Christian, was slightly concerned that hiring Jackson, with the singer's reputation of child molestation, would not only go against his own principles but would harm his company's reputation, and needed reassurance. Randy Phillips, who had been wooing Jackson for three years, explained to the singer why he felt London was the perfect venue for the singer's comeback and, in turn, Jackson explained his own ambition to branch out into films. It just so happened that Philip Anschutz owned the largest cinema chain in the USA, so it seemed the fit was right. Together they discussed their wishes for a new live show and when the meeting ended, Michael Jackson had shaken hands on a series of 10 live comeback concerts at the O2 in London in 2009.[94]

Everything was now aligned to drive Jackson to his tragic end.

4

At the beginning of 2009, thanks to the efforts of Tom Barrack in restructuring Jackson's finances, and AEG Live working towards the comeback concerts, the prospect of Michael Jackson eventually being able to stand on his own two feet again financially was looking a distinct possibility.

Two weeks after the meeting with representatives of AEG Live in Las Vegas, Jackson agreed to return to Los Angeles to begin work on the forthcoming O2 shows. Staying in a suite at the Hotel Bel Air, arranged for him by Tohme Tohme, Jackson commenced work on the show behind closed doors to start proving to himself, and the world, that he was still the King of Pop. By coincidence, an album of that name, released by Sony on Jackson's fiftieth birthday, had reached the top of the charts everywhere that it had been released.[1] It seemed that, globally, there was still an appetite for Michael Jackson's music and, for AEG Live and their forthcoming concerts in London, this was just the reaction they wanted.

In an effort to provide anything that was needed to ensure Jackson was primed for the comeback, AEG agreed to move the singer out of the Hotel Bel Air and rent him and his children a $100,000 a month house, once owned by Sir Sean Connery, in the exclusive neighbourhood of Holmby Hills. Built in 2000, the property at 100 North Carolwood Drive was an elegant and sophisticated French chateau estate with seven bedrooms, 13 bathrooms and more than one acre of lush grounds surrounding it. Inside, the walls were lined with various nineteenth-century watercolours, while the floors were covered with oriental rugs, and the various nooks and crannies were stuffed with Asian ceramics and sculptures. The $100,000 per month rent, being paid by AEG as part of an advance, was set against Jackson's earnings from the forthcoming O2 concerts.

At the end of January 2009, Jackson signed the initial contract with AEG Live, LLC[2] for the London concerts. By signing the contract, Jackson accepted $6.2 million from AEG and a further Letter of Credit for $15 million, to help him purchase a home in Las Vegas,[3] on the basis that he would perform 10 concerts at the O2. Of the $6.2 million, $3 million immediately went to Two Seas Records, the record company owned by Sheikh Abdullah who had sued Jackson for reneging on his recording deal, and $1.2 million was an advance to cover the rental of his Carolwood home. If Jackson didn't fulfil his contract, a clause stated that the singer would forego to AEG every asset he owned, including the prized Sony/ATV catalogue.

However, Jackson unwittingly failed to notice that the contract wasn't for 10 shows, as he had thought, and which had previously been discussed and agreed over a handshake with AEG owner Philip Anschutz. So when the singer actually signed the contract on 26 January 2009, he had either not read the document thoroughly or had not had his attention brought to Clause 3 of the contract which stated quite clearly that: 'Artistico[4] hereby pre-approves up to thirty-one (31) Shows, or such other greater number as agreed by Artistico and Promoter, at the O2 Arena in London, England between July 26 and September 30, 2009.'[5]

It seems strange that there appears so much confusion about the number of concerts Jackson was agreeing to perform in London. Is it conceivable that Dr Tohme Tohme, Jackson's self-appointed business manager, failed to alert the singer to this major discrepancy of a contract for 31 shows, when he had only agreed to do 10? Can we really believe that Randy Phillips, of AEG, didn't highlight to Jackson the increased number of shows in the contract, significantly different to what had been previously discussed and agreed with a handshake? In an article in the *Daily Mail*, author and journalist Randall Sullivan claims that, 'AEG prepared plans to at least double the number of O2 concerts. When Jackson found out, he burst into a tearful rage, insisting ten shows were all that he had agreed.'[6] Even before the initial shows were announced in London, the AEG President and CEO, Tim Leiweke, stated that Jackson would probably do more: 'We'll announce 10 shows. I think you'll see 20, 25 dates at the O2. His production budget is… Wow…' Leiweke told an audience at the *Billboard* Music & Money Symposium at the St Regis Hotel in New York City on 5 March 2009.[7] Jackson's former business and financial overseer, Leonard Rowe suggested he had spoken to Michael about the increase from 10 to 31 shows and wrote, 'In fact, Michael told me personally that he only originally agreed to do ten shows but, evidently, contractually this number was increased to thirty-one.'[8]

Perhaps the reason Jackson signed the document was that, on closer inspection, it appears the contract wasn't a contract at all, but a Letter of Intent, and the document is signed 'Very truly yours' by AEG Live's President and CEO Brandon K. Phillips,[9] a style of signing off more associated with a letter than a contract perhaps. Moreover, the document certainly wasn't a final agreement as on the final page it explicitly states, 'By signing below each party acknowledges its agreement to the foregoing and agrees to negotiate the definitive agreement expeditiously and in good faith'.[10] Maybe Jackson was aware that this was not a final agreement by any means and simply wanted to get the ball rolling so the initial advance could be paid to him as quickly as possible.

One other item in the document that the singer failed to notice or amend was that the document was not addressed to him, but to Dr Tohme Tohme, a man whose position in relation to Jackson was yet to be formally established. Throughout the document, all references to decision making in the future about the concerts, the schedules, the finances and the rewards, state that any discussions will be between AEG and The Michael Jackson Company, LLC ('Artistico' in the contract).[11] This, effectively, takes Jackson out of any decision-making process and means that Dr Tohme Tohme could be construed as the sole representative of Jackson's company and, therefore by default, of Jackson himself. It might be that the singer was anticipating renegotiating or amending this document with the help of Tohme Tohme prior to it becoming the final contract and such negotiations may have included increasing or decreasing the number of concerts to be performed at the O2.

Whatever the document actually was, one thing *was* certain: by signing it – and Clause 16.9 of the document deemed that '… facsimile copies of photocopies of signatures shall be as valid as originals'[12] – the singer was tying himself into a deal that would benefit virtually everybody except himself. The document appears to indicate that the 'Production Costs' of the show would be covered by Michael Jackson. These would include, as laid out in the document under Clause 8, 'Production Costs':

…sound and lights, rigging motors, staging elements, video, pyrotechnics, photos and bios of Artist, televised broadcasts, the cost of all musical instruments as well as the cost of transporting, storing and insuring them, personnel costs for the tour Party (including transportation, feed and accommodation), salaries, wages, per diems, payroll taxes and expenses, union dues and other labour costs and benefits of musicians and dancers and other non-management members of the tour Party, obtaining cancellation insurance, and the actual costs of Artist-related management and staffing including the services of Dr Tohme Tohme, which should not exceed $100,000 per month.

In addition, Jackson would also be liable for:

…the costs of travel and transportation including trucking, bussing and freight and local ground and show transportation for the tour Party, tour design fees and tour creative art, visa & immigration costs for the tour Party and all such other costs for which an artist (or its furnishing company) is customarily responsible including, without limitation, adequate worker's compensation and liability and other insurance.

Finally, Clause 8(i) once again stated that: 'cancellation insurance, if available and mutually approved, to cover the risk of loss of Artistico's profits and Production Costs in an amount which, at a minimum, is equivalent to or exceeds any unrecouped portion of the Advances and costs relating to naming Promoter as a loss payee on such insurance.'[13]

This insurance required within Clause 8(i) of the document

appears to indicate that AEG Live were concerned about Michael's ability to sell enough tickets to cover the costs of the production as well as making a profit. Consequently, this insurance would place all the risk on Jackson as any insurance payments from this policy, should the shows fail to recoup its investment and make a profit, would go directly to the Promoter, in this case AEG Live (or Concert West as they were also trading as).

The document also stated that: 'Artist shall approve and reasonably co-operate in Promoter's acquisition of life-insurance, non-performance, cancellation and other insurance, subject to reasonable confidentiality restrictions.'[14] The clause goes on to state, 'Artistico hereby represents and warrants that Artist does not possess any known health conditions, injuries or ailments that would reasonably be expected to interfere with Artist's first class performance at each of the Shows during the Term.'[15]

Whilst it is only natural that any promoter would want to take out both life insurance and cancellation to cover the artist and their own investment, Jackson's health was already questionable and the rumours about his continued dependency on drugs were circulating everywhere. In December 2008, author Ian Halperin[16] disclosed to the world that Michael Jackson had only six months to live owing to emphysema and chronic gastrointestinal bleeding. He claimed a source close to the singer said Jackson: '…wants to have the lung transplant but because of other illnesses he's fighting, he's too weak to undergo such a major procedure. He's taking one painkiller after another.' In an interview with journalist Daphne Barak in June 2009, the nanny to Jackson's children, Grace Rwaramba, recalled his drug abuse by disclosing that she had to frequently pump his stomach after he had taken dangerous cocktails of prescription drugs. She claims she had even asked the singer's mother, Katherine, and his sister, Janet, to intervene to help Jackson face his addiction to painkillers.[17]

With AEG Live in line to receive all insurance payments should the shows be cancelled and all production costs being paid for by Jackson before he would get any 'artist's compensation' from the 'net pool revenue', it appears AEG Live were undertaking no risks in putting on this series of concerts, yet were to gain huge financial rewards whether the concerts went ahead or not.

At the bottom of all this was the fact that if Michael defaulted on his promissory note, signed as an addendum to the document on 26 January, which stipulated the $6.2 million advance would have to be repaid to AEG Live – and given his poor health and drug addiction it seemed almost inconceivable that Jackson wouldn't default – then AEG potentially stood to gain the entire Michael Jackson catalogue, including his half of the Sony/ATV catalogue.

Five weeks after signing this document (whether it was a contract or an agreement) Jackson, accompanied by his children, flew to the UK, still in the belief that he was going to perform 10 shows at the O2 Arena. They stayed at the Lanesborough Hotel in Knightsbridge, overlooking Hyde Park, and, with rumours of a major announcement in the offing, fans were already camping outside the hotel hoping to catch a glimpse of their idol.

On 5 March 2009, a press conference was scheduled at the O2 in London to announce the forthcoming Jackson shows. For Randy Phillips, it was a major relief that Jackson had actually turned up in London; he had been trying to contact the singer during the week before the trip but couldn't get a response from Jackson. Testifying in court following Jackson's death Phillips said about the trip to London, '…I was flying blind. I didn't know what was happening in Jackson's camp.' Phillips could only get in touch with Jackson through the singer's manager, Dr Tohme Tohme, but Jackson was now not talking to Tohme Tohme either, or returning any of his calls as he was furious that Tohme Tohme had decided to sell off some of Jackson's belongings at auction to raise money.[18]

Completely in the dark, Phillips arrived at the Lanesborough Hotel on 5 March to accompany Jackson to the O2, and only then did he find out, first-hand, exactly what was happening in Jackson's camp. It was in chaos. The singer, apparently drunk and despondent, was holed up in his hotel room and Phillips had to try to sober him up.[19] Dr Tohme Tohme later referred to it as, '…a little issue', continuing that, '…Michael got drunk'. There seemed little prospect that Jackson would be in a fit enough state to attend the press conference and, with time ticking and the O2 on the other side of London, Phillips was, in his own words, '… sweating bullets'.[20]

Fully aware of the significance and profile of the press conference, Phillips tried to talk to Jackson but the singer confided to him that he was concerned that nobody would turn up at the O2 and the whole event would be a disaster. Phillips began screaming at Jackson and slapped him[21] and, together with Dr Tohme Tohme, they dressed Jackson ready to face the media – he couldn't even fix his cufflinks unaided owing to the state he was in. Phillips would later say it was the scariest thing he had ever seen.[22]

There were 5,000 fans waiting for Jackson at the O2 together with nearly 400 members of the world's press, but they were all unaware of the drama unfolding back at the hotel as Phillips struggled to cajole Jackson out of his room. Leaving the hotel, Jackson was seen to stumble and fall on the steps to the Ford SUV waiting outside to take him and his entourage to the O2.

As helicopters followed the convoy across London, another shock awaited Phillips inside the SUV when he realised that no script had been written for the press conference. Arriving at the O2 90 minutes late, Phillips hastily scribbled a brief script for Jackson to read off the teleprompter. Despite his drunken persona at the hotel, Jackson emerged, with aviator shades and a sparkly jacket, as well as a hunched gait, through the scarlet silk curtains at the O2 with a beaming smile across a face caked in make-up. A giant video screen above the stage relayed images as his fans screamed and shouted their love for him and cameras flashed away. Jackson seemed jittery and unsure what to do or say. Eventually, in a strange bass-like voice that was unlike the voice the public had heard from Jackson before, he spoke the words that Randy Phillips had recently scribbled during the journey in a brief four-minute appearance on stage:

I love you so much. Thank you all. This is it. I just want to say that these [sic] will be my final show performances in London. This will be it. When I say this is it, this really means this is it. Because, I'll be performing the songs my fans want to hear. This is it. I mean, this is really it. This is the final curtain call. OK, I'll see you in July. And I love you. I really do. You have to know that. I love you so much, really, from the bottom of my heart. This is it, and see you in July.

As Jackson left the stage, without fielding any questions from the press, the bemused host, Dermot O'Leary confirmed that there would be 10 concerts beginning on 8 July 2009 and announced tickets would go on sale on Friday, 13 March 2009.

With news of the impending concerts now official, the world began talking about Michael Jackson again. But while the excitement about the concerts spread throughout his fan base, particularly in the UK, there was also a theory circulating, especially across the internet, that the man who faced the press at the O2 wasn't Michael Jackson at all, but an impersonator, or, perhaps worse, an imposter. Numerous sites began springing up rapidly with various

71

theories and 'photographic proof' that a lookalike had stood in for Jackson at the O2. The various forums suggesting an impersonator pointed to the hunched walk, the deeper voice, the straightness of his teeth, the fact that the star's chin was too square and even the differences in his left hand when compared to photos from a decade previously. Could it really have been a lookalike on the stage rather than the King of Pop? If this were true, it certainly wouldn't have been the first time. It had been rumoured that Jackson used doubles to avoid paparazzi and even get access to prescription drugs. One instance took place on 17 October 1999, when the population of Barnstaple, a sleepy Devon town, was shocked to see Michael Jackson arrive in a stretch limousine to perform at an awards ceremony at the Queen's Theatre for children. The 450 people in attendance were all happy to accept they had been in the presence of Jackson himself, despite his record company assuring the press that the singer had been in Los Angeles all week. To this day, many of those who were there on that cold North Devon day remain convinced that it was actually Michael Jackson they saw, rather than an imposter.[23]

Following the press conference, Michael Jackson took his two youngest children to London's Drury Lane to see the theatre production of *Oliver!* His fears about nobody turning up at the O2 had been proved wrong, with a crowd of thousands attending to witness his press conference. Any further doubts he might have had about his popularity, in the UK at least, would have been thoroughly dispelled as he was also mobbed by adoring fans outside the theatre. At the show, Mark Lester, an old friend of Jackson's, who had played Oliver in the original 1968 film, joined the singer and his family to watch the show.[24]

While in London, Jackson discovered that, without his knowing, Dr Tohme Tohme and Randy Phillips had discussed, and made a provisional arrangement for, additional concerts at the O2 if ticket demand was substantial enough. Jackson was still convinced he was only going to perform 10 shows and that would be it. To find out that this might be extended, without anybody discussing it with him, caused Jackson to threaten Tohme Tohme and Phillips with cancelling of the shows.[25]

At the outset, Randy Phillips had yet to be convinced about the drawing power of Jackson as a live performer. This was hardly surprising, given that Jackson hadn't performed a major tour for 12 years, had suffered child sex abuse allegations and hadn't released an album of fresh material since *Invincible* in 1991. But when AEG Live announced a 'pre-sale' window for tickets to the 10 concerts and 1 million people applied for this window within 24 hours, Phillips knew he was on to a winner and, with Tohme Tohme, planned to increase the number of concerts to 20.

When Michael discovered their plans he confronted them with his threat to pull out of the shows. However, Tohme Tohme was able to convince the singer that his finances were in such dire straits that he had to earn at least $100 million to avoid bankruptcy[26] – and bankruptcy would mean losing his prized Sony/ATV catalogue. Backing down, Jackson agreed to perform the 20 shows and then, upon learning that Prince had performed 21 sell-out shows at the O2, Jackson demanded he outdo his rival by performing 31 shows.[27] Strangely, 31 shows was the exact number written in the document that was signed by Michael Jackson on 26 January 2009, some six weeks earlier. By the time negotiations had finished, Jackson was committed to performing a staggering 50 shows at the O2,[28] all of which sold out almost immediately, with expected returns of around $125 million when additional revenue sourcing was taken into consideration.

Part of the deal for undertaking these concerts was that Jackson would be provided with an estate near London to act as a temporary home during the concert run as well as having a personal trainer and a chef/nutritionist on hand and, most important of all, a personal physician needed to be hired to look after all aspects of Jackson's health. In return, Jackson would be contracted to only appear onstage for stretches of no longer than 13 consecutive minutes and that lip-synching could be used if appropriate. Despite fans knowing or suspecting this, tickets for the sold-out concerts were soon going for thousands of dollars on various internet auction sites.

Nobody knew how much Jackson would make from the concerts. During the trial after his death, accounting expert Arthur Erk suggested Jackson could have made around $1.5 billion if he could perform 260 shows over three years,[29] while AEG were content to suggest it would more likely be around $132 million from the O2 concerts alone. What Tohme Tohme envisioned was a lucrative residency in Las Vegas once Jackson had completed his UK concerts and, quite possibly, a world tour.

Returning to the USA from his press conference in London with such figures being bandied around in the press, Jackson found himself, once again, being surrounded by vultures all after the potential riches or the debts he owed them. Amongst them, naturally, was his family, who he'd been careful to keep at arm's length, with the exception of his mother, for some time.

It was Michael's father, Joe Jackson, who was one of many jockeying to get close to Michael and share the spoils of his potentially lucrative return. When he landed back in Los Angeles, the singer found a whole host of different managers purporting to represent him. Apart from his own team, led by Dr Tohme Tohme, there was a new group circling – AllGood Entertainment Inc. – and they threatened to scupper the entire O2 concert run.

AllGood Entertainment Inc. was founded in New Jersey in 2002 and describes itself on its website as, '…a promoter of live concert events which feature international acts ranging in ethnic diversity from rock acts, adult contemporary artists and comedians to Latin, R&B, Hip-Hop, Reggaeton and Old School artists.' They had established a strong reputation for producing shows in the USA and the Caribbean with artists as diverse as Stevie Wonder, Sting, Bon Jovi and Julio Iglesias, amongst others.

Joe Jackson had been in talks with AllGood Entertainment Inc. towards the end of 2008 with a view to staging a lucrative Jackson Family Reunion Concert[30] with Michael and all his performing brothers and sisters joining together on stage for a worldwide Pay Per View event which included, for Michael, the single biggest offer to an artist in the history of the concert business[31] – $20 million for Michael alone and his family splitting another $20 million.[32] Joe recommended Patrick Allocco, the principal partner of AllGood Entertainment Inc. should meet with Frank Dileo who was, according to Joe, now looking after the singer's affairs.[33]

Following a meeting on 26 November 2008, Jackson's old manager, Frank Dileo, accompanied by his business partner, Mark Lamicka,[34] signed an agreement[35] with AllGood Entertainment Inc.[36] after Dileo claimed he represented Jackson and that he had had several phone calls with the singer who was supportive of the reunion concert.[37] On 1 November 2008 however, Jackson had released a statement via his business advisor, Dr Tohme Tohme, which read, 'My brothers and sisters have my full love and support, and we've certainly shared many great experiences. But at this time I have no plans to record or tour with them. I am now in the studio developing new and exciting projects that I look forward to sharing with my fans in concert soon.'[38] Dileo failed to notify AllGood Entertainment Inc. of this statement and, consequently, was in position to earn a $550,000 retainer, plus commission, to secure Jackson and his family for the reunion concert.[39]

AllGood Entertainment Inc. started to get cold feet about the deal with Dileo when they discovered his business partner,

Mark Lamicka, was facing legal action connected with defrauding a promoter.[40] When Joe Jackson heard about this he struck up a partnership with Leonard Rowe who had been the promoter behind Michael's *Off The Wall* tour in the late 1970s, as well as working with the likes of Barry White, Marvin Gaye and Kool & The Gang. But Rowe had a murky past, he had served two prison sentences for fraud and writing dud cheques,[41] and been convicted for wire fraud as well as being arrested for possession of marijuana.[42] In 2008 he was ordered to pay the singer R. Kelly $3.4 million after losing a lawsuit connected to booking fake concerts.[43]

On 1 January 2009, AllGood Entertainment Inc., who were keen to revive the deal for the reunion concert now that Dileo appeared to be out of the picture, contacted Rowe. The deal that was on the table now would see Jackson receive $15 million for his one performance and his brothers $1 million each.[44] Rowe was all too aware of Michael's reluctance to take part in the concert but realised that, perhaps, the way to get to him to agree, or at least consider it, was to involve his mother Katherine, the only member of the family the singer hadn't cut himself off from.[45] Rowe suggested that AllGood Entertainment Inc. pay Katherine $1 million and that such an offer might sway Michael Jackson.[46] The only problem was, Rowe didn't have direct access to Michael Jackson so he called Katherine Jackson and asked her to get Michael to call him, which he did the following evening. During that call, Rowe told Jackson of the incredible deal he had on the table and the singer suggested Rowe fly to Los Angeles to meet with Dr Tohme Tohme.[47]

In Los Angeles, Rowe presented the deal to Tohme Tohme but was told that Michael was currently involved in another deal that was near closure, a deal that might be worth up to $300 million for Jackson.[48] Rumours had been circulating that AEG were negotiating with Jackson and Rowe assumed this must be the deal Tohme Tohme was referring to.[49] AllGood Entertainment Inc. had heard similar[50] but Frank Dileo, who was still marauding around Los Angeles claiming to be Michael Jackson's manager, was telling anyone who would listen that the AEG London shows would never happen and that there was no deal with AEG.[51]

On 21 January 2009, however, AllGood Entertainment Inc. heard that Michael Jackson *was* committed to the AEG deal[52] so arranged, hastily, to meet with Rowe and Katherine Jackson to explore how they could move forward. Katherine was concerned that Michael didn't seem in any fit shape to undertake a run of shows[53] and the AllGood Entertainment Inc. offer of one family reunion special, during which Michael would be contracted to only sing two songs with his brothers and appear on stage for 90 minutes in total, was extremely appealing.

By the time Patrick Allocco of AllGood Entertainment Inc. and Leonard Rowe managed to meet with Michael Jackson's representatives on 12 February 2009 to discuss their plans for the singer, it was too late.[54] Discovering for a fact that Michael had already signed up with AEG, AllGood decided to abandon the idea of a reunion show and instead focus on a Michael Jackson solo concert with 'guest appearances' from his brothers for a $30 million payout. [55]

Within the Jackson camp, Michael Amir Williams had now assumed a greater role and had the ear of the singer.[56] Williams felt Dileo represented a better option for Jackson than Tohme Tohme as business advisor and so manipulated the situation to encourage Jackson to think that Tohme Tohme had served him poorly by manoeuvring Jackson into a position where he was being forced to do 50 shows in London against his will.[57] At the same time, spurred on by the lure of a personal payout that had been increased to $2 million by AllGood Entertainment Inc., Katherine Jackson had managed to open the door to her son to Leonard Rowe and Joe Jackson.[58] On 21 March 2009, Michael Jackson allegedly called Leonard Rowe, suggesting he come and work for the singer and stated that he was unaware what was happening with the AEG Live deal and that he had only agreed to do 10 shows in London, but was now faced with 50.[59]

On 25 March 2009, Michael finally met face-to-face with his father and Leonard Rowe to hear about their concert plans[60] and Rowe introduced the notion that the singer should sign some form of agreement that he would present at a later date.[61] One day later, Rowe met with Frank Dileo[62] and a press release was issued from Champion Management saying that, 'Michael Jackson, universally claimed as the King of Pop, today named Leonard Rowe, the legendary concert promoter from Atlanta, as his new Manager. Rowe succeeds Dr. Tohme Tohme.'[63] On 14 April 2009, Leonard Rowe met with Michael Jackson at his Carolwood home.[64] Already present was Joe Jackson, and in Rowe's possession was the letter for Michael to sign. Addressed to Randy Phillips it began, 'Dear Mr. Phillips, Please be advised that effective from the date of this letter,[65] Mr. Leonard Rowe is my authorized representative in matters concerning my endeavours in the entertainment industry.'[66]

Bizarrely, around the same time, Frank Dileo, perhaps hedging his bets, laid claim to a letter allegedly composed and signed by Michael Jackson, stating that he was Jackson's sole manager and representative.[67] Not only was Dr Tohme Tohme now out of the picture, but Dileo's claims caused a significant rift between Rowe and Dileo, with Dileo's loyalty appearing aligned to AEG and not the singer. This may have been confirmed in Rowe's mind when Dileo subsequently managed to convince AEG Live that he alone could negotiate successfully with Michael Jackson and ensure that the London shows happened.[68] On 25 May 2009,

Michael Jackson wrote a letter to Leonard Rowe that renounced any business agreement the two of them had had and, effectively, stopped in its tracks any possibility of a Jackson reunion show.[69] Responding to this, AllGood Entertainment Inc. filed a lawsuit against Jackson and Dileo for $40 million, claiming they had agreed to the reunion concert and that the agreement to perform at the O2 had been a breach of contract on Jackson's and Dileo's part.[70] There was confusion all round, and the only certain fact was that the AllGood deal to stage a concert with Michael Jackson in Texas in whatever capacity was dead in the water.

The AEG Live concerts in London seemed more definite however, and as they loomed on the horizon, it wasn't entirely clear who was representing Michael Jackson in any of his affairs[71] despite the fact that with the apparent contract signed, the 'This Is It' concert run would begin on 8 July 2009 at the O2. There wasn't much in Jackson's life at that point that was constant, except, perhaps, his financial turmoil.

Meanwhile, lurking in the darkness, there was a secret that Jackson had continuously refused to acknowledge publicly, and it was a secret that he was growing increasingly dependent on as the countdown to London continued. Since his accident filming the Pepsi commercial in 1984, Jackson had become exposed to prescription medicine and had become more and more dependent on these drugs, to a point of chronic addiction. He had first been prescribed painkillers following the 1984 accident. The initial prescription to Jackson after the accident was routine and was nothing unusual, but the singer was in such constant pain over the coming years for a wide variety of ailments that he continually resorted to these drugs, which, ultimately, resulted in an addiction.

Desperate to be seen as the clean-cut and pure King of Pop, Jackson had always shied away from drugs, despite being exposed to them from an early age in the clubs, bars and strip joints that he used to perform in with his brothers as The Jackson 5. In his autobiography, *Moonwalk*, released four years after the Pepsi incident, Jackson describes how he has never taken drugs:

> I myself have never tried drugs — no marijuana, no cocaine, nothing. I mean, I haven't even tried these things. Forget it. This isn't to say we were never tempted. We were musicians doing business during an era when drug use was common. I don't mean to be judgmental — it's not even a moral issue for me — but I've seen drugs destroy too many lives to think they're anything to fool with.

But analysis of the medical records compiled during Jackson's stay in hospital[72] shows that he was prescribed Darvocet-N, an oral analgesia, for what was described as '...control of moderate to severe pain'.

Darvocet-N was withdrawn from the USA market in November 2010, some six years after it was banned in the UK. A report found the drug put patients at risk of abnormal or even fatal heart rhythm abnormalities, but this news was too late for 2,000 or more people in America alone who had already died from side effects of taking Darvocet-N. The drug was also known to be 'habit-forming'.[73]

In addition, the medical notes show that Jackson[74] was already taking Plaquenil and Atabrine and had had nasal surgery – a rhinoplasty after breaking his nose. Plaquenil and Atabrine, both previously prescribed to the singer, were used to treat *Lupus Erythematosus*, an autoimmune condition that causes joint pain, skin rashes, swelling and rheumatoid arthritis, from which Jackson was suffering.

Neither Plaquenil nor Atabrine are addictive, but Darvocet-N most certainly is, and during his first night in hospital, Jackson was prescribed Darvocet-N every three hours. This was, primarily, to control the pain from the burns. Dr Hoefflin's report (he was the doctor who treated him initially for burns) stated that Jackson was admitted in a 'quite shaken-up state'. He goes on to record that Jackson '…had a burn the size of a palm over the apex of the scalp, there was surrounding singed burned hair, he had a central 25-to 50-cent piece area of deeper burn'. Jackson was admitted overnight and, although being advised to stay in hospital for a few days the next morning, he asked to be discharged so he could rest more comfortably at home. The final paragraph of the report, after the doctors had agreed to Jackson being discharged early, states that he will be sent home on 'Percocet 1 every 3 hours prn or Darvocet-N 100mg 1 to 2 every 3 hours prn'.[75]

Twenty-five years after this accident and his first exposure to prescribed painkillers – a prescription given in the best of faith and with Jackson's medical recovery solely in mind – it was found that Jackson had been a long-term user and abuser of drugs, specifically painkillers. He had managed to keep this addiction hidden from all but those closest to him over the years. However, in 2009, the singer's chronic dependency on these painkillers was to reach a tragic conclusion.

Throughout his adult life, the health of Jackson and his ever-changing appearance had aroused significant interest in the world's media. His first exposure to plastic, and then later cosmetic, surgery was in 1979 after he had broken his nose whilst performing a complex dance routine. By 1986, Jackson had had four nose alterations and a cleft created in his chin but denied, in his autobiography, any work being done on his cheeks, eyes or lips.

In 1986, Jackson, as previously mentioned, also became a regular client of Dr Arnold Klein,[76] a man described in the *Beverly Hills Times Magazine* as, 'The most innovative & famous cosmetic dermatologist in the world'. He was also a man who claimed that

Albert Einstein was his great-great-uncle.[77] Dr Klein was known as the father of modern cosmetic dermatology and prided himself on the innovative injection techniques he developed for the cosmetic use of Botox, Collagen and Restylane. Following Jackson's accident filming the Pepsi commercial in January 1984, Klein, having known Jackson for almost a year, spent the evening with Jackson in hospital, reassuring the singer and a bond between them developed (Klein, himself, was badly burned as a two-and-a-half-year-old child). For Dr Klein, the chance to be affiliated to Michael Jackson, the man he 'adored' according to another patient,[78] was simply overpowering and for Jackson, Klein was to become his key to unlocking the door of prescription drugs, and this meeting, borne out of an accident, was life-changing for the both of them.

Dr Klein was soon to become one of Jackson's chief physicians and was the central figure in treating Jackson's skin conditions, such as *vitiligo*. He was also the physician who prescribed Benoquin to Jackson, a cream that bleached Jackson's skin and a cream that Jackson even used to bleach his scrotum. Combined with this treatment for his skin, Klein also used the wrinkle-reducer Botox and the filler Restylane on Jackson, injecting them into his cheekbone, chin, nose and below his right eye. Later, towards the end of the singer's life, Klein was also injecting Botox into the singer's groin and armpits to reduce excessive sweating, and these particularly painful injections required Jackson to receive up to 300mg of Demerol after every injection. Demerol is a highly addictive opioid painkiller and, according to some within Jackson's inner circle, he was addicted to Demerol as early as 1984.[79] Back then, Jackson underwent long and painful treatment for the burns on his head, which involved inserting expanding balloons under his scalp in an attempt to stretch the skin, which would then be stitched over his injuries. In order to bear the excruciating pain of these operations, Dr Steven Hoefflin, in good faith and with the best of intentions, prescribed large doses of Demerol over a significant period. This reconstructive surgery was unsuccessful and, as a consequence, Dr Klein suggested Jackson fire Dr Steven Hoefflin, but by that point, the singer was probably already addicted to Demerol.[80]

Marc Schaffel[81] was part of Jackson's inner circle, being Jackson's video producer, and in an interview with ABC News in 2009[82] said the singer had a 20-plus year addiction to Demerol and that he, along with others close to Jackson, was planning to stage an intervention to help Jackson break his dependence on drugs in 2003. This never happened, but his close friend, actress Elizabeth Taylor, had staged a similar intervention in 1993. On 12 November that year Jackson abruptly cut short his *Dangerous* tour in a move that even seemed to take some of his associates by surprise. Travelling at the behest of Taylor and her husband, Larry Fortensky, to London via Canada and Iceland, Jackson entered rehab in London for eight weeks. The aim was to treat him for his dependency on drugs, an already chronic addiction that had been exacerbated by the stress of the child molestation allegations he faced at the time.

But by the mid-1990s, Jackson was back on drugs and, by now, was not only using Demerol, but also the powerful anaesthetic drug Propofol.[83] During tours in the 1990s, Jackson was struggling to sleep after each show. He would come off stage buzzing with adrenaline and began to rely on Demerol to wind down after the shows and to be able to sleep. But it was following another accident, this time in Munich, that Jackson moved on to Propofol. He had arrived in Munich on the afternoon of 27 June 1999 to headline two concerts at the Munich Olympic Stadium. During the first concert, as he was performing 'Earth Song', a crane that had risen from the stage to allow him to perform above the crowd, suddenly fell violently to hit the ground at rapid speed with Jackson on-board. Incredibly, Jackson managed to finish the song before collapsing in his dressing room, upon which he was rushed to hospital.[84] After an examination, he spent the night in hospital under medical observation. But the impact of the drop caused Jackson significant pain in his back, which required more than Demerol to ease the pain and make him sleep. According to his then-wife, Debbie Rowe, Jackson's Munich hotel room was transformed into something resembling a surgical suite.[85]

Dr Allan Metzger, one of Jackson's physicians back in the USA, had been contacted by Jackson and Rowe following the Munich accident, and he put together a medical team in Germany to administer Propofol to the singer.[86] This German medical team explained to Jackson the dangers of Propofol and the procedure of administering it. After an initial medical examination, they constantly monitored the singer while he was under the influence of Propofol. Debbie Rowe was particularly worried about the consequences of Jackson dying while taking the drug, but Jackson himself was more worried about not sleeping.[87] Throughout this tour, Jackson's friend, Frank Cascio, was travelling with the singer extensively and recalls paying the anaesthetist, who showed up two or three times a week, in cash.[88] This anaesthetist would apparently stay with Jackson for up to four hours to monitor the Propofol administration, and revealed to Cascio how dangerous and risky the treatment was but, even then, Cascio refused to believe Jackson had a drug problem as he had grown accustomed to the singer being visited by doctors during times of stress.[89]

As well as Propofol and Demerol, Jackson was also addicted to Xanax and his relationship with Dr Klein allowed him the perfect avenue to gain the prescription drugs easily. One of Klein's employees was a Certified Nurse Anaesthetist named David Fournier.[90] He recalled an incident when Jackson, under sedation, stopped breathing during a procedure with Dr Klein in 2003 and that Fournier administered Propofol to Jackson 14 times between 2000 and 2003. Fournier's professional relationship with Jackson ended in November 2003 when he refused to sedate Jackson on the suspicion that the singer was lying to him about his drug use.[91]

Jackson used aliases often to keep his medical treatment (and drug use) secret – names such as Omar Arnold, Paul Farance, Josephine Baker and Fernand Diaz, amongst others – and if he couldn't get what he wanted from Klein, the singer had a host of other physicians he could get prescription drugs from.[92]

In 2009, Jackson was still seeing Dr Klein regularly for facial injections of Botox and other dermatological procedures and made 18 visits that are recorded to Klein between April and June 2009. Despite this, Jackson was seemingly unable to get Propofol from Dr Klein and he had begun to look for other sources of the drug.[93]

At the end of January, shortly after Michael Jackson had signed the 'contract' for the O2 concerts, Cherilyn Lee received a phone call from the singer's Head of Security, Faheem Muhammad. Lee specialised in holistic nutritional health care and had been working as a practitioner since the 1970s, and Jackson was keen for her to see his children who had coughs and runny noses. Arriving at the house, she checked the lungs of all three children and set them up with Vitamin C powder. When they told their father that they felt much better, Jackson started talking with Lee, asking her what else she did. When Lee replied that she used holistic approaches to help people and give them more energy, explaining the course of treatment in such instances to him, Jackson became intrigued and asked her to return at a later date as he felt he might be anaemic.

When she came back on 2 February, Lee tested Jackson's blood, measured his red blood cells and did a full examination of him before working out a nutritional plan, full of vitamins, to help him increase his energy levels. Throughout his treatment with Lee, Jackson didn't want to discuss any of his previous surgeries and he also wanted to use an alias on all the medical records. The name he chose was David Mich.

His chief complaint, apart from thinking he was anaemic, was that he suffered from fatigue, especially around midday, and had been doing so for several months. Questioning Jackson during this initial examination, Lee asked him if he was taking any prescription medicines or had taken any in the past year. The only drug Jackson mentioned to her was Tylenol, which he said he took for insomnia '…every now and then'.[94] He also mentioned that, over 12 years or so ago, he had taken Xanax, Ativan and Ambien. He never mentioned Demerol, Meperidrine, Diprivan or Propofol, and failed to mention he had gone into rehab in 1993 for a dependency on painkillers. Throughout this initial meeting, Cherilyn Lee felt Jackson was telling her the truth and that he simply wanted to dedicate himself to becoming healthy.

Upon examining Jackson for the first time, Lee thought he seemed in good shape, but she was concerned about the amount of Red Bull he appeared to be drinking. She also suggested he gain some weight but the singer said he could not carry any weight during a concert if he wanted to perform to his high standards, and was happy with his weight as it was. When the results for Jackson's blood tests came back, they showed he was hypoglycemic with low blood sugar, primarily caused by skipping meals and drinking too many caffeine-based drinks, so she devised a nutritional plan for him that involved him drinking smoothies that would help his hypoglycemia and also the low folic acid and Vitamin D level (caused by his reluctance to go out in the sun) that he was showing.

Lee continued to see Jackson throughout February, documenting his progress, which was going well, and stopping his apparent reliance on Red Bull. At no point did Jackson mention to her any other drugs or medications, or the names of any other doctors he might be visiting.

This was an act of deception on Jackson's part; Jackson hadn't seen Dr Klein during January and February, but he had made contact once again with Dr Allan Metzger who, up until 2003, had been the singer's main physician whenever he was in Los Angeles. Jackson had only spoken to Metzger once since 2003, when the pop star called him in 2008 to talk about skin care, a back strain and general health issues whilst he was in Las Vegas.[95] On 26 February 2009, Jackson called Metzger out of the blue. He wanted to discuss the forthcoming O2 concerts and the anticipated stress and pressure he was facing. During the phone call, Jackson talked about doing the concerts to 'redeem his image' following the various accusations and allegations against him. To cope with the forthcoming stress, Dr Metzger suggested Jackson tried hypnosis. When the topic of the phone call switched to Jackson's potential insomnia, Metzger suggested they find someone in London to look after him, somebody '…who knows what they're doing'. They also mentioned Xanax, because that had worked for Jackson in the past, but there was no discussion regarding Demerol or Propofol. The phone conversation ended with Jackson asking if Metzger would come and visit him at a later date, a visit that, as it would turn out, would be both social and medical.[96]

Meanwhile, on 9 March, Cherilyn Lee visited Jackson at his Carolwood mansion (where every one of their meetings took place) to tell him that his treatment with vitamins and nutritional supplements was working well. Still, Jackson made no reference to his call to Dr Metzger and failed to notify Lee of a series of appointments he was about to begin with his dermatologist, Dr Arnold Klein, in just a few days time.

On 12 March 2009, Michael Jackson took the short trip to the clinical offices of Dr Klein to have Restylane filling work done on the cleft in his chin. He was to visit him twice more in March 2009: on the 17th, when Jackson had more Restylane filling work done, and on the 23rd, when Jackson had Botox injections under the eyes. Each time, Jackson was given a 200mg injection of Demerol directly into his face to act as a painkiller.[97]

A day later, on 24 March 2009, Cherilyn Lee visited Michael again. During this meeting, Jackson complained of '...feeling very tired'. Lee continued to give Jackson his intravenous vitamin therapy but Jackson said to her, 'Thank you for bringing the natural sleep products but I don't think this is going to work'. Cherilyn Lee gave him herbal tea to try to help him sleep and advised him that he should try to turn off the lights and the music and not play DVDs when it was time to sleep, but he responded by saying that was the only way he could really sleep (the natural products were helping him to sleep up to five hours a night by this stage). In addition, Lee suggested that perhaps Jackson undergo a sleep study to identify what might be preventing him sleeping but, once again, he declined the offer.

In April, Jackson stepped up his visits to Dr Klein. On 6th, 9th, 13th and 15th he received 200mg injections of Demerol following Restylane filler being injected into his cheeks. But on 17 April, the level of Demerol injections increased significantly to 300mg following Botox injections into Jackson's armpits. Was this a sign of Jackson's increased tolerance to the drug? Confirmation of his demand for higher levels of Demerol to satisfy his growing addiction, perhaps? Whatever the reason, the levels of Demerol intake continued to increase – during the week beginning Monday, 13 March 2009, Jackson had been injected with 700mg of Demerol and over the course of the following week this had increased to three injections, amounting to a total of 1050mg of

Demerol over his several visits to alleviate the pain as Jackson was injected with Botox into the groin, with the aim of controlling excessive perspiration. The final week of April saw Jackson receive 900mg of Demerol in three separate visits to Klein. In addition to the Demerol, Jackson was also receiving Prednisone, prescribed to him on 25 April by Klein to cope with the pain levels Jackson was suffering from eye and lip Restylane injections.[98]

In the midst of all this, Cherilyn Lee visited Michael Jackson on 19 April, still unaware he was visiting any other medical practitioners or was being prescribed drugs. During this visit, Jackson, who Lee remembers as not being himself that morning, expressed a concern to Lee about sleeping and said he wanted some additional help to make him sleep. Out of the blue, he mentioned to her a drug called Diprivan and how it had helped him to sleep in the past. Lee was unaware of this drug so, taking the opportunity, she left the house and called a friend to see if they could shed any light on this drug. When her friend told her that Diprivan was an anaesthetic, also known as Propofol that was used in surgery, Lee went back into the house to try to convince Jackson that it was not a safe drug for him to be taking at home and that it definitely wasn't a medicine for insomnia.

However, Jackson wasn't prepared to take her advice on board. He told her that she didn't understand and that he had been told the drug was safe. His demeanour became insistent and upsetting; he was desperate for a good night's sleep and wanted the drug, but Lee knew it was extremely dangerous. She showed him her reference book to illustrate the risks of the drug but he kept telling her she didn't understand and that doctors had told him it was safe. Becoming desperate herself, Lee told Jackson: 'I understand you want a good night's sleep and want to be knocked out, but what if you don't wake up?' Jackson responded with, 'You don't understand. Doctors have told me that the medication is safe just as long as I'm being monitored.' Lee was anxious to know who these doctors were, but he refused to tell her any names. [99]

The conversation continued with Jackson complaining he didn't want to wait the hour it took for the other medications he was consuming to knock him out. He wanted to be asleep immediately, upon demand, and as far as he was concerned, Propofol was the only drug that could do this for him. But despite Lee continuing to warn him that using Propofol at home could result in death, Jackson was insistent that other doctors had assured him it was safe – if monitored. Finally, Lee convinced Jackson to take the cocktail of vitamins she had prepared for him to sleep. It was past midnight now and Jackson was anxious to get a good night's sleep as he told Lee he was due to have '…a big rehearsal tomorrow, and I have to be ready for my rehearsal tomorrow'. So Lee made him a cup of herbal tea and, after tucking him into bed, started his vitamin intravenous drip. For the rest of the night, Lee sat in a chair opposite the bed and observed Jackson sleep until 4:30am, when he awoke with a start and actually stood up on the bed before he spoke to Lee, saying in an agitated manner, 'I told you I cannot sleep all night'. He then jumped off the bed and ran to the bathroom. When he came back into the room, Jackson again stated his need for Diprivan (Propofol) and accused Lee of potentially destroying his day by not giving it to him. He suggested, in the future, she should bring an anaesthetist with her who could administer it properly and safely.

When Cherilyn Lee left Jackson's Carolwood mansion on the morning of 20 April, after that eventful night, she didn't realise it would be the last time she would ever see him. Unable, or unwilling, to administer Propofol to him, Cherilyn Lee was no longer of any use to Jackson. He was still seeing Dr Klein throughout April, and getting increasing doses of Demerol through injections. But Klein wasn't administering Propofol to Jackson. And with his Los

Angeles physician, Dr Metzger also refusing to give Propofol to Jackson, the singer was running out of options to get the drug he felt he really needed to make him sleep.

However, unknown to those around him, Michael Jackson had already approached another doctor in Las Vegas about the possibilities and practicalities of this doctor being able to lay his hands on Propofol; this Las Vegas doctor was already known to Jackson. Being a doctor he could get quantities of Propofol, as well as other painkillers, and had already proved to Jackson he could access the drug. What's more, this doctor was seriously in debt and with a newborn baby by his mistress to support. He needed a financial escape route, and Michael Jackson was just the person to provide it.

The physician Jackson had found was Dr Conrad Murray.

5

Peter had seen many tragedies, but he had forgotten them all.
J.M. Barrie, *Peter Pan*

Dr Conrad Murray first met Michael Jackson in 2006. The singer was, by then, living in Las Vegas, and in December of that year, he became concerned that his daughter, Paris, was coming down with influenza. One of Jackson's security guards at the time happened to be the son of a patient of Dr Murray, a cardiologist with offices in Houston and close to Jackson's mansion in Las Vegas, and so the security guard suggested that Murray be called over to the house.

When he arrived in his silver BMW, wearing blue scrubs, Dr Murray had no idea who the patient was, but when Michael Jackson opened the door to him, the star-struck Murray was stunned. The meeting with the pop superstar was, for Murray, a far cry from his poverty-stricken childhood, but the pinnacle of all he had hoped for when he left his native Caribbean to seek his fame and fortune in the 1980s, at precisely the moment when Michael Jackson was the undisputed King of Pop.

Grenada is a small, but lush, Caribbean island at the southern end of the Grenadines. Originally subjugated by the French in 1654, it was ceded to the British in 1763. Eighty years later, a merchant ship en route to England from the East Indies left a small quantity of nutmeg trees on the island. Some curious locals planted these trees and, now, Grenada supplies almost 40 per cent of the world's annual nutmeg crop lending Grenada the moniker, the 'Spice Island'. It was amongst the smell of spice, on the western edge of the island, in the parish of St Andrew's, that Conrad Robert Murray was born on 19 February 1953, to the unmarried Rawle Helyn Andrews and Milta Murray.

Grenada might be a lush and stunning Caribbean island, but to the child Conrad Murray it was the backdrop to a harsh upbringing. With his father having moved away to live in Texas, where he worked as a doctor in Houston,[1] the young Conrad was raised by his grandparents who scraped a living in Grenada's barren agricultural industry.

At the age of seven, Conrad left Grenada with his mother to return to her native Trinidad and Tobago. They settled in El Socorro, a squalid, crime-ridden district of the capital, Port of Spain. The young Conrad Murray was an enthusiastic scholar and worked hard at school while his spare time was spent playing cricket, showing skills as a wicket keeper, in the streets of the surrounding slums with his friends. All about them, as they played, were scenes of despair, decay and desperation. Cocaine addiction was rife throughout the neighbourhood, and occasionally the young boys were tempted to 'escape' their surroundings thanks to a local female drug-dealer called 'The Coke Queen'.

Unlike many of his friends though, Murray never gave into temptation and kept cocaine at arm's length. He had dreams of following his father into medicine and wanted to escape the deprivation that was threatening to envelop him. His ambition, like his father's, was to travel to the USA and become a physician with the aim of making his fortune before returning to Trinidad, where he could provide care for poor Trinidadians who couldn't afford proper healthcare.

Devoting himself at an early age to his education, Murray was the only child amongst his class to pass enough exams at the age of 12 to be given a place at high school in Trinidad. By this point, his mother had remarried and had a daughter, a stepsister for Conrad, called Suzanne Rush, but for all the apparent domesticity at home, Murray had still yet to meet his natural father. He had heard his father was a successful physician in the USA, but there had been no time spent together. Despite this, the young Conrad Murray continued to dream of following in his father's footsteps and pursuing a medical career. In order to save enough money to travel to the USA and study medicine, Conrad passed through a number of jobs in Trinidad, from teacher to customs clerk to an insurance underwriter.

Already, before he had even started his medical training, the young Conrad Murray would cruise around Trinidad in his cream and brown Dodge Avenger as the sun set, or invite himself to weddings, always in the pursuit of eligible young women, bragging to them confidently that he was a junior doctor. By the time he was accepted into Texas Southern University in Houston at the age of 27, Murray had already established a reputation on the island for his womanising, and had fathered at least one child.[2]

Relocating to Texas, Murray completed an undergraduate degree in Houston before going on to study medicine at Meharry Medical College in Nashville, Tennessee, from where he graduated in 1989 – but left with debts of around $71,000 in student loans, debts that still hadn't been settled some 20 years later. It was an early indication that Murray seemed to struggle to control his finances, and this struggle was to impact on his personal and professional life for the next two decades, ultimately resulting in him accepting the invitation to become Jackson's personal physician.

During the 1990s, Murray performed his medical residency at Loma Linda University Medical Center in California, before undertaking fellowships in cardiology at the University of Arizona in 1995 and interventional cardiology at the Foundation for Cardiovascular Medicine in San Diego. Licensed to practise medicine as a cardiologist in Texas, California and Nevada,[3] it was in 2000 that Murray founded Global Cardiovascular Associates in Las Vegas and then, in 2006, opened an office in the Armstrong Medical Clinic in North Houston.[4]

In Houston, Murray was eager to follow in his father's footsteps.[5] His father was extremely well respected for bringing medical care to the impoverished African American neighbourhood of Acres Homes in northwest Houston. Conrad Murray wanted to continue this legacy and was lauded for bringing medical treatment to areas where others feared to go, treating poor, predominantly African American, patients who could rarely pay Murray's normal rates. This meant Murray lost money with almost every patient he saw at his Acres Homes Cardiovascular Center in Houston. Even in Las Vegas, his clientele seemed to cover the entire Las Vegas caste system, those less fortunate and barely able to avoid treatment could find themselves sharing the same facilities as members of the Las Vegas governmental elite.

Becoming increasingly successful, or so it seemed, Murray used a $1.66 million loan to purchase a four-bedroom, 5,268sq ft mansion with stunning swimming pool, close to the 18th hole of the glitzy, gated Red Rock Country Club in Las Vegas in October 2004.[6]

With a glamorous address, silver BMW, two clinics and his stature in the community assured, owing to his position as a cardiologist caring for those less fortunate, the journey of Conrad

Murray from a poor child growing up in a red-brick house amongst the drug addicts of Trinidad to renowned physician in the USA appeared almost complete.

But Conrad Murray had many skeletons in his closet. He'd had run-ins with various authorities ever since his arrival from Trinidad to the USA in the 1980s. He still had the student debts of $71,000 from Meharry Medical College hanging over his shoulders, a debt that officials were fervently chasing. In addition, while at Meharry, Conrad Murray had been arrested by police in November 1985 at the behest of a girlfriend who had accused him of a fraudulent breach of trust. Murray posted a bond of $2,000 and the case was eventually dismissed in January 1986.

Six years later, in June 1992, Conrad Murray further exhibited his inability to control his finances when he filed for bankruptcy in California. Less than a year after that, the State of California placed on record that Murray had failed to pay $1,578 in state taxes.

In February 1994, Conrad Murray was charged with domestic violence over an incident in Arizona while he was undertaking his cardiology fellowship at the University of California. It was alleged that he threw his then-girlfriend, Janice Adams, to the ground after she had accused him of having an affair. This alleged incident happened while their baby was apparently sitting crying on the floor. Murray stood trial for this offence in July 1994 but was ultimately acquitted of the charge.

In May 2001 the State of California reported that Murray had failed to pay state taxes once more, this time amounting to $19,457, and in April 2003, Murray again was reported for not paying state taxes, this time owing a sum of $21,084. And in 2003, Murray was one of several defendants named in a civil lawsuit brought by Canada Life Assurance Co. This suit was eventually settled and dismissed but in March 2008, Siemens sued Murray and his company, Global Cardiovascular Associates, for unpaid fees stemming from equipment lease and personal guarantee. They claimed $309,046 from the company and $123,033 from Murray himself and the Nevada court ruled in Siemens' favour. In addition, Murray owed a former business partner almost $70,000 over the failed launch of an energy drink named Pit-Bull.[7] [8] [9] [10] [11]

Murray also had over $13,000 outstanding in child support payments. By this point, he had allegedly fathered six children by five different women and his difficulty in keeping up with alimony payments, or at least remembering to keep up with alimony payments, had seen him sentenced to jail twice. In 2007 he was sentenced to 25 days in jail for non-payment of child support in connection with a child he had with Nenita Malibiran, a nurse who had worked with Murray in Sharp Memorial Hospital, San Diego, California,[12] and, on 29 April 2009, he was again sentenced to jail for 25 days for failing to pay Malibiran child support. On each occasion, Murray avoided incarceration by swiftly paying the money he owed. None of this should have been a surprise; in 1999, during a child custody hearing, Murray revealed himself that he had a history of fathering children before abandoning their mothers.

Murray's first wife was Zufan Tesfai, who he married in Texas on 17 October 1984. But during this marriage he began an affair with Patricia Mitchell, who bore him a child and was the same woman who accused him of a fraudulent breach of trust in November 1985. Murray and Tesfai eventually divorced on 26 August 1988, but he then went on to have two daughters with Janice Adams while working in Tuscon, Arizona. Adams was the woman who reported Murray on domestic violence charges for which he was acquitted. By 2009, Murray had married his current wife, Blanche Yvette Bonnick Murray,[13] with whom he had two children, born in 1990 and 1996, and who were living in his Las Vegas mansion at this time.

However, unbeknown to Blanche, Conrad Murray had many more mistresses scattered around the country; there was Sade Anding, a cocktail waitress he had met in Houston when he gave her a $110 tip for an $11 drink, and two strippers, Michelle Bella, whom he had paid $1,100 for her services, and Bridgette Morgan.

There was also 29-year-old Nicole Alvarez. She was an aspiring actress[14] who Murray had met in 2005 in the VIP lounge of the Crazy Horse strip club. Alvarez had given Murray a private dance, after which Murray gave her a cheque for $3,500. Besotted with her, Murray rented her a flat in Santa Monica and paid the monthly rent of $2,564. It was the least he could do – Alvarez was pregnant with Murray's seventh child, becoming the sixth woman to bear him a child, and the baby was due in March 2009.[15]

As well as all the women in his life, Conrad Murray had another secret he wanted to keep.

His father, Rawle Andrews, MD had been, for many years, a revered and respected doctor in Houston and had been practising in his Andrews Medical Clinic since 1964. But, in 1994, Dr Andrews had his medical licence restricted by the Texas Board of Medical Examiners for over-prescribing 'controlled substances and substances with addictive potential' to two patients for 'extended periods of time without adequate indications'.

In their report, the board highlighted four 'dangerous' painkilling drugs that Dr Andrews had overly prescribed: Stadol,[16] Nubain,[17] Phenergan[18] and Talwin.[19] Following his medical licence being restricted, Dr Andrews was required to complete courses on pain management and the prevention and treatment of drug abuse. In addition, he had to keep separate records of prescribed controlled drugs for the remainder of his career and appear before the board once a year. Dr Andrews was allowed to practise medicine once more in 1999 after he had complied with all the provisions laid down in the restrictions. He continued to work in his Houston clinic until two months before his death on 12 July 2001.[20]

Dr Conrad Murray would have known that his father had suffered disciplinary action for prescribing dangerous and addictive painkillers for extended periods. Although the parallels might be coincidental, it was a dark shadow that already existed on the Murray family's professional medical history.

In the early months of 2009, Conrad Murray was in deep financial trouble – his two clinics were facing legal actions totalling hundreds of thousands of dollars and he was threatened with individual claims for similar amounts. In addition, he had tens of thousands of dollars of child support to pay, and another child on the way by his mistress, whose rent he was also paying. And, if all that wasn't enough, Murray was also facing repossession of his $1.2 million Las Vegas mansion as he had fallen almost $100,000 behind on mortgage repayments.[21]

Coincidentally, or perhaps not, the company holding the mortgage on Conrad Murray's property was Sunrise Colony, a company owned by, amongst others, Tom Barrack, the same Tom Barrack who had saved Neverland from being repossessed by paying off Jackson's debt on the property, and the same Tom Barrack who had introduced AEG's Philip Anschutz and Randy Phillips to the singer with a view to creating the forthcoming O2 concerts. Curiously, Tom Barrack's partner in Sunrise Colony is William Bone, the same William Bone that owned Sycamore Valley Ranch before Michael Jackson purchased it in 1988 and renamed it Neverland. It seemed everyone circling Jackson was connected in some way.

Murray needed a way out, some opportunity to make a lot of money very quickly in order to put all his financial problems behind him and to enable him to keep his house on the Red Rock Country Club, a resort that was also owned by Sunrise Colony.

So, financially, he was in a similar situation to Jackson. It might have been on a far lesser scale than the singer, but for Murray, trying to service all his debts, while appearing to those around him as though everything was in order, was becoming all consuming. In addition, it now appears both Murray and Jackson were in debt, either directly or indirectly, to Tom Barrack, Colony Capital and Sunrise Colony. And, for Murray in particular, with no publishing royalties, back catalogue or potential sell-out concerts, there seemed to be no end in sight.

However, for Conrad Murray and Michael Jackson, everything was beginning to align. From very different backgrounds, the two of them were about to come together in an ultimately fatal encounter. One was a fading pop superstar, riddled with addictions to painkillers, with a face corrupted by plastic surgery, drowning in half a billion dollars worth of debt, and forced to go back on the road one more time; the other was a womanising doctor, with a trail of failed relationships behind him, a man with increasing debts and decreasing morals. The temptation to indulge the King of Pop's desperate addiction for painkillers in exchange for the financial pay-off that would settle his own debts might well have been huge.

Michael Jackson had been impressed by the way Conrad Murray had treated his daughter, Paris, back in Las Vegas in December 2006. Murray had visited Michael Jackson a further seven times between 2006 and 2008 when the singer resided in Las Vegas. Not once did Murray prescribe any painkillers during these visits, although he did prescribe Jackson a sedative in 2008 when the singer complained of insomnia.

In the spring of 2009, prior to rehearsals taking place for the 'This Is It' concerts, AEG Live raised the issue of Michael Jackson requiring a personal physician. Given Jackson's well-documented health issues over the past two decades, it was only natural that

AEG Live felt the performer's well-being was a major concern as the July concerts deadline loomed on the horizon. The singer's continued association with dermatologist, Dr Arnold Klein, was also causing a level of apprehension amongst the AEG Live fraternity, despite the fact Jackson hadn't paid Klein a visit during January and February of 2009.

Seeking a comprehensive insurance policy to cover Jackson failing to fulfil his commitments to them, AEG Live began negotiations about taking out a $17.5 million policy with Lloyd's of London in February 2009. The policy would cover the first 30 concerts at the O2 Arena, meaning that, in announcing 50 concerts, AEG Live effectively had 20 concerts that weren't yet insured. Lloyd's of London demanded that Jackson undertake a physical examination and so, on 4 February 2009, Jackson, under the name of 'Mark Jones', received a visitor to his Carolwood mansion: the New York ear, nose and throat specialist, Dr David Slavit, who was hired for the physical by Lloyd's themselves.[22] [23] [24]

In New York, Jackson underwent what has been described by Randy Phillips as a '…pretty gruelling five-hour physical'.[25] [26] Dr Slavit was aware that Jackson was intending to tour in London and had asked to see Jackson's medical records for the previous five years in order to make an accurate assessment. Slavit requested these records as the insurance broker had already raised questions regarding Jackson's health, including anything relating to his heart, lungs, weight or prior drug use, if any. The brokers were specifically questioning Jackson's breathing capacity and his pulmonary status.

As it turned out, Dr Slavit never received any documents relating to Jackson's medical history for the previous five years prior to overseeing the examination. The only information he received regarding Jackson's medical history was that which Jackson volunteered to him during the physical. During their one-to-one examination, held behind closed doors, Dr Slavit asked Jackson if he was taking any medication, to which the singer replied that he was on antibiotics for his nasal cold and didn't mention anything about painkillers. Jackson also failed to mention anything about having trouble sleeping or whether he was in pain.

During the medical examination, Dr Slavit took Jackson's temperature, blood pressure and pulse readings. He examined Jackson's ears, nose and throat, examined his heart and lungs as well as his abdomen, skin and peripheral pulses. The report states that Jackson weighed 127lbs, but Dr Slavit didn't weigh the singer, he merely relied upon what Jackson told him.

To conclude the examination, Dr Slavit took blood samples from Jackson at 1:44pm, which upon examination by Westcliff Medical Laboratories, resulted in normal and consistent findings. Reviewing the report with Jackson, Dr Slavit asked him to respond truthfully to item number 4, a question, which read, 'Have you ever been treated for or had any indication of excessive use of alcohol or drugs?' In his own hand, Jackson circled the answer, 'No'.

Based on the information Dr Slavit now had at his disposal, and based upon the understanding that the examination was to find out whether Jackson was physically capable or in physically good shape as far as moving forward with the aspect of performing, he concluded that the singer was in excellent condition. Following this, the insurance broker announced that Jackson had passed with flying colours, despite having a little hay fever. The insurance policy, finally completed in April 2009, had a clause in it however that stated the insurers are exempted, should the concerts be cancelled because of death, or if Jackson was involved in the possession of or 'illicit taking of' drugs.

Dr Slavit's report[27] fails to mention anything about Jackson's painkiller addiction or narcotic abuse. It doesn't make any reference to his frequent cosmetic surgery. There is no reference to any of the ailments, some apparently life-threatening, that Jackson was suffering from, and which the global press were always keen to offer up in international tabloids.

But there is one entry that is particularly interesting, one name included in the report stands out specifically, that of Dr Conrad Murray. Dr Slavit writes, 'Dr Conrad Murray in Las Vegas, Nevada, follows Mr Jackson on a regular basis'. It appears that, during the examination, Dr Murray was identified by Jackson as his personal physician and he even reported seeing Murray when needed, most recently a couple of months ago for a general check-up. Jackson went on to tell Dr Slavit that he thought Conrad Murray was a good doctor, who was caring towards him and that he was satisfied with the treatment he was receiving from Murray. But nobody within Jackson's inner circle seemed to be aware that Murray was, at this point in time, Jackson's personal physician. And why would they be? Jackson was now living in Los Angeles; Murray's clinics were in Houston, Texas and Las Vegas, almost 300 miles away.

Not only is Murray's name of interest in Dr Slavit's report, the date is also significant. If, as indicated in Slavit's report, Jackson was referring to Conrad Murray as his personal physician in February 2009, and had been seeing Murray two months previously, in December 2008, for a routine check-up, then this is the first indication that Murray was already entrenched in Michael Jackson's life and didn't assume his role solely as a result of the O2 concert schedule. Certainly, those around the singer seemed totally unaware of Murray in such a pivotal role. Bill Whitfield and Javon Beard, Jackson's Las Vegas-based bodyguards, recall seeing Murray in 2006 and on rare occasions since but generally to only check on his children's well-being. Kenny Ortega said in his testimony that he never met Murray until April 2009 and even Faheem Muhammad, Jackson's Head of Security, hadn't encountered Murray before March 2009.

In his interview with Los Angeles Police Department on 27 June 2009, two days after Jackson's death, Conrad Murray stated to the police that he had been working for Jackson for '...a little over two months',[28] which would suggest he started working for the singer directly in April 2009 following a phone call from Michael Amir Williams.

So why was nobody within Jackson's team seemingly aware of Murray in the early months of 2009?[29] Or earlier? And why did Murray, himself, tell police he had only worked for Jackson for a little over two months[30] when, in February 2009, Dr Slavit's[31] report[32] quite clearly mentions Murray as Jackson's personal physician?[33] [34] In fact, closer inspection of Murray's medical records in relation to Jackson, or often 'Omar Arnold'[35] shows Murray was treating him regularly from 12 April 2007 and had seen him at least three times in 2008, including an appointment on 19 November 2008 when Jackson (or 'Arnold') was complaining of insomnia and anxiety, for which Murray prescribed Xanax and Restoril.[36] This meeting correlates with the information Jackson had given to Dr Slavit about Murray being his personal physician for a couple of months before his February medical.

Exactly how close Murray was to Jackson during the early part of 2009 can be judged by an examination of Dr Murray's relationship and communications with Tim Lopez, the owner of Applied Pharmacy Services in Las Vegas, Nevada. This might provide some answers to the importance Murray had, and was being groomed to have, by Jackson.

Applied Pharmacy Services was a pharmacy on West Flamingo Road in Las Vegas where Tim Lopez was owner and chief pharmacist. It was opened as a corporate entity in May 2000 and was what is known in the USA as a compounding pharmacy, which meant that medicines are made specifically for patients rather than stocking general medicines found in regular retail pharmacies. The pharmacy had traded successfully except for a case in July 2008 when the Nevada State Board of Pharmacy had taken action against Allied Pharmacy Services pharmacists Jessica Nguyen and Timothy Lopez for failing to keep proper records and for failing to have the education and experience in filling a prescription properly. They were fined $1,225 and instructed to complete an educational course.[37]

Another dubious record of the pharmacy was the employment of Kenton Crowley in 2002. Crowley was an experienced pharmacist in California, but he had his licence revoked in 1999 owing to his own drug abuse, notably addiction to Demerol, and the fact that he had been prescribing medications to an addict and also sending medications across state lines without a prescription. Crowley had also spent time in jail for drug-related crimes. Despite his tarnished reputation, he successfully applied for his Nevada pharmacy licence in 2002 and it was issued on a probationary basis, whereupon Lopez, who had supplied a letter of recommendation to the board, hired him. Crowley stopped working for Lopez in July 2008, shortly after he was arrested for driving on a suspended driver's licence and speeding (he had been convicted of DUI in 2007). He never met Murray or dispensed prescriptions to Jackson but it's curious that Lopez should willingly employ a character with such a background.[38] [39]

In November 2008, Tim Lopez received his first phone call from Dr Conrad Murray. Murray identified himself as a cardiologist from Las Vegas and described himself as an African American. He stated that a lot of his patient clientele were also African American and that they suffered from a condition known as Vitiligo. The reason for his phone call, so he said, was to enquire about a chemical treatment for that condition called Benoquin.

It was well known that Michael Jackson suffered from Vitiligo,[40] a chronic disorder that causes depigmentation of patches of the skin. During the 1980s, many onlookers had noted that Jackson's skin was getting paler and the tabloids even suggested the singer bleached his skin and changed his features to appear European. Throughout the 1990s, Jackson continued to get paler and paler and, given the severity of his condition, it was decided by his dermatologist, none other than Dr Arnold Klein, that the easiest way to treat the condition, rather than drugs and ultraviolet light treatments, was by using creams to make the darker spots fade so the pigments could be evened out across the body. The cream that Klein used on Jackson was Benoquin, the same cream Conrad Murray was enquiring about when calling Tim Lopez in November 2008.

Was Murray calling Lopez out of the blue in 2008 to discuss Vitiligo and Benoquin in order to provide treatment to none other than Michael Jackson? Certainly, if Murray was Jackson's personal physician by now – even if not officially – as indicated in the report written by Dr Slavit in February 2009 (in which Jackson himself alluded to Murray having been his personal physician for at least two months), it would be a necessary treatment for Murray to acquire for his client.

Conrad Murray didn't follow up his phone call with Tim Lopez immediately. Instead, the next time Lopez heard from Murray was in March 2009 when Murray called him asking why Lopez hadn't called him back to follow up on his request for Benoquin. Lopez offered that he might have lost Murray's contact information. Murray enquired again about Benoquin and Lopez went off to check the sources of availability. Locating a limited quantity of the cream, Lopez called Murray back on 1 April 2009, saying that he had found some of the desired cream and that it would have to be considered a special order. He was able to offer Murray 40 tubes of 30 grams each and Murray placed the order. At no point did Murray reveal the names of any patients he would be using the cream for, and suggested it would be used on a trial basis. When the order was ready to be collected, Murray arrived in person at the offices of Allied Pharmacy Services to pick up the consignment. This was the first occasion Lopez actually met Murray face-to-face. They discussed the cream and Lopez offered to make any changes to the formula if it was required following Murray's trial period. Murray paid by company cheque and then he asked Lopez if it was possible to send any future orders direct to his offices. Lopez confirmed that this wouldn't be a problem as long as Murray left him a credit card on file.[41]

Two days later, on 3 April 2009, Murray called Lopez to state he was happy with the cream. This timescale means that Murray only had 2 April to treat Jackson with the Benoquin, given that Murray had to travel back from Las Vegas to Los Angeles. It is known that Jackson had started to see Dr Klein again in March and April but, conveniently, Jackson did not visit Klein between 23 March, when he was given 200mg of Demerol following Botox injections under the eyes,[42] and 6 April for Restylane injections into the cheeks as well as a further 200mg of Demerol. During this period, Jackson didn't receive treatment from nurse Cherilyn Lee either; he saw her on 26 and 31 March. Therefore, if he needed it, Murray had uninterrupted access to Jackson between 1 April and 3 April to administer Benoquin to the singer and, possibly, discuss other medicines that Murray might be able to get hold of.

Whatever Murray and Jackson discussed at the beginning of April, it can't be any coincidence that during a phone call with Tim Lopez on 3 April, Conrad Murray enquired about the availability of saline bags for IV drips and, more interestingly, Propofol and its package sizes and price. Lopez was unable to provide Murray with the information he requested at that precise moment but promised to research the drug and its availability.[43]

On 6 April, while Jackson was visiting Dr Klein, Murray made another phone call to Tim Lopez, during which Lopez confirmed he could access Propofol and saline bags for Murray. Immediately, Murray placed an order over the phone for 10 x 100ml vials and 25 x 20ml vials. In addition Murray ordered nine saline bags and 40 x 30 gram tubes of Benoquin, and requested the entire package be sent to his office in Las Vegas.[44] But when the courier arrived at Murray's Las Vegas office, Murray requested that part of the order be taken, instead, to a location in Santa Monica. The address he gave to the courier was that of his mistress, Nicole Alvarez.

But before the courier left, Murray removed several vials of Propofol.[45] Why did he do this? Was it to take them to Jackson to prove that he could get access to the drug? Had Jackson and Murray been having conversations about Jackson's desire for the drug, particularly with his forthcoming concert schedule? Did Jackson promise Murray the exclusive role of personal physician in London if he could provide a steady stream of Propofol for him?

One of the stipulations that Jackson had made of AEG Live during the negotiations for the London O2 shows was that AEG Live pay for the services of a personal physician. Jackson referred to himself as 'the machine', telling those around him that they had to '…take care of the machine'. AEG Live knew this, particularly given Jackson's previous record of health-related issues and his known predilection for pulling out of concerts at the last minute. Consequently, they had agreed to provide and pay for Kai Chase, a personal chef and nutritionist and had also hired Lou Ferrigno, once known as TV's 'Incredible Hulk', as his personal trainer. Randy Phillips was reluctant, initially, to pay for a personal physician, particularly when Jackson demanded that a person of his choosing would fill this role. But, reflecting that a personal physician might reduce Jackson's dependency on Dr Klein and therefore the drugs Klein was believed to be supplying to Jackson, AEG Live agreed to pay for a private physician. Little did they know that they were breaking the drug cycle with Klein, who was providing Jackson with Demerol, but were unwittingly about to introduce Jackson to a gateway to his drug of choice, the more dangerous Propofol.

Propofol, also known as Diprivan, and sometimes Milk of Amnesia, is an extremely strong anaesthetic used primarily during surgery and administered via an injection through a needle placed into a vein, with a maximum dose of 250mg, with 40mg given every 10 seconds until anaesthetic induction is reached. However, if a longer period of sedation is required it can be continuously infused by an IV drip. It is never given as an aid to sleeping. Propofol is extremely fast acting, its effects occur within a matter of seconds, and works by slowing brainwave activities and the nervous system. It works for short periods, for example three to five minutes generally, enabling doctors just enough time to perform a short painful procedure on a patient, such as cardiac shock or to fix a joint dislocation. However, it also wears off rapidly, allowing the patient to wake within a short time with reasonably full alertness. Deadly in the wrong hands, Propofol is only designed for use in a medical setting where ventilation support and monitoring of cardiovascular functions is available and must only be administered by a trained professional, although there is no DEA licensing requirement, meaning any physician can use it. The main issue with Propofol is that it can make the patient's brain forget to breathe. Excess sedation can occur if Propofol is used in conjunction with drugs such as Diazepam, hence the reason that constant monitoring of the patient is essential and critical at all times.[46]

Without any DEA licensing requirement, Murray was legally able to administer Propofol but it would be highly irregular and irresponsible to attempt to administer the drug anywhere except in a hospital where access to monitoring and resuscitation technology was immediately available.

Tim Lopez never questioned why Murray wanted the Propofol and never asked where it would be used. In fact, the only checks Lopez carried out on Murray were to verify his medical degree and determine his designation, the name, address, phone and fax number of his clinic, his licence number and his DEA number.[47]

On 8 April, the courier delivered the packages of Propofol to the home of Nicole Alvarez in Santa Monica. By now, she had given birth to Murray's child and had been introduced to Jackson by Murray some months before, visiting the singer's home on two or three occasions.[48] In March 2009, Murray had also told Nicole Alvarez that they would be going to London when he revealed that Jackson was getting ready for his concert tour. All this was happening before Murray had been officially approached by anyone other than Jackson about being his personal physician on tour and without anything detailed in writing. When the first package arrived at her flat on 8 April, Alvarez signed for it, but didn't open it. However, she made sure that Murray knew a package had arrived for him at her apartment. For Murray, knowing that the delivery had arrived from Allied Pharmacy Services was important because, in April 2009, they weren't the only medical suppliers he was ordering goods from.

SeaCoast Medical is a company based in Omaha, Nebraska. Opened in 1991, they provide pharmaceutical products and services to non-acute physician offices throughout the USA. They had had dealings with Conrad Murray since December 2006 but since his last order from them on 16 December 2008, transactions between Murray and the company had stopped. However, on 25 March 2009, they received a call from Connie Ng in Murray's Las Vegas office enquiring about obtaining an IV fusion set. The order was placed over the phone with delivery noted as being to Murray's

Las Vegas office. But the credit card used to pay for the order was declined and, a week later, nothing had been resolved regarding the payment.[49]

On 13 April 2009, Connie Ng rang SeaCoast again. During this call, Ng asked SeaCoast representative, Sally Hirschberg, if the package could be sent to a residential address in California instead of Murray's office in Las Vegas. This unusual enquiry raised a red flag in Hirschberg's mind and she refused to complete the order. But the following day, another order was placed for a whole variety of medical goods, ranging from Sodium Chloride to injection components for an IV device, to syringes and saline bags. Two further orders were made by Murray's office in April: on the 16th there was an order for 25 tubes of Lidocaine and on 21 April an order for a blood pressure cuff and components and IV catheters. All of these supplies were delivered to Murray's Las Vegas offices.[50] How much of it was to treat Jackson is unknown, but the fact Murray wanted shipments directed to Santa Monica instead of his Las Vegas offices, can only mean that some, if not all, was meant for the singer. It indicates that Murray was stockpiling a significant amount of medical paraphernalia in Los Angeles. Was this because Jackson had already promised him the role of personal physician in London?

Certainly, as April progressed, Murray was becoming the only potential source of Propofol for Jackson. By 19 April, nurse Cherilyn Lee had been dispensed of when she refused to supply Propofol and despite Jackson's frequent visits to Dr Klein – he had visited him five times by 19 April and across these visits received a total of 1,100mg of Demerol from him – the dermatologist was also refusing to administer Propofol. Murray had proved he could lay his hands on Propofol, as his successful order via Tim Lopez on 6 April had shown and, as such, had manoeuvred himself into a position in Jackson's inner circle as Kenny Ortega, the man who was directing the 'This Is It' shows, confirmed when he spotted Murray at Carolwood in April.[51]

Murray wasn't finished yet. On 28 April he placed another Propofol order with Tim Lopez, this time for 40 individual vials of 100ml of Propofol and 25 vials of 20ml of Propofol. Again, Murray stipulated that the order should be delivered to the Santa Monica address of Nicole Alvarez and just two days later, on 30 April, Murray ordered injectable forms of both Lorazepam (10 x 10ml) and Medazepam (20 x 2ml). This package was also shipped to Nicole Alvarez's address.[52]

So, by the end of April 2009, without so much as a formal commitment and operating solely on some sort of verbal agreement with the singer that he was to be Jackson's personal physician, and with a potentially lucrative trip to London ahead of him, Dr Conrad Murray had already ordered some 5,900ml of Propofol. To put this amount into some sort of perspective, a typical hospital with nine anaesthetists working 10-hour days every day of the week would use around 5,000ml a week.

Dr Murray was a qualified cardiologist and not an anaesthetist who would have a more detailed professional knowledge of Propofol, its uses and its dangers.

Despite this, Murray hadn't stopped ordering Propofol or other drugs, as his continued business with Tim Lopez's wholesale pharmacy in Las Vegas shows.[53]

In fact, as April ended and May began, he had only just got started.

6

When people grow up, they forget the way.

J.M. Barrie, *Peter Pan*

On 1 May 2009, another package arrived at Nicole Alvarez's Santa Monica flat. This package consisted of vials of Lorazepam and Midazolam that Murray had ordered the day before from Tim Lopez of Allied Pharmacy Services in Las Vegas. While Murray was placing his order with Lopez on 30 April, Michael Jackson was, once again, visiting Dr Arnold Klein at his clinic in Beverly Hills to have injections of Restylane and Intralesnl+7.[1]

Meanwhile, rehearsals for the 'This Is It' concerts at the O2 in London were well underway in Burbank, California, even without its superstar main attraction. A supremely talented seven-piece backing band, alongside four backing vocalists, had been assembled under the musical directorship of Michael Bearden[2] and thousands of dancers from all over the world flew into Los Angeles in May to audition for the show in front of the 'This Is It' co-creator and co-director, Kenny Ortega.[3]

Born on 18 April 1950, in Palo Alto, California, Ortega had known Jackson since the 1990s *Dangerous* tour when he was the director of the production and also when he was Jackson's co-creator/partner on the *HIStory* tour in 1996, as well as working together on a small number of one-off concert productions for charity subsequently.

Ortega had vast experience as a stage and television dancer and choreographer, and had worked on films in the 1980s such as *Xanadu, Pretty In Pink, St. Elmo's Fire* and *Dirty Dancing*. During the 1990s and the early part of the millennium, Ortega's credits were mostly connected with television shows such as *Chicago Hope* and *Ally McBeal* – before he scored a massive hit in 1996 as choreographer and director of *High School Musical*.

As early as February, Ortega had been having meetings with Jackson to discuss the music, the effects, the lighting and all the relevant details of the show. They would meet three or four, sometimes even five, times a week as the rehearsal schedule gathered pace, to construct the conceptual elements of the show. At first, these meetings were at Jackson's Carolwood mansion, but once actual rehearsals began, these meetings generally took place at the Center Stages in Burbank, California. Joining them was choreographer Travis Payne.[4]

Payne had first worked with Jackson as a dancer in 1992 on the short film, *Remember The Time*. Following this, Payne worked as a dancer and choreographer on the *Dangerous* tour.[5] In early 2009, Payne was working with Kenny Ortega at the Wynn Hotel Casino in Las Vegas and, following Jackson's London press conference, went to meet the singer at his Carolwood home to discuss working together on the new show. Later, Payne discovered he would be the associate director and choreographer on the 'This Is It' tour. Deciding they should get the best dancers in the world, Payne, Ortega and associate choreographer, Stacy Walker,[6] auditioned some 5,000 dancers to select, in April, the most suitable 11 candidates for the shows.

In his court testimony following Jackson's death, Ortega recalled the singer being very excited in mid-April at the potential of doing something really important and wonderful with the 'This Is It' shows, and having the opportunity for his own children to witness him perform live – something they had never before had the chance to see.[7] The shows certainly promised to be spectacular, with pyrotechnics, giant puppets, a flaming bed and a 3D *Thriller*-inspired haunted mansion. The co-owner of Center Staging in Burbank, Johnny Caswell, told *USA Today* on 29 June 2005, 'He [Jackson] was trying, and succeeding, in structuring the biggest, most spectacular live production ever seen. By the time he left my facility, he had graduated through several studios and was on a soundstage taking up 10,000 square feet.'

However 'excited' Jackson seemed to Ortega, there was still concern about his health amongst many of those around the singer. He didn't seem to be attending as many rehearsals as he was scheduled to appear at. In her court testimony, associate choreographer Stacy Walker said that Jackson wasn't at rehearsals as often as he should have been. Was this because of illness or fatigue? Was it because he was visiting Dr Klein and under the effect of Demerol? Or was it simply because he was rehearsing at his Carolwood home with choreographer Travis Payne, who was helping the singer refresh his memory on the dances that already existed to then change and improve them with Jackson's input?

These rehearsals at Jackson's home were scheduled for five days a week but Payne was unsure who was setting the rehearsal schedule for Jackson.[8] The fact that Payne was scheduled to rehearse with Jackson at his home for five days a week certainly offers a reason why Jackson might not have been attending rehearsals at Center Staging. But there might have been another reason. During his testimony Payne was asked, 'How often did you rehearse with Mr Jackson?' His response was, 'It varied. I would go for private rehearsal at Carolwood. Michael would not turn up until Tuesday.' Was this because Jackson was either visiting Dr Klein or recovering from visiting Dr Klein? An inspection of the record of his visits to Dr Klein shows he visited him on Monday, 23 March and then on Monday, 6th and Monday, 13 April, which means he wouldn't have turned up for rehearsals until Tuesday, but the list of the singer's visits to Dr Klein in April shows Jackson couldn't have attended rehearsals on 6th, 9th, 13th, 15th, 17th, 21st, 22nd, 25th, 27th, 28th and 30th, as he was at Dr Klein's on those days.[9]

Perhaps this is why, during the first week of May, Randy Phillips and Paul Gongaware (both of AEG) supposedly, according to an action brought in September 2010 by Katherine Jackson against AEG Live, complained to Jackson that he was not participating in enough of the show's preparations.[10] Jackson had been photographed leaving Klein's clinic on a number of occasions, so there could be no doubt that AEG Live were aware that Jackson was still visiting the dermatologist.

Consequently, AEG Live may have thought that by acquiescing to Jackson's insistent demands for a personal physician, and hiring Dr Conrad Murray to fulfil the role, the singer might stop seeing Klein and, therefore, be less exposed to the drugs that people around Jackson thought he was obtaining from Klein. In the 2010 case brought by Katherine Jackson against AEG Live, it explicitly claims that, 'AEG instructed Michael Jackson to stop seeing and taking medications from his current doctor and to instead start seeing a doctor that AEG would provide.'[11] Dr Robert Waldman, an addiction specialist, was already of the opinion that Jackson had exhibited signs of a developing tolerance to Demerol by late April and by early May he believed the singer was dependent on Demerol and possibly addicted to opioids.[12][13]

During the first week of May, Jackson's personal assistant at the time, Michael Amir Williams, or Brother Michael as he was also known, called Dr Murray to tell him the singer wanted him to be his personal physician in London for the O2 concerts, as well as the build-up to the shows. Williams told Murray to expect a call from Paul Gongaware to formalise the arrangement. Paul Gongaware was the co-CEO of AEG Live. He had begun working for Concerts West in the mid-1970s[14] and had worked with stars such as The Beach Boys, Led Zeppelin and Elvis Presley, amongst others. In fact, Gongaware was working alongside Colonel Tom Parker, Presley's manager, when Elvis died in 1977 in a case coincidentally also related to prescription drugs, this time given to Presley by *his* doctor, Dr Nick.[15] In an email written by Gongaware on 5 July 2009, to Gabe Sutter, a computer technician involved in an earlier Jackson tour, Gongaware wrote: 'I was on the Elvis tour when he died so I kind of knew what to expect.'[16]

Gongaware knew that Jackson had an issue with prescription drugs and was aware that he had been in rehab following the *Dangerous* tour in 1993.[17] During this tour, Gongaware had been acting as tour manager and had been responsible for logistics with what was known as the 'B' party.[18] This tour suffered from a number of cancellations, such as in Bangkok when Jackson took painkillers to help with the pain he was suffering from after surgery on his scalp, and it was one of these cancellations, in Mexico City, that spurred Elizabeth Taylor to recommend Jackson enter rehab in London.

Despite his background knowledge of Jackson's predilection for painkilling drugs and the singer's known unreliability towards actually turning up for scheduled performances, Gongaware was specifically involved in AEG Live trying to secure Michael Jackson for the O2 shows. AEG Live felt it was vital to secure Jackson as they attempted to overtake Live Nation as the world's biggest concert promoters.[19] To have a series of Jackson concerts would significantly increase the standing and value of AEG Live.

As far back as 26 September 2008, Gongaware and AEG Live were considering the prospects of a Michael Jackson tour. On that date, Gongaware sent an email to Randy Phillips saying, 'Net to Mikey, 132 Million' and then continued, 'It's a big number, but this is not a number MJ will want to hear. He thinks he is so much bigger than that. If we use show income, it's over a quarter of a million dollars. His net share works out to be 50% after local, venue and advertising costs, which is quite good. His gross will approach half a billion dollars. Maybe gross is a better number to throw around if we need numbers with Mikey listening.'[20]

In an article in the *New York Post*, Richard Johnson wrote, 'Greedy concert promoters tricked a drug-addled Michael Jackson into signing up for his grueling final concert series by overstating his cut of revenues and softballing how hard he'd have to work.'[21]

Certainly, it appears that well before undertaking any formal discussions with Jackson, AEG Live had already thought about the potential of more than the 10 shows initially proposed to Jackson, as the September 2008 email continues, 'We play out O2 London. Who knows? 30 shows maybe. Then go play out Berlin and other European centres, as many as we can get. Take a break, ship the gear by sea freight (cheapest way), then play out the next continent. We'll be all arenas in America, Europe, Australia stadiums in some places where it makes sense. We finish in America.'

On 5 January 2009, Gongaware sent an email to David Campbell[22] and Jessica Koravos[23] in the UK on the subject of Michael Jackson's potential O2 dates.[24] In the final paragraph of the email, Gongaware wrote, 'We seem to be at or near the final draft of the contract.' He then continued, 'Although it's not going as fast as we would all like, the idea is to get it done any way we can.'

Three weeks later, on 26 January 2009, Michael Jackson had signed a document for 31 shows but still seemed to believe in his mind that he was only going to do 10.[25] By the end of February 2009,

AEG Live were gearing up for the press conference in London at the beginning of March, but Gongaware, with his previous experience of working with Jackson, was already airing his concerns about the possible problems ahead and whether the singer would even turn up to the press conference at the O2. On 27 February 2009, in an email to Randy Phillips, Gongaware wrote, 'We cannot be forced into stopping this, which MJ will try to do because he's lazy and constantly changes his mind to fit his immediate wants.'[26]

Gongaware knew that, in London especially, Michael Jackson was known as 'Wacko Jacko' within the press and media, and any prospect of Jackson not showing up to his own press conference would only fuel the frenzy of ridicule towards him.

In March 2009, Gongaware wrote another email, this time to his assistant, Kelly Distefano, which said, 'Fix the sizing for May. Change the color for the actual shows to something like – like the first one you used, like a light tan or something. I don't want the shows to stand out so much when Michael looks at it. Less contrast between work and off. Maybe off days in a contrasting soft colour. Put 'off' in each day after 8 July as well. Figure it out so it looks like he's not working so much.' It seems that, as early as March 2009, AEG Live already had concerns about not only Jackson's work schedule, but also his reliability in carrying out what was expected of him. Rehearsals had yet to begin, but the number of concerts had already been increased from the initial 10 shows to 50. Gongaware knew how unreliable Jackson was and how important it was to cajole him towards the London dates by appearing not to be putting too much pressure on him, especially when the pressure the singer was already facing from his financial woes was increasingly overwhelming.

Perhaps Jackson was already beginning to exhibit signs of pulling out of the shows? Maybe he was baulking at the workload ahead of him? The concert schedule had dramatically increased and no one, least of all Jackson, had any idea whether he was physically up to performing 50 shows.

In her testimony at the trial after Jackson's death, his make-up artist Karen Faye[27] offered an interesting insight into the way Jackson worked. While on the witness stand in the Jackson v. AEG Live case, Faye read from an email she had sent in March 2009 upon meeting Jackson in preparation for the concerts,

> I see his pattern once again emerging with his caretakers. He uses them to finance his life, and then moves on when he cannot deliver on his promises. I am not saying his original intent isn't to fulfill his obligations, but I'm merely speculating that he becomes paralyzed with fear. I see so many people invest in his success and believe in him. Then I have to watch him self-destruct. I have seen with my own eyes him deteriorate physically in a month. I have seen him do this several times in my relationship with him.

She suggests that therapy might be a perfect treatment for him being able to succeed before concluding with, 'He hurts himself most of all'.

However, the jeopardy to AEG Live at this point was negligible; there was little financial risk to them as, according to the document Jackson had signed, he was bearing all the production costs and AEG Live hadn't had to pay out to hire the O2 Arena because they owned it. What this March email does show is that AEG Live, through Paul Gongaware, were already aware that the schedule for May, which included predominantly rehearsals, had to be carefully adjusted and presented to Jackson in order to keep him placated while, at the same time, ensuring the rehearsals went ahead.

By the time Gongaware was phoning Dr Murray in early May,

Jackson had already signed the contract document for the O2 shows.[28] Jackson had specifically instructed Gongaware and Michael Amir Williams to hire Murray as his personal physician at the beginning of May 2009, and on a permanent basis for the period of the tour. But why was Jackson so insistent that Murray should assume the role? Was it really as simple as Jackson being familiar with Murray? After all the singer had told Dr Slavit he was satisfied with the care he was receiving from Murray. Was it because Murray had proven to the King of Pop that he could easily acquire Jackson's drug of choice, Propofol? Or was it because Brother Michael had supposedly urged Jackson that he hire a black doctor?[29]

Whatever the reason, neither Jackson nor AEG appeared to explore more about Murray's background. A simple check would have revealed Murray's previous encounters with the law, his romantic liaisons and extra-marital affairs and his financial woes. And it appears that AEG Live failed to conduct exhaustive inquiries into the medical and personal background of Conrad Murray. In his testimony to the court following Jackson's death, Paul Gongaware replied to a question about AEG Live's investigation into Murray, regarding whether they checked out '...his background and qualifications, and everything like that', by replying, 'No, we didn't do that. When we check out someone, we check out – we either rely on if we know the person, or if they're known in the industry, or if they're recommended by the artist. And in this case, Dr Murray was recommended by the artist. In fact, the artist insisted.' Certainly, Gongaware confirmed at the same trial that he never saw an investigation report into Dr Murray.

Despite not doing detailed background checks, Paul Gongaware telephoned Dr Murray in Las Vegas on 8 May 2009 and, according to the Joe Jackson v. Conrad Murray trial, told him that AEG was interested in hiring Murray as Jackson's personal 'concierge' physician. Gongaware also supposedly explained to Murray that Jackson had a drug problem and that AEG Live wanted Dr Murray to 'wean' Jackson off his medications and to reduce his dependence on them.[30] It seems unlikely, given their lack of background checks, that AEG Live were aware that Murray had, by this point, already ordered a considerable amount of Propofol and was, to all intents and purposes, already Jackson's exclusive personal physician.

Gongaware knew that Jackson had already passed a medical – Bob Taylor had given him the information from the insurers – but it appears that at no point did Gongaware actually see the report. Gongaware didn't even seem to know, when he talked to Murray on the first occasion, who Murray was or what his medical specialty was.

During this initial phone call, Gongaware, despite having no background information about Murray, asked the doctor how much he wanted to accept the job. As Randall Sullivan wrote in his book *Untouchable*, 'The call that came out of nowhere offering him a job as Michael Jackson's personal physician must have seemed to Murray a miracle cure for all that ailed him.'[31]

Consequently, Murray stated that he wanted $5 million, saying that he would have to close four clinics and lay some people off.[32] Gongaware told Murray that this simply wasn't going to happen and ended the call.

Later that week, Gongaware spoke once more with Murray.[33] At that moment Gongaware was in a car with Michael Jackson and the singer told Gongaware to offer Murray $150,000. Gongaware said to Murray that he had been authorised to offer $150,000 and Murray immediately began protesting, saying he '…can't do it for that' and that he needed more. But Gongaware cut Murray off mid-sentence and told him that the offer came directly from the artist, upon which Murray immediately accepted,[34] therefore going from $5 million to $150,000 a month within seconds.[35]

During this conversation, Gongaware specifically asked Murray if he was licensed to go to London. Murray didn't say 'yes' but he did tell Gongaware 'Don't worry about the licensing. I'll take care of that.'[36] In addition, Murray specified that he would need an assistant in London as well as some medical equipment. Gongaware finished by saying that AEG Live would, from that moment on, work on contract negotiations with Murray, as they were in the process of doing with other parties of the forthcoming Jackson tour, through Timm Woolley, the tour business manager.[37]

While all this was going on, Michael Jackson had checked in once again at Dr Klein's clinic. On 4, 5, 6 May he received three injections totaling 800mg of Demerol[38] following treatment for acne scars with Restylane, as well as five injections of Latanoprost for Jackson's eye hypertension.

On 8 May 2009, as expected, Timm Woolley made contact with Conrad Murray. During their phone conversation, the two of them discussed the details of Murray's engagement and Woolley confirmed the points raised in their discussion in an email sent to Murray later that day. Amongst the topics the email refers to are Murray's mode of travel: 'most likely with Artist on charter, but 1st Class if not', and he confirms that Murray's accommodation in London is within '…easy proximity of the Artist – that might be a guest house on the grounds of the property rented for Artist'. The email also states to Murray that, 'AEG contract would not cover more than one month in lieu of notice if there was a curtailment or cessation of the tour', and concludes with the offer of $150,000 per month, payable mid-month.

Two days later on Sunday, 10 May 2009, without responding to this email, Conrad Murray visited Michael Jackson at his Carolwood home. What happened that day remains a secret, but what is known is that Murray made an audio recording of Michael Jackson on his own iPhone. In the recording, we hear the barely recognisable voice of Jackson speaking in a rambling, slow and semi-comatosed manner, seemingly under the influence of drugs.

In the four-minute recording Jackson slurs out the following words:

Elvis didn't do it. Beatles didn't do it. We have to be phenomenal. When people leave this show, when people leave my show, I want them to say, 'I've never seen anything like this in my life. Go. Go. I've never seen nothing like this. Go. It's amazing. He's the greatest entertainer in the world.' I'm taking that money, a million children, children's hospital, the biggest in the world, Michael Jackson's Children's Hospital. Going to have a movie theatre, game room. Children are depressed. The… in those hospitals, no game room, no movie theatre. They're sick because they're depressed. Their mind is depressing them. I want to give them that. I care about them, them angels. God wants me to do it. God wants me to do it. I'm going to do it, Conrad. Don't have enough hope, no more hope. That's the next generation that's going to save our planet, starting with…we'll talk about it. United States, Europe, Prague, my babies. They walk around with no mother. They drop them off, they leave… a psychological degradation of that. They reach out to me: 'Please take me with you'. I'm going to do that for them. That will be remembered more than my performances. My performances will be up there helping my children and always be my dream. I love them. I love them because I didn't have a childhood. I had no childhood. I feel their pain. I feel their hurt. I can deal with it. 'Heal the World', 'We Are The World', 'Will You Be There', 'The Lost Children.' These are the songs I've written because I hurt, you know, I hurt.

After Jackson stopped speaking here, there was silence until Murray asked if Jackson was okay. Eight seconds of silence followed before Jackson finally replied with an eerily foreboding, 'I am asleep'.

Why did Murray make this recording? What purpose did he hope it would serve? Was it an opportunistic keepsake, snatched when the singer was barely able to function? Or was it, possibly, an insurance policy taken out by Murray,[39] proof that Jackson was under the influence of drugs when he returned from visits to Dr Klein? After all, Paul Gongaware from AEG Live is supposed to have requested that Murray helps to 'wean' Jackson off Demerol[40] and those close to Jackson confirmed during the trial that the singer talked with a slower speech pattern with a slur in the speech after a visit to Dr Klein's clinic.[41]

But, if this recording was made on Sunday, 10 May 2009,[42] any connection to Dr Klein, and the Demerol he might have been giving to Jackson, is irrelevant as the singer hadn't visited Klein's clinic since Wednesday, 6 May and Demerol is likely to be out of a person's system in 10 to 20 hours following administration.[43] It is possible, of course, that Jackson administered Demerol himself, but he was known to have a phobia of needles and so self-administration seems highly unlikely.

In an exclusive interview with Don Lemon broadcast on CNN on 26 June 2014, Conrad Murray was questioned about the iPhone recording. After Don Lemon had played an extract from the recording he pressed Murray about why he felt the need to record Jackson in such a state:

Don Lemon: Dr Murray, that is disturbing. Anyone in that condition, why would you continue to give him drugs and then give him Propofol? And why would you record that?
Murray: Well, first of all I was accused of recording that so that I can take advantage of Michael down the road. And that was not

the case. I did not even recognise or realise that that recording was actually on my phone. Michael had asked me, well, as far as I could look back, how much he snores at night. And I would speak to him about that. He wanted to record that, not only on tape, but on camera. I actually had just learned from my daughter who taught me to do talks and one of the apps on the phone.

Don Lemon: How to work it?

Murray: Right.

Don Lemon: But the question behind that is, so you were trying to monitor his sleep pattern, whether or not he was snoring, and that's how you got that recording.

(Crosstalk)

Murray: That's exactly how that was done when I look back in retrospect, yes.

Don Lemon: So why then would you continue? Because if he was…

(Crosstalk)

Murray: Interestingly – good question. If you look at my – if you listen to that recording, you hear a man that is clearly in the sleep state of going to sleep. But he is alert. His conversation makes sense.

Lemon: His mind is still active, even though he's in a state of sleep.

Murray: Yes. But if you look at my statement to the police, I explained to them, to the police, all that Michael Jackson wanted, including the children's hospital. Michael was just reiterating his dream to me. At the end of that state, of that recording, did you hear what he says at the end? He says, 'I'm asleep'.[44]

In this interview, Murray fails to reveal much and it remains impossible to know what drugs Jackson had been taking prior to the audio recording being made, if any. But maybe the next order that Murray made to Applied Pharmacy Services can shed some light. No contract had yet been signed between Murray and AEG Live and negotiations were still at the discussion stage but, within two days of making this recording, Murray had already begun spending nights at Jackson's Carolwood home[45] and on 12 May he called Tim Lopez in Las Vegas to order another 40 x 100ml vials of Propofol, 25 x 20ml vials of Propofol and 20 x 2ml vials of Midazolam.[46] This order of Propofol was equal in quantity to the order Murray had made on 28 April.

The order Murray made on 12 May also contained 10 x 0.5ml of Flumazenil. This was the first occasion that Murray had ordered Flumazenil since he had been working with Jackson. Flumazenil is a medicine that is specifically used as an antidote to reverse the effects of certain types of sedatives known as benzodiazepines. Midazolam and Lorazepam are benzodiazepines, and Murray had ordered both in April and May. Could it be that Murray was concerned about the side effects and potential dangers of the various prescription drugs he now had at his disposal, hence the reason he recorded the audio clip on his iPhone? And his order of Flumazenil would ensure, quite correctly, that he had an ability to reverse the effects of benzodiazepines if needed.

Certainly, it appears that by mid-May Murray was injecting, or considering injecting, Michael Jackson as, on 14 May, Conrad Murray phoned Tim Lopez to enquire about Lidocaine cream, and asked specifically about getting access to an increased strength of the cream.[47] Lidocaine cream is used as a local anaesthetic on the skin of a patient to cause numbness or loss of feeling before certain medical procedures, such as injections. Michael Jackson had a phobia of needles and Murray's initial order of Lidocaine was for a 2% cream and now, on 14 May, Murray was asking Lopez to increase the strength to 4%.

At this point in May, Jackson was taking a more pro-active role in the rehearsals, although his attendance was still irregular and unpredictable despite the fact that on 12 May 2009, the *Los Angeles Times* reported that:

> Four mornings a week, an SUV with darkened windows bears Michael Jackson through the gates outside a nondescript building near the Burbank airport. He spends the next six hours on a soundstage in the company of 10 dancers and pop music's best-known choreographer.

He certainly wasn't at rehearsals four mornings a week every week throughout most of May and his lack of attendance was becoming increasingly frustrating for those involved in the forthcoming shows. In fact, a report in the *Daily Mail* on 22 May 2009 claimed that '…Michael has so far only shown up for two days of rehearsals, while his dancers have been working every day for 45 days.'[48] But he had instigated changes in his life in May, whether at the behest of AEG Live or not, to seemingly improve the chances of him actually performing at the O2.

He had stopped seeing Dr Klein (his last visit to the dermatologist was on Wednesday, 6 May and he didn't revisit him until Friday, 15 May) and he now also had his own personal physician, Dr Conrad Murray, who was in contract negotiations with AEG Live. The report from the *Los Angeles Times* that he was suddenly attending rehearsals, turning up in an SUV four mornings a week, fits with a gap between visits to Klein and certainly allows for a period when Jackson was likely clear of Demerol, 7 to 14 May, and therefore able to attend rehearsal for four mornings prior to the report being written, on any combination of 7, 8, 9, 10 and 11 May.[49]

If Jackson were suddenly attending rehearsals regularly, and for six hours a day in the company of dancers and choreographers, he would need to be fit and alert and, most importantly, awake. He would have needed a good night's sleep before to get through such a schedule, not an easy task for a man suffering from insomnia. And, by this point, according to his LAPD interview, Dr Murray had been administering Jackson Propofol.[50]

On 15 May 2009, Dr Murray responded by email to AEG's initial contract offer, made by Timm Woolley a week earlier. In his email, which essentially agreed to the contents of the previous email from Woolley on 8 May and confirms that he is ready to sign a contract after showing it to his attorney, Murray concludes by writing, 'As for good faith with my client I am sure you are aware that my services are already fully engaged with Mr Jackson.'

But despite Jackson having his own personal physician – the one he had insisted upon – as well as Lou Ferrigno as his personal trainer who worked on conditioning, toning and increasing the flexibility and stamina of the singer's body, there was still concern amongst many behind the scenes that Jackson was in no fit state to open the tour on 8 July. He had frequently missed rehearsals and his health was still questionable. These lingering doubts about his ability to pull off his remarkable comeback prompted AEG Live, on 20 May, to delay the opening four nights of his O2 concert tour. The opening show, scheduled for 8 July 2009, was pushed back by five nights while the shows scheduled for the 10, 12 and 14 July were moved to dates in March 2010.

The official line was that the delays were at the behest of Michael Jackson and Kenny Ortega, and were down to the nature of the planned shows. In a statement, Randy Phillips said,

> Kenny and Michael are, at the same time, both creative pioneers and perfectionists. The show has grown in size and scope, thereby necessitating more lead time for manufacture of the set, programming the content

for the massive video elements and, most importantly, more time for full production and dress rehearsals. As much as we agonized over this change in the original schedule, we are sure the fans will understand when they experience the level of entertainment Michael Jackson intends to deliver.

Seven hundred and fifty thousand fans had already bought tickets and, despite all the apologies and excuses, it was a bitter pill for them to swallow, and, for many of them, the official line was treated with scepticism.

Across international media outlets, all sorts of rumours accounting for the delay started to circulate. Many attributed the reason to Jackson's notorious reputation for cancelling concerts, but most suggested health fears with stories ranging from cancer scares to Jackson needing a lung transplant. The odds of him actually making the first night in London were cut dramatically and author Ian Halperin reported that 'Behind the scenes, Jackson's mental and physical health was rapidly deteriorating.'[51] Halperin, quoting a member of Jackson's household staff suggested that the singer was 'terrified' by the forthcoming concerts and wasn't eating or sleeping and, when he did manage to sleep, he was having nightmares that he was going to be murdered. Halperin's source ends by saying, 'His voice and moves weren't there any more. I think he maybe wanted to die rather than embarrassing himself onstage.'

The *Daily Mail* also had their own take on the postponement. On 22 May, reporter Alison Boshoff wrote that a 'perfectly placed Jackson family source' insisted that the singer is simply 'not able to pick himself up out of the stupor he is in'. She added: 'The suggestion that they need more time to set up the show in London is a joke.'[52]

While the announcement was being made on the 20 May 2009 that the London shows had been postponed, Jackson was back in Beverly Hills visiting Dr Klein. He attended Klein's clinics on the 19, 20, and 21 May and had 100mg of Demerol injected into him on each of these days. These were Jackson's last visits to Klein during May. By this point in time, Dr Murray was spending an increasing amount of time at Jackson's Carolwood home, particularly at night. He had been seen by the nutritionist hired to prepare food for Jackson, Kai Chase, who recalled observing Murray carrying canisters of oxygen down the stairs each morning.[53] [54] Murray had been asked to 'wean' Jackson off Demerol; with Jackson scaling back his visits to Dr Klein, his main provider of Demerol, could it be that Murray was actually succeeding in his aim? But, if so, at what cost?

On 22 May, Conrad Murray sent another email to Timm Woolley at AEG Live, this time with his bank account information and a request for his May payment of $150,000. When this hadn't arrived in his account almost a week later, Murray sent another email on 28 May to Woolley stating that: 'I gathered from your last email that my contract is taking a little more time to develop than usual. In the meanwhile I have performed and continue to fulfill my services to the client in good faith.' Further on in the email, Murray points out that the usual date of payment is 15 May and that, therefore payment is 13 days overdue. He concludes with, 'I would appreciate it if you would look into this matter immediately so that we can go forward amicably as we have done to this point.' This, despite the fact that no contract had been formally agreed, presented or signed between AEG Live and Murray. Woolley replied, almost immediately, with an email in which he said,

> The legal department has not yet completed the agreement which is rather specialized since it is a

rare event that a physician is engaged to accompany a touring artist. In any other circumstance I would agree that payment should be made as close as practicable to the due date, But AEG policies dictate that payment can only be made under a fully executed agreement.

At this point, Jackson was still not attending rehearsals regularly and AEG Live were anxious that Murray continue to do whatever he could to get the singer to the rehearsals. The non-payment and non-completion of the contract was threatening to become an issue. But Murray was in such a financial position that he couldn't survive without Jackson, Jackson needed Murray to have access to Propofol, and AEG Live needed Murray to get the singer to the rehearsals. It was becoming a vicious circle for all concerned.

On 30 May 2009, the *Los Angeles Times* printed an article in which it hinted at trouble ahead. It claimed, 'Even as Jackson's deep-pocketed benefactors assemble an all-star team – *High School Musical*'s Kenny Ortega is directing the London concerts – there are hints of discord.'

This was against a backdrop of the same article featuring comments stating that AEG Live has proposed a three-year tour with Randy Phillips suggesting estimated ticket sales for the global concerts would exceed $450 million with the hope that Jackson would receive 50 per cent of that. The article ends with Randy Phillips acknowledging the concerts are a do-or-die moment for Jackson saying, 'If it doesn't happen [the O2 concerts], it would be a major problem for him [Jackson] career-wise in a way that it hasn't been in the past.'

When Randy Phillips acknowledged the O2 concerts were a pivotal moment for Michael Jackson, nobody around him, least of all Jackson himself, could realise how prophetic the do-or-die comment was as the main players in this tragedy entered June 2009.

7

Take care, lest an adventure is now offered you, which,
if accepted, will plunge you in deepest woe.

J.M. Barrie, *Peter Pan*

On Monday, 1 June, the rehearsal schedule for the 'This Is It' tour entered its seventh week. But, as had happened so often before, Michael Jackson was once again conspicuous by his absence. While the musicians and dancers did what they could without the main attraction, under the supervision of Kenny Ortega, Michael Jackson was back visiting his old friend, Beverly Hills dermatologist, Dr Arnold Klein. Here, Jackson received an injection of Restylane, accompanied by another 200mg of Demerol.

Despite the instructions laid down to Dr Murray by AEG Live that he was to 'wean' Jackson off Demerol, the singer's visits to Dr Klein continued well into June. It is known from medical records and invoices, despite Klein insisting otherwise in an interview with Harvey Levin of TMZ on 6 November 2009,[1] that Jackson visited Klein on 1, 3, 10, 16 and 22 June. By the time Jackson made his final visit to Dr Klein on 22 June, the singer had undergone 179 procedures and received 51 injections,[2] including 21 of Demerol totalling 5,250mg of the drug, in a three-month period. When Dr

Klein's attorneys submitted an invoice for these procedures, which they sent to the creditors following Jackson's death, the bill came to almost $50,000.[3]

By now, owing to the increasing scale of the production, the rehearsals had moved from Center Staging in Burbank to The Forum in Inglewood, California. Opened in December 1967 at a cost of $16 million,[4] The Forum is a multi-purpose arena that Michael Jackson knew well. It was at The Forum, on 20 June 1970, that The Jackson 5 performed to a crowd that broke the venue's attendance records, with 18,675 people paying to see the group. Jackson had also appeared there in 1981 when he joined his old friend and mentor, Diana Ross, onstage for a performance of her hit single 'Upside Down', recorded for her television special.

However, while the production had moved to The Forum, Jackson had yet to be seen at rehearsals there and, for AEG Live, this was causing major concerns, not least because they had discovered at the end of May that their initial outlay for the O2 concerts had more than tripled. Initially a $7.5 million outlay towards the production budget had been agreed by AEG Live, but now, when artist advances and the rent on Jackson's house were taken into account, AEG Live were almost $29 million out of pocket. And the main attraction was nowhere to be seen.[5] Somehow, AEG Live had to persuade and cajole Jackson to attend rehearsals as a matter of urgency.

One of the people who could help them was Dr Conrad Murray. He had still not agreed to, or signed, a contract for his services, yet he was devoting himself to his role as Jackson's personal physician almost exclusively by the beginning of June. But while Jackson was visiting Dr Klein, Murray had no patient to treat, as Jackson would travel to see Klein without Murray. Still, Murray kept himself busy and, on 1 June 2009, he placed another order with SeaCoast Medical. Amongst the items ordered were an airway-kit (priced at $2.02) and an Ambu Bag, a manual hand-held resuscitator used by medical professionals in preference to mouth-to-mouth ventilation in out-of-hospital settings when the patient's breathing is insufficient or has ceased completely. Ideal, perhaps, to resuscitate a drug addict suffering cardiac arrest.

On 2 June, Kai Chase began her employment as Michael Jackson's chef and nutritionist. Jackson had already been working with Lou Ferrigno as his personal trainer, and the implementation of a chef and nutritionist was seen as a vital cog in the efforts to get Jackson ready for the London concerts. However, within a few days of her employment, Chase became aware that tensions were running high throughout the Jackson camp.

Shortly after Chase was hired, a meeting was called at Carolwood mansion to discuss the problems of Jackson not attending rehearsals. Kenny Ortega was concerned that the singer wasn't coming to enough rehearsals and, when he did, was taking it nonchalantly. Others within the production camp would suggest that when Jackson did actually turn up to rehearsals, he would often be 'woozy' and not as focused as he should be. But when Ortega put his concerns to Jackson, the singer told him that he wanted Kenny to build the house and then the pop star would come in and paint the front door.[6]

The meeting that took place at Carolwood was, supposedly, a heated one. It was heated enough, as Kai Chase testified, for a vase to be sent crashing to the ground and voices to be raised. According to Chase's testimony in court, Jackson attended the meeting wearing a surgical mask and layers of clothing as he was complaining about feeling very hot, then extremely cold.[7] These are classic withdrawal symptoms of an addict coming down from Demerol and it's possibly no coincidence that Jackson visited Dr Klein twice in the first week of June and received two injections, totalling 400mg of Demerol.

The meeting was attended by Dr Murray, Frank Dileo, Michael Jackson and Randy Phillips. Kai Chase suggested that Jackson was an emotional wreck at the time; that he was scared, fearful and anxious about the meeting. She had to go in and out of the room refilling beverage glasses but didn't overhear anything while she was briefly in the room but did, however, hear raised voices when she had left. On one occasion when she returned to fill the glasses she noticed a vase was lying broken on the floor and it wasn't long after that Dr Murray stormed into the kitchen having escaped the meeting and exclaimed: 'I can't handle this shit!' before leaving via the back door.[8]

On 3 June, Jackson visited Klein's clinic once more after filming parts of 'The Drill' in 3D at Culver Studios,[9] and perhaps as a result of the heated meeting, he soon began attending rehearsals more frequently. On 4[10], 5, 6, 8, 9, 10[11] and 11 June, Jackson turned up to rehearsals at The Forum and Conrad Murray was also spotted accompanying him there for the first time.[12]

Jackson would generally attend during the evening as, at certain points during 1 to 11 June, the singer was also going to Culver Studios in Culver City. Here he was shooting *The Dome Project* which consisted of seven short film works and vignettes, either adaptations of earlier videos or totally new film elements: 'Smooth Criminal', 'Thriller', 'Earth Song', 'They Don't Care About Us', 'MJ Air', 'The Final Message' and 'The Way You Make Me Feel' were the songs that had new film elements created for them, mostly in 3D.

Jackson's reappearance at rehearsals was a relief to many. Amongst others, choreographer Travis Payne[13] was aware of Jackson missing rehearsals at The Forum. He knew Jackson wasn't showing up but never asked the singer why when he saw him at their private rehearsals. As far as Payne was concerned, Jackson was busy with other projects, such as an album and a book. Payne also thought Jackson seemed tired and recalled the singer saying to him that he had trouble sleeping. Furthermore, Payne noticed Jackson was losing weight throughout the rehearsal period. He asked the singer about it: 'I'm getting down to my fighting weight,' Jackson told him.[14]

The singer's make-up artist, Karen Faye,[15] was also aware Jackson was periodically missing rehearsals at The Forum, or turning up late, and Stacy Walker, the associate producer of the show, recalled in her testimony that: 'I don't remember how many times he came or not, it's difficult. I remember being frustrated at the time, when we thought he would come and he didn't.' The general consensus amongst most of the production team was that Jackson was rehearsing on his own or with Travis Payne, working on other projects, or spending time with his children.

On 8 June, the eighth week of rehearsals began. Jackson was rehearsing at The Forum on Monday 8th to Thursday 11th, although he visited Dr Klein's clinic on the 10th where he underwent acne surgery and Botox injections under the eyes, as well as receiving a 200mg injection of Demerol. It was on the 10th that choreographer Travis Payne recalled Jackson turning up at rehearsals wrapped in a blanket suggesting the singer was cold, once again a classic withdrawal symptom of Demerol.

That same day, while Jackson was at Klein's Beverly Hills clinic, Dr Murray ordered more Propofol from Tim Lopez – this time 40 x 100ml bottles and 50 x 20ml bottles, some 5,000 additional millilitres of Propofol. This meant that, between 6 April and 10 June, Dr Murray had ordered 255 separate vials of Propofol, totalling some 15.5 litres of the drug, equivalent to 3.49 gallons. Just based on these orders alone, Murray had ordered in those 80 days enough to give Jackson 1,937mg of Propofol every single day.[16]

On 12 June, Jackson attended rehearsals at The Forum once more, but it didn't go well and the next day, Saturday 13 June,

Michael Jackson cancelled rehearsals on doctor's orders.[17] The following day, emails were exchanged between Kenny Ortega, Paul Gongaware, Randy Phillips, Travis Payne and Frank Dileo about Jackson's lack of appearances at rehearsals.

Ortega sent an email to Paul Gongaware, which said:

> Were you aware that MJ's doctor didn't permit him to attend rehearsal yesterday? Are Randy and Frank aware of this? Please have them stay on top of his health situation. Without invading MJ's privacy it might be a good idea to talk to his doctor to make sure everything MJ requires is in place, who is responsible for MJ getting proper nourishment/vitamins/therapy everyday? Personally, I feel he should have a top nutritionist and Physical Therapist working with him on a regular basis. The demands on this guy are mentally and physically extraordinary! The show requirements exhaust our 20 year olds. Please don't underestimate the need to stay on top of this.

Travis Payne, himself becoming increasingly concerned about Jackson's well-being, suggested the singer should consider a regular massage, but Jackson flatly refused, as he thought it would be a violation of his personal space.

Karen Faye shared Payne's concerns about Jackson. Having worked with Jackson as his make-up artist for over 25 years, she had noticed, as rehearsals progressed, the singer getting thinner and thinner each month, and she also noticed that he was beginning to repeat himself often, saying the same thing over and over again. Faye was aware that not all was right, a feeling confirmed during a visit to Paul Gongaware's office where she heard Gongaware screaming down the phone to Michael Amir Williams because

Michael Jackson had locked himself in his bathroom and wasn't coming out.[18]

Faye was so concerned that Jackson was missing rehearsals that she went to people higher up the production chain to share her thoughts about the singer's psychological well-being. She once even encountered Randy Phillips in the hallway of the rehearsal facility and told him how everybody was sad that Jackson was missing rehearsals. Phillips replied with the anecdote that he had had to get a drunken Jackson off the floor in London to ensure he turned up to the O2 press conference. This confirmed her fears for Jackson's health and when she realised the singer was constantly cold to the touch, she communicated her concerns directly with Frank Dileo, by now Jackson's manager again.

Making a phone call to Dileo when Michael Jackson was late to rehearsals once more, probably on 16 June,[19] she expressed her concerns to the management but, as she later testified, she felt she wasn't listened to by either Dileo or Ortega, and recalled that Kenny Ortega even told her to not listen to what Jackson was saying to her.

But, two days earlier, on 14 June, the consequences of Jackson's frail health and the impact it was having on rehearsals with an opening night in London looming on the horizon had alerted those much higher up the production chain than Karen Faye. By 14 June, Paul Gongaware had almost certainly discussed the significance of everybody's concerns with Frank Dileo. Gongaware had written an email to Randy Phillips saying that they had requested a face-to-face meeting with Dr Murray on Monday 15 June, at which they were going to remind Murray that it was AEG, not Jackson, who was paying his salary. Consequently, they wanted Murray to '…understand what is expected of him'.

On 15 June, the draft contract for Dr Murray's services, which were still being performed in good faith, was close to being finalised.

Kathy Jorrie, a lawyer from Los Angeles, was responsible for drafting the contract for services involving Conrad Murray and Michael Jackson. On 15 June she sent a draft agreement to Timm Woolley at AEG Live, part of which contained a clause that AEG Live were actively looking to secure housing for Dr Murray in London. The anticipation was that this contract, stipulating the provision of first-class airfare, housing in London and the provision of medical equipment as requested by Murray, would be signed by 3 July 2009. But, on the first draft agreement being sent to Murray the next day, 16 June, it was stated as commencing on 1 May 2009, some six weeks previously. This draft agreement was forwarded to Murray via email, and it obviously provided Dr Murray with a sense of security that the job appeared to be definitely going ahead as, later that day, he sent a letter to all his clients telling them that, 'Because of a once in a lifetime opportunity, I had to make a most difficult decision to cease practice medicine indefinitely.'

It wasn't the only business Murray was doing around that time. On 15 June, Murray placed another order with Tim Lopez, this time for 20 vials of Midazolam and 10 vials of Lorazepam while, at the same time, Dr Murray's account representative in his Las Vegas clinic, Connie Ng, phoned Sally Hirschberg at SeaCoast Medical to talk about a potential order of urine bags, specifically asking for small urine collection bags.[20] [21]

While Murray was confident enough in his position to announce to his clients that he was closing his clinics, the production team still had little confidence in the ability of Jackson to pull off the shows. Kenny Ortega wrote in an email that Jackson is '…not in great physical shape, I believe he is hurting, he has been slow at grabbing hold of the work', and, following rehearsals on the 16th, the band's musical director, Michael Bearden, sent an email to Kenny Ortega regarding Michael Jackson's singing ability at that point of rehearsals. He wrote:

MJ is not in shape enough yet to sing this stuff live and dance at the same time. He can use the ballads to sing live and get his stamina back up. Once he's healthy enough and has more strength, I have full confidence he can sing the majority of the show live. His voice sounds amazing right now, he needs to build it back up. I still need all big dance numbers to be in the system so we can concentrate on choreography.

It's hardly surprising that both Ortega and Beardon felt this way around the 16 June rehearsal date as it's the date when Karen Faye referred to Jackson as looking frightened but stoic following his latest visit to Dr Klein's clinic for treatment, which involved yet another injection of Demerol.

There might have been another reason for Jackson's increasing anxiety on 16 June: that day his representatives were in court on his behalf to face the charges filed against him by his ex-manager, Raymone Bain. Bain was formerly the singer's publicist, but in 2003 became his spokesperson and later his personal manager. In 2006 she signed an agreement with Jackson, which appeared to guarantee her a 10 per cent finder's fee on any agreement Jackson entered into as a result of Bain's work. Jackson dismissed Bain in 2007, but she was now suing the singer for $44 million over allegations that Jackson '...elected not to honour the financial obligations of our contractual relationships.'[22] This action, brought by Bain, was the latest in a long line of legal claims faced by Jackson as he prepared for his comeback[23] – he had already been to court to prevent the contents of Neverland being sold; he had been sued by John Landis, the director of the 'Thriller' video, claiming Jackson had failed to pay Landis his 50 per cent cut of the net proceeds of the video; he had also been sued by former *Playboy* model Ola Ray who played Jackson's girlfriend in the 'Thriller' video, seeking the unpaid royalties she felt she was owed for her role; and he had been sued for $7 million by the son of the King of Bahrain. As well as these, there were countless other lawsuits pending.[24]

With increasing stress impacting upon his life at so many levels, it is hardly surprising that Jackson was having trouble sleeping. He was in a financial mess, he was facing lawsuit after lawsuit and he had the tension of his impending comeback at the O2, upon which so much was riding. To help Jackson sleep, Dr Murray was giving the singer Propofol on a daily basis, in fact he had been doing so for six weeks and Jackson was, probably, by now dependent on the drug. Murray was also administering Jackson benzodiazepines and these drugs together meant the singer was often unable to communicate properly with his closest friends and wasn't able to make sense as he continually repeated himself during conversations.

On 18 June, Michael Jackson, once again, failed to turn up at rehearsals. As a result, Randy Phillips, Kenny Ortega, Paul Gongaware and Frank Dileo travelled to Jackson's home. This meeting was referred to as a 'drug intervention', the aim of which was to try to get the pop star to stop his dependence on drugs, and to focus and attend rehearsals. Dr Murray was invited to attend this meeting at AEG Live's discretion.

While it was true that Jackson had stepped up his attendance at rehearsals, there was still the concern that he was distracted. In an email at the time, Randy Phillips said of the singer, 'Getting him fully engaged is difficult and the most pressing matter as we are only 20 days out from the first show.'

AEG Live had already pushed back the opening date by five days, but it was inconceivable they could make yet another schedule change. Kenny Ortega had severe concerns that Jackson simply wouldn't be ready in time, even with the new opening date. He would question Jackson by asking, 'Are you going to show up? Are you really going to be here? You need to do this.' As far as Ortega was concerned, they could placate Jackson no longer; it was time for 'tough love'.[25] Kenny Ortega wasn't alone in realizing how critical it was that Jackson showed up for rehearsals. Everyone knew that Jackson was the fulcrum of the production and the whole show, and that naturally, everything revolved around him. Frank Dileo, however, had a different view of how crucial Jackson was to the rehearsal schedule. Dileo referred to Jackson as '…a gamer' in his relationship to the rehearsal process: 'He's the quarterback. He's the star of the team, and in practice, quarterbacks are easy going. But game day, he's turning it on', Dileo would say.[26]

Dileo's reassurances didn't hold much weight with the others in the production team and it was Ortega's concerns that were shared by others. Even when Jackson did turn up at rehearsals his lacklustre performances worried many. The meeting on 18 June would see Jackson being read the riot act about failing to turn up at rehearsals, AEG demanding he put in maximum effort when he was there and, most importantly perhaps, the need for him to address his dependency on drugs. During the meeting Phillips and Gongaware urged Jackson to stop seeing Dr Klein. They were under no illusions that Klein was providing the singer with drugs that went some way to making the singer sleepy, lethargic and unable to rehearse properly. They demanded that Jackson only take the medications prescribed to him by Dr Murray, apparently totally unaware of the medications Murray was *already* prescribing him. The situation was extremely serious for all concerned, especially Jackson. According to a complaint filed with the Medical Board of California in 2010, Joe Jackson alleges that in this meeting Phillips and Gongaware also told Jackson that he turned up for rehearsals or AEG were going to 'pull the plug' on the show, his house and his doctor.[27] This would naturally be followed by lawsuits and Jackson's career would be over.

Joining in, Ortega is supposed to have told Jackson that he had to get his 'shit' together before Phillips confirmed that Jackson must no longer see Klein, or take his drugs, because they had hired Murray to be Jackson's doctor, not Klein.[28] As far as they were concerned, Jackson had to do what Dr Murray instructed him to do. Then, turning on Murray, Phillips and Gongaware allegedly, according to a claim made in the Katherine Jackson v. AEG Live Complaint For Damages, told the doctor that he had to make sure Jackson got to rehearsals, and if he didn't, the shows would be cancelled and Murray's employment terminated.[29]

Many of the production crew present at rehearsals had little idea that Jackson was specifically under the influence of drugs. Travis Payne, for example, had never seen Jackson taking any prescription medication during rehearsals. He did observe the singer being under the influence of something, but had no idea what. Payne referred specifically, to instances when Jackson attended rehearsals after visiting Dr Klein when he noticed Jackson appearing '…you know, just a little loopy'.[30] And even though Kenny Ortega was aware that Jackson hadn't been turning up to rehearsals, he had no idea why and didn't even suspect the singer was addicted to prescription medication. Ortega was told that Jackson's no-shows were to do with scheduling and while it impacted on his rehearsal, he had no reason to doubt it, or to suspect anything else was going on.[31]

However, there was, by now, grave concern that if Jackson continued to miss any rehearsals then it was very possible that the production wasn't going to be able to open in London in July. Following the meeting at Carolwood, during which Jackson had been read the 'riot act' by Phillips, Gongaware and Ortega, the singer made his way to that night's rehearsals. He arrived at The Forum at 9:30pm that evening, but those who saw him arrive said he appeared visibly shaken. In fact, Jackson was furious. He was under no illusion that the choice before him was a stark one: he had to accept AEG Live's demands or suffer catastrophic financial consequences. Karen Faye confirmed this in a text she sent to her boyfriend when she arrived home at 2:30am on the 19th. In the text, she referred to a meeting having taken place between Jackson and Randy Phillips and wrote:

> Kenny told me AEG [Randy Phillips] is funding his entire life right now. His house, food, kids, school, everything. They told him they will 'PULL THE PLUG IF HE DOESN'T GET HIS SHIT TOGETHER. IF HE DOESN'T DO THIS, HE LOSES EVERYTHING, PROBABLY EVEN HIS KIDS.'[32]

It was too early to know what effect the meeting might have had on the singer, but that night AEG Live moved forward with Conrad Murray's contractual agreement. At 11:11pm Kathy Jorrie forwarded the written agreement to Conrad Murray. In it was a clause stating that AEG Live would have to provide CPR equipment and a nurse to Murray but otherwise, with the exception that the agreement required Michael Jackson's signature, it was identical to the agreement Murray had held discussions about on 8 May 2009.[33]

Later that evening, when Jackson returned home from rehearsals, Dr Murray gave the singer a cocktail of Ativan (Lorazepam), Valium (Diazepam), Versed (Midazolam) and Propofol to enable Jackson to sleep. It was a 'cocktail' of drugs that Murray had been giving to Jackson nightly for six weeks. These drugs, known as powerful benzodiazepines, are central nervous depressants and constant use of them could result in an addiction to these multiple 'downers' or depressants. They are not normally lethal when used on their own, but when mixed with other central nervous depressants, such as alcohol for example or, worse, Propofol, they can be fatal.[34]

The following day, 19 June, Jackson appeared at The Forum for rehearsals, but it was quickly apparent to all concerned, especially Kenny Ortega, that the singer was unwell both physically and psychologically. Ortega recalled that Jackson 'wasn't right' and that '…there was something going on that was deeply troubling me.' Ortega also remembered Jackson, on that night, appearing 'lost'. He would later testify that Jackson was, 'Just lost and a little incoherent. Although we were conversing, and I did ask him questions and he did answer me, I did feel that he was not well…at all.' Ortega was full of concern, he had never seen Jackson in such a state before. The thought now occurred to him that throughout the weeks of rehearsals, it was possible that Jackson might have been on drugs.[35]

The singer was upset, not coherent, and seemed drugged and disoriented to those around him. The production manager, John 'Bugzee' Hougdahl, sent an email to Randy Phillips saying, 'I have watched him deteriorate in front of my eyes over the last eight weeks', and Travis Payne recalled the singer being on edge that evening, as well as being cold, exhausted and paranoid. These observations seemed to back up Karen Faye's comments that Jackson was '…cold like ice cubes', and that he was shivering and shaking.

With no prospect of Jackson being able to rehearse, Kenny Ortega offered the stricken singer food, which Jackson accepted. Deeply concerned, Ortega fed him chicken soup, put a blanket around him, rubbed his feet and put a heater in the room next to him. The two of them talked and Jackson said to Ortega, 'Can I sit with you tonight and watch rehearsal; I would really like that. Could Travis go on stage and perform and could I sit with you and watch rehearsal?' Naturally, Ortega agreed as Jackson seemed so weak and so frail, and the two of them sat together for two hours watching the rehearsal performance before the singer left early, at Ortega's suggestion.

At 2:04am on the morning of 20 June, Ortega sent an email to Randy Phillips from his office at The Forum, which said,

> Randy, I will do whatever I can to be of help in this situation. If you need me to come to the house, just give me a call in the morning. My concern is now that we've brought the doctor into the fold and have played the tough love, now or never card, is that the artist may be unable to rise to the occasion due to real emotional stuff. He appeared quite weak and fatigued this evening. He had a terrible case of chills, was trembling, rambling, and obsessing. Everything in me says he should be psychologically evaluated. If we have any chance at all to get him back in the light, it's going to take a strong therapist to help him through this as well as immediate physical nurturing. I was told by our choreographer that during the artist's costume fitting with his designer tonight they noticed he's lost more weight. As far as I can tell there is no one taking care responsibility (caring for) for him on a daily basis.[36] Where was his assistant tonight? Tonight I was feeding him, wrapping him in blankets to warm his chills, massaging his feet to calm him and calling his doctor. There were four security guards outside his door, but no one offering him a cup of hot tea. Finally, it's important for everyone to know, I believe that he really wants this. It would shatter him; break his heart if we pulled the plug. He's terribly frightened it's all going to go away. He asked me repeatedly tonight if I was going to leave him. He was practically begging for my confidence. It broke

my heart. He was like a lost boy. There still may be a chance. He can rise to the occasion if we get him the help he needs. Sincerely, Kenny.[37]

With alarm bells ringing following the aborted rehearsal, Frank Dileo called Conrad Murray that evening and left a voicemail message in which he said,

Dr Murray, this is Frank Dileo, Michael's manager, I'm the short guy with no hair. I'm sure you know Michael had an episode last night; he's sick… I think you need to get a blood test on him today. We gotta see what he's doing.[38]

That same day, Saturday 20 June, another meeting was called at Jackson's Carolwood home. Attending the late-morning meeting was Jackson, Conrad Murray, Kenny Ortega and Randy Phillips. They had a frank and heated discussion about the singer's health and stamina, particularly about what had happened the previous evening at rehearsals. During this discussion, Murray took a hostile tone with Ortega, who he saw as meddling in the doctor's area of expertise. Dr Murray, who had jurisdiction to organise Jackson's rehearsal schedule, was apparently upset that Ortega hadn't allowed the singer to rehearse on the 19th and had, instead, sent Jackson home after the singer had sat out some of the rehearsals. This despite Ortega's protestations at the state he had found Jackson in. One of the phrases Murray was supposed to have used towards Ortega was a stern, 'I am the doctor, not you. You direct the show and leave Michael's health to me'. Murray continued by confirming that Jackson was both physically and emotionally fine and more than capable of handling all of his responsibilities for the show.[39]

In response to Murray's outburst, Ortega asked Jackson to back him up and explain to Murray that the decision not to rehearse was a joint decision that was agreed between the singer and Ortega. Michael Jackson informed Murray that this was, indeed, what had happened and told Ortega that he felt '…ready to take the reins'. He continued by telling Ortega that he shouldn't be afraid, that he was perfectly capable of handling the responsibilities and that he wanted Ortega to stay by his side. He concluded by saying, 'I'm fine Kenny, I promise you', before they both embraced.[40]

In the documentary, *Michael Jackson & The Doctor: A Fatal Friendship*,[41] a film made with the participation of Dr Murray as the actual trial took place, Murray recalls a meeting with Randy Phillips at Jackson's home where Phillips took Murray aside, according to claims made in the documentary by Murray, to warn him of the dire financial outcome to Jackson if he failed to make the tour and the concerts were cancelled. Murray doesn't state when this meeting took place, but, according to him, it was a crisis meeting, and it was at Carolwood. 'That's when I got the shock. Randy Phillips just asked that I step out the living room when the meeting had ended', Murray claims. Once outside, Phillips spoke with Murray.

And this is him, you know, grinding his teeth. He [Jackson] does not have a fucking cent. A fucking cent. What's this bullshit all about? Listen, this guy is next to Skid Row. He's going to be homeless. The fucking Popsicles that his children are sucking on, look, those kids, what's that all about? Nine security guards, why does he need that? I'm paying for that shit. I'm paying for the toilet paper he wipes his arse with. He doesn't have a fucking cent. And if he don't get this show done, he's over. This is it. This is the last chance he has to earn any kind of money. He's ruined. Financially he has nothing. Zero.

In the 2011 trial, Randy Phillips denied ever saying this to Murray, or having any such conversation.[42]

Following the meeting on 20 June, no rehearsals took place on the 21st and 22nd as the whole production relocated to the Staples Center for what was planned to be the final two weeks of rehearsals.

But the concern about Jackson's well-being amongst the production crew continued to grow and, on 20 June, Karen Faye took it upon herself to send Frank Dileo some emails she had been receiving from concerned fans, worried about his state of health. These fans were often to be found waiting outside the rehearsal studios, hoping to get a fleeting glimpse of their idol as he was whisked in and out of the building, and perhaps be lucky enough to get an autograph, a photo with Jackson or even snatch a brief conversation with him. One of these fans had been invited onto the set of the 3D *Thriller* shoot at Culver Studios. Following this invitation, the fan had sent an email to Karen Faye describing how they had managed to meet Michael Jackson while at the location and were trying to persuade him to wear a jacket they had brought along for him as a gift. They managed to cajole the singer into trying the jacket on and, during this process, the fan managed to catch a glimpse of Jackson's torso and his back. What the fan saw was shocking:

> He took his jacket off and we saw something horrible, a skeleton and then we saw his back and we were still in shock. We don't know if he is anorexic and stopped eating, or if it's something more complicated than that. Well, in the [sic] case, if he has stopped eating, here is what I want to tell you. If you do nothing he will die. I know that it is humanly impossible for a human being to be a skeleton and dance for two hours straight and not be in danger.[43]

152

Karen Faye echoed the thoughts of the writer of the email when she forwarded it to Dileo. Faye wrote: 'Frank, unfortunately she is right… he will make himself so sick he will die.'[44][45]

For nearly a quarter of a century Jackson was the centre of a world where those around him were only too eager to pander to him and to provide him with whatever he wanted, and painkillers were top of his list. The decades of Demerol abuse and reliance on other painkillers had caught up with him. Now, with a major series of shows to contend with, countless legal claims against him and the turmoil of his finances hanging like a shadow over him, Jackson was facing levels of stress few can comprehend. The medication that had brought him to this level was now his only escape. Jackson was caught in a maelstrom of confusion. Everyone around him, however well intentioned they might seem to the singer, had their own agenda. And a large part of that was to add to the confusion that was increasingly surrounding the singer. In doing so, they could potentially open up a direct avenue to Jackson and manoeuvre themselves into an indispensible position of influence, generally with their own interests at heart rather than those of Jackson. Combined with Jackson's blurred reality from the effects of his addiction, perhaps it's no wonder that Jackson didn't know which way to turn, who to believe and who to turn to.

One of the few people around Jackson who had said 'no' to him was holistic nurse, Cherilyn Lee. Now, almost two months since the singer had abruptly dispensed with her services when she refused to get Propofol for him, Cherilyn Lee received a call out of the blue from Jackson's security team on the night of 21 June. At the time, Lee herself was in hospital in Florida. She had been attending a seminar in St Petersburg but found herself completely overworked so admitted herself to hospital and ended up being hospitalised for two days. The call from the security guards on the night of the 21st found them asking if Lee could come to the house immediately. The call wasn't from Jackson himself, but Lee could hear him in the background saying, 'Tell her, please tell her that one side of my body is hot, one side of my body is cold'. These are classic symptoms of Demerol withdrawal and Jackson hadn't seen Dr Klein, his main source of Demerol, for five days. Lee told them that there was no way she could come to the house, as she was now in Florida, but suggested that, on the basis of what she had heard, Jackson should be taken to hospital without delay.[46]

But Jackson wasn't taken to hospital. Instead, the following day, 22 June, he was taken once more to Dr Klein's clinic in Beverly Hills, his source of Demerol. There seemed to be nothing out of the ordinary about this visit, Jackson was treated with Restylane and had 100mg of Demerol, but the people present in Klein's clinic that day had a weird feeling about Jackson's visit. Many had the unnerving feeling they were seeing him for the last time. Both Klein and Jason Pfeiffer, Klein's assistant, recalled the singer saying goodbye to everyone in the clinic, as though for the final time, and they were all creeped out about it.[47]

Pfeiffer had got to know Jackson well through his visits to the clinic and, on many occasions, had answered the phone to Jackson when the singer was 'out of it' and desperately seeking drugs, as Pfeiffer recalled in an interview in 2013.[48] Pfeiffer said Jackson had a 'death wish' and that '…it was inevitable that something was going to go wrong'. He even recalled Jackson begging for Propofol, telling Pfeiffer: 'I do it all the time to sleep'. Pfeiffer, like Klein, refused to give Jackson Propofol, but Pfeiffer was ready to admit that Jackson was hooked on Demerol during his visits to the clinic: 'The main reason he came into the surgery so often, was to get a fix of Demerol during his procedures. He begged everyone to give it to him.' Pfeiffer suggested Jackson was an addict who used cosmetic procedures as an opportunity to get a fix of Demerol, even inventing and faking medical issues in order to receive the drug. Often, Jackson would plead with the clinic to give him four times the regular amount of Demerol. 'Michael felt he was immune to normal volumes,' said Pfeiffer, 'and begged for extra quantities.'[49]

Karen Faye felt that something was going on and, on 22 June, sent another email to Frank Dileo asking him to intervene as Jackson was suffering from '...serious stuff physically and mentally and... concerts not worth jeopardizing his life for.' Frank Dileo failed to respond to her emailed concerns.[50] Others around Jackson, like Faye, were unnerved about the state of the singer and were worried something terrible might happen. Jackson's son, Prince, recalled seeing his father being left in tears after talks with Randy Phillips just days before he died. 'After he got off the phone, he would cry. He'd say, "They're going to kill me, they're going to kill me."'[51] And in the final week of rehearsals Jackson purportedly asked the producers of the show, 'You aren't going to kill the artist are you?'[52]

On 23 June, with Jackson out of Klein's clinic, rehearsals resumed. By now the production was installed in The Staples Center, a 950,000sq ft multi-purpose arena in downtown Los Angeles. By all accounts, this was one of the most successful rehearsals with Jackson appearing strong and optimistic, looking towards the future and keen to get the tour off the ground and head to London.[53] He was full of energy, full of a desire to work and full of enthusiasm. Stacy Walker remembers them doing half the show on this rehearsal night with Jackson's performances being '...great in the numbers.'[54] In fact, Walker was so excited after that rehearsal that she called her mother to tell her to get tickets for the opening night as soon as possible. Ortega would later refer to the singer as being '...a different Michael'. By this point in rehearsals, however, Jackson was using a teleprompter, a piece of equipment on stage, out of view of the audience, which displayed song lyrics. Jackson had never used a teleprompter before in any of his performances, but now felt he needed one to help him remember the song lyrics, even for the songs he had sung thousands of time before.

While the rehearsal was taking place, Dr Murray was overseeing Jackson's care. At 5:33pm, Connie Ng sent an email to Murray under the subject of 'Omar Arnold – Progress Notes'. A minute later, Ng sent another email to Murray with the subject of 'Omar Arnold – 2D – Echo'. This contained a report referring to an echocardiograph on 17 January 2007. Ng sent another email at 5:38pm under the subject heading of 'Omar Arnold Medication Log'. These emails proved, beyond doubt, that Murray was indeed treating Jackson[55] as early as 2007.

As well as these emails, Dr Murray also received a revised employment agreement from Kathy Jorrie, on behalf of AEG Live. There were minor changes to the agreement following discussions that had been ongoing, most notably the fact that Murray would not be paid until the contract was signed by both Murray and Michael Jackson.

Conrad Murray finally signed the agreement the following day, 24 June 2009, and faxed it to AEG Live. That same day, Michael Jackson turned up three hours late to rehearsals at The Staples Center. There were only eight more rehearsals in Los Angeles before the whole production would be shipped to London for two weeks of full dress and technical rehearsals. But, according to production manager, John 'Bugzee' Hougdahl, 'The company is rehearsing right now, but the doubt is pervasive.'[56]

Despite Jackson turning up late this was, like the day before, a successful run-through with Jackson fully participating not only in rehearsals, but also other areas of production. 'Earth Song' was the final song to be rehearsed that night, and those who witnessed Jackson's performance of this composition had goose bumps when it finished. Even Randy Phillips said, 'I had never seen such exultation in the cast and crew'.

Around midnight, as he was about to leave, Jackson was particularly excited as the next day they were due to rehearse an illusion that was going to be a major part of the tour, a tour that Jackson had by now intimated to Ortega might go worldwide and eventually end up in the USA. Jackson loved magic and illusions, and often used them within his shows. This illusion planned for 25 June would see Jackson standing on a bed with silk flames partly obscuring him. When the silk flames came down Jackson would vanish before suddenly rising up on a cherry picker and flying out over the audience. As he left, Ortega recalled the singer was feeling great. 'He looked at me and he asked me if I was happy and I said I was happy. I asked him if he was happy and he said he was very happy', Ortega recalled.

Just before he left the Staples Center, Jackson asked Ortega to thank everybody and to tell them that he loved them – the dancers, the singers, the band, and the crew. Ortega told Jackson that he would make sure everything was prepared for the illusion rehearsal the next day and told him that he loved him. Jackson returned the compliment, saying he loved Ortega more, then they hugged, and Michael Jackson left the Staples Center.

As he left the arena around 12:30am, Jackson turned to Ortega and said, with a big smile on his face, 'I'll see you tomorrow'.

But Michael Jackson never returned.

8

Two is the beginning of the end.
J.M. Barrie, *Peter Pan*

At around 12:30am on the morning of 25 June 2009, Michael Jackson made preparations to leave the Staples Center after what most of those present had thought was a successful rehearsal. Michael Amir Williams, Jackson's personal assistant,[1] recalled saying to Jackson that he thought the rehearsal was extraordinary. 'Oh Brother Michael,' replied Jackson, 'it's just thirty, forty per cent. I don't go a hundred until the show time.'

With a black robe wrapped around him and covering the length of his body, Jackson shuffled towards the golf cart which, driven by Alberto Alvarez, would take him to his waiting SUV. As he made his way slowly to this golf cart, Jackson was accompanied by two bodyguards, with his manager, Frank Dileo, following on behind. Before he got into his SUV, Jackson saw Randy Phillips from AEG Live. The singer went over to him, put his hand on Phillips' shoulder and said, 'You got me here. Now I'm ready. I can take it from here'. Jackson and Phillips embraced before the singer got into his vehicle and headed back to his Carolwood home. Neither Randy Phillips, nor any of those attending rehearsals that night, could possibly have thought they would never see Jackson alive again.

Before Jackson got into the motorcade at the Staples Center, Michael Amir Williams had already made a phone call to Dr Conrad Murray at 12:10am, telling the doctor that Jackson had finished rehearsals and that he wanted Murray at Carolwood by the time Jackson was due home. This was a regular pattern following rehearsals, and one that both parties were used to.[2]

Leaving the Staples Center, Jackson's car, driven by Faheem Muhammad with Michael Amir Williams in the front passenger seat, slowed down to allow the singer to greet his fans who, even at that time of the morning, continued their vigil outside the rehearsal studios. While Jackson did this, another car went ahead to prepare for his arrival home.

While Jackson was leaving the rehearsal venue, Dr Murray made his way, alone, to Jackson's home and his silver BMW 650 convertible passed through the security gates at the singer's Carolwood mansion at approximately 12:45am. Michael Jackson had yet to arrive home so, once in the house, Murray went straight to Jackson's 'medication' room on the first floor.

Jackson's car, with Michael Amir Williams accompanying him, arrived back at Carolwood, just over 10 minutes later, around 12:58am, as part of a three-car convoy. Amir Williams was relieved to see Dr Murray's car already parked in the driveway. Arriving home, Jackson, after once again stopping outside the gates to greet the small band of loyal fans waiting there, went straight into the house. Alberto Alvarez would be waiting by the door to greet the singer and open the front door for him. As Jackson entered, Alvarez wished him goodnight. A few minutes earlier, Alvarez had arrived back in the first car of the cavalcade carrying all of Jackson's paperwork, bags and gifts from fans that had accumulated during the evening. Alvarez unloaded all of this from the vehicle and left it at the bottom of the stairs. It would likely be Michael Jackson, Prince or the housekeeper who would carry them upstairs the following morning.

Once inside, Michael Amir Williams would usually say goodnight to Jackson and then go into the security trailer, which stood near the front door, for a debriefing with the rest of the security staff, before making his way to his own home, leaving the security detail to keep watch over the property throughout the night.

The security of Jackson's property was taken care of by a Los Angeles-based firm, called Security Measures, a company owned by Steven Echols, a self-avowed member of the Nation of Islam.[3] This company was personally selected by Michael Amir Williams to secure the contract and Williams was also a member of the Nation of Islam. The trail of the Nation of Islam ran deep within Jackson's empire; other members of the security firm working at Jackson's property, such as Larry Muhammad, Isaac Muhammad and Patrick Muhammad, were all members of the Nation of Islam. Alberto Alvarez was also apparently a member of the group and Grace Rwaramba, the woman employed by Jackson to look after his children, had close ties to Louis Farrakhan, who was the leader of the Nation of Islam in 2009. The connection went even deeper – Farrakhan's son-in-law and chief-of-staff, Leonard Muhammad, was previously chosen to oversee Michael Jackson's business affairs, despite the fact that he had a somewhat dubious business background selling unproven Aids treatments to deprived areas of Chicago.[4] [5]

For a number of years, there had been rumours that Michael Jackson was becoming increasingly influenced by the Nation of Islam, and many of those close to him feared that the financially vulnerable singer could be open to exploitation by the organisation. This was despite the fact that, in November 1984, Louis Farrakhan,[6] the leader of the Nation of Islam, said of Jackson, '[His] Jheri curl, female-acting, sissified-acting expression is not wholesome for our young boys, nor our young girls.'[7] It was a view that was to change significantly in 1993, following Jackson's first molestation scandal, when Farrakhan said Jackson was being treated like, '...a slave on a plantation'.[8] Later that same year, during a rally in New York, Farrakhan said, 'The powers that be can't stand to see Michael Jackson politically aware and using his money for the advancement of his people.'[9]

The Nation of Islam is an Islamic religious and political movement that was founded in Detroit, Michigan on 4 July 1930 by Wallace D. Fard Muhammad.[10] The organisation combined the elements of traditional Islam with black, nationalist ideas and would bring Malcolm X into the spotlight in the twentieth century. Following the mysterious disappearance of its founder in 1934, the new leader, Elijah Muhammad was convinced the twentieth century was the time for black people to assert themselves and encouraged followers in the USA to drop their 'slave' names in favour of Muslim names or simply an 'X', signifying they had lost their identities in slavery. During the 1980s the Nation of Islam, and Louis Farrakhan, its new leader, had a record of violent pronouncements against Jews, whites, Christians and homosexuals, but, since then, the organisation has attempted to sanitise its public image by promoting the work its security companies, such as Security Measures, have done in eliminating drugs and crime from public housing projects.

In December 2003, the *New York Times* published an article[11] in which it was suggested officials from the Nation of Islam had moved into Jackson's Neverland ranch, and had begun to make decisions regarding his business affairs, associates, friends and legal strategies. Coincidentally, that month, Jackson's official spokesperson, Stuart Backerman, resigned in protest at the Nation of Islam's presence in Jackson's life and the fact that he was concerned that the singer's multicultural message to the world was in contrast to the Nation of Islam's philosophy of black separatism.[12] An associate of Jackson said the group were 'brainwashing' him and suggested that they had tried to do the same with Whitney Houston.[13]

Jackson's brother, Jermaine, had already converted to Islam in 1989 and many think it was Jermaine, and Michael Jackson's nanny, Grace Rwaramba, who introduced the singer to the Nation of Islam.[14] It is more likely that the actor Eddie Murphy was the first figure to entice Michael Jackson to the group. On his *Bad* tour in 1988 and 1989, Murphy had provided the singer with some tapes of Louis Farrakhan's speeches and these sparked Jackson's interest. Before long, the singer had donated $25,000 to Farrakhan's Million Man March,[15] a gathering, en masse, of African Americans in Washington D.C. to 'convey to the world a vastly different picture of the Black male'. However, if the Nation of Islam had hoped Jackson might convert to Islam, they would be disappointed. Jackson was, and remained, a Jehovah's Witness.[16]

So why did Jackson align himself so closely to the Nation of Islam in 2003? Was he really a follower of the Black Muslim movement? Or was there something else going on behind the scenes? One theory in circulation during 2003, and connected to Jackson's further trials regarding child molestation, was that Jackson was cultivating a relationship with the Nation of Islam to provide him with protection inside the United States' prison system should he be convicted of any wrong-doing. Certainly, as far as Farrakhan was concerned, he was only too keen to exploit any association with the King of Pop (and the cash Jackson was supposedly filtering his way) given that his group had only 20,000 followers at the time, and any publicity that the pop superstar could give them would be welcome.

As it turned out, Michael Jackson didn't go to jail, and he soon fired a number of members of his entourage who were affiliated to the Nation of Islam, but rumours of the singer's association with the group continued over the next few years – Grace Rwaramba was gaining considerable influence over the singer, the Nation of Islam provided Jackson with security during his 2005 trial for child molestation, and there were even rumours that the Carolwood mansion was owned by the Nation of Islam and that the rent they charged the singer, $100,000 per month, was considerably more than elsewhere in the neighbourhood.

Despite him being a Jehovah's Witness, stories and rumours about Michael Jackson converting to Islam also began to surface. Jackson helped fuel these rumours in 2005, when, following his acquittal of child molestation charges, he went to live in Bahrain as a guest of Sheikh Salman bin Hamed Khalifa. Two years later, in January 2007, Reuters published a headline proclaiming 'Jermaine Jackson wants Michael to convert to Islam', and on 21 November 2008, *The Sun*, under the title, 'The Way You Mecca Me Feel', ran an 'exclusive' which reported that Michael Jackson had converted to Islam. The article stated that,

> Michael Jackson has become a Muslim – and changed his name to Mikaeel. The skint superstar, 50, donned Islamic garb to pledge allegiance to the Koran in a ceremony at a pal's mansion in Los Angeles, *The Sun* can reveal. Jacko sat on the floor wearing a tiny hat after an Imam was summoned to officiate.[17]

After Michael Jackson's death, his brother, Jermaine, confirmed that the singer didn't ever convert to Islam, but his ties to the Nation of Islam had been close in the weeks leading up to his passing.[18]

***

By 1am on Thursday, 25 June 2009, Dr Conrad Murray, was already in the singer's Carolwood mansion awaiting the arrival of the King of Pop. Later Murray claimed that the night before he had been successful in getting Jackson through a whole night of sleep without using any anaesthetics, such as Propofol. It was apparently his plan to wean the superstar off his Propofol dependency (Murray had given it to him for 60 consecutive nights to help Jackson sleep) and, for the past 72 hours, he had tried to slowly withdraw the drug from Jackson's nightly cycle. According to Murray it had worked the previous night, but Murray was never sure what frame of mind Jackson would be in when he returned after rehearsals.

Murray had made his way upstairs upon arrival and had settled in, as normal, into one of Michael Jackson's two bedrooms. The second floor at Jackson's rented Carolwood home, reached by a large and winding staircase, was a maze of bedrooms, bathrooms, closets and foyers that spanned out from the landing. Four bedrooms occupied this floor: there was the Master Bedroom and Bedroom Two, separated from each other by a large foyer area that led from the landing into Bedroom Two. The Master Bedroom was accessed directly from the landing at the top of the winding stairway. Both bedrooms had their own closets and bathrooms. The two other bedrooms were considerably smaller, but both still had their own closets and bathrooms. Prince used one of these smaller bedrooms, while Paris and Blanket shared the other bedroom.

The room that Murray always inhabited was Bedroom Two, but to all intents and purposes it was considered the 'medication room'. It was here that the doctor had his medical equipment laid out ready to receive Jackson when he returned.

Haunting photographs taken by LAPD investigators on the day Jackson died, and released during the trial, provide a fascinating window into how the singer lived, and died. The medication room looked out over an expansive back garden and had a large double bed that faced the window. In the corner of the room a doorway led to the bedroom's large closet room and then on into the bathroom. This room, despite having a feature fireplace, gold-leaf mirrors and upholstered French period chairs, resembled the squalid lifestyle of a drug addict. Tables were strewn with medical paraphernalia such as vials of drugs, syringes and tubes. Plastic bags, scattered on tops of chairs and tabletops, contained latex gloves, creams and saline bags. In the corner of the room, 11 oxygen tanks stood upright next to an electric fan which was perched on a seat, while Murray's medical holdalls were lying open on the floor, on chairs, on table surfaces and even stored in cupboards. Opened cans of Sprite lay scattered on the floor, while various tubes of pills and tablets – some closed, some open – could be found on shelves.

Next to the bed was a dressing table with three more oxygen tanks beside it. On the dressing table stood a number of plates featuring photos of babies or young children and a Michael Jackson DVD. Propped up against this dressing table was a large photo of a black infant smiling, with the words 'Sweet Baby' printed next to the child's face.

A cheap television had been placed on a small round table that stood between two upholstered chairs while a sofa faced away from the bed towards an unused fireplace. Numerous DVDs and CDs were stacked high on a portable shelving unit with the top shelf covered in empty bottles and more medical paraphernalia. A black fedora was placed on one chair. An oxygen canister, attached to a device that allowed it to be wheeled around the room after the patient, stood near the foot of the bed.

Next to the bed was a bedside table with a number of bottles of pills, some bottled water, a bronze figurine and, tucked underneath out of sight, a telephone. In the closet, suitcases and travel holdalls were piled on top of each other and next to them stood a Walt Disney bag. In another area a mauve suitcase lay on the floor, its top open and clothing spilling out of it, while another beige suitcase stood upright and unopened next to a cardboard box full of rolled posters. In front of them, on the floor, was a cushion with the image of Michael Jackson staring back.

The bed itself was a double bed, with an elaborate golden headrest. Beneath the sheets on the bed was a waterproof mattress liner to cater for Jackson's supposed incontinence. On the bed rested a porcelain doll with curly golden hair, dressed in a beige romper-suit with images of animals adorning its chest. A black electric fan stood at the base of the windows ready to direct cool air over the bed as all the windows were closed and the heavy gold curtains drawn. The narrow toilet cubicle was adjacent to a dressing room with a sink. The whole area was strewn with medical equipment, cans of Red Bull, disposable latex gloves, paper on the floor and bags left opened but piled high in the corners.

It was in the bedroom, amongst the mess, that the doctor had his medical equipment laid out ready to receive Jackson when he returned, including a hanging IV bag, primed to administer intravenous fluids.

Emerging from Bedroom Two and exiting the foyer onto the landing, a sharp right turn would lead to the Master Bedroom, a room that Jackson regarded as his inner sanctum. He was the only person, except for his children, who was allowed access to this bedroom. Even the cleaners weren't allowed entry. Conrad Murray later described how Jackson would spend long periods of time in this room spraying himself with Cologne, perhaps to obscure the smell from this unclean and unkempt room. Like the other bedrooms, this bedroom had a bathroom and closet, but they dwarfed anything else on the floor and were larger than most living rooms. There was also a mirror in this Master Bedroom, upon which Jackson had written a message to himself: 'TRAIN, perfection, March, April. FULL OUT May'. It seems Jackson always had two rooms to himself, no matter where he was living or staying. His reason for this was that he never trusted anyone coming into his room. As a result, this room was constantly in a terrible state.

Despite the fact that generally nobody was allowed into this room, Dr Murray suggested he was actually once permitted to enter, and in an interview with *The Mail on Sunday*,[19] he referred to it as one of the '…happiest days of his life'. In this interview Murray recalled being granted rare access into this inner sanctum, which smelled terribly and in which there were clothes strewn everywhere. Once Murray was inside, the singer reached out to grab his hand and said, 'There are only four people in my family now, Paris, Prince, Blanket and you, Dr Conrad'.

According to Murray's testimony and other evidence from the later trials, the night unfolded broadly as follows.

Around 1:05am, Michael Jackson joined Dr Murray in the bedroom. As always, the two of them had a brief conversation, enquiring about each other's day. On this particular night, Jackson told Murray he was tired and fatigued, and complained that he was being treated like a machine, before following his normal routine – leaving Murray and having a shower before returning to the bedroom where Dr Murray would apply a dermatological cream to Jackson's body, primarily his back, after which the singer would put on his pyjamas. This was a nightly ritual for Murray and Jackson and would involve Benoquin, a treatment cream Jackson had been using for decades.

As soon as Murray had applied the dermatological cream to Jackson's body, as well as fitting a condom catheter, the singer was desperate to get to sleep. Only an hour or so before, however, Jackson had been on stage, driving himself through rehearsals. Consequently, even at this time of the morning, the singer was still buzzing from the natural highs of performing and was unable to sleep. The fact that Jackson was still drinking Red Bull, that his bedroom was fully lit and that he insisted on playing loud music as he tried to sleep might have been a factor in him not being able to drift off easily, but, according to Murray, Jackson was adamant he needed these distractions in his bedroom to help him sleep.

Initially, Dr Murray attempted to talk with Jackson, to try to calm him down a little,[20] but this had no effect on the singer who remained awake and restless. According to his police interview, Dr Conrad Murray then placed an intravenous drip into Jackson's leg, just below the knee.[21] This IV technique is the most common form of IV medication and is known as the Peripheral Cannula method. This method ensures the IV is injected into the veins peripherally in either arms or legs. The injected cannula contains an injection port that is separate from the regular tubing through which injections can also be administered alongside the saline.

By now it was around 2am. The singer seemed to be no closer to sleeping and was growing increasingly anxious. According to Murray's interview, he then gave Jackson an oral pill of 10mg of Valium, a sedative to reduce anxiety. Jackson sat on his bed, waiting for the Valium to have any effect, but one of the issues with Valium is that the effects are delayed, and Jackson needed to sleep, so Murray turned to the IV drip. Following the oral dose of Valium, Murray began to give Jackson Lorazepam in an IV form. He gave him 2mg in total, injected through the port, which was diluted with saline and pushed slowly into Jackson's veins. This was a standard dilution and would usually suffice in sedating most normal adult patients. But Jackson wasn't a normal patient; his years of drug abuse had given him a level of tolerance to sedatives that meant this initial dose was nowhere near enough to send him to sleep.

Waiting, and hoping, that the Lorazepam would work, Dr Murray sat in a chair next to Jackson's bed and observed him, but after an hour the singer was still wide awake and continuing to complain to Murray that he had to sleep. Dr Murray then decided to give Jackson a different agent, this time Midazolam. He went ahead and injected 2mg of the drug slowly into Jackson at about 3am. Midazolam is a potent sedative that requires slow administration. It can also cause serious and life-threatening cardiorespiratory failure so Murray would have needed to monitor the singer constantly. Murray waited again by Jackson's bedside observing the singer and waiting for the drug to take effect. But, once again according to Murray, there was little, if no, impact on Jackson. Murray asked Jackson if he felt even a little bit drowsy, but he was wide awake. 'Do you think your eyes are telling you to sleep?' Murray asked the singer, but the response was a firm 'No'.

Murray's next move was to encourage Jackson to try to meditate. Changing the lighting of the room to a more tenebrous setting and lowering the music, Murray began rubbing Jackson's feet in the hope that it would make him relax. Reluctantly, Jackson started to meditate and Murray watched him for 10 to 15 minutes until the singer's eyes began to close and he drifted off at around 3:20am. Murray kept watching Jackson as he slept, hoping that, at last, the drugs had worked, but within 10 to 12 minutes, Jackson woke up again with a start, as is generally the case with Midazolam, where rapid awakening is one of the results of levels of the drug dropping quickly after administration is terminated.

It was, by now, around 3:30am. Jackson, desperate to sleep, was surprised that the meditation had worked, albeit briefly, and asked Dr Murray if they could continue trying it. But an hour later their further efforts at meditation had failed to work and the singer was still wide awake. It was at this time in the morning that Jackson's mood began to change significantly. Apparently he started complaining more forcefully to Dr Murray. He told Murray, 'I got to sleep, Dr Conrad, I have these rehearsals to perform. I must be ready for the show in England. And tomorrow I will have to cancel my performance. I have to cancel my trip, because, you know, I cannot function if I don't get my sleep.' The pressure on Dr Murray was beginning to grow as Jackson put the cancellation of the entire tour on his shoulders. The responsibility of getting Jackson to sleep, the only way in which he could function and therefore fulfil his commitments to the rehearsal process and, eventually the tour, was at that moment transferred to Dr Murray.

Responding to the increasingly agitated Jackson, Dr Murray suggested that they continue to try meditation. He reported saying to Jackson, 'I want you to try. Just try, you know. So you have to close your eyes'. The singer would follow his instructions but continued to be restless on the bed, moving his feet constantly and shifting around incessantly. He started to complain once more to Murray. 'Oh, I just can't sleep,' Jackson said, 'The medicine doesn't work.' Looking at his watch, Murray worked out it was almost three hours since he had first given Jackson a dose of Lorazepam so, at around 5:00am, Murray felt it appropriate to administer another 2mg of Lorazepam to the wide-awake singer, but, like before, this had absolutely no effect. Jackson was, by now, increasingly troubled and becoming more and more anxious at his inability to sleep and the subsequent effects it would have on the concerts. He continued to pressurise Murray, once more saying that he couldn't perform, that he'd have to cancel rehearsals again, which would put the show behind and disappoint his legion of fans. Murray told Jackson that, 'If I got the medicine that I gave you, I'd be sleeping until tomorrow evening, a normal person's way. You are not normal.'

At 5:54am, while Murray was reportedly trying to placate Jackson, he received an email on his iPhone from Bob Taylor of Robertson Taylor Insurance Brokers in London. Murray recalled reading the email quickly. It began, 'Hi Conrad' and asked questions about issues of well-being with Jackson, press reports about the artist and issues of full disclosure needed for an insurance policy for the singer. In the email Taylor urged Murray to realise that they were '…dealing with the matter of great importance', and reminded the doctor that his '…urgent attention will be greatly appreciated'. Despite the urgency of this, and the priority everyone else seemed to be giving it, Dr Murray decided not to reply to the email immediately, and waited almost six hours before doing so. Why did he wait so long to answer?

This email was critical, as it followed an email trail from the previous evening concerning the matter of the cancellation insurance policy for AEG Live regarding the O2 concerts. In order to obtain the insurance necessary (and AEG Live were looking to obtain the maximum available to them at that time, some $17.5 million in insurance cover for cancellation), the insurers were requesting access to Michael Jackson's medical records for the past five years, as well as Jackson submitting to a new medical in London. For much of the evening of 24 June and the early morning of 25 June, Paul Gongaware and Bob Taylor had been emailing each other[22] with increasing concern about getting hold of Jackson's records and getting him to agree to undertake the medical. In fact, AEG Live had already booked 6 July as the date of the medical in London at a private suite in Harley Street.

It was rapidly becoming a critical situation, and one that Dr Murray was an increasingly integral figure in. Paul Gongaware had copied Murray in on the email chain at 7:08pm and at 8:32pm, Bob Taylor had replied, again copying Murray in, saying, 'I await hearing from Dr. Murray'.

For the two days leading up to 25 June, AEG Live had also been emailing Murray with details of his proposed contract. These emails had been arriving into Murray's inbox with increasing urgency, and, after deciding he was happy with what he was seeing in the proposed agreement, Murray signed the contract on 24 June.

Why was there a sudden desire to get the contract to Murray? Was it because AEG Live realised that, in order to get access to Jackson's medical records, they were dependent solely on Dr Murray? They hadn't signed the contract yet, so Murray had no guarantee of getting paid anything, and he had already worked for two months without getting a dime of the $300,000 that was owed him. So is it possible that AEG Live were holding Murray to ransom; get Jackson's medical records and get the singer to agree to a London medical and then, and only then, will AEG Live sign the contract guaranteeing Murray the money he so desperately needed? Of course, Michael Jackson would need to sign the contract too, but if Murray could persuade the singer to agree to releasing his medical records and undergoing the London medical, then surely Jackson *would* sign the contract. All it needed was for Murray to get Jackson to agree. And now, it was incumbent on Murray to do so for his own long-term financial future and for AEG Live's insurance policy, which, with Jackson unable to convince anybody of his ability to carry out the 50 shows at O2, was becoming increasingly vital to AEG Live.

Murray was already aware of the importance of getting the medical records and his role in the entire process as, two days earlier, on the evening of 23 June, Murray had been in constant touch with his office in Las Vegas in an attempt to locate and source as many of Jackson's medical records as he could. As the evening of the 23rd progressed, one of his office workers, Connie Ng, had been emailing him various medical notes and files connected to Jackson or, in the case of these records, Jackson's alias, Omar Arnold. But while Murray had actually managed to get hold of Jackson's medical records, he still hadn't got permission from the singer to release these to AEG Live, or agreement from the singer to undergo another medical. As far as Jackson was concerned, he had already passed a medical and was refusing to undertake another one. Suddenly, Murray realised the whole tour, and consequently his own financial salvation, might hang on his ability to convince Jackson to release his medical records and undergo another examination in London at the behest of AEG Live and their insurance brokers.

But it seems that Jackson was refusing to back down. He was already at loggerheads with AEG Live over their demands for so many shows at the O2 and had supposedly professed the opinion, according to later reports, that they were '…going to kill him'.[23] [24] As far as Jackson was concerned, he was doing, and had done, all that was required of him.

At 6:31am, a text was logged on Murray's iPhone and at 7.01am, Murray made a call to Andrew Butler, a friend and patient of his in Nevada, from his Sprint phone.[25] The call lasted for 25 seconds. Perhaps Jackson drifted off momentarily allowing Murray the brief window to make this call. Whether he did or not, from this moment on, there appear to be a number of discrepancies between Dr Murray's version of events as told in his LAPD interview on 27 June 2009 and what actually happened.

As the sun rose on 25 June 2009, Jackson was still wide awake, still talking, and still pressuring Dr Murray to help him sleep. At 7:30am, Dr Murray prepared and gave Jackson another 2mg of Midazolam, still to no effect whatsoever. Thinking there might be something wrong with the IV site as Jackson wasn't responding to any of the drugs, Dr Murray checked it to ensure the IV was flowing into Jackson and not over the bed sheets, but there was no sign of any of the drugs escaping.

Before administering the Midazolam, Murray supposedly made Jackson urinate. The singer wore a condom catheter while under Murray's care, a flexible sheath that covered Jackson's penis just like a condom. Dr Murray would roll the catheter onto Jackson's penis every evening before the singer went to sleep and then attach it with either double-sided adhesive or a strap. The catheter would then be connected to a tube that would drain Jackson's urine into a drainage bottle, which stood on the floor nearby. The condom catheter was necessary, according to Dr Murray, as Jackson was incontinent,[26] but it is more likely that Murray used both an incontinence pad placed beneath Jackson on the bed (one was photographed by LAPD when they arrived at the scene of Jackson's death) and a condom catheter mainly because the singer was apparently under anaesthetic every night and unable to control his urination rather than medically incontinent. Dr Murray said that he made Jackson stand up and urinate through his condom catheter, and that the singer filled a bag that he had attached to him. Murray emptied this bag into a portable jug that stood beside the bed on a table before administering the further 2mg of Lorazepam through the IV but, once again, there was little effect on Jackson and he remained awake.

Elsewhere in the Carolwood mansion, the chef and nutritionist Kai Chase arrived for her day's work at 8am as usual.[27] Upon arrival she would generally prepare breakfast for Prince, Paris and Blanket Jackson and help get them ready for school[28] before getting lunch and dinner prepared. She would also make breakfast for Michael Jackson, usually granola and juices, always organic. Preparing these various breakfasts, Chase opened the fridge in the kitchen and noticed that the dinner she had made the previous evening for Jackson and Murray, a white bean soup, was unusually still in the fridge and untouched.

Jackson would generally come down into the kitchen in the mornings, as he was very hands-on and interested in his children's nutrition, but on this particular morning, Jackson didn't appear, and neither did Dr Murray, who would normally come down around 10am on most days to collect the singer's breakfast and take it up to his room. But Chase didn't think anything of this, she was aware of his rehearsal schedule and the strains that this routine was putting on Jackson, and frequently saw oxygen tanks lined up in the security booth, which she assumed must have been for Jackson. Shortly after preparing the food, Chase left to visit the local market to buy some fresh produce.

Meanwhile, between 7:30am and 10am, upstairs in Jackson's bedroom, Dr Murray, according to his testimony to the LAPD, continued to watch the singer while trying to encourage him to meditate as Jackson still wasn't sleeping. Jackson was getting increasingly anxious and continued to berate Murray, telling him that because he cannot sleep he will have to cancel the day and therefore the rehearsal and, consequently, everything will be thrown off schedule (a schedule that was already tight given that they now had little time left before they were supposed to leave for England).

During this period of time, Murray received and sent a number of text messages from Texas. These occurred at 8:36am, 9am and 9:11am. He also received two phone calls: one at 8:49am from Antoinette Gill, a patient and friend in Nevada seeking a referral from another physician which lasted for 53 seconds, and the other one at 9:23am which came from Marissa Boni, a friend of Murray's daughter in Nevada. This phone call lasted for 22 minutes. So, between 8:36am and 9:45am, a total of 69 minutes, Dr Murray had been on the phone for 23 minutes and sent or received three texts. Murray had previously said he had spent the time between 7:30am and 10am watching and talking to the singer, trying to encourage him to go to sleep. It would be reasonable to assume that, during the phone calls from 8:49am to 8:50am and 9:23am to 9:45am, Murray had either left Jackson's bedroom to talk freely, or the singer was asleep; either scenario being contrary to Murray's later testimony to LAPD.

At approximately 10am on 25 June, according to Murray's police interview, nine hours after he returned home from rehearsals, Jackson was still wide awake and continuing to complain that he wasn't sleeping and that the rehearsal would have to be cancelled. It was now, as testified by Murray, that Michael Jackson said to him, 'I'd like to have some milk. Please, please give me some milk so that I can sleep, because I know that this is all that really works for me.' 'Milk' was Michael Jackson's name for Propofol.[29] Dr Murray was aware that everything he had used throughout the night hadn't worked on Jackson, and Murray knew that the singer had to be up and about by a certain time in order for his participation in the rehearsals to be productive.

If Dr Murray's recollections, as told to the LAPD, are correct, then he was now caught between a rock and a hard place. He had to heed a different set of warnings and threats from AEG Live – that if he didn't get Jackson to rehearsals there would be no show in London, and if there was no show, then Murray wouldn't get paid.[30] For a man in his own perilous financial straits, Conrad Murray was banking on the $150,000 a month from this job, to help sort out his own affairs. Any prospect of the tour not going ahead, and him not receiving the money, would be a financial and personal disaster. Consequently, Dr Murray had to get Jackson to sleep, even if only for a few hours, so he would be fit for the rehearsals later that day.

Supposedly a conversation took place between Murray and Jackson in the singer's bedroom at around 10am, with Jackson on the bed, desperate to go to sleep: 'If you got Propofol now,' said Murray, 'how much time, how much sleep [do] you expect to have? You know, you [are] going to be needed to be up no later than noon.' 'Just make me sleep,' replied Jackson, 'Doesn't matter what time I get up.' Murray responded with, 'What will happen to you? Your rehearsal is already scheduled for today.' Jackson came back with, 'I can't function if I don't sleep. They'll have to cancel it. And I don't want them to cancel it, but they will have to cancel it.'

AEG Live had made it plainly clear that it was Murray's responsibility to get Jackson to rehearsals, and with the concerts looming, there was an added urgency for Jackson to attend, despite his apparent ambivalence towards them. Murray knew that AEG Live were growing impatient with Jackson, and with the demands for Murray to get him in a fit state suitable for rehearsals, the pressure on Murray was growing. He knew that he depended on this job and if he couldn't do what AEG Live required, then the whole tour could be cancelled. And that would be a financial disaster for Murray.

Dr Murray stated to the LAPD that it was roughly 10:40am when he began giving Michael Jackson Propofol. He diluted it with Lidocaine, to avoid Jackson suffering any burning sensation during the administration of the drug, and then pushed in 25mg of Propofol. It took Murray between three and five minutes to administer the drug and, within 15 minutes, according to Murray, the singer had fallen asleep. While Jackson was falling asleep, Dr Murray said he began taking all the precautions he possibly could, given that he was administering Propofol, a drug that Murray realised could have potentially lethal effects. He ensured that the oxygen canisters were at the bedside and that Jackson was using an oxygen nasal cannula. He claimed he also put a pulse oximeter over one of Jackson's fingers to check the singer's oxygen saturation level and his heart rate.[31]

Dr Murray had given Michael Jackson Propofol every day for two months, so was aware how the singer had reacted to the drug in the past. But for the three days leading up to 25 June 2009, Murray insisted that he had been trying to wean Jackson off Propofol in order for the singer to assume a more natural pattern of sleep. In their discussions some weeks before, Murray had been surprised at Jackson's pharmacological knowledge. He found it odd that

178

the singer seemed to know so much about Propofol but quickly discovered through conversations with him, that Jackson had taken it multiple times in the past having been given it by a number of other doctors in various places around the world.[32] Murray also learnt that Jackson knew all about the anti-burn precautions required such as using Lidocaine before injecting Propofol, as injections of Propofol in the past had set his '…limbs on fire'. [33]

During these discussions, according to Murray, Jackson claimed that other doctors had allowed him to infuse Propofol himself, but Murray refused to allow Jackson to do this, much to the singer's annoyance. 'Why don't you want me to push it?' Jackson asked Murray. 'You know, it makes me feel medicine is great.' Dr Murray was adamant that he would not let Jackson administer the drug himself and responded, 'Well, if I'm going to give you an agent that is going to put you to sleep immediately and be so quick to act, I don't want you ever to infuse such a substance when I'm present. I'll do that. So sorry about the other doctors who have done this. I would not.'

As far as Dr Murray was concerned, he was trying to wean Jackson off Propofol and return the singer's sleep patterns to a more physiological state. He also reported being concerned about Jackson's reliance on the drug once he had finished the tour. He asked Jackson, 'If this is your pattern, what's going to happen when the show is over? Are you going to continue like this?' Jackson responded by saying, 'No, I think I'll do fine. I think I'll be able to sleep without it.'

But that was all for the future. Right now, following a restless night, Jackson was insistent that he have his 'milk'. So, at 10:40am on Thursday, 25 June 2009, Dr Murray pushed 25mg of Propofol slowly into the singer. By 11am, according to Murray, Jackson had fallen asleep. It wasn't a deep sleep, as Jackson snored while he was sleeping deeply and he wasn't snoring now, so Murray was hesitant, aware that the singer might suddenly jump out of his sleep, as he was prone to do, and reach for the IV site as he had done in the past. According to Murray's police interview on 27 June 2009, he stayed and monitored Jackson. He checked his oxygen saturation, which was in the high-nineties and saw that his heart rate was roughly in the seventies. It seemed that everything was stable with Jackson but Murray continued to sit and watch him '…for a long enough period that I felt comfortable'. After this, Murray testified that he needed to go to the bathroom himself, as well as having to empty some of Jackson's urine from the bottle that he had collected overnight. To reach the bathroom, Murray had to leave Jackson's bedroom, pass through another chamber, similar to a dressing area, and into a third vault, which is where the bathrooms were.

But Murray's phone records indicate a different pattern of events and contradict the story he gave to the LAPD. At 10:14am Murray used his iPhone to call his clinic in Houston, Texas. This call lasted for two minutes. At 10:22am his Sprint phone received a call from Dr Joanne Prashad in Houston regarding a patient and some medications. Murray answered all her questions knowledgably without even having access to the patient's medical records, which somewhat surprised Dr Prashad. This phone call lasted one minute and 51 seconds, and it appeared to Dr Prashad, that there were no other distractions occurring about Murray while the call was held.

At 10:34am, Murray called his personal assistant, Stacey Ruggles on a San Diego number, with regards to a letter for the London Medical Board concerning the forthcoming London tour. This phone call lasted for eight-and-a-half minutes and, once again, Murray sounded normal and not distracted in any way.[34]

None of this activity matches with Murray's account that he administered the Propofol to Jackson at 10:40am. He also told the

LAPD that it took three to five minutes to administer slowly, which means that he would have been occupied with the administration of the drug from 10:40am to 10:45am, at exactly the same time the records indicate he was talking on the phone to Stacey Ruggles.

Murray also said to the police that he was having a conversation with Jackson around 10am, and it was during this conversation that the singer first asked for Propofol. But from 10:14am to 10:43am, Murray had spent much of the time on the phone, so it's hard to envisage how he could have had such a pivotal conversation with the singer. Dr Murray's phone activity between 8:36am and 10:43am was such that it is likely Michael Jackson was actually asleep during these 127 minutes. For a patient to be sedated for that long much more than 25mg of Propofol is required. In fact, it has to be continuously infused through the IV line. During such administration, the patient's brain can forget to breathe, so the patient has to be monitored constantly, and a person with the skills to breathe for the patient is required to stand guard at all times next to them in case of emergency. If Dr Murray was on the phone so frequently during those 127 minutes, as phone records suggest, then it seems doubtful he would be focusing his entire attention on monitoring the well-being of his patient.

While all this was happening on the second floor of Jackson's home, Kai Chase had arrived back from her shopping trip to the market. When she returned to the kitchen, she noticed nothing unusual; Jackson's three children were all playing together in the den, and she began unloading the groceries, putting things away before starting to prepare the lunch around 10:15am.

At 11:17am, Dr Murray finally responded to the email he had received earlier that morning from Bob Taylor. He wrote:

Dear Bob, I am in receipt of your email. I spoke with
Mr. Jackson and requested his authorization for

181

release of his medical records in order to assist you to procure a cancellation policy for his show, however authorization was denied. I therefore suggest that someone from AEG should consult kindly with Mr. Jackson as to its relevance for he is of the opinion that such a policy is already secured in the U.S. As far as the statements published by the press, let me say they're all fallacious to the best of my knowledge. Sincerely, Conrad Murray.

After sending this email, Murray then held a phone call with his office in Las Vegas that (according to records) started at 11:18am and ended at 11:49am. During this phone call, at 11:26am, he received an incoming call from Bridgette Morgan, one of his 'mistresses', but he was unable to answer this call owing to the fact he was already on the phone to his office. Immediately following the phone call to his office, Dr Murray called one of his patients, a man named Bob Russell at 11:49am. Russell didn't answer the phone so Murray left a brief message: 'Just wanted to talk to you about your results of the EECP. You did quite well on the study. We would love to continue to see you as a patient, even though I may have to be absent from my practice for, uh, because of an overseas sabbatical.'[35] This phone call to Bob Russell ended at approximately 11:51am.

Given that Murray sent an email to Bob Taylor at 11:17am, which would have taken at least a minute or two to compose, and then immediately followed this at 11:18am with a call lasting almost 32 minutes to his office and then another one to Bob Russell that lasted a further couple of minutes, it seems that Dr Murray was on the phone or composing emails for at least 34 minutes consecutively in the hour after he had supposedly given Jackson 25mg of Propofol, a drug which requires constant and close observation of the patient. How could Murray monitor his patient after giving him 25mg of Propofol if he was engaged in emails and phone conversations? And even if he had given him 25mg of the drug, Jackson had now been asleep for over an hour; it would usually require 60–200mg of Propofol to knock out an adult for that long, particularly one who had developed a tolerance to the drug, unless the patient was being continually administered the drug via an IV drip.

To revisit Murray's story, he told the LAPD that he had administered Propofol at 10:40am and then monitored Jackson until he was asleep at 11am before going to the bathroom to relieve himself and empty a urine bottle. It is possible that he then made all his emails and phone calls until 11:51am, from the bathroom area, but this would have meant that Murray had definitely neglected the care of his patient, who had just been injected with a potentially lethal drug.

Moreover, Murray wasn't finished with the phone calls yet. Immediately after his call to Bob Russell, Murray made another call. At 11:51am, he called Sade Anding, another one of his 'mistresses', and right from the outset of the call Anding said she felt that Murray '…didn't sound like himself at all'. What could she mean by this? Why wasn't Murray sounding 'like himself'?

Without knowing it, this call placed Anding at the heart of a moment in pop history as Dr Murray entered the 83-minute window that was to make him notorious around the world.

9

To die would be an awfully big adventure.

J.M. Barrie, *Peter Pan*

At 11:51 on the morning of Thursday, 25 June 2009, Dr Conrad Murray dialled the phone number of Sade Anding, a 24-year-old waitress in a steakhouse and cocktail bar in Houston, Texas. After meeting Anding, Murray had pursued her for seven months, despite her having a boyfriend and Murray having a wife and children as well as a 28-year-old former stripper and actress, Nicole Alvarez, as his mistress.[1] At their initial meeting Murray had boasted to Anding about how successful he was and how he had come from Trinidad to start a clinic in Houston. At the bar on their first encounter, Murray had given her a $100 tip for a $10 drink after they had talked for 15 minutes, during which, at no time, did Murray mention his wife, a girlfriend, or any children he might have had.[2] He did tell her that she was '… too beautiful to be waiting on people – at a place like this.'[3]

Murray began frequenting the bar and was keen for Anding to personally serve him every time he visited. He continued to tip well and soon they were speaking on the phone at least once a week. 'I told him I had a boyfriend. I was his confidant,' Anding recalled. 'I felt like I was important to him. I felt like he needed me to get things off his chest. He would call me and tell me about his day and his problems. We just talked about stuff.'[4]

Before long, Murray told Anding, whom he referred to as his 'girlfriend', that he had landed the role as Michael Jackson's personal doctor. He told her that he had been good friends with the singer for a while since he had treated Prince, Jackson's son. From the moment he revealed he was Jackson's personal doctor, Anding noticed that Murray began showing off more and becoming flashier with his cash. On one occasion he handed her $450 after taking her out for a pizza. He also bought her a black strapless dress, and gave her a $500 cheque as he sat on a hotel bed. 'Looking back I think he was hoping I would join him on the bed, but I said I had to go,' she remembered during an interview with *The Sun*.[5] Murray even promised to take her to England to meet Michael Jackson at his London O2 concerts, despite also making Nicole Alvarez a similar promise.

At 11:51am on 25 June, Anding answered Murray's call, which arrived somewhat out of the blue. She was in Houston at the time and had not heard from him since they had had dinner in Texas in May. When she answered Murray said, 'It's Conrad'. She asked him how he was doing and commented that they hadn't spoken for a while, but sensed, quite quickly, that he was not his normal self and was distracted. Murray simply responded by saying, 'Well', and then failed to say anything else. Determined to break an awkward silence, Anding said brightly to Murray, 'Okay, let me tell you about my day.' Again, Murray didn't respond. Not sure what was going on, Sade Anding began talking to Murray. It was a one-way conversation and she only stopped when, instead of silence, Anding heard a lot of commotion coming down the phone line.

Both confused and alarmed, she became aware that something was wrong as she pressed the phone to her ear and heard coughing and mumbling coming from the room Murray was in, and she didn't believe the mumbling she heard came from Dr Murray. 'Hello? Hello? Hello? Are you there? Are you there?' she started to call into the mouthpiece, but Murray was not responding. The indistinct noise she was hearing convinced her that Murray had been distracted and had put the phone in his pocket without turning it off or perhaps had dropped it somewhere where a lot of noise was being made. Sade Anding hung up and immediately called Murray back, but she got no answer. She tried texting him, but, again, no response from the doctor:

> I knew there was something really wrong. I felt like this stabbing pain in my chest. For him to get off the phone like that without saying anything to me was not normal, and with all the commotion, it seemed to me like an emergency.[6]

It was now 11:57am. Sade Anding had hung up with Dr Murray not talking to her and involved in some sort of commotion. But what exactly was going on with Murray? The times of the phone calls, times that have been verified by Edward Dixon, a Senior Support Engineer with AT&T under oath, contradict considerably the story that Dr Murray gave to the LAPD on 27 June 2009. Murray's AT&T mobile phone showed that at 11:51am he made a phone call that lasted 11 minutes. This was the phone call to Sade Anding, and followed directly his phone calls at 11:18am to his office and 11:49am to Bob Russell. It was during the 11:51am phone call, that Murray became distracted and was when Anding indicated she heard a 'commotion' and 'coughing and mumbling'. However, Murray had told the LAPD that he had administered Propofol to

Jackson at 10:40am, then observed and monitored the singer until 'everything looked stable' before going to the bathroom sometime between 10:50am and 11am. 'I leave his bedside. I walk through another chamber, which is like a dressing area. And then I get into the third vault, which is where the bathrooms are and the, and where I can urinate', Murray told the LAPD. He then revealed he was gone for about two minutes before he came back into Jackson's bedroom to find the singer not breathing. What followed, according to Murray, were his frantic efforts to revive the King of Pop. So frantic that it seems he stopped at 11:07am to receive a call from his assistant, Stacey Ruggles, in San Diego, and then halted his efforts again at 11:17am to email Bob Taylor in London, before taking time out to call his Las Vegas clinic at 11:18am for 32 minutes. After this call, he left a message for his patient Bob Russell before calling Sade Anding at 11:51am. It was during this call that Anding heard the commotion in the room that Murray was in along with coughing and mumbling. So, in all likelihood, this was the moment when Murray actually noticed that Jackson was not breathing, not approximately 50 minutes earlier as he had claimed – unless the phone call was part of an elaborate alibi.

In an interview for Channel 4, conducted by Steve Hewlett on 30 October 2011, one week before the conclusion of Dr Murray's trial, the doctor was questioned about the timeline of phone calls:

Steve Hewlett: In the initial statement, having given Michael Propofol and waited until he fell asleep and felt reasonably comfortable, you then say you left the room for two minutes to visit the lavatory and then when you came back Michael was in some form of distress. That timeframe doesn't make sense because you were on the mobile phone talking to various people for something like forty-five or fifty minutes.
Murray: I would say, this is what I can tell you I have done.

So he got medicine about 10:50, he drifted into sleep around five minutes, I sat there. As I said in my statement I waited as long as I felt I was comfortable that the effects of the medicine, Propofol, was gone.

Hewlett: And then you left the room.

Murray: How long was that? So normally Propofol would last about… the effective, end organ, sleep state would be gone in ten minutes. I sat there for at least thirty minutes. If you look at the calls as they were coming through, I think the very first call that came through was from my daughter. I did not even pick it up.

Hewlett: But the point is you're out of the room for a lot more than two minutes.

Murray: No, I'm still at the bedside.

Hewlett: Taking calls at the bedside?

Murray: Let me clarify for you. After giving him his Propofol I sat there long enough, with Mr Jackson, looking at him, checking his vital signs, checking his oximeter, making sure his pulse is all fine, making sure he was asleep, and he was asleep but not as deep as he would normally sleep because he was not snoring. And then by 11:20, 11:25, I decided well, look, if the calls are going to start coming in and if I need to call and he's now comfortable the effects of Propofol is more than twenty minutes gone…

Hewlett: Okay, but the point is this, you never mentioned the phone calls to the police.

Murray: They never asked me.

Hewlett: But you're supposed to…you're telling them what's happened.

Murray: Listen to me. I just sat there and we never interrupted the policemen, we never told them what they could ask, what they couldn't ask. They did not ask me the question. I did not think it was important.

Whether this version of the timeline is true or not, one thing is certain; when Murray dialled Anding at 11:51am, it would be another 83 minutes before the gurney carrying the stricken body of Michael Jackson was rushed into the ER of the Ronald Reagan UCLA Medical Center and an incredible 134 minutes after Murray, according to his statement, had come back into Jackson's bedroom after going to the toilet to find the singer not breathing.

It becomes quickly evident that Murray's statement to the LAPD cannot be relied upon when comparing it to the statements and testimonies of the various witnesses who appeared in court subsequently as well as all the various phone and data records available. All these paint a very different picture of what really happened on the morning of 25 June 2009.

What is beyond doubt is that Murray was making a phone call to Sade Anding between 11:51am and 12:02pm. At some point during this phone call, probably around 11:57am, Murray returned to Michael Jackson's bedroom and found the singer not breathing.

Clearly Murray had left the room, but not at 11am just to go to the toilet as he had previously stated to the LAPD. It is likely that he did leave the room around 11am, possibly to go to the toilet, but more likely to guarantee some privacy for the emails and phone calls he was about to make. According to phone records, from 11:18am Dr Murray was constantly on the phone without interruption and it was only when he re-entered Jackson's bedroom probably at approximately 11:57am, that he responded to the stricken superstar.

Speaking in the documentary *Michael Jackson & The Doctor: A Fatal Friendship* before he was found guilty of involuntary manslaughter, Conrad Murray said of the moment he noticed something was wrong with Jackson, 'He was not breathing. So my concern was has those agents... the Valium, the Ativan, the

Versed, acting in concert, has now overwhelmed him once he went to sleep. Not 25mg of Propofol.'[7]

Finding the singer not breathing, Murray said he was torn between what to do. Instead of calling 911 he attempted to revive Jackson. He leaned in to Jackson and felt for a pulse. There was no sign of a pulse in Jackson's neck or wrist so Murray pulled back the sheets covering Jackson and thrust his hand down Jackson's pyjama front to try and locate a femoral pulse in Jackson's inner-thigh. According to Murray's interview with the LAPD, he found a '…thread pulse in the femoral region'. He said that Jackson's body was warm and there was no change in his colour so Murray assumed that everything had happened very quickly, '…just about the time I was gone, within that time and coming back'. He was referring here to the two minutes he had told the LAPD that he had been away from Jackson to visit the bathroom. Immediately, Dr Murray began to perform cardiopulmonary resuscitation (CPR) on Jackson while the singer was still lying in bed, as well as mouth-to-mouth resuscitation.[8] Murray started with chest compressions before resorting to mouth-to-mouth to get oxygen into him and said that he saw Jackson's chest rise and fall appropriately. While he was doing this, Murray noticed the telephone on the stand beside Jackson's bed, but this telephone, like the rest of the telephones within Jackson's Carolwood mansion, were disconnected to avoid nuisance calls coming in. All calls had to be made on mobile phones.

The time was now around noon, and Murray still hadn't called 911 and, instead, kept going with CPR. 'The only way I can get help is, well, I know that he lives at 100 North Carolwood. I don't know the zip code,' Murray told the LAPD. 'To speak to a 911 operator would be to neglect him. I don't have that availability. I want to ventilate him, do chest compression, enough to give me an opportunity.' In order to carry out his CPR efforts efficiently,

Murray said he had to improvise as the bed Jackson was lying on was not firm enough for his CPR to be effective. Consequently, Murray laid his left hand under Jackson's body, between his shoulder blades, to provide additional support and a harder surface while performing a non-standard form of CPR on the singer with his right hand only. It would have made sense to get Jackson onto the floor and to continue CPR with both hands, but Murray said he couldn't move the singer off the bed himself, despite Jackson weighing only 136lbs (62 kilos).[9]

Sade Anding heard the beginning of the tragedy unfold before she hung up at 12:02pm. Nobody else at Jackson's Carolwood mansion was aware of what was happening upstairs at that moment. His three children were all playing in the den, under the supervision of the nanny, Rosalind Muhammad,[10] and Kai Chase was in the kitchen preparing a spinach Cobb salad with organic turkey breast for lunch, which was always served to Jackson and his children at 12:30pm.

Thirty-four-year-old Alberto Alvarez had arrived at Carolwood a couple of hours earlier, some time between 10am and 10:30am. Alvarez had worked for Jackson, on and off, since 2004 and his title in June 2009 was Director of Logistics. His main duties involved performing advance route surveys, checking venues and getting them ready for the arrival of Jackson, ensuring that everything around the singer was secure. Upon arrival at Carolwood he checked into the security office, a plain but functional white trailer that stood on a driveway by the side of the property. As far as Alvarez and the rest of the security detail were concerned, everything was okay. Jackson had arrived home early in the morning, they had seen him into the property, there had been no intruders on the grounds overnight or any other security scares, and their only tasks for the day might be the odd mundane chore before accompanying Jackson to another rehearsal at the Staples Center later in the evening.

As it happened, Alvarez soon found himself alone in the security trailer on the morning of 25 June, as his colleague for the day, Faheem Muhammad, was sent off to run an errand at the local bank.[11] Originally hired as a driver,[12] Muhammad, who had known Jackson's personal assistant, Michael Amir Williams, for the previous 10 years, had worked for Jackson for approximately 10 months and been rapidly promoted to Jackson's Chief of Security. At around 11:45am, Faheem Muhammad left Carolwood in one of the security team's SUVs and headed for the nearby bank.

Meanwhile, Michael Amir Williams was yet to even arrive at Jackson's Carolwood home. He was still at his own home in Downtown LA, getting ready for the day ahead. He was now described as the singer's Chief of Staff and referred to himself as a friend of Jackson's, as well as the liaison between Jackson's security and major staff. Amir Williams was a confirmed fan of Jackson, often trying to sneak in at rehearsals to watch the singer performing, but he was usually on errands or doing other tasks for Jackson, so didn't get as many opportunities to witness him singing and dancing as he'd hoped, but he was sure that the opportunity would present itself in London during the upcoming 50 shows at the O2. At noon on 25 June, Amir Williams was oblivious to the idea that he would never get to see the singer perform at the O2.

At 12:05pm, Kai Chase, working in the corner of the kitchen with music playing in the background, saw Dr Murray for the first time that day. Murray had not appeared earlier in the day, as was usual, to pick up the juice she had made for Jackson. This had slightly surprised her, but not as much as the state Murray was in when she saw him running down the stairs in a panic. Murray stopped at the third bannister and leant over to scream out to her to get help urgently and call for security. He also told her to, 'Go get Prince!' Chase immediately dropped what she was doing and ran to the den to get Jackson's son. But Prince had already been alerted to the commotion and screaming going on, and was coming towards the kitchen when Chase reached him. She instructed Prince to hurry to Dr Murray who, by now, had made his way back up the stairs towards Jackson's bedroom.

Prince made his way through the kitchen, past the two housekeeping assistants, Jimmy and Blanca, who had started to cry but who were unaware exactly what was going on. Kai Chase remained in the kitchen, without ever calling security as Murray had screamed at her to do, and returned to her work as Prince headed towards Murray who was standing at the top of the stairwell.[13] Seeing Prince, Dr Murray began descending the stairs to halt the child's progress towards the bedroom. He tells Prince that there's something wrong with his dad before instructing him to go back downstairs and stay in the kitchen. Murray ends with a reassurance, telling the child that everything will be all right.

The two housekeepers had told Kai Chase that they suspected there must be something wrong with Michael Jackson and when Prince came back, to join his siblings, the nanny, Chase and the housekeepers in the kitchen, all grouped together and began consoling each other while praying and crying. Chase recalled the energy in the house had suddenly changed and that something was not right. She remembered Carolwood as normally being a happy house, full of music and children and animals playing. Now, it was different, the whole house seemed to be almost at a standstill.

Murray's interview with the LAPD once again throws up contradictions in the timeline. In his interview, Murray stated that he had called Michael Amir Williams about Jackson's predicament and given Jackson a 0.2mg injection of Flumazenil, a drug specifically used to reverse drowsiness, sedation and other effects caused by benzodiazepines[14] before he went to call Kai Chase to get Prince. In his interview, Murray said he reached for his mobile phone to call Jackson's assistant as he continued

CPR with his '…left hand singularly', the same left hand that he earlier said he had placed under Jackson's body. Managing to grab his mobile phone, Murray said he then called Brother Michael, who didn't answer and left a voicemail message, which said, 'Brother Michael, you need to send security up to Mr Jackson's room immediately. We have a problem.' Murray then returned to Jackson's body and continued CPR but noticed that the singer didn't have a pulse now, so he tried lifting Jackson's legs to give the singer what he referred to as an autotransfusion.[15] But with nothing to prop Jackson's legs up, Murray lowered them once more to continue with CPR before injecting Flumazenil into the IV port. Was Murray aware of the benzodiazepines reacting with the Propofol he had already given to the singer? The benzodiazepines would not be dangerous when used by themselves, but when mixed with central nervous system depressants, such as Propofol, they can be lethal. It was only after carrying out all of these actions that Murray said he *then* raced out to the kitchen where Kai Chase was. But Kai Chase testified that Murray had shouted to her at 12:05pm while phone records show that it wasn't until 12:12pm when Murray called Michael Amir Williams, or Brother Michael as he was known, for the first time. So yet again Murray's version of events seems at odds with official phone records.

At 12:13pm, after stepping out of the shower, Michael Amir Williams noticed he had a missed call from Dr Murray. The doctor had left a voicemail for him and after Amir Williams dialled the number to access it, he heard a frantic Dr Murray: 'Call me right away, Hurry. Call me, Call me right away'. Amir Williams immediately called Murray back. It was 12:15pm. Murray answered quickly, asking Amir Williams where he was. Amir Williams told him he was at home. 'Get here right away,' Murray urged. 'Get here right away. Mr Jackson had a bad reaction. He had a bad reaction. Get someone up here.' It wasn't just what Murray had said that shocked Amir Williams, it was the way he had said it. Something serious was up. But, throughout the call, Murray had never asked Amir Williams to call 911.

Murray had instead asked Amir Williams to 'Get someone up here' so, before leaving his house, he called Faheem Muhammad, as he knew Jackson was comfortable with him. Faheem was still on the way to the local bank at this point and took the call on his mobile in the SUV at 12:16pm. 'Where are you?' asked Amir Williams when Faheem answered. 'I just left the property. I went to the bank,' replied Faheem. Amir Williams ordered Faheem to turn around immediately and when questioned about what was going on said, 'I don't know, but something. Get back right away.'

Amir Williams, still unsure what was going on at Carolwood, now called Alberto Alvarez. He tried him three times in succession but failed to get through. He then tried another member of the security detail, Derrick Cleveland, but couldn't get through to him, either. He then dialled Alberto Alvarez one more time. This time he managed to get through. It was 12:17pm when Alvarez answered. He was sitting in the security trailer outside the house but left quickly when Amir William said, 'I don't know what's going on, but get back to the front door.' Carrying his mobile phone to his ear, with Amir Williams still on the line, Alvarez started walking towards the front door. 'Are you walking? Okay, walk faster,' said an increasingly anxious Amir Williams. Alvarez started running towards the front door.

When Alvarez reached the front door, he found it locked. He rattled the handles, pulling at the doors, but they wouldn't open. He peered through the glass and saw the nanny, Rosalind Muhammad, quickly making her way to open the door for him. Behind her he spotted Paris and then further back the chef, Kai Chase. Looking up towards the stairway, Alvarez saw Murray standing at the top.

As Alvarez entered the property, Amir Williams heard Dr Murray's voice over the still connected phone line and understood that '…a lot is going on'.[16] Murray called to Alvarez from the top of the stairs, saying, 'Alberto, come. Come quick.' Suddenly, Alberto Alvarez hung up on Amir Williams who, by now desperately worried, had thrown on some clothes and rushed to his car to make the drive to Carolwood. During the drive, Amir Williams continued to try to contact Alvarez to get an update on events, but he was unable to get any response.

Alvarez had run up the stairs as soon as he had entered the building, skipping steps as he did so. The stairs were on the left-hand side of the foyer and it was the first time that Alvarez had ever been upstairs in Jackson's house. Dr Murray was standing at the top calling down to Alvarez, 'Alberto, come quick, come quick', before he disappeared into the bedroom. Alvarez followed him through the small foyer before he entered Jackson's bedroom. What Alvarez saw as he entered the bedroom left him 'frozen'. Michael Jackson was lying flat on the bed with his head on the pillow and his mouth open. His hands were down by his sides, his head leaning slightly to the left and his eyes were half-open. Alvarez noticed that Jackson's penis was out of his pyjamas and that it had something plastic covering it. He also saw an IV stand with a drip on it.

Dr Murray was on the right side of the bed and was continuing to administer his one-handed CPR. When Alvarez entered Murray said to him, 'Alberto, he had a bad reaction. Mr Jackson had a bad reaction.' The situation in the room seemed frantic as Murray asked Alvarez to help him perform CPR by carrying out the chest compressions while Murray continued his attempts at mouth-to-mouth resuscitation.

It was now 12:20pm, and outside Faheem Muhammad had returned from his aborted trip to the bank. Before entering the house, Faheem called Michael Amir Williams who, himself, was racing towards Carolwood. Faheem made the call to ensure that what Amir Williams had previously ordered him to do, to go back to the house and to rush upstairs, was correct as there was an unwritten rule that no members of staff were allowed to go upstairs within the property.[17] Amir Williams confirmed with Faheem that he should go ahead and go upstairs to see what's going on and check on everything.

Meanwhile, in the bedroom, the call to 911 still hadn't been made. In his interview with the LAPD, Dr Murray discussed the moment when Alvarez entered the room, which, according to phone records, would probably have been 12:17 or 12:18pm. Murray, however, had told the LAPD that he, himself, had returned to Jackson's bedroom, shortly after 11:00am, after a two-minute toilet break, to find the singer not breathing. This, if we believe the LAPD interview, would indicate that Murray had carried out CPR himself for over an hour, perhaps from 11:02am to 12:12pm, before calling Michael Amir Williams. Of course, phone records indicate that Dr Murray had been making numerous phone calls between 11:18am and 11:51am, culminating in his call to Sade Anding, so it seems inconceivable that he was administering CPR to Jackson at this time. So when Murray said to the LAPD, 'That's when the gentleman you hear on the 911 call comes upstairs. The door is open. He gets inside there. I said "Call 911". While he's doing 911, I am doing chest compressions. I'm doing mouth-to-mouth resuscitation. But I want 911 to be called now, even though he's still on the bed, because I would still need help to move him off the bed and place him at an appropriate site on the floor, where I would have a firmer surface,' he was almost certainly referring to 12:17pm or 12:18pm, the moment when Alvarez entered the bedroom.

But, according to the testimony of Alvarez, Dr Murray wanted him to do something entirely different before he called 911, and it wasn't assisting with CPR.

Alvarez recalled, during his testimony, that at one point, Murray froze and was simply surveying the situation within the room, glancing around at the scene before him. Then, suddenly breaking out of this trance, Dr Murray grabbed a handful of vials from a nightstand beside Jackson's bed, before handing them across the bed to Alvarez and ordering him to put them in a bag. Alvarez managed to find a plastic grocery bag within reach and held this bag open while Murray dropped the bottles and vials into it. Then Murray pointed and ordered Alvarez to '…put them in the brown bag'. Alvarez saw a brown canvas bag, which looked like a reusable lunch bag with a white lining inside it. Alvarez did as he was instructed and dropped the plastic bag into the brown bag. Not yet finished, Dr Murray pointed to the saline bag hanging from the IV stand and told Alvarez to '…remove that and put it in the blue bag'. As he went to do as ordered, Alvarez noticed there was a small bottle lying inside, at the bottom of the saline bag. The saline solution inside the bag was mixing with a milk-like substance, which was likely to be Propofol. Alvarez removed this saline bag, but left another one, which had no bottle inside it, hanging on the stand. Once this was done, Dr Murray told Alvarez to put everything he had gathered into the closet.

It was now 12:21pm and the call to 911 was finally made. Alvarez made the emergency call while Dr Murray continued with the CPR on the bed. The 911 dispatcher at Beverly Hills Police Department answered the call:

911 Operator: Paramedic 33, what is the nature of your emergency?
Alvarez: Yes, sir, I need an ambulance as soon as possible.
911 Operator: Okay, sir, what is your address?
Alvarez: Carolwood Drive, Los Angeles, California, 90077.
911 Operator: Is it Carolwood?

Alvarez: Carolwood Drive, yes [inaudible]

911 Operator: Okay, sir, what's the phone number you're calling from and [inaudible] and what exactly happened?

Alvarez: Sir, we have a gentleman here that needs help and he's not breathing, he's not breathing and we need to – we're trying to pump him but he's not…

911 Operator: Okay, how old is he?

Alvarez: He's 50 years old, sir.

911 Operator: Okay, he's unconscious and he's not breathing?

Alvarez: Yes, he's not breathing, sir.

911 Operator: Okay, and he's not conscious either?

Alvarez: No, he's not conscious, sir.

911 Operator: Okay, all right, is he on the floor, where is he at right now?

Alvarez: He's on the bed, sir. He's on the bed.

911 Operator: Okay, let's get him on the floor. Let's get him down to the floor. I'm gonna help you with CPR right now, okay?

Alvarez: [inaudible]…we need to…

911 Operator: We're on our way there. We're on our way. I'm gonna do as much as I can to help you over the phone. We're already on our way. [inaudible] did anybody see him?

Alvarez: Yes, we have a personal doctor here with him, sir.

911 Operator: Oh, you have a doctor there?

Alvarez: Yes, but he's not responding to anything. He's not responding to CPR or anything.

911 Operator: Okay, okay, we're on our way there. If you guys are doing CPR instructed by a doctor you have a higher authority than me. Did anybody witness what happened?

Alvarez: Just the doctor, sir. The doctor's been the only one here.

911 Operator: Okay, did the doctor see what happened, sir?

At this point in the phone call, Alvarez begins to relay the question to Dr Murray, who was still working on Jackson in the background. But Alvarez was abruptly cut off by someone, it could only be Murray, speaking angrily in a foreign language that cannot be identified.[18] After being halted in his attempts to try to relay the questions to Murray, Alvarez returns to the phone call.

Alvarez: Sir, you just, if you can please…
911 Operator: We're on our way. I'm just passing these questions on to my paramedics while they're on their way there.
Alvarez: Okay. He's pumping his chest but he's not responding to anything, sir. Please…
911 Operator: Okay, we're on our way. We're less than a mile away. We'll be there shortly.

The paramedics who were rushing to Jackson's home were coming from Station 71 on South Beverly Glen Boulevard in Bel Air, about four minutes away from Jackson's Carolwood mansion. Opened on 11 May 1948, Station 71 was one of 106 neighbourhood fire stations under the 471 square-mile jurisdiction of the Los Angeles Fire Department who, as well as providing firefighting and fire prevention services, also provided emergency medical services. The call was relayed to them from the 911 operator at 12:22pm and a Fire Department Rescue Ambulance and Engine,[19] with a crew consisting of Firefighter-Paramedic Richard Senneff, Paramedic Martin Blount, Paramedic Mark Goodwin, Firefighter Brett Herron, Fire Captain Jeff Mills, Engineer Gary Burgandy and EMS Supervisor Bob Linnel, was dispatched immediately.

Martin Blount, who became a paramedic in 1999, was driving the rescue ambulance. Alongside him in the front was Richard Senneff, a firefighter-paramedic who had worked in this capacity for the Los Angeles Fire Department since 1984 and who had worked as a paramedic since 1982. He would ride on the LAFD rescue ambulance part of the time and the remainder of the time he'd ride on a fire engine, which is also a paramedic assessment engine. On 25 June, Senneff was in the attendant position on the rescue ambulance, working as a paramedic.[20]

In front of him, Senneff had a teletype readout[21] which told him they were speeding to a cardiac arrest at 100 North Carolwood and that the casualty was a 50-year-old male. It also stated the incident time was 12:21pm and the dispatch time was 12:22pm. It only took four minutes for the ambulance to arrive at Jackson's mansion, pass through the gates and park beside the front door to the property. It was now 12:26pm. The call to 911 had been made five minutes previously, but those five minutes had witnessed more incredible scenes within Jackson's bedroom.

As soon as Alberto Alvarez had finished making the 911 call, he went to help Dr Murray move Michael Jackson's body onto the floor, where Murray could perform more effective CPR with both hands, using the floor as a firm support. Alvarez went to grab Jackson's legs but hesitated when he noticed a needle was still stuck in one of the singer's legs. This needle was connected to a clear plastic tube, which led to the bag on the IV that Alvarez hadn't been told to remove earlier. Dr Murray, seeing Alvarez's hesitancy, came across and removed the needle and tube from Jackson's leg and then, with Alvarez grabbing the singer's legs and Murray his upper body, they moved Jackson from the bed to the floor.[22]

Once Michael Jackson's body was on the floor, Dr Murray placed a pulse oximeter on the singer's fingertip. Alvarez asked Murray what the device was and was told that it was like a heart monitor. In fact, a pulse oximeter is nothing like a heart monitor as it instead monitors a person's pulse rate and the percentage of a patient's red blood cells that have oxygen attached to them, not a heart rate. The percentage of red blood cells that have oxygen attached to them should always be 95 per cent or above and, on most pulse oximeters, the default low oxygen saturation alarm setting is 90 per cent. But the pulse oximeter that Murray was using was a Nonin 9500, a device that comes with instructions that say it '...must be used with other methods of assessing clinical signs and symptoms. This device has no audible alarms and is intended for spot-checking'. This model retails for $275, but Nonin Medical produces other pulse oximeters that contain visual and audible alarms. They retail between $750 and $1,250. It appears that the device that Murray was using was a cheaper option without an alarm and one not sufficient enough for his duty of care to Jackson at that moment in time.[23]

Dr Murray and Alberto Alvarez were then joined by Faheem Muhammad, who had been given the all clear by Michael Amir Williams to enter the house, and who had subsequently rushed upstairs to see what was happening. Approaching Faheem, Alvarez said, 'It's not looking good'. Then, to the amazement of both Alvarez and Faheem, Dr Murray suddenly asked, 'Does anyone know CPR?' Alvarez looked at Faheem before going to assist Dr Murray once more. Alvarez performed chest compressions on Jackson while Dr Murray, on his knees, continued mouth-to-mouth resuscitation. As he was doing so, Murray breaks away to say, 'You know, this is the first time that I give mouth-to-mouth, but I have to do it, he's my friend.' The fact that a trained cardiologist had never given mouth-to-mouth before may have shocked Alvarez and Faheem who understood Murray to be Jackson's personal physician and, therefore, a professional trained in, and with experience of, medical procedures.

Faheem could only see Jackson's legs and feet from where he was standing, so he moved around to the left side of the bed. Here he was able to look down on the singer. Jackson's eyes and mouth were wide open and, to a layperson like Faheem, the singer looked dead.

The whole tragic scenario was suddenly made worse when Paris and Prince walked into the room to see Murray and Alvarez attempting to revive their father. Prince was standing at the doorway, a couple of paces inside, gently weeping with a look of shock on his face at seeing his father stricken on the floor. Paris, however, had crumpled to her knees instantly, screaming 'Daddy' and beginning to cry hysterically.[24] Murray shouted out, 'Don't let them see their dad like this.' Faheem ushered the two children away from the scene and took them downstairs to Rosalind, their nanny, telling her to take them back to the den. As soon as he had done this, Faheem instructed security to prepare the cars, in the event that they would have to go to the hospital.

It had been a frantic five minutes. Five minutes which had culminated with the arrival of the rescue ambulance at 12:26pm.

Firefighter-Paramedic Richard Senneff was the first out of the ambulance. His role on 25 June was that of the Radio Man. The Radio Man is, medically speaking, in overall charge of the patient once on location. He looks after communication with those in the immediate vicinity and the receiving hospital, and is in charge of information gathering and information dispersing on site.

Senneff was escorted into the house by several members of Jackson's external security team, all looking the part – wearing dark suits, dark ties and white shirts.[25] As soon as he entered the house, Senneff began asking questions of the security detail that greeted him. He asked one of them, 'What's going on?' and was simply told, 'There is a man who needs your help upstairs.' As Senneff led the way, Paramedic Martin Blount, Firefighter Herron and Paramedic Mark Goodwin followed him. They all galloped up the stairs, still totally unaware of the identity of the patient needing their help.

As soon as Senneff entered the bedroom, he saw Dr Murray reaching over the patient from the far side of the bed. Both Alberto Alvarez and Dr Murray say in the court testimony and

LAPD interview that they had moved Jackson's body to the floor by the time the paramedics arrived to administer CPR in a more regulated manner, but this contradicts the testimony of Senneff and Blount, who both say they saw the patient on the bed. 'I saw what appeared to be a thin, pale, patient wearing pyjamas,' Senneff said, before going on, '…and a shirt opened up, laying on the bed.' Blount was even more specific in his testimony when questioned by District Attorney Walgren:

Blount: I observed a male lying on the bed, very pale, very thin and, at that time, the next time I saw him was when the guys in front of me got him off the bed and put him on the floor.
Walgren: Okay, well, when you saw the patient, was he on the floor?
Blount: No, sir. He was in the bed.[26]

Why did Murray and Alvarez say they had moved Jackson to the floor before the paramedics arrived when, quite clearly, they hadn't? Was it in an attempt to suggest they had carried out proper CPR procedures? One-handed CPR on a soft bed certainly goes against best advice. Did the two of them come up with this version of events before the paramedics arrived to give a different impression of the care that Murray was giving Jackson? If so, what did Alvarez stand to gain from such misleading statements if it was, indeed, his intention to mislead? Certainly, there was a lot of frantic activity and confusion in the bedroom, but this evidence suggests Murray was already starting to cover his tracks as the paramedics arrived.

Later in his evidence, Senneff stated that he '…saw the doctor attempting to move the patient from the bed to the floor. He was about halfway between the two.' In his own testimony, Murray had told the LAPD that he was unable to move Jackson by himself earlier, yet here it seems as though he was making efforts to get the singer off the bed, but wasn't quite quick enough to avoid being spotted by the LAFD when they burst into the room.

Upon meeting the paramedics, Dr Murray introduced himself as the patient's doctor.[27] Paramedic Martin Blount was at the rear of the group of emergency personnel as they entered the room, but recalled seeing Dr Murray immediately and noticed him sweating profusely and acting in an agitated manner.

Senneff, meanwhile, was quickly looking around, surveying the scene that had greeted him. He noticed an IV stand on the same side of the bed as Dr Murray and that the patient still had an IV tube attached to his right leg. He also noted a number of medical vials and bottles scattered about the room.[28] Immediately, Senneff began trying to obtain information from Dr Murray. He asked what the patient's underlying medical condition was. At first, Murray didn't answer, so Senneff asked him again. This time Murray responded, 'There isn't any', he said. Senneff found this unusual and irregular, and pursued his questioning of Murray. 'I did pursue it,' said Senneff in his testimony, 'because it is unusual to come to someone's home, I've been to a lot of homes through the years, and have an IV pole and a personal doctor there. That is just not usual.' But that wasn't all that was unusual in the room.

Senneff thought the patient was anyone but the King of Pop: 'And the patient, he appeared to me to be pale and underweight. I was thinking along the lines of, this is a hospice patient.' He also said he could see the patient's ribs and, at that point, couldn't recognise who the patient was. He even questioned Dr Murray about whether the patient had a 'Do not resuscitate order' as the patient looked so poorly. As far as the paramedic was concerned, it just didn't add up, especially when Dr Murray told him that the patient had no problems. 'He is fine,' Dr Murray explained to Senneff, 'He was practising all night. I'm just treating him for dehydration.' What Senneff saw in front of him, however, was an underweight, thin person lying in bed with an IV pole, a personal doctor around him and items scattered about the room suggesting someone who was under the care of a physician for a chronic illness. But Martin Blount was under no illusions as to who the patient actually was, he recognised Michael Jackson immediately.[29] He went to Jackson's head straight away and began to provide air support to the singer by inserting a tongue suppressor, tilting Jackson's head back, and using an Ambu Bag connected to an oxygen tank that he had wheeled in himself.[30] Following this, he did advanced life support with an endotracheal tube, ensuring 100 per cent of the oxygen was going directly into Jackson's lungs.

While Blount was doing this, Senneff was asking Dr Murray if the patient was taking any medications. 'No, none. He is not taking anything,' replied Murray. Unconvinced, Senneff repeated the question. This time Murray gave him a different answer, 'Well, I gave him a little bit of Lorazepam to help him sleep.' As testified by the paramedic, this was the only information regarding medication that Murray gave to Senneff. He didn't mention any other medicines or narcotics, and he certainly didn't mention Propofol.

The next question Senneff asked Dr Murray was crucial, not only in determining how to treat the patient, but also in how the truth would manifest itself later. Senneff asked Dr Murray how long the patient had been in this condition, how long he had been down. Murray replied by saying, 'It just happened right when I called you.'[31] At that point, Senneff thought, with the patient only just down and a doctor present who surely must have been doing CPR, they might have a chance to revive the patient. But once Senneff touched Jackson to move him to a different area to work on, he had second thoughts.

Walgren: Now, despite Dr Murray telling you the patient had just been down when he called, did the patient, in your expert opinion, appear to have been just down?

Senneff: Initially, when he told me that, sure. Sounds fine. Then as soon as I picked him up, his legs were quite cool, cool to the touch.

Walgren: How about his eyes?

Senneff: His eyes, the moisture in his eyes, his eyes had become dry.

Walgren: What does that mean?

Senneff: Time has elapsed.[32]

Senneff also noticed that Jackson's hands and feet were tinged blue, meaning there wasn't any respiration going on and no circulation, and his eyes were also 'blown' and dilated. A few minutes earlier, Murray had placed the cheap version of a pulse oximeter on Jackson's finger-tip, but this had no audible alarm on it so would not have alerted Dr Murray, if he needed to be alerted, that Jackson was already cyanotic.[33] This also confirmed to Senneff that time had elapsed and he formed the opinion that Jackson was already dead when the paramedics arrived at the scene. Paramedic Blount also felt Jackson was cool to the touch and was certain that the singer had been down for a while despite Murray's comments.

The paramedics, specifically Mark Goodwin, then hooked Jackson up to an EKG machine[34] while Blount continued to try to get oxygen into Jackson's lungs. The EKG machine was flat lining, showing Jackson was asystole, a dire form of cardiac arrest in which the heart is at a total standstill. As far as Senneff was concerned, this confirmed the event hadn't just happened, as Murray had told him, but guessed it must have occurred, at the very least, within the last 20 minutes but could well have been considerably longer.

Throughout all of this, Alvarez and Faheem Muhammad could do little but stand by and watch as the paramedics struggled, in vain, to revive Jackson. Downstairs, in the kitchen, Kai Chase, the nanny, the housekeepers and Jackson's three children all huddled together, praying and consoling each other. Michael Amir Williams was still in his vehicle rushing towards Jackson's Carolwood home and, outside the gates, tour buses stopped momentarily to enable the tourists to take photos while the singer's devout fans and a few paparazzi gathered beside the gates, totally unaware of what was happening inside Jackson's bedroom.

Up to this point, the number of paparazzi waiting outside Jackson's home had been slowly diminishing for some months. Other celebrities had appeared on the scene for photographers to trail and the value of a Jackson photo was not what it once was. One of the few paparazzi waiting outside Jackson's home on 25 June was 31-year-old Ben Evenstad. He was the co-founder of the National Photo Group Agency and had been fascinated by Jackson for years. 'As a pap, you spend most of your time chasing sex symbols, but M.J. was different, almost like a Howard Hughes character. With the masks and the umbrellas and the mystery, I thought Michael was more interesting than any other celebrity, and he has more interesting fans than any other celebrity – this group, mostly female, who would follow him all over the world. If he went to Ireland, France, Bahrain, Neverland, they were there. The same individuals. Nobody else had what he had. I set out to document why,' said Evenstad in an interview with *Vanity Fair* in June 2009. It was this quest to document what Jackson had that led Evenstad to be standing outside Jackson's Carolwood home on the afternoon of 25 June 2009.

Evenstad set his agency up in 2007 after spending the previous eight years as a paparazzo for another photo agency who had begun to express concerns at the amount of time Evenstad was spending chasing Jackson when photographs of him were not of great value. Upon founding his own agency Evenstad offered a job to his close friend, Christopher Weiss, and trained him up to be a paparazzo. Weiss really wanted to be a doctor, and was in the process of getting his paramedic's licence, but he was also becoming increasingly anxious about the debt he was accruing to fund his medical training. Evenstad's offer seemed to Weiss to be a convenient way out of his potential debt and he quickly started to become fascinated by the job. When Jackson moved into the Hotel Bel Air in Los Angeles in late 2008, Evenstad sent Weiss to sit outside the hotel and wait for any Jackson photo opportunity. Evenstad was eager for his agency to become known for its photo scoops of Jackson. When Jackson moved out of that hotel, Evenstad discovered that the singer would be living in Los Angeles at Carolwood. No other photo agency had this information ensuring that Evenstad's agency was the only one for some time with a photographer outside Jackson's house.

But on 25 June, neither Christopher Weiss nor Ben Evenstad was outside Jackson's home to begin with. Weiss was, instead, setting up camp outside the home of Brad Pitt and Angelina Jolie, some eight miles away from Jackson's home. Pitt and Jolie were Hollywood's hottest couple at the time and Weiss had already photographed Pitt but was waiting to capture a photo of Jolie when he suddenly received a phone call from Ben Evenstad who had, in turn, received a call from one of his other agency photographers, Alfred Ibanez, who was situated outside Jackson's house. Ibanez told Evansted that there was an ambulance at Jackson's home and instructed him to get there as quickly as he could. Evansted made his way there as fast as possible, but told Weiss to rush there immediately too.

Weiss arrived first to find only two fans and three autograph hunters waiting outside the gates of Jackson's house. A number of other paparazzi were there also, but they were all from Evansted's agency as the call Evansted had made to Weiss was one he had made to every other photographer on his books. But none of these other photographers had the medical background that Weiss had, and he was able to analyse an image that Alfred Ibanez had already taken with his telephoto lens. Ibanez had zoomed in to snap a picture of the call screen inside the window of a fire truck that was parked on the street outside Jackson's property. When Weiss looked at Ibanez's digital image, he was able to read '50-year-old-male... not breathing...'. With his medical background, Weiss knew that this was more serious than simply an anxiety attack but as time passed – and during this period Ben Evansted had turned up to join Weiss – he assumed that it was probably nothing life threatening. 'We were there for 20 minutes,' Weiss recalled, 'and if you've got a full arrest the paramedics usually load and go within 8 to 10 minutes.'

While the paparazzi waited outside the gates, wondering what was going on and speculating with the handful of onlookers, inside the house efforts were still being made to revive Jackson.

It was now 12:40pm and despite the singer's EKG showing he had flat-lined, and the capnography[35] reading 16 instead of the normal 36 to 40, the paramedics had been administering both Epinephrine and Atropine since 12:34pm.[36] Epinephrine is adrenaline and it can kick-start the heart, while Atropine is used to take the brakes off the heart so it can accelerate. But the paramedics found administering these drugs into Jackson wasn't straightforward as they struggled to find a vein in the singer's arms. Paramedic Goodwin inserted a needle a number of times into Jackson's arms but each time failed to locate a suitable vein.[37] They had noticed that Jackson had an IV in his right leg, but on investigation discovered it wasn't flowing properly. An urgent discussion ensued to decide whether they should administer drugs down the endotracheal tube, which is an approved method of administration in emergency situations, but as they were debating this, Senneff found he could get an IV into

Jackson's jugular vein and they were able to administer the first round of drugs via the left jugular vein in Jackson's neck.

While they were administering these drugs, Senneff was in contact with a care nurse at the base station of the Ronald Reagan UCLA Medical Center. This was standard protocol for paramedics. The nurse at the hospital is charged with radioing back care for the patient under the supervision of an attendant at the hospital, in this case Dr Richelle Cooper. Dr Cooper began working at UCLA in 1994 after graduating from the UCLA David Geffen School of Medicine, the UCLA EM Residency, and the UCLA EM Research Fellowship. Highly experienced, Dr Cooper was viewed as one of UCLA's finest clinicians and also received some of the highest evaluation scores from the residents for her bedside teaching with a specialty in emergency medicine. Unaware who the patient was, this was simply another emergency call for Dr Cooper.

Senneff constantly relayed back their actions to UCLA. At no point, did he or any of the medical team feel any indication of a pulse in Jackson. After administering the first round of starter drugs, Senneff relayed to UCLA that there was no sign of life but suggested that they wanted to continue. After the second round of starter drugs, Senneff fed back to UCLA again and, once more, stated that there was no sign of life. This time UCLA was ready to pronounce Michael Jackson dead. But, at this point, Dr Murray suddenly indicated that he had identified a femoral pulse again in Jackson's groin area.[38] Senneff didn't see any sign of a pulse or electrical activity on the EKG heart monitor and instructed two members of his paramedic team to check the area, but neither of them found any sign of a pulse either. The paramedics even stopped CPR to see if the heart was functioning by itself. But there was no visible activity.

At this point, Martin Blount's attention was drawn to some vials of medicine he saw scattered on the floor. Looking closer he saw that they were vials of Lidocaine and, moreover, that three of them were open and had been emptied. Lidocaine is a drug administered with Propofol to ease the burning sensation. These three opened vials could only have been used by Murray to treat Jackson whilst administering Propofol to him. In Volume 97, Issue 2 of the journal *Anesthesia & Analgesia*, it states categorically that 'Lidocaine is widely used to reduce the pain associated with injection of Propofol, administered either mixed with Propofol or as a separate injection.' But the most vital part of the article is the conclusion which states, 'The use of a freshly prepared mix of Propofol 1% Lidocaine 1% in a 10:1 volume did not affect the dose of Propofol required for the induction of anesthesia.' This potentially means that if Murray used three vials of Lidocaine, then it is conceivable that ten times as much Propofol could have been used on the singer, based on this 10:1 ratio. And at this point, Murray hadn't even revealed to any of the paramedics on the scene that he had given Jackson Propofol earlier in the morning.

With two rounds of starter drugs failing to have any effect on Jackson, and UCLA ready to pronounce him dead, the paramedics administered one final round of starter drugs at 12:40pm. Again, there was no sign of life in Jackson and at 12:57pm, UCLA base station, through Dr Richelle Cooper, advised that further resuscitation efforts on Jackson would be futile and that they could pronounce him dead.[39] Hearing this verdict over the radio, Dr Murray said, 'No, I don't want to call it. I want to keep trying'. Murray was convinced he could feel another pulse in Jackson, this time inside one of the singer's elbows. UCLA were aware that Murray was in the room, but not that he was a doctor and when Senneff told them that the patient was a very high profile VIP and that 'the physician on the scene doesn't want to call it,' Dr Richelle Cooper asked if Murray was willing to assume control of the call by saying, 'If the doctor wants to try, if he accepts the care, that will be fine.' As Murray had a valid California medical licence, this was all within protocol.

Murray was eager to assume control. He felt that UCLA were slow in giving orders and that the 20 minutes they had tried to revive Jackson was an unnecessarily limited amount of time given the fact that he said he had only been out of the room for two minutes. He didn't want to pronounce Jackson dead. Not there. And not then.

Detective Martinez: Okay, and they want to give up, and you don't want to give up.
Dr Murray: I said, 'No'.
Detective Martinez: So they transfer care to you.
Dr Murray: Yeah.
Detective Martinez: Okay.
Dr Murray: I mean, I love Mr Jackson. He was my friend. And he opened up to me in different ways. And I wanted to help him as much as I can. You know, he was a single parent. You don't always hear that from a man. But he would state that, you know, he was a single parent of three. And I... I always thought of his children, you know, as I would think about mine. So I wanted to give him the best chance.

So, once he had assumed control, Murray suddenly had power over the paramedics within the room. Senneff relinquished responsibility and stopped the radio call with the base station at UCLA a few seconds later and began to follow instructions from Dr Murray.

Murray had his own ideas about what should be done; he wanted to give Jackson some bicarbonate, he wanted to administer a central line and he also wanted to give Jackson magnesium.[40][41] But most of all, Murray wanted to get Jackson to hospital.

Following Murray's instructions, the paramedics gave Jackson bicarbonate before preparing to transport him to hospital. They had to transfer the singer down a flight of stairs so Paramedic Herron rushed out to get the backboard, which they would use to carry Jackson down the stairs to the waiting gurney. As Herron left the room he bumped into Alberto Alvarez who was waiting outside. Alvarez wanted to know what was happening and Herron told him that they were preparing to bring Jackson out. Alvarez thought for a moment then followed Herron down the stairs before heading into the kitchen.

By now, Faheem Muhammad himself was in the kitchen, and when Alvarez walked in he demanded to know where Jackson's children were. One of the housekeepers told Alvarez that they were in the den with the nanny. Alvarez implored the housekeeper to make sure they stayed in the den, as the paramedics were about to bring their father down to the ambulance.

Meanwhile, up in the bedroom, Herron had returned with the backboard and the paramedics carefully slid Jackson onto it before securing him with binds and ties. During this time, Martin Blount saw Murray scooping Lidocaine bottles off the floor and putting them into a black bag.

The paramedics gathered up as much of their equipment as they could, but couldn't carry it all while transferring Jackson down the stairs, so Senneff left some of their equipment in the room to collect later.

At 1:07pm, they started taking Jackson out of the room. As they left, Dr Murray told them he'd join them in a few moments and remained in the room as the paramedics carefully made their way down the stairs and into the ambulance. As his colleagues secured Jackson in the ambulance, Richard Senneff headed back to Jackson's bedroom to collect their equipment that they couldn't originally carry down. But as he entered the bedroom, he was met with a startled Dr Murray who was standing next to the nightstand, holding a plastic trash bag, and picking things up and placing them in the bag. After collecting up all the paramedics' remaining equipment, Senneff left Murray and went back to the ambulance. Outside the house, they waited briefly for Murray to join them before making the short trip to the hospital. Nobody asked what Murray had been clearing up in the room.

Michael Amir Williams finally arrived at Carolwood after the 40-minute journey from his home just as the medics were carrying the gurney to the ambulance. He saw Dr Murray come down and get into the ambulance as well, and later described Murray as looking frantic at this time. During all of this, Alberto Alvarez was desperately trying to distract Jackson's children, so they wouldn't see the paramedics bring their father down and load him into the ambulance.

Despite the apparently grave situation and the need to get Jackson to hospital as quickly as possible, the nature with which the ambulance left Jackson's Carolwood home was quite remarkable, and all filmed by the gathering group of onlookers outside the gates. Firstly, the ambulance reversed out slowly making no effort to turn around in the driveway to make its exit easier and quicker. Secondly, the ambulance failed to use its sirens. And thirdly, as the ambulance slowly exited the gates, it actually stopped to allow a bus of Japanese tourists to crawl by as they all took photos of Jackson's home, totally oblivious to the fact they were witnessing the tragic end of the King of Pop.

The ambulance slowing down gave the waiting paparazzi the opportunity to take photographs. Ben Evenstad had been anxiously waiting outside Jackson's house with his team of agency photographers gathered around, including Christopher Weiss. Evenstad was well aware that something was happening and, as the ambulance slowly came out of the gates he shouted at his photographers, 'This might be the biggest picture ever, so get up to the windows of that vehicle and shoot. I don't care if you can't see. Just shoot.' Weiss went into action and managed to get to within a foot of the ambulance window, but Evenstad was convinced all he'd get was a picture of his own reflection as the flash went off. Nobody knew what was going on inside the ambulance and they were just hoping they would get something on camera. Jumping in their cars to follow Jackson's entourage as it made its way to hospital, Weiss checked a few of the photos he had tried to take through the window, but all he found was photos of a reflection on the glass. He was depressed, convincing himself that he'd missed a massive photo opportunity.

As the ambulance carrying Jackson to UCLA made its way along the freeway, it began to gather a following of press cars, photographers on motorcycles and helicopters in the air, all alerted that something serious might be going on.

Behind the ambulance, Alberto Alvarez was following, as was Michael Amir Williams with Jackson's children in the vehicle, whilst in the ambulance everything was being done by the paramedics to help Jackson. Dr Murray, however, was making a phone call from the back of the ambulance. At 1:08pm, he called his mistress, Nicole Alvarez. The call lasted for two minutes and Martin Blount heard Murray tell her, 'It's about Michael, and it doesn't look good.'

At 1:13pm, the ambulance arrived at UCLA. As they pulled up Dr Murray asked if the paramedics had a towel they could put over Jackson's face as they wheel him into the hospital to avoid him being recognised. The paramedics find a towel and drape it over Jackson's lifeless face as they move the gurney from the ambulance and towards the hospital.

At 1:14pm, the gurney carrying Michael Jackson crashes through the door of the UCLA emergency room. It had been

83 minutes since Murray had called Sade Anding from outside Jackson's bedroom, the call that was interrupted when he re-entered the room to find Jackson not breathing.

So much had happened in those 83 minutes, but for Jackson it was 83 minutes too long. As the hospital staff waited to do what they could, and whilst Ben Evenstad began scanning the digital images taken by his photographers to see if he had struck gold, it slowly began to dawn on Dr Conrad Murray that there was no hope for his patient.

And, consequently, no hope for him.

10

When people grow up they forget the way.
J.M. Barrie, *Peter Pan*

At 1:14pm, the gurney carrying the body of Michael Jackson was rushed into the ER of the Ronald Reagan UCLA Medical Center. The team of 14 doctors and nurses in the ER were prepared for his arrival, and were waiting to jump into action, but none of them knew that the patient they were about to receive was Michael Jackson.

Firefighter-Paramedic Richard Senneff helped to push the gurney directly into the ER as he informed the team of respiratory therapy medics, EKG staff and x-ray technicians of the protocols his team had already carried out on location and in the ambulance on the journey to UCLA. Once the gurney was in place in the ER, Senneff's duty was done. He went off for a debriefing with his chief and then dedicated his time to getting the ambulance ready for his next call, which came around 6:00pm that day.

As the gurney was rolled past her, Dr Richelle Cooper was introduced to Dr Murray. Dr Cooper was aware that the patient had a personal physician present at the scene of the initial cardiac arrest, as she had been the person at UCLA who had handed care of the patient over to Murray at 12:57pm when she had given authorisation for the pronouncement of death. Now, for the first time, Dr Cooper and Dr Murray came face-to-face.

While Jackson was being put on a monitor in the ER and initial drugs were being administered and began circulating round his body, Cooper asked Murray to explain what had happened. He reported to her that Jackson had been in his usual state of health and had not been ill, but had been working very hard. He stated that he thought Jackson may be dehydrated and that he had also had trouble sleeping so he had given the singer 2mg of Lorazepam through an IV.

Like Paramedic Senneff before her, Cooper questioned Murray what medications the patient was on and what had been administered. She asked again and again. All Dr Murray told her was that he had given Jackson 2mg of Lorazepam at some point in the morning and had later on given another 2mg of the same drug before he witnessed the patient arrest.[1] Cooper immediately assumed that, by saying he 'witnessed the arrest', Dr Murray must have watched Jackson die in front of him: 'If I was in a room with a patient and the patient's eyes rolled back, he stopped breathing and didn't feel a pulse, I would report that while I was in the room I witnessed an arrest. I'm not sure if you would call that art of medicine. That is what I would take as witnessing the arresting in the room at the time,' she testified later.

Meanwhile, outside the hospital, rumours were beginning to circulate about Jackson's well-being, especially on the internet. The USA celebrity website, TMZ.com[2] posted a short story suggesting that Jackson had been rushed to a Los Angeles hospital having suffered a cardiac arrest which had been treated with CPR by paramedics. Once this had been published online, a number of other news agencies from around the globe were alerted to the potentially breaking story. As the minutes ticked by, TMZ.com continued to update what it knew and published an exclusive of a distant photo, which they claimed showed the King of Pop arriving at UCLA. They also suggested his mother was rushing to be with him. But nobody could verify the story.

While this news was beginning to spread on the Internet, inside the UCLA Medical Center, Dr Cooper continued to ask Murray about the patient's history of drug use or current drug use as she tried to determine exactly what had happened, while also managing Jackson's care. 'I had a 50-year-old male who was dead. I didn't know why,' she said. 'I was trying to think of reasons for something I may be missing or something related to the event that would explain, and it is a common question when you are taking history, is what is the past medical history and what other drugs may be used.' Murray told her that he knew Jackson was taking Flomax[3] and Valium but, other than that, he reported no other drug use (except the Lorazepam he had already admitted to administering) and no past medical history. Murray also stated that there had been no reports of chest pain or anything of that nature prior to the cardiac arrest. Dr Cooper was later to tell the court 'I assumed I was receiving a clear testimony. "I was at the patient's bed. I gave 2mg of Lorazepam. I witnessed arrest. I instituted CPR. 911 was called." My assumption is this was all approximate to the paramedics arriving and the patient arriving to me.'

With Jackson now under the care of Dr Cooper, an ultrasound was placed on his chest to see if there was any cardiac motion. The scan did show some movement of the heart muscle and movement of the valve but Dr Cooper reported that it was not what could be considered good heart function in terms of a heart that was pumping. However, Dr Cooper was informed by Dr Murray that he had felt a faint pulse (despite the report from the paramedics who said that there wasn't a pulse) so, from the moment Jackson arrived in the ER, she made the decision to attempt resuscitation, and the team of doctors and nurses were working on him constantly.[4]

Although the team working on him quickly realised their patient was none other than Michael Jackson, it was vital that they used an alias in all manner of patient registration and sample labelling. This was to prevent a delay of care from an inability to label items while Jackson was being treated, and, also, to avoid any information about their VIP patient being leaked outside of the hospital. Despite being cocooned in the ER, everyone was becoming aware of the press quickly gathering outside the doors of UCLA and the hospital's management were rapidly preparing a room to hold a press conference. In circumstances where an unknown patient needs a name, or where a celebrity needs an alias, the hospital had a list of names to be used. The most obvious one was 'John Doe', but Jackson was assigned the name of 'Trauma WM0241 Gershwin'.

While the medical team was valiantly doing all they could in the ER, Michael Amir Williams had arrived at UCLA in his vehicle, bringing with him Jackson's three children and Rosalind, their nanny. With Amir Williams trying to block the cameras from recording their arrival, the children were ushered into the hospital through the back doors. Once inside, they were shown to a stark, empty room with a security guard standing by the door. The children had no option but to sit there and wait for any news.

Amir Williams, however, managed to get to the area where the medics were frantically working on Jackson's body. Realising the true seriousness of the situation, Amir Williams broke down and took himself off to the bathroom to cry privately.

Paul Gongaware was still at his home in Hermosa Beach, an affluent beachfront city in Los Angeles County, about 18 miles from UCLA. Gongaware had received a phone call at his home from Randy

Phillips who had, in turn, received a phone call from Frank Dileo telling him to get over to Jackson's house immediately as something was going on.[5] Randy told Gongaware that as he arrived at Jackson's home, the ambulance was pulling out of the house, so he followed it to UCLA. Despite this news, Gongaware opted to remain at home and not travel to the UCLA Medical Center.

By now, the news was spreading that there was something seriously wrong with Michael Jackson. While TMZ.com continued to monitor and update its story, the *Los Angeles Times* became the first 'mainstream' news organisation to reveal the drama happening by claiming that, when the paramedics entered his Carolwood home, Michael Jackson was not breathing. But at the Staples Center, where rehearsals were continuing for the forthcoming London shows, nobody had any idea of what was happening to Michael Jackson. All the dancers were onstage rehearsing with the band and Kenny Ortega was getting Jackson's disappearing illusion ready in preparation for the singer turning up later. As far as all those in attendance at the studios were concerned, Michael Jackson would be arriving later that evening to join them for rehearsal.

Back at UCLA, one of the team working alongside Dr Cooper was Dr Thao Nguyen. She was a Cardiology Fellow, a physician-in-training, at UCLA. She was then in her fourth year and doing post-doctoral research. Nguyen was elsewhere in the hospital when Jackson arrived but she was called to the ER when she received a page saying help was needed with a VIP patient. When she arrived in the ER, Dr Cooper introduced Nguyen to Dr Murray, whom Nguyen described as appearing 'devastated'. Nguyen began by asking Murray, who was giving her his full attention throughout, about the situation and the patient, and Murray explained to her that he was Jackson's physician and that the singer had been preparing for a concert tour in England but had been tired and had been having

223

trouble sleeping, which required some medications for sleep. When Nguyen asked what medications Murray had given to Jackson to help him sleep he told her he had administered 4mg of Ativan (a brand name for Lorazepam) to the singer. Nguyen asked Murray if he had attempted to reverse the effects of the Ativan, but his reply was 'No'.

Continuing her questioning of Murray while the rest of the team worked on reviving Jackson, Nguyen asked Murray what had happened after he had administered Ativan to the singer. Murray's response was that he, '...later found the patient not breathing'. But when Nguyen asked Murray *when* he found the patient not breathing, Dr Murray was unable to give her a proper answer, simply saying he '...did not know the time'. She grilled him further to get an estimate of the time he'd found Jackson not breathing in relation to the 911 call, but Murray simply replied that he '... had no concept of time'. As he had earlier done with Dr Cooper, Dr Murray never mentioned to Dr Nguyen any medications other than Ativan (Lorazepam) that he had given to Jackson.

Murray did, however, continue to plead with Nguyen to not give up on Jackson and to make sure everybody tried their best to save him. In his interview with LAPD, Murray made sure he told Detectives Martinez and Smith that 'I think they may have given up earlier [if I] hadn't been insisting and giving him every opportunity.'

While in ER, Jackson was given Epinephrine, sodium bicarbonate and Vasopressin.[6] In addition to which, a Dopamine drip was started. He was continuously ventilated and chest compressions were being constantly done from the moment he arrived at the hospital. The team was also monitoring his cardiac output at all times. During this period, the team would occasionally stop compressions to see if Jackson's body was spontaneously creating a pulse but at no time did Dr Cooper feel or observe a pulse that was independent from either CPR or chest compressions.

Dr Murray was keen to assist wherever he could and, initially, he put on some medical gloves and was making attempts to feel a pulse. But before long, Dr Cooper instructed Murray that he was not allowed to provide medical care in the ER, although he was expected to remain in discussion with her as treatment progressed. Despite their discussions, throughout the time that Dr Murray was in the ER with Dr Cooper, he failed to tell anyone that he had administered Propofol to Jackson.[7][8]

At 1:21pm, however, a nurse in the room said they felt a weak femoral pulse in Jackson, which had been noticed without CPR. Dr Cooper looked at the monitor and saw a slow, wide rhythm, essentially indicating no activity and a 'dying heart'.[9] She put the ultrasound on Jackson's heart and saw the same lack of cardiac activity and was unable to detect a pulse when she felt for one. Nevertheless, at 1:22pm she ordered CPR to be continued.[10]

Meanwhile, back at the Staples Center, while rehearsals were continuing, news was beginning to filter through that something had happened to Jackson. Stacy Walker was on stage with the dancers when, at around 2pm, her colleague Travis Payne called her on her mobile phone to talk about the news he was hearing on the radio in his car. Payne was travelling to Carolwood for his home rehearsal with Jackson as planned, and had received a call a few minutes earlier, first from his cousin in Atlanta and then from his mother to tell him that she had seen news reports about the singer. Payne had told his mother that he was sure everything was fine, but as he got closer to Jackson's home, he heard further reports on his car radio concerning the singer. Becoming anxious at what might be happening, he called Stacy Walker to ask if anything was up or if anyone at the Staples Center knew what was going on. Stacy went to find Kenny Ortega who told her that he was aware that Jackson had been taken to hospital, but that was as far as it went[11] and Walker went back to her rehearsals while Travis Payne continued his drive to Jackson's home. Jackson's musical director for the tour, Michael Bearden, remembers hearing the first snippets of news coming through: 'My mother called me. I hadn't spoken to her in a while and she said, "Well, I heard something about Michael". She heard it on a gossip channel,' he said. 'I said, "Don't believe that. I just left Michael. I just saw him. He's fine." And then I started getting call after call.'[12]

At UCLA, the medical team was continuing to do all they could. But when further efforts at CPR appeared to be fruitless, they decided the next course of action would be to place an intra-aortic balloon pump directly into Jackson.[13] This decision was partly reached following the requests by Murray to the team '… to not give up easily', and the fact that Murray was convinced he could feel a pulse in Jackson. Dr Nguyen couldn't feel a pulse and neither could another of the medical team in attendance, Dr Cruz. Both felt using the balloon-pump was a futile attempt at reviving Jackson and as far as Nguyen was concerned, this was a 'last ditch effort'. She was far from optimistic that it would work based on the observations and readings that were available to her.

In his police interview, Murray said of the decision to use a balloon-pump, 'I asked the cardiologist. I said, "Do you think that it will be effective?" He said he had done it before and he had good results. I said, "Then fine." It's not something I would do, because I don't think balloon-pumps help you if there's no blood pressure. But he wanted to try, and I was willing to give him any effort that was necessary. So I said, "Proceed."' Despite this statement, Dr Murray had no authority in the medical treatment of Jackson once he arrived at UCLA, so it wasn't up to him to make the decision to proceed or not.

A balloon-pump can be extremely effective for drug-induced cardiovascular failure as it decreases the effort required by the heart by increasing the oxygen supplied directly to the heart.[14] Before inserting the balloon-pump, an understanding was reached between the medical team and Dr Murray that if this method should fail to revive and resuscitate Jackson successfully then all further efforts at reviving him would stop immediately. Despite the balloon-pump being inserted successfully, it had no effect on the singer, therefore Michael Jackson was pronounced dead in the ER at 2:46pm. 'We wanted Mr Jackson to depart with dignity and respect, so we decided to end our efforts,' recalled Dr Nguyen.

Outside the ER, Michael Amir Williams was pacing up and down in a corridor. Frank Dileo had just arrived at UCLA and he sat down beside Randy Phillips on a gurney that was in a hallway beside a wall. Amir Williams joined them there and they were all asking each other what was going on.

At that moment a nurse emerged from the ER, saying nothing but shaking her head disconsolately. Amir Williams and Dileo feared the worst. The nurse looked at them sitting on the gurney before saying, 'I'm sorry.' Frank and Randy got up to hear her continue, 'I'm sorry to tell you Mr Jackson has passed away.' Upon hearing the news, Frank Dileo collapsed, only being held up by Phillips who had managed to grab him. They were all totally devastated and barely believed what they had been told until it was confirmed to them a few moments later when a sombre Dr Murray emerged from the ER and simply said to them, 'He's dead.'

With Jackson pronounced dead, the issue of who was going to sign the death certificate arose. Almost immediately, Dr Murray refused to do so. 'I wouldn't want to sign the death certificate on Mr Jackson when I don't understand the cause of his death,' Murray told the LAPD.

Murray left the ER, devastated at the death of Jackson. He talked with a Detective Porche from LAPD, gave him his mobile phone number and then felt it his duty to console Katherine Jackson, Michael's mother, who had arrived at the hospital within the past hour. Murray was concerned about how they would break the news to her, especially as she had a heart condition of her own.[15] Accompanied by an ER doctor, Murray went into a room further down the hall where Katherine Jackson was waiting. According to Murray, the ER doctor began explaining to the elderly Katherine Jackson that her son had been brought in to UCLA while he was having difficulty breathing and that they had done everything in their power to revive him. Katherine Jackson apparently said, 'Well, how is he? He's not dead, is he?' When the doctor replied that her son was dead, Katherine Jackson broke down. Dr Murray said that he stayed with Katherine, holding her hand, after the ER doctor had left them. Concerned for Katherine's welfare, he supposedly asked for the social workers to come in or a hospital psychologist, whichever was available at the time. When a social team and the hospital's Head of Security arrived, Murray apparently asked them to take care of Mrs Jackson.

Then, according to his LAPD interview, Murray became concerned about Jackson's three children. He was unsure whether they had been brought to the hospital or not. Discovering that they were in another room, he decided that the children had to know what had happened. But what was the best way to tell three young children that their father had died? Murray decided to speak with Frank Dileo. Dileo agreed that he would go in with Dr Murray to inform the children of their father's death, but Murray suggested that someone else should accompany the two of them, someone who had a good relationship with the children. The ideal candidate was Michael Amir Williams and so the three of them went into the room where Prince, Paris and Blanket had been kept under supervision. When they entered the room, the children were just sitting there, having something to eat, knowing something was going on with their father but unsure what. Amir Williams recalled that Prince said to them as they entered, 'Make sure you tell the doctor that Daddy is allergic to this and that'. The children were then told that their father had passed away by Frank Dileo, who blurted out the news, 'Your daddy had a heart attack and died.'

All three children burst into tears at the news and Dr Murray was horrified by Dileo's insensitivity. 'No, no, no,' Murray said, 'Don't tell them that. We don't know what happened.' Dr Murray said that he stayed there to comfort them all, especially Blanket, whom he referred to as the 'little guy'. According to Murray's LAPD interview, he said Paris Jackson was particularly affected by the news. She was crying and saying that she didn't want to be an orphan and Murray, empathetically tapping into his own experience of fatherhood, told her that they would take care of her. Frank Dileo also reassured her, committing himself to looking after her and her brothers, too.

Murray then said to the LAPD detectives, perhaps in an effort to depict himself as a caring and trustworthy doctor that the whole family had relied upon, that Paris had said to him, 'Dr Murray, you said you save a lot of patients. You know, you save people with heart attacks, and you couldn't save my dad.' I said, 'I tried my best.' And she said, 'I know that, Dr Murray. At least I know. I know you tried your best, but I'm really sad. You know, I will wake up in the morning and I won't be able to see my daddy.'

Paris then asked to see her father. Upon hearing this, Murray said that he 'pulled a psychology team together' and informed them that some help was needed and asked whether the psychological team thought that the children seeing their father's body was a good idea. According to Murray, someone within the psychological team said it probably would be a good idea and suggested that it may well bring closure to the tragedy. Murray questioned whether the children were mature enough to understand the situation, but the psychological team apparently reassured him that they would be able to cope with viewing the body.

By now the news was beginning to spread rapidly, on the Internet and through global media, that Jackson was in hospital suffering, it was suggested, from a cardiac arrest. Nobody, outside of the hospital, was yet aware of the tragic truth. Travis Payne, who had been on his way to Carolwood to see Jackson, had been diverted from his journey and told to drive instead to the Staples Center immediately as he had been informed that there had been an emergency at Jackson's house. When he arrived at the rehearsal venue, Travis and the rest of the dancers and musicians continued with their day, rehearsing 'Smooth Criminal', as though nothing had happened, but some of them were beginning to sense all was not right.

Then, abruptly, the rehearsals were halted. Kenny Ortega received a phone call from Paul Gongaware of AEG Live. Gongaware had remained at home while Jackson was in hospital but was becoming increasingly anxious about what might be happening with the singer. After he hadn't heard from Randy Phillips for a while, Gongaware took it upon himself to call Phillips' mobile phone to find out what was going on. Randy Phillips simply told him that Michael Jackson had died. After he had spoken to Phillips, Gongaware was in shock, and couldn't understand how it had happened as Randy had given no explanation. Gongaware then immediately called Kenny Ortega at the Staples Center. His words to Ortega were simple and straightforward, 'Our boy is gone', he said. At first Ortega didn't believe him, and wasn't even convinced it was Gongaware on the other end of the phone. 'I'm not trusting that this is really Paul Gongaware,' Ortega said, 'Tell me something that only you would know that can prove to me that this is really

Paul Gongaware telling me this.' Ortega was in a state of total shock and denial as Gongaware responded, 'You have to sit down and get a hold of yourself and listen to me. Michael has gone.' Ortega couldn't believe what he was hearing. He didn't want to believe what he was hearing. 'I wanted to believe it was some weirdo on the phone calling me and telling me something and I… I think I made him call me back, or I think I made him… I don't even remember. I just remember that it was a very awkward telephone call, and I… and I didn't want to believe what he was saying as the truth.'

Ortega went into the hallway and found Karen Faye, Jackson's hair and make-up artist. He went up to her, put his arms around her and told her that Michael Jackson had passed away. Stacy Walker went into what she described as a motherly mode. She consoled all the dancers, telling them not to worry and saying that everything would be okay. Just like Ortega, Walker didn't want to believe the news coming through. 'It's not that I didn't believe that he wasn't in hospital. I just thought that he would be okay,' she said. 'We were just all there the last two nights and it had been great and we just did 'Thriller' and 'Beat It' and then he was just gone.'

Travis Payne recalled the moment the call came through: 'I remember Kenny saying: "Tell me something that will make me know it's you and that this is true." Well, apparently he got recognitions on the phone. I remember him collapsing in his seat and crying.' After Ortega broke the news to everyone gathered together, Payne recalled they became silent, 'We prayed and then we ultimately got the call. They said he had passed, and that was very hard.'[16]

While this was going on at the Staples Center, Dr Murray approached Michael Amir Williams in the hallway at UCLA Medical Center and made a discreet request that Amir Williams found odd. Murray said to Amir Williams, 'Brother Michael,

Mr Jackson has some cream in his room that I know he wouldn't want the world to know about. Can you have one of the guys give me a ride back to the house to get the cream?'

It was a strange request, especially in such distressing circumstances. Amir Williams suspected that it was impossible to go back to the house[17] but told Murray he would check. Amir Williams went to find Faheem Muhammad and said to him, 'Faheem, Dr Murray said something about a cream and wants to get back to the house. You know, we can't give him a ride back to the house.' Faheem replied in agreement, 'No, we can't give him a ride back to the house. I'm not giving him a ride.' Between the two of them, they agreed to tell Murray that the police had taken their keys. Upon hearing this, Murray simply said, 'Oh, okay.'

Meanwhile, after a social worker had talked to Jackson's children again, they joined their grandmother, Katherine, in a larger room at the hospital, one that resembled a conference room. Murray witnessed this occurring and said he noticed that, of the three children, only Paris 'went to the grandmother'. Murray told the LAPD that, 'I'm not sure how close they are, because the two boys [Prince and Blanket] are still kind of running away from a distance. And Paris was more comforted by a [another] relative versus the grandmother.' While the family was together and in the same room, Dr Murray made arrangements for Michael Jackson's body to be made as presentable as possible so that the children would be able to view it and say goodbye to their father.

During this period, Dr Murray also said he noticed that Michael Jackson's family started to trickle in to the hospital. He noticed Jermaine and La Toya and some other cousins that he was less familiar with come into the room, and Murray stayed to hold hands with Katherine and La Toya. He asked them if they had any questions. Naturally, they were desperate to have an explanation for Michael's death. Murray said he had no idea. Because of this,

Murray recommended that the family request an autopsy, not only for their own piece of mind but also for his. Murray claimed that he too wanted to know why the singer had died.

Once the body was ready for viewing, the social workers accompanied the children and other members of the family to see Jackson's body. Dr Murray watched the procession of people coming in and weeping from behind a glass partition but one person who didn't view the body was Katherine Jackson, Michael's mother. Somewhat surprised, Dr Murray went back into the large conference room to check with her whether she wanted to see her son, but she was adamant that she didn't. Someone perhaps conspicuous by his absence from the hospital that day was Jackson's father, Joe. But the 81-year-old was almost 300 miles away in Las Vegas, unable to rush to Los Angeles, and was restricted to providing TMZ.com earlier in the day with the quote that his son was 'not doing too well'.[18]

Meanwhile, Dr Murray persisted in his efforts to get back to Jackson's Carolwood home. He tracked down Michael Amir Williams again, and this time asked about getting some food, as he told Amir Williams he hadn't eaten all day. Amir Williams simply told Murray that they couldn't take him anywhere. Suspicious of Murray's motives once again, Amir Williams went to Faheem Muhammad and asked him to call security at the house and tell them to lock it down. 'No one in. No one out,' was the instructions. That day, 25 June 2009, was the last time Amir Williams saw Dr Murray.

There was only a two-hour window for Jackson's body to be viewed before it was taken to the coroner, yet still members of Jackson's family were arriving at the hospital. Dr Murray was concerned about what would happen to Jackson's children for the remainder of the day. After being turned down by Amir Williams in his efforts to get back to the house, Dr Murray apparently asked

233

a security guard if they could be taken home. The guard informed Murray that Jackson's house was in lockdown now, and that nobody could enter it as detectives and forensics experts from the LAPD were expected there soon.

Murray continued to wait in the hospital. It was difficult for anybody to leave owing to the huge crowds of concerned fans and legions of expectant paparazzi that had joined the burgeoning news crews who were, by now, broadcasting whatever they knew about the situation to a global audience. Murray sought out Randy Phillips, who had arrived at the hospital some time earlier and then spoke with Frank Dileo and Michael Amir Williams about what to do next. Murray wanted to know from them if there was anything else he could do at the hospital. They told him there was nothing to be done but said they now may all have to be airlifted out of the hospital because of the crowds gathering outside.

Moving to another area within UCLA, Dr Murray found himself introduced to the Jackson family's lawyers, who were keen for the family to release a statement to the press. According to Murray, Randy Phillips and Jermaine Jackson were eager for Murray to review the proposed press release to make sure he was happy with it. Murray scanned it and made a few small changes, adding that the cause of death will not be known until an autopsy is performed. Around this time, Dr Murray and Jermaine found themselves sitting together in the corner of the room. A brief conversation ensued, during which Jermaine asked Dr Murray where he was from as he was curious about his accent. After telling Jermaine he was from Trinidad in the Caribbean, Murray asked him if there was, 'Anything else I can do for you?' Jermaine said that there wasn't so Murray told him he was tired and that he was going to try to make his way home, despite the furore outside the hospital.

Meanwhile, at 5:20pm, Elissa Fleak, the coroner investigator for the Los Angeles County Coroner, arrived at UCLA to perform an external body examination on Michael Jackson. This is a standard procedure to look for wounds and obvious trauma, but she found no such evidence on Jackson's body. She preserved the vials of blood taken from Jackson for future toxicology testing and then began making her way to Jackson's home to investigate the scene where Jackson lost consciousness to try and determine what the details and circumstances surrounding this tragic event were.

At this time, 5:30pm, the celebrity website TMZ.com was the first media outlet to break the news of Jackson's death when they updated their earlier story about his hospitalisation after suffering a cardiac arrest. On their webpage they said 'Update – Michael Jackson passed away today at the age of 50.' The news, released online, was at first met with disbelief by many. A lot of people felt that the singer's death couldn't possibly be verified until a more established and mainstream news organisation confirmed it. Just minutes before the nightly network news began, the story was finally verified by the *Los Angeles Times* and, shortly afterwards, The Associated Press. Very quickly, social media networks exploded with the news. Twitter had over twice the normal amount of tweets per second and the internet saw web traffic to news sites increase by about 50 per cent. The Google news section saw such an increase in 'Michael Jackson' enquiries within 20 minutes of TMZ.com announcing his death that it thought the network was under some sort of malware attack. By the end of the day, Jackson's Wikipedia page had almost 2 million visits, as well as 650 edits being made.

Inside the hospital, cut off from global news outlets but obviously aware of the worldwide significance of the story and the gathering of news crews outside, Dr Murray then approached Faheem Muhammad and told him that he was tired and had to leave. Faheem said to Murray that he was unable to leave himself and then could only watch as Dr Murray walked out through the large glass doors of UCLA. That was the last conversation Faheem Muhammad had with Murray, and the last time he saw him.

Almost four hours after Michael Jackson's death, at 6:18pm, Jermaine Jackson appeared in front of a gathering of news crews at a hastily arranged press conference to confirm to the world that his brother had died. 'This is hard,' Jermaine Jackson told the world,

My brother, the legendary King of Pop, Michael Jackson, passed away on Thursday, June 25th 2009. It is believed he suffered cardiac arrest in his home. However, the cause of death is unknown until the results of the autopsy are known. His personal physician, who was with him at the time, attempted to resuscitate my brother, as did the paramedics who transported him to Ronald Reagan UCLA Medical Center. Upon arriving at the hospital at approximately 1:14pm, a team of doctors, including emergency physicians and cardiologists, attempted to resuscitate him for a period of more than one hour. They were unsuccessful. Our family requests that the media please respect our privacy during this tough time. May Allah be with you, Michael, always. Love you.

Jermaine Jackson then left the room.[19]

Within two minutes of Jermaine confirming the news to the press, TMZ.com were also able to have verification of the story they had led with an hour earlier. At 6:20pm they published confirmation: 'We've just learned Michael Jackson has died. He was 50. Michael suffered a cardiac arrest earlier this afternoon at his Holmby Hills home and paramedics were unable to revive him. We're told when paramedics arrived, Jackson had no pulse and they never got a pulse back. A source tells us Jackson was dead when paramedics arrived. A cardiologist at UCLA tells TMZ Jackson died of cardiac arrest. Once at the hospital, the staff tried to resuscitate him but he was completely unresponsive. A source inside the hospital told us there was "absolute chaos" after Jackson arrived. People who were with the singer were screaming, "You've got to save him! You've got to save him!" We're told one of the staff members at Jackson's home called 911. La Toya ran into the hospital sobbing after Jackson was pronounced dead. Michael is survived by three children: Michael Joseph Jackson Jr, Paris Michael Katherine Jackson and Prince "Blanket" Michael Jackson II.'

The news that the King of Pop had died flared throughout the world. Within six minutes of Jermaine Jackson's press conference, the entire Top 15 albums on Amazon.com were Michael Jackson albums. Nine out of ten trending topics on Twitter were Michael Jackson-related; the TMZ website went down at multiple points, as did the blog of Perez Hilton.[20] Within a few more minutes, USA tennis star Serena Williams, competing at Wimbledon at the time, posted this on Twitter: 'My heart goes out to the entire Jackson family.' An hour later, the British Prime Minister, Gordon Brown, released a statement saying that, 'This is very sad news for the millions of Michael Jackson fans around the world. The Prime Minster's thoughts are with Michael Jackson's family at this time.' Sir Paul McCartney, who had recorded and performed with Jackson, and also lost his stake in his Beatles catalogue to him, said, 'It's so sad and shocking. I feel privileged to have hung out and worked with Michael. He was a massively talented boy-man with a gentle soul. His music will be remembered forever and my memories of our time together will be happy ones.' Madonna expressed her condolences by saying, 'I can't stop crying over the news,'[21] while Elizabeth Taylor was said to be 'too devastated' to issue a statement. Quincy Jones, the producer who had done so much with Jackson to shape the *Thriller* album, said, 'I'm absolutely devastated. I just don't have the words. I've lost my little brother today and part of my soul is gone.'

Ben Evenstad, a huge Jackson fan, was equally distraught. Evenstad headed back to the offices of his photo agency with the memory cards he had collected from all his paparazzi photographers who were outside Jackson's home as the ambulance pulled away. Not only was Evenstad personally devastated at the news coming out about Jackson's death, but he was also depressed that his agency had missed the opportunity to capture a shot of Jackson in the ambulance as it left his home. But as he started scanning and editing the images, Evenstad quickly realised that his boyhood friend, Christopher Weiss, one of the men he had sent to Carolwood, *had* in fact captured the one and only shot of Jackson in the back of the ambulance with his face in profile as paramedics worked to save his life. As Evenstad looked at the photo, he realised he had the last ever picture of Michael Jackson, a picture that was soon to be worth over a million dollars.[22]

Now that the news of Jackson's death had been confirmed, it didn't take long for people to speculate about the cause. Within hours of Jermaine Jackson announcing his brother's death, the Showbusiness Editor of *The Telegraph*, Anita Singh, published an article, which reported that, '…the 50-year-old singer had been given a painkilling injection shortly before his death.' The report continued by quoting the Jackson family's lawyer, Brian Oxman, who said, 'I do not know the extent of the medications that he was taking, but the reports that we have been receiving in the family is that it was extensive and this is something which I feared and something which I warned about. I don't know the cause of all this so I can't tell you what the ultimate result of it is going to be, but I can tell you for sure when you warn people that this is what's going to happen and then it happens, where there is smoke there is fire.'[23] ABC News quoted a senior law enforcement official who had been briefed on the initial investigation and who suggested drugs played a part, referring to Jackson being 'heavily addicted' to Oxycontin and receiving daily doses of Demerol.[24] And Fox News reported that the pop icon was '...taking a cocktail of prescription drugs including antidepressants.'[25]

But the true cause of death remained unknown as dusk fell on 25 June 2009. Later that evening, Detective Martinez, one of the LAPD detectives on the case, tried several times to call Dr Murray but his efforts would go straight to voicemail. He even tried texting Murray a couple of times but received no reply. Murray, however, was seemingly already under instruction from his own lawyer to leave his phone off until they met.

Michael Amir Williams went back to Jackson's Carolwood home on the evening of 25 June. It hadn't been his intention to return to the property but, as Katherine Jackson and the other members of his family were also getting ready to go to Jackson's home, Amir Williams felt it his duty to create a diversion to allow the family to slip away. Amir Williams, along with Alberto Alvarez, Faheem Muhammad and Isaac Muhammad got in two cars at the hospital and started to drive away from the hospital to cause the necessary diversion. But during this drive, Michael Amir Williams received a phone call asking him to go back to Jackson's Carolwood home, and so both cars made their way back to the property. When they arrived there, the Los Angeles Police Department and coroners were already present and beginning their investigation, part of which involved Amir Williams giving a statement to the police, recalling the events of the previous 24 hours. Amir Williams remembered it being frantic when he got back to Carolwood.

The coroner investigator, Elissa Fleak, had already been at the house for some time when Amir Williams returned. She had begun her on-scene investigation in Jackson's bedroom by taking photographs to document items she felt relevant to the investigation, such as vials of prescription medicines and making an inventory of evidence she found which included several bottles of pills next to Jackson's bed. Amongst the prescription medications she discovered scattered around the room were Flomax, Trazadone, Lorazepam, Clonazepam, Diazepam, Temazepam and Tizanidine. She also found 19 tubes of Lidocaine and a bottle of Benoquin. She noted from the prescription details on the bottles that the Clonazepam and Trazadone was prescribed by Dr Metzger, the Tizanidine was prescribed by Dr Klein, but all the remaining medications were prescribed by Dr Murray.

On the bedside table, Fleak found three prescription pill bottles, three prescription medicine bottles, a bottle of over-the-counter Aspirin and a couple of empty juice bottles. A number of prescription bottles also lay in a wastebasket nearby.

She also discovered a syringe on the table with the plunger completely depressed, while on the floor she discovered a needle on the left side, a couple of feet away from the bed, as well as an oxygen tank and an Ambu Bag. At the foot of the bed she saw an IV stand with an IV kit attached. She also found a jug that appeared to have urine in it and urine pads nearby.

Elissa Fleak also found, when looking on the floor, an empty vial of Flumazenil and an empty vial of Propofol. They were both found to the left of the bed, beneath the nightstand, which was adjacent to the bed. Fleak was looking mainly for pills as, in her work, many of her cases involved pills or tablets. She didn't realise the significance of the Propofol and the use of the IV drip to possibly administer it until a couple of days later. As it was, Elissa Fleak seized these items and took them to the Coroner's Office where they were logged to await further investigation. Continuing her search, Elissa Fleak only glanced into the other rooms, scanning them but not searching them.

A further search was to happen a few days later when Fleak returned to Carolwood. Detectives had informed her that additional information had been gathered following an interview with Dr Murray and there was now the possibility that medical evidence remained in the house, specifically in the closet.

And so it was on 29 June 2009 that Elissa Fleak returned to Carolwood and searched a wardrobe in Michael Jackson's closet.

In it was a bag. And in the bag was the evidence later used to convict Dr Conrad Murray.

11

Dreams do come true, if only we wish hard enough. You can have anything in life if you will sacrifice everything else for it.

J.M. Barrie, *Peter Pan*

The day after Jackson's death, the world woke up to the news with a huge sense of shock. 'A Star Idolised and Haunted, Michael Jackson Dies at 50' was the headline in *The New York Times*. 'The King is Dead', pronounced *The Guardian* in the United Kingdom. Rio de Janeiro's *Extra* simply devoted its front page to an image of Jackson's single diamond-studded white glove resting against a black background, under the title 'Michael Jackson 1958–2009'.

Other headlines, however, began suggesting a sense of inevitability in Jackson's death and started looking for clues as to the cause of his passing. 'The Thriller Is Gone – Death of "King of Pop" at 50 Remains Mystery' said the *Daytona Beach News Journal*, while the UK's *Daily Express* asked on its cover, 'Did Injections Kill Michael?'. New York's *Daily News* proclaimed, 'He Saw It Coming – King of Pop had a chilling premonition of own death'.

On the Hollywood Walk of Fame, the singer's star was covered by a film premiere that was taking place so fans started laying flowers on another star bearing the name Michael Jackson on the Walk of Fame, a star that actually honoured a talk-show host with the same name and not the King of Pop.[1] Elsewhere in Los Angeles, fans were holding vigils outside Jackson's Carolwood home where they played his music, danced and cried. Curious onlookers gathered to watch similar tributes in cities across the USA. In Gary, Indiana – Michael Jackson's hometown, hundreds of people made the pilgrimage to the simple house where the singer spent much of his childhood. Some lit candles or left teddy bears while others placed personal notes at the shack.

Such was the level of grief worldwide that even Nelson Mandela made a brief and rare public appearance to comment on Jackson's life and legacy. The world's largest online fan club, MJJcommunity. com, reported that 12 Michael Jackson fans had apparently committed suicide following the singer's death. Gary Taylor, head of the fan club, told Sky News that, 'It is a serious situation that these people are going through but Michael Jackson would never want this. He would want them to live.'[2] Throughout Jackson's international fan base, there was a great sense of depression, sadness and anger.[3] One of Jackson's closest friends, the Reverend Jesse Jackson, identified this and encouraged the singer's fans to support each other: 'This is a time when hearts are heavy. There is great pain but great cause to celebrate Michael's life. It made Michael happy saying "We Are The World". Don't self destruct.'[4]

Across the radio, airwaves were filled with music from throughout Jackson's career while the music channels on television showed the singer's groundbreaking videos on a continuous loop.

Meanwhile, as Jackson's musical legacy was being played out on televisions, radios and the Internet worldwide, on the morning of 26 June 2009, Dr Christopher Rogers, the Chief of Forensic Medicine at the Los Angeles County Coroner's Office was preparing for Autopsy Case Number 2009-04415 to determine the cause and manner of death of Michael Jackson.

At around 6:45pm the previous day, a helicopter had ferried Jackson's body to the Los Angeles Coroner's Office. A news channel filmed the moment when hospital workers placed the singer's body, wrapped in a white sheet, onto a stretcher and then into a waiting van. It had lain overnight in the mortuary at Lincoln Heights until 10:00am on the morning of 26 June, when a three-hour autopsy was performed by Dr Rogers and the Chief Medical Examiner, Lakshmanan Sathyavagiswaran,[5] with Detective Scott Smith of the LAPD witnessing the procedure.

Dr Christopher Rogers had been employed with the LA County Coroner's Office since 1988. Previously he had attended medical school at the University of California in San Diego, after which he undertook a pathology residency at Los Angeles County USC Medical Center before training in forensic pathology. In the course of his career he had performed thousands of autopsies and, given the nature of his location in California, a number had been on celebrity figures. But Michael Jackson wasn't just a celebrity, he was a global superstar, at one time perhaps even the most famous man on the planet. People wanted to know how, and why, he had died. The rumour mill was already beginning to spin out of control, and it was hoped the autopsy would provide the answers to the singer's cause of death.

The autopsy report reveals Dr Rogers' observations regarding his initial external examination: 'The body is identified by toe tags and is that of an unembalmed refrigerated Black male who appears the stated age of 50 years. The body weighs 136 pounds, measures 69 inches in length, and is thin.'[6]

It had seemed for many months, perhaps years, people around Jackson had been concerned about his health but, in fact, one of Dr Rogers' early observations was that the singer's general health was excellent. There were some incidental findings: Jackson had an enlargement of the prostate gland, he had Vitiligo, a polyp on his colon, some inflammation and scarring of his lungs, and traces of arthritis, particularly in his spine.

Dr Rogers was particularly surprised by the health of Jackson's heart. It had no abnormalities and, in particular, did not have coronary artery atherosclerosis,[7] which virtually everybody at Jackson's age would be expected to have to some degree. There was also no sign whatsoever of Jackson suffering from any form of cardiac disease. And he found no observations or evidence of any trauma or natural disease that would have caused Jackson's death. In fact, the only signs of trauma to Jackson's body were as a result of the desperate struggle to save his life: his chest showed some bruising and there were a number of cracked ribs, almost definitely caused by the CPR. The intra-aortic balloon-pump remained in Jackson's heart and the singer was still wearing a condom catheter. Dr Rogers noted 'numerous' puncture marks on both arms and additional puncture marks on Jackson's left knee and right ankle, an indication, perhaps, of Jackson's prior drug use or simply sites for IV drips.

What Dr Rogers' autopsy report did show was that Michael Jackson had a number of cosmetic tattoos. Both eyebrows and the areas beneath his eyes – his lower eyelids – had dark tattoos around them and his lips had a pink tattoo on and around them also. There were a number of scars that indicated cosmetic surgery: one scar behind his left ear and another behind his right ear, each measuring approximately three quarters of an inch in length and suggesting Jackson had had either a limited facelift or that both his ears had been pinned back as the result of having skin grafts due to the burns he suffered in 1984. On each nostril Dr Rogers discovered more scarring which would have undoubtedly been connected to cosmetic surgery on the singer's nose, probably a result of removing excess skin during a nose procedure.[8]

While scarring on his face was expected owing to his prolific history of cosmetic surgery, Dr Rogers also found scarring on other parts of Jackson's body. On his left arm, the singer had a quarter-inch scar just below the bicep. This could have been scarring that had built up from multiple IV entries. There was also a scar on both wrists and one on his right hand, all of which were probably resulting from ligament surgery. On his torso, Jackson had a scar that suggested an appendectomy and two small scars around his belly button, which would indicate that a type of liposuction (likely a procedure known as BodyTite Fat Reduction) had been carried out on the singer. More scarring on his right leg, specifically around the knee area indicated possible knee surgery.

Given the fact that Jackson had suffered third degree burns to his head in 1984 as a result of his accident while filming the Pepsi commercial, it was not surprising that Dr Rogers' autopsy would find anomalies with Jackson's scalp. There was evidence of the singer going bald above his forehead, while the rest of his hair was short and tightly curled. This had been completely covered up by the style of wigs Jackson had appeared in during the last few months of his life. The bald part of Jackson's scalp, the area that had been significantly affected by the accident, had been darkened by a tattoo that covered the top of his scalp from ear to ear and which would have been used to hide scars from burns and hair loss resulting from the accident.

After concluding the autopsy, Dr Rogers was unable to point to a specific cause of death. He had found evidence that Michael Jackson had taken prescription medications, but everyone would have to wait for the results of the toxicology tests before establishing whether this had any bearing on his death.

Craig Harvey, the Chief Investigator for the Los Angeles County Coroner's Office stated that, at that moment, there was no evidence of trauma or foul play and continued, 'There will be no final ruling as to the cause and manner of death until requested test results have been received and reviewed in context with the autopsy findings.' It was anticipated that these tests would take between four and six weeks to complete, which only meant that speculation would continue as to the cause of Jackson's passing. In the meantime, Jackson's body was released to his family although the *Los Angeles Times* suggested that the coroner had probably kept Jackson's brain in order to conduct a neuropathology test to determine whether the singer's brain had been damaged by drug abuse.[9]

Around the world, all manner of theories were beginning to emerge as reporters, analysts, investigators and fans dissected every bit of information they could find out about Jackson's last few days alive. There were even theories that the singer had faked his own death to escape the complex and serious financial difficulties he had found himself in and that the body discovered and being investigated was actually that of a Jackson lookalike who had terminal cancer and, in return for a substantial payment to his soon to be bereaved family, had died in place of the King of Pop.

Of course, the man who could provide many of the answers was Dr Conrad Murray, but he was nowhere to be found. The Los Angeles Police Department had made efforts to contact him on the evening of Thursday 25 June, the day Jackson had died, but Murray had slipped out of UCLA Medical Center and wasn't responding to any attempts to call him via his mobile phone and had seemingly disappeared into thin air.

The LAPD continued to try to contact Dr Murray on 26 June, but it wasn't until much later in the day on the 26th, after the initial autopsy had been completed, that Murray's attorney, Michael Pena, contacted the LAPD on Murray's behalf. Speaking to Detective Orlando Martinez, Pena suggested that they should meet, along with Dr Murray who wanted to talk, on Saturday, 27

June 2009. Michael Pena said he would call back on the Saturday with a convenient time and location.

Meanwhile, on Friday 26th, the Jackson family, having just taken possession of the singer's body, demanded that a second autopsy be carried out. They had been gathering together at their estate in Encino since the singer's death but were becoming increasingly frustrated by the unanswered questions surrounding the tragedy. 'We don't know what happened. Was he injected, and with what? All reasonable doubt should be addressed,' said the Reverend Jesse Jackson after he spent time visiting the Jackson family.[10] In fact, TMZ.com reported that the new autopsy was already underway at a secret Los Angeles location.[11] It was debatable whether this second autopsy would do anything but confirm what was discovered in the first autopsy. 'The organs have already been dissected once, and with the second autopsy, you are not getting the same pristine blood samples that you got in the first', Dr Stephen Cina, Deputy Chief Medical Examiner of Broward County in Florida, and one of the pathologists involved in the autopsy of celebrity *Playboy* pin-up Anna Nicole Smith, told *Time* magazine.[12] What the Jackson family might have been hoping for, however, was that this second autopsy, conducted by a private pathologist, might provide answers quicker than the LA County Coroner who probably had a backlog of cases to investigate.

The Jackson family had every right to ask for a second autopsy. They also had every right to be suspicious of Dr Murray. After all, it emerged that none of them had ever met Murray although he claimed to be Jackson's private physician. The Reverend Jesse Jackson spoke about the uncertainty that the Jackson family were feeling regarding the death of the singer and the role Dr Murray might have played in his passing: 'Michael was in good shape, he was in good health, practising three to four hours a day. There is a gap between him going to bed and the next day when we got a call that he was not breathing. All we know is that something happened to Michael with the doctor present. How long had he stopped breathing, how long was he unconscious?'[13]

On Saturday, 27 June, as agreed, Michael Pena called Detective Orlando Martinez and suggested they meet at the Ritz Carlton Hotel in Marina del Rey on Westside, Los Angeles County at 4pm. Martinez travelled with Detective Scott Smith to the location where they met Michael Pena, Dr Conrad Murray and, also, Ed Chernoff.

Ed Chernoff was the leading attorney of the firm Chernoff Law, based in Houston, Texas. After attending the University of Houston Law Center, Chernoff joined the Harris County District Attorney's office where, during his time there, he only lost one felony trial. In 1991 he started Chernoff Law and, according to his website in 2015, he '...currently holds the record for the quickest acquittal in the Southern District of the United State Courts, as a jury acquitted his client after 15 minutes of deliberations'. He was just the type of attorney Dr Murray needed. Despite Murray not being suspected of any wrongdoing at this stage and considered solely to be a witness in events surrounding Michael Jackson's death, newspapers were beginning to delve into his background and revelations were emerging about Murray's financial past and the string of debts and missed alimony payments that were connected to him.

The meeting between Dr Murray, his representatives and the LAPD took place in a boardroom at the Ritz Carlton Hotel and lasted for approximately three hours. Murray told the detectives that he had met Jackson initially in 2006. Later, he said, Jackson wanted him to be his personal physician on the London tour. He told them he was an interventional cardiologist and also stated that he was aware Jackson was seeing other physicians and that, upon a cursory physical exam, he found little wrong with the singer.

They discussed the treatments Jackson was receiving at Carolwood and, naturally, the night that Jackson died. Murray gave a comprehensive account of all that had happened on the night of 24 June and the morning of 25 June, and revealed the sedatives he had given to the singer throughout the period. During the interview, Dr Murray mentioned Propofol to the detectives, referring to it in the beginning by the term 'milk', the word that Jackson would himself use.[14] Murray told the detectives he gave Jackson 25mg of Propofol between 10:40am and 10:50am and Jackson was asleep by 11am, upon which Murray went to the bathroom for two minutes before returning to find the singer not breathing.

Murray went on to tell the detectives he was trying to wean Jackson off Propofol at the time of his death and that he was aware other doctors had given it to Jackson multiple times.[15] Throughout the rest of his interview, Murray described his efforts at resuscitation and the arrival of the paramedics before the journey to hospital where Jackson was pronounced dead.

It was towards the end of the interview when Dr Murray first mentioned a bag he had placed in one of Jackson's cupboards in the closet. It came about during an exchange in which the detectives had been questioning Murray about the syringes that were being used on the final night. Dr Murray revealed he used two syringes:

Detective Smith: These… the evening that this was going on at Mr Jackson's house, his final night, these different syringes or one syringe was used when you injected it into his IV drip down below?
Dr Murray: Yeah, one syringe for that, yeah.
Detective Smith: I'm sorry.
Dr Murray: Yes.
Detective Smith: One syringe was used for the various medications you gave him, or…

Dr Murray: No, I had…

Detective Smith: Each time it was a…

Dr Murray: No, I had two syringes, and they were… I would recap them, if I needed it. And you know, I would use the medication, and then I would draw some saline to have them mix. Right away then I would use it.

Detective Smith: What did you do with those syringes when you were done with them?

Dr Murray: Well, I usually have my bags right there. Everything I use, I would put it quickly into the bags and, you know, just put it into the cupboard, because he wanted me to not have anything hanging around.

Detective Smith: Where's your bag where those syringes would be at now?

Mr Chernoff: Oh, really?

Dr Murray: I don't have them.

Mr Chernoff: I thought you left it there.

Dr Murray: Yeah, I did.

Detective Smith: Where? Where did you leave it?

Dr Murray: In that same bedroom, in the closet, where it always stays.

Detective Smith: Okay. Which closet? It's a mess.

Detective Martinez: It's forty-five cupboards.

Dr Murray: Yeah, if you walk into the dressing room and you turn right, the high level top, the bags are right there with the items in it and the medication.

The detectives were alerted by the prospect of the bags containing material relevant to the investigation. The bags hadn't been found in the search of Jackson's Carolwood property so far and they were curious as to what they might contain. They continued their discussions with Murray, focusing specifically on the bags:

Detective Smith: Black attaché bags?

Dr Murray: Three bags. There were three. One is a little Costco bag. One is a black small bag. The other one is a little blue bag that has a zipper at the top of it.

Mr Pena: And you left it there because you went directly with the EMTs to the hospital and never went back to the house, right?

Dr Murray: Oh, but… yeah, but they would have stayed there anyway until I came back the next night and help him, because, you know, it has the IV catheters and everything is in there.

Dr Murray left the hotel after the three-hour interview with his aides. It was to be the last time he would talk to any authority about the death of Michael Jackson.

Meanwhile, the LAPD switched their attention to finding the bags in the closet that Murray had referred to, in order to see what they contained and whether the contents would be crucial evidence in the investigation into Jackson's death. On Monday, 29 June, Elissa Fleak returned to Carolwood to recover the bags that Murray had mentioned. On her previous search of the property, this closet hadn't been thoroughly investigated, as the team was more interested with the actual scene of Jackson's cardiac arrest, the second bedroom or his medication room, as it was known. Now, returning to the scene, Fleak passed through Jackson's bedroom and found the closet. Going to the cupboard in the closet that Murray had identified as containing the bags, she found them stored on the top shelf. As Dr Murray had said, there was a black bag with a zipper, a larger dark blue bag and a light brown and blue bag with side pockets.

Examining the contents of the bags, Elissa Fleak discovered a collection of medical supplies including a plastic bag full of tubes of Benoquin lotion, a blood pressure cuff and three bottles of Lidocaine in the small black bag, two of which were empty and one partly empty. In the large blue Costco bag, Elissa Fleak found a 100ml vial of Propofol inside a cut-open IV saline bag. Inside the blue bag was also a second vial of Propofol, measuring 20ml, one vial of Lorazepam and two vials of Midazolam. There was also a bloody piece of gauze, a bag of miscellaneous medical packaging that had been crumpled up, supply packaging and a finger pulse monitor. In the light blue and brown bag she found two 100ml unopened vials of Propofol, four 20ml vials of Propofol (also unopened) and three 20ml bottles of Propofol, all of which had been opened. She also found two 30ml bottles of Lidocaine, both open, but both with liquid in them. There was also one unopened 30ml vial of Lidocaine, one 10ml vial of Midazolam, which had been opened, two 10ml unopened vials of Midazolam, one 5ml bottle of Flumazenil, which was open with liquid inside, one 4ml bottle of Lorazepam, which was also open and a similar bottle that hadn't been opened. She also found a red pill bottle with no label that contained fourteen red and black capsules, another tube of Benoquin, over-the-counter eye drops, an IV clamp and a blue strip of rubber. Alongside all of this were five business cards for Dr Conrad Murray. In total, she had found 11 bottles of Propofol with contents totalling 460ml of the drug, 180ml of which had been used. Another empty bottle of Propofol had also been found on the floor of Jackson's bedroom.

In his testimony, Alberto Alvarez recalled being instructed by Dr Murray to put bottles into bags before he called 911. He specifically remembered a brown bag, into which he put a plastic bag containing some bottles and he also remembered a blue bag, into which he put the IV bag, which, as he recalled, had a bottle inside the saline bag. Alvarez's testimony suggests that these were the bags found in the cupboard and seemed to indicate that Murray may have been determined to hide them as best he could. Murray knew the authorities were rushing to the location following the 911 call and may have assumed that he would be able to return to Carolwood later to remove the evidence before the house was searched. Perhaps this was why he was so keen to get a lift back from the hospital to the singer's home on the evening of Jackson's death.

The amount of Propofol found was a major turning point in the investigation into Jackson's death. At that time there was no conclusive proof that detectives were looking at a criminal case or homicide, but such a substantial amount of one drug, seemingly hidden away, aroused their interest. However, for the time being, they would have to wait until the results of the toxicology tests arrived back.

In the meantime, Jackson's music sales had skyrocketed. On the same day that Elissa Fleak was discovering the bottles of Propofol in his home, he topped the UK album chart once more and four of his other hit albums reappeared in the UK Top 20. Six of his singles also entered the UK singles chart and he had sold 300,000 records in just two days. By 3 August, he had sold 2 million records in the UK alone in the week since his death. HMV reported that sales of Jackson's records were 80 times greater than they had been up to the day before he died and online retailer, Amazon, had sold out of all Jackson's and The Jackson 5's CDs within minutes of the news of his death. In Australia, 15 of Jackson's albums were back in the Top 100 and he had 34 singles in the Top 100 singles charts, including four in the Top 10. In *Billboard*'s European Top 100 albums, eight of his albums were in the Top 10. In the USA, Jackson occupied all of the top nine positions on *Billboard*'s Top Pop Catalogue Albums and in the third week after his death he was to occupy the entire top 12 positions. His album *Number Ones* saw a 2,340 per cent increase in sales in the USA, and he became the first artist ever to sell over 1 million downloads in a week. By the end of 2009, six months after his death, Jackson had sold over 8 million albums in the

USA alone, and in the year following his death Michael Jackson sold 35 million albums worldwide and generated revenues of approximately $1 billion for his estate.

While everyone waited for the results of the toxicology tests (the second autopsy yielded nothing that wasn't already evident in the first autopsy), plans were being made for a public memorial service in advance of Jackson's funeral. The date set was 7 July and the venue would be the Staples Center where Jackson had completed his final rehearsal only hours before he died. AEG Live, the promoters of his now-cancelled London shows at the O2, were in charge of organising the memorial and if they weren't already facing enough of a backlash from Jackson fans, some of whom thought they might be partly responsible for his death by creating an impossible schedule for the singer, then claims that AEG were going to charge fans $25 for tickets to the memorial service were a PR disaster.[16] Unsurprisingly, within a week, AEG Live had backtracked on their apparent decision and confirmed they would not be charging and that 11,000 tickets would be made available, free of charge, to fans and distributed via a lottery system.[17]

After the memorial service, Jackson would be taken to Forest Lawn Cemetery in Hollywood Hills, California, where he would be buried. But in the week leading up to the funeral, rifts were already evident within the Jackson family. According to a story in the *Daily Mail*,[18] some within Jackson's family wanted a shrine to the singer erected at Neverland but they were over-ruled by Katherine Jackson and the pop star's sisters. It also seemed that his brothers in The Jackson 5 wanted an open coffin and for the singer to be driven through the streets of Los Angeles, enabling mourners and devastated fans the opportunity to throw flowers. Once again, Katherine Jackson had the final say. She felt an open coffin would be 'ghoulish' and might affect and harm the children.[19] It seemed that Katherine was determined to respect her religious principles while the brothers were eager for the funeral to reflect Jackson's showbiz pomp.

But Jackson's mother had other matters to deal with as well as the funeral. On the day before her son was due to be buried, a Los Angeles judge denied her control of Michael Jackson's multi-million dollar estate for the immediate future. Instead, Jackson's former attorney, John Branca and the record executive John McClain were appointed temporary administrators of the Jackson estate until 3 August, while the authorities attempted to determine the validity of Michael Jackson's 2002 will. In this will, Michael Jackson inserted a no-contest provision, meaning Katherine Jackson risked losing the 40 per cent of the assets left to her by her son if she contested the will. However, her lawyers suggested Katherine Jackson wasn't contesting the will, merely trying to preserve her role as the administrator.[20]

Bizarrely, this will was signed on 7 July 2002, exactly seven years to the day before his funeral. In the will it said that his estate is left to the 'Trustees of the Michael Jackson Family Trust'.[21] These three trustees were John Branca, John McClain and Barry Seigel. However, on 26 August 2003, Seigel signed a letter saying he no longer wished to be an executor of the trust. The will went on to intentionally omit Jackson's former wife and mother of two of his children, Debbie Rowe. Jackson's mother, Katherine, was named to serve as the guardian to his children. If she was unable, or unwilling, then the back-up guardian was none other than Diana Ross. At no point in the will are any provisions made for Jackson's father, Joe, or any of the singer's eight siblings.

Given that Katherine Jackson was entitled to 40 per cent of her son's estate, why was she battling for control of it and challenging the will? Was it connected to the fact that, although Jackson's will was dated and signed at 5pm on 7 July 2002, a number of other people had suggested Michael Jackson was actually in New York on that date, taking on the former president of Sony Records, Tommy Mottola, in court? Jackson's former manager, Leonard Rowe, was one of those not convinced that Jackson had actually signed the 2002 will in Los Angeles. He had received a call from Randy Jackson in the weeks after Michael's death and Randy suggested he had proof that Michael was definitely in New York on the date the will was supposed to have been signed in Los Angeles. This proof was in the form of a tape from the Reverend Al Sharpton, who was in court with Michael Jackson at the time.[22] The executors and administers of the 2002 will were John Branca and John McClain (now that Barry Seigel was no longer an executor). With Michael Jackson dead, they acquired full power to administer his estate, which included the lucrative Sony/ATV catalogue. But, as Leonard Rowe pointed out in his book *What Really Happened To Michael Jackson?*, John Branca had been fired by Jackson from his role as his attorney on 3 February 2003 and in the termination letter to Branca, Jackson wrote, 'I have asked Mr LeGrand[23] and Ms Brandt to obtain all of my files, records, documents, accounts for myself and all companies I won or control which may be in your possession. You are to deliver the originals of all such documents to Mr LeGrand immediately.' Leonard Rowe suggests that, while John Branca handed over the other files as requested, he '… secretly refused to turn over the purported July 7th, 2002 will and March 2002 trust. No will was ever turned over to Michael's new attorney.'[24] On 17 June 2009, just eight days before Jackson died, Branca reappeared when he was re-hired by Michael Jackson. Within a few days, Branca would have control over all of Jackson's assets. Of course, the will might simply have been assigned the wrong date, perhaps Branca, McCain and Seigel flew to New York to meet with Jackson instead, or maybe the singer's signature was forged, although there is no evidence of this and no suggestion of it made by anybody. Whatever occurred, John Branca was now in a strong position with regards to administrating Jackson's will and overseeing the finance streams coming in and going out. But the whole affair created an unsavoury backdrop to Jackson's impending funeral.

As it turned out, Michael Jackson's funeral was a combination of showbiz and spirituality. On the morning of 7 July, Jackson's long-time make-up artist, Karen Faye, prepared his body for the family to say their final goodbyes at Forest Lawn Cemetery. Faye, along with Jackson's costume designer Michael Bush, dressed the singer in a black tunic on which was laid white pearls and a gold belt. Faye glued fake eyelashes onto Jackson and then applied three coats of his favourite mascara, a coat of pale foundation and rose-pink lipstick. The final touch was his jet-black wig.

When his family had said their final goodbyes, the solid bronze casket (which cost a reported $25,000 and had been finished with 14-carat gold-plating and lined with blue velvet), was closed and transported to the Staples Center. The freeways along the 11-mile route were closed and the casket arrived at 10am with the service due to begin at 10:30am.

All of Michael Jackson's brothers sat in the front row, each wearing a single white sequined glove. Other guests included Berry Gordy, Lionel Richie, Smokey Robinson, Stevie Wonder, Magic Johnson, Kobe Bryant, Mariah Carey and John Mayer. Debbie Rowe did not attend as, according to Attorney Marta Almli, 'The onslaught of media attention has made it clear her attendance would be an unnecessary distraction to an event that should focus exclusively on Michael's legacy. Debbie will continue to celebrate Michael's memory privately.'[25]

The service was broadcast around the world and is reported to have been watched by up to 1 billion people, although with the advent of Twitter, blogs and other new media, it could have been significantly higher.[26] They witnessed Stevie Wonder,

Mariah Carey and Jennifer Hudson singing the King of Pop's songs and Jermaine Jackson singing his brother's favourite song, Charlie Chaplin's 'Smile.'[27] They saw film clips illustrating his entire career, an array of speakers from the worlds of show business and rights movements, and a dance spectacular choreographed by Kenny Ortega. Jackson's daughter, Paris, delivered a short, but emotionally charged few words before being escorted off the stage in tears by her family: 'I just want to say, ever since I was born, Daddy has been the best father you could ever imagine… and I just want to say I love him… so much.' The onlookers in the crowd were silenced by her show of raw emotion.

Afterwards, the casket was carried from the Staples Center as an instrumental version of Jackson's 'Man In The Mirror' played. At 12:48pm, the memorial service finished and the coffin was taken back to Forest Lawn Cemetery where the plan was to bury the singer on 29 August – what would have been his fifty-first birthday.[28]

The final cost of Jackson's funeral was over $1 million, paid for by his estate. His crypt in the Great Mausoleum[29] at Forest Lawn Cemetery, dubbed the 'New World's Westminster Abbey' by *Time* magazine, cost $590,000. Other costs included the guest invitations totalling $11,716. The cost of security and the fleet of luxury cars was $30,000 and the sum for the florist was $16,000. The funeral planner charged $15,000 and an Italian restaurant in Pasadena, where guests went after the service, billed the estate $21,455.

While Jackson's funeral was taking place and while the Jackson family were starting to get embroiled in a bitter battle about the validity of the singer's will, the law enforcement agencies in Los Angeles were beginning to turn their attention to Dr Conrad Murray and the possibility that he had more to do with Jackson's death than anyone might have thought.

Officers raided Murray's Houston offices on 22 July 2009

and seized a number of items, including computer hard drives and a 'Texas Department of Public Safety controlled substance registration'. However, they failed to find any Propofol, the drug that was now dominating their investigation. They were still waiting for the results of the toxicology analysis, and the actions of LAPD in seeming to target Dr Murray was causing his attorney, Ed Chernoff, a great deal of concern: 'Based on Dr Murray's minute-by-minute and item-by-item description of Michael Jackson's last days, he should not be a target of criminal charges,' Chernoff said to CNN. 'Dr Murray was the last doctor standing when Michael Jackson died and it seems all the fury is directed at him. Dr Murray is frustrated by negative and often erroneous media reports. He has to walk around 24-7 with a bodyguard. He can't operate his practice. He can't go to work because he is harassed no matter where he goes.'[30]

It seemed the whole world was waiting for the toxicology results. Dr Murray was still a free man and guilty of no crime, but William Bratton, the Los Angeles Police Chief, made it clear in an interview with CNN that the coroner would determine the exact cause of Jackson's death based on the results of the toxicology tests: 'Are we dealing with a homicide, or are we dealing with an accidental overdose?' he said.[31]

One person confident that there was foul play involved was Jackson's sister, La Toya. She was the driving force behind getting the second autopsy carried out and she was under no illusions about what had happened to her brother. 'I believe Michael was murdered. I felt that from the start. Not just one person was involved, rather it was a conspiracy of people,' she told *The Mail on Sunday* in July 2009.[32] 'Less than a month ago, I said I thought Michael was going to die before the London shows because he was surrounded by people who didn't have his best interests at heart. Michael was worth more than a billion dollars. When anyone is worth that much money, there are always greedy people around them. I said to my family a month ago, "He's never going to make it to London". He was worth more dead than alive.'

While La Toya was certain her brother was murdered, there was still no definitive evidence or smoking gun to suggest anything sinister had happened. Dr Murray still seemed the man most culpable as he was with the singer when he had died and throughout the rest of July and August, police continued to raid Dr Murray's home and offices in Las Vegas. The pharmacy belonging to Tim Lopez in Las Vegas, which supplied many of the drugs that Murray administered to Jackson, including Propofol, was also raided when the authorities established a link between Murray and the pharmacy.

Whilst the LAPD were focusing their investigation with ever-greater intent on Dr Murray, the eight-page toxicology report that everyone was waiting for had arrived on Dr Christopher Rogers' desk.

But, before that, a team from the LA Coroner's Office had another task. On 6 August 2009, six weeks after Jackson's death, LaToya Jackson accompanied three officials from the Coroner's Office as they went to Forest Lawn Memorial Park. Among them were Craig Harvey, the Chief of Operations, Jose Hernandez, a forensic technician, and Jaime Lintemoot, a senior criminologist. The reason for them being there was to take hair samples from Michael Jackson's head for potential toxicology testing. His body had yet to be buried and when it was brought to La Toya and the team of coroners, they found Jackson 'supine in a yellow casket with blue lining. The majority of the decedent was covered with multiple white towels/sheets leaving only the hands and top of the head exposed'. [33] Just as when he was alive, a wig of long, dark hair covered his head, but it was what lay beneath that the team were interested in. Carefully and precisely, with gloved hands, samples of Jackson's natural hair hidden beneath the wig were collected. Gently plucked out one by one, these one and half inch strands would potentially provide evidence that would show, beyond reasonable doubt, just how long Jackson had been taking drugs, whether it be Propofol, benzodiazepines or any other chemical influences.

As it turned out, these hair samples weren't required as Dr Rogers had, by now, received the toxicology report and had analysed it. Completed on Wednesday, 15 July, the toxicology report showed a cocktail of drugs in Jackson's body. Propofol, Lorazepam, Midazolam, Lidocaine, Diazepam and Nordiazepam were found in Jackson's blood samples. Propofol, Midazolam, Lidocaine and Ephedrine were found in his urine. Propofol and Lidocaine were found in his liver tissue, Propofol was identified in his vitreous humour (the gel between the eye's lens and retina), and Lidocaine and Propofol were found in his stomach contents.

The report showed the amount of Propofol found in Jackson was 3.2mcg/ml in his heart blood, 4.1mcg/ml in his hospital blood and 2.6 mcg/ml in his femoral blood. Dr Selma Calmes, the anaesthetist consultant concluded that, 'The levels of Propofol found on toxicology exam are similar to those found during general anaesthesia for major surgery (intra-abdominal) with Propofol infusions, after a bolus induction.'[34] Basalt's textbook *The Disposition of Toxic Drugs and Chemicals in Man (7th edn)* mentions that in five fatal cases of acute Propofol poisoning, post-mortem Propofol levels ranged from 0.5–5.3mcg/ml. The levels found in Jackson were within this range.

On 19 August, Dr Rogers concluded that:

> Toxicology studies show a high blood concentration
> of propofol, as well as the presence of benzodiazepines
> as listed in the toxicology report. The autopsy did not

show any trauma or natural disease, which could cause death.

The cause of death is acute propofol intoxication. A contributory factor in the death is benzodiazepine effect.

The manner of death is homicide, based on the following:

1. Circumstances indicate that propofol and the benzodiazepines were administered by another.
2. The propofol was administered in a non-hospital setting without any appropriate medical indication.
3. The standard of care for administering propofol was not met (see anaesthesiology consultation). Recommended equipment for patient monitoring, precision dosing and resuscitation was not present.
4. The circumstances do not support self-administration of propofol.

This coroner's report was released on 27 August 2009, and one day later the Los Angeles Police Department said that they had sent the case to prosecutors, who would decide whether or not to file criminal charges.

Dr Murray, meanwhile, had released a video on YouTube just a few days previously. Filmed by a Houston-based production company, Murray used it to deliver a message to his friends and supporters. Lasting barely a minute, it featured an emotional Murray saying,

I want to thank all of my patients and friends who have sent such kind emails, letters and messages to let me know of your support and prayers for me and my family. Because of all that is going on I'm afraid to return phone calls or use my email. Therefore I recorded this video to let all of you know that I have been receiving your messages. I have not been able to thank you personally, which you know is not normal for me. Your messages give me strength and courage to keep going. They mean the world to me. Please don't worry. As long as I keep God in my heart and you in my life, I will be fine. I have done all I could. I told the truth and I have faith truth will prevail.

In reality, Dr Murray's legal team was in the process of negotiating the terms of his surrender. Murray had returned to Houston in the aftermath of Jackson's death and had kept a low profile while he made plans to revive his clinics in Houston and Las Vegas. It was reported that his finances were deteriorating (his home was eventually repossessed in May 2010), he had not been paid a dime by AEG Live, but, according to his attorney, it appeared many of his patients wanted him to return to medicine. However, as the net began to close in on him and speculation about his role in Jackson's death grew, Murray flew from Houston to Los Angeles at the end of January, prepared to surrender after his advisors spoke with members of Los Angeles County District Attorney's Office. These discussions were centered on whether Murray should be arrested or whether he should be allowed to turn himself in. There was, however, a considerable amount of concern and anger at the prospect of Murray simply being allowed to surrender. The LAPD were worried that, with an impending arrest, Murray might actually flee to another state or even abroad, and they were also aware that the sight of Murray surrendering and handing himself him to the police without being arrested might give the impression that he was receiving preferential treatment. Detectives were keen to arrest him on

Friday, 5 February 2010, but negotiations eventually allowed Murray to turn himself in on Monday, 8 February.

Almost eight months after the death of Michael Jackson, Dr Conrad Murray walked into a courthouse in Los Angeles, as onlookers shouted 'murderer', and surrendered. Superior Court Judge Keith Schwartz charged him with involuntary manslaughter. The charge was that Murray, 'did unlawfully and without malice, kill Michael Joseph Jackson... in the commission of an unlawful act, not a felony: and in the commission of a lawful act which might have produced death, in an unlawful manner, and without due caution and circumspection.' Dr Murray pleaded not guilty to the charge, which carried with it a maximum sentence of four years in prison, and was released after posting $75,000 bail money and surrendering his passport. He was also granted permission to continue practising medicine on one condition: as long as he didn't administer anaesthesia.

While everyone waited to see how the charges against Dr Murray would play out, the Jackson family was still haggling over the will. For the last few months of 2009, Katherine Jackson had been going back and forth in her legal challenges against the 2002 will made by her son. Initially dissuaded to challenge it by her lawyers, who realised that such a challenge would be fruitless, Katherine reiterated her desire to have John Branca and John McClain removed as executors to the will, believing they had undue influence. However, Katherine eventually dropped her challenges towards Branca and McClain only to see her husband[35] Joe Jackson take up the baton. In the will, Joe Jackson had been left out entirely and was set to receive nothing from his son's estate, an estate that was beginning to look increasingly lucrative in the months after his death. Michael, and some of his other siblings, had claimed that Joe had physically abused Michael as the child was growing up and, at times, apparently merely the sight of his father made Michael want to throw up.[36] La Toya had written that Joe beat his children and even molested her sister, Rebbie.[37] With these allegations in the background, it's perhaps no wonder that Michael struck him out of his will.

But despite this, Joe continued to challenge all and sundry in an effort to get what he perceived as his legitimate share of the will. He said he needed over $15,000 per month simply to cover his expenses[38] and, seeing how much money the estate was making since the death of his son, was eager for people to know that he should be due a share. He even stated during an *Extra* TV show appearance that his son was, '…worth more dead than alive'.[39] But for all his legal challenges, Joe Jackson was ultimately unsuccessful and was destined to survive by selling perfume in a Las Vegas Strip mall. That was until the mall shut down his operation as the perfume contained an image of Michael Jackson that Joe couldn't prove that he had the licensing rights to. While Katherine received over $1 million a year from Michael Jackson's estate, Joe received nothing. He moved to Las Vegas where he lives in a condo near the Stratosphere Casino and attempts to charge a $50,000 per appearance fee to anyone who will have him, but there appear to be few bookings.[40]

With Murray now under arrest, and the challenges to the will seemingly at an end, the executors of the will began to address the financial situation surrounding the estate of Michael Jackson. There were substantial claims against the estate in the wake of Jackson's death, and John Branca was determined to restructure the estate in order to service the debts that had accrued over the past few years; debts which totalled in excess of half a billion dollars.[41]

AEG Live were also anxious to recoup as much as they could. They had sold over 750,000 tickets for the O2 concerts and were sitting on roughly $85 million. They faced having to refund all of it until they came up with an intriguing and potentially lucrative plan. As well as offering full refunds to anyone who wanted their money back, they also offered ticket holders the option to receive the actual tickets they had purchased for the concerts, tickets that AEG Live suggested Michael Jackson had personally had a major part in designing. But in receiving the actual tickets, the holders would forfeit their option to a full refund. AEG Live have never released the figures regarding this refund offer, nor how many people took up the option to receive their souvenir ticket in exchange for its purchase price. But suffice to say that if only 50 per cent asked for a full refund, AEG Live would still be making in excess of $42 million, in addition to the cancellation insurance they had taken out on the singer.

John Branca, along with AEG Live, then saw footage that had been shot during the 'This Is It' rehearsals. This was originally private footage, intended only to be seen by Jackson as the show developed in rehearsals, and after the tour to be hidden away in his own personal archives.[42] Branca, however, quickly identified the financial potential of this raw footage. Kenny Ortega was a willing cohort in the possibility of producing a film from the footage, especially when fans bombarded him with requests to see it once they discovered some of the rehearsals had been filmed: 'At first I got so many messages from fans around the world asking to see the shows, asking to see the footage and eventually I realised the journey wasn't over and we had to do this.'[43] But the real reason to make the film was money and AEG Live had 100 hours of footage to exploit. The deal that was eventually struck, after much legal wrangling in the courts, was that Sony Pictures paid at least $60 million for the film rights,[44] with Jackson's estate entitled to share 90 per cent of the profits with AEG.[45] When tickets for the film went on sale they sold out within two hours and it made over $23 million in the USA on its opening weekend.[46] Despite some fans of Jackson's boycotting the film, complaining that AEG Live were partly responsible for Jackson's death and now profiting out of it, the film became the most successful music film of all time raking in over $261 million at the international box office.[47] It made an additional $45 million in DVD sales in the USA and topped DVD charts worldwide, selling particularly well in Japan and Europe. John Branca had also negotiated a deal with Sony to put out Jackson's unreleased material and existing recordings that could be exploited at certain appropriate anniversaries for a fee reported to be up to $250 million,[48] and he entered a deal with Cirque du Soleil for a Michael Jackson-themed show called 'Immortal', which has brought in another $300 million since its opening.[49] In fact, the money required to pay off all of Jackson's debts had been raised by Branca within five months of Jackson's death. The estate still faced six major lawsuits, including one claim of $300 million from AllGood Entertainment, who were suing for losses, claiming Jackson had pulled out of a reunion concert with his brothers that was scheduled to be on television,[50] but it was a remarkable turnaround for an estate that only a few months earlier was deep in debt. In fact, it has been hailed as '...the most remarkable financial and image resurrection in pop culture history' by CBS's '60 Minutes'.[51]

Facing a more uncertain future, however, was Dr Conrad Murray. It was at the end of July 2010, following a major investigation into not only Murray but into all of the doctors who had treated Jackson in the past, that justice officials revealed that only one of these physicians would face charges. That one was Dr Murray.

The trial started on 27 September 2011 in Los Angeles County Superior Court with the presiding judge being Judge Michael Pastor. Throughout the proceedings, Dr Murray refused to take the stand, relying solely on the interview he gave to LAPD detectives two days after Jackson's death. However, it quickly became evident that the various witnesses called to give testimony had accounts of the night of 24 June and the morning of 25 June 2009 that differed widely from the account given by Murray.

The prosecutors[52] in the trial told the jury that, '…misplaced trust in the hands of Murray cost Jackson his life.' In response, Murray's attorney, Ed Chernoff said that Jackson was tired from rehearsals, took eight tablets of Lorazepam and, 'When Dr Murray left the room, Jackson self-administered a dose of Propofol that, with the Lorazepam, created a perfect storm in his body that killed him instantly. The whole thing is tragic, but the evidence is not that Dr Murray did it.'

As the trial progressed, details of Murray's orders of Propofol from Tim Lopez started to emerge and when Elissa Fleak, the Los Angeles County Coroner, was called to the stand and stated she found evidence of numerous prescription medicines in Jackson's bedroom, including empty bottles of Propofol, the noose began to tighten around Murray's neck. Earlier, Alberto Alvarez had described how he was told to pack away vials of medicine quickly before the paramedics arrived and how one of the IV bags had a bottle with a milky substance actually inside the saline bag, and a bottle inside a saline bag, regardless of its contents, is an extremely irregular procedure. This milky substance could only have been Propofol.

On day 10 of the trial, Dr Christopher Rogers took to the stand and, based on his autopsy and the subsequent toxicology report, concluded that the cause of death was acute Propofol intoxication with contributory effects from benzodiazepines. When asked about the manner of death, he testified it was homicide and quashed suggestions that Jackson could have self-administered the Propofol. He said that the '…circumstances do not support self-administration' as Jackson would have had to wake up, self-administer the drugs (and he was needle-phobic), let the drugs circulate through the bloodstream to the brain, and then be found not breathing, all in the space of the two minutes that Murray claimed he was out of the room. Instead, it was likely, in Dr Rogers' professional opinion, that Dr Murray was estimating the doses given to Jackson and that '…Murray accidentally gave too much'. Additional evidence to support his theory was found in the shape of a cut in the rubber stopper of the Propofol vial inconsistent with a needle but known in medical circles as a 'spike', which is used to allow the drug to flow out of the vial constantly. [53] [54]

D.A. Walgren asked Dr Rogers whether, if Jackson had self-administered the Propofol and/or Lorazepam, would it still be homicide because of negligence by Murray? Dr Rogers replied simply, 'Correct'.

Dr Alon Steinberg, a cardiologist, found Dr Murray exhibited 'six separate and distinct extreme deviations from the standard of care' and suggested these contributed to Jackson's untimely death.[55] Dr Steven Shafer, a Professor of Anaesthesiology at Colombia University and a worldwide expert who has published numerous papers concerning Propofol and has a particular interest in mathematically modelling Propofol dosage, concentration and effort, found 17 'separate and distinct egregious violations'[56] of the standard of care Murray gave to Jackson, and when asked whether, 'Each one of the seventeen egregious violations is individually likely or expected to result in injury or death to Michael Jackson?' Shafer replied with, 'Yes'.[57]

As key figures from the events leading up to and including 25 June testified – figures such as Randy Phillips, Cherilyn Lee and Kenny Ortega – Dr Murray's defence seemed to be in tatters and his interview to LAPD appeared obviously misleading. Ex-patients of his were called to try to portray him as an angel of mercy, but they did little to sway the jury and on 7 November 2011, after nine hours of deliberation, Dr Conrad Murray was found guilty of involuntary manslaughter and was taken into custody pending sentencing. On hearing the news, Jackson's sister LaToya screamed out and Jermaine Jackson consoled his weeping mother, Katherine. Outside the court, Jackson fans cheered and burst into applause.

On 29 November 2011, Murray was sentenced to the maximum penalty of four years incarceration[58] for the involuntary manslaughter of Michael Jackson with the judge[59] saying, 'Dr Murray created a set of circumstances and became involved in a cycle of horrible medicine. The practice of Propofol for medicine madness, which violated his sworn obligation for money.' The Jackson family was in court and released a statement before sentencing:

> We are not here to seek revenge. There is nothing you can do here today to bring Michael back. We respectfully request that you impose a sentence that reminds physicians that they cannot sell their services to the highest bidder and cast aside their Hippocratic oath to do no harm. The Bible reminds us that men cannot do justice. They can only seek justice. That is all we ask as a family. And that is all we can ask for here.

As he was led away, Murray blew a kiss to his mother and his girlfriend while, outside the court, Katherine Jackson said to the waiting media, 'Four years is not enough for someone's life. It won't bring him back, but at least he got the maximum. I thought the judge was very, very fair and I thank him.'

However, Jermaine was more direct outside the court and alluded to the wider picture saying of Murray, 'He's just a finger to a bigger hand,' before pointing to a sign held by a Jackson supporter that read 'AEG needs to be investigated'.[60]

Almost two years later the Jackson family launched a lawsuit against AEG Live in April 2013, seeking some $40 billion in damages. This claim was based on the presumption that AEG Live were negligent in hiring Dr Murray as Jackson's personal physician, and ignoring the fact that Jackson was already in poor health before he died. AEG Live countered by saying Jackson's drug abuse began long before he came into contact with Dr Murray and that, in fact, they hadn't chosen the physician but, instead, Jackson had personally selected him. In their closing statement, AEG Live attorney Marvin Puttnam told jurors that, 'AEG would never have agreed to finance this tour if they knew Mr Jackson was playing Russian Roulette in his bedroom every night'. After five months in court, a jury in Los Angeles exonerated AEG Live, finding that they played no part in Jackson's death. The verdict was a huge blow to Katherine Jackson and Michael's three children.

Another big blow for the family came a month later when Dr Murray was released from prison at 12:01pm on 28 October 2013, two years ahead of schedule owing to prison overcrowding in California and his good behaviour. Upon his release, his legal representative said, 'He's pretty confident that he'll be able to practise medicine again somewhere'. With his medical licence revoked in Texas and suspended in California and Nevada, there was only one place for Dr Murray to go. In 2014 he headed back to his native Trinidad where he secured a job, but only on a voluntary basis, with the Trinidad Ministry of Health, consulting local heart surgeons.[61] [62]

Meanwhile, the Michael Jackson estate continued to rake in money at an astronomical rate. The combined earnings of Jay Z, Taylor Swift and Kanye West since Michael Jackson died come nowhere near the revenues Jackson has earned for his estate after his death, with some estimates putting the sum at $1 billion dollars in the 12 months following his death alone.[63] That year *Billboard* suggests Jackson made $429 million from music sales, $392 million from film and television, $130 million from music publishing,

$35 million from licensing and touring, and $31 million from his recording contract.[64] He has sold over 50 million albums since he died and remains the biggest selling artist on iTunes.[65] Even ringtone revenues give a net value of $5 million. And, of course, his estate still holds a 50 per cent share in the Sony/ATV catalogue, a catalogue now valued at $2 billion.[66]

Michael Jackson has never been richer. As Joe Jackson said, as Frank Dileo said, as even John Branca said, 'Michael Jackson is worth more dead than alive'.

12

Sometimes, though not often, he had dreams, and they were more
painful than the dreams of other boys. For hours he could not be
separated from these dreams, though he wailed piteously in them.
They had to do, I think, with the riddle of his existence.

J.M. Barrie, *Peter Pan*

Upon his release from jail in October 2013,[1] Dr Conrad Murray gave few interviews, but when he did talk, he continued to proclaim his innocence with a vigorous, some might say deluded, determination. 'By the end Michael Jackson was a broken man,' he told *The Mail on Sunday*,[2] 'I tried to protect him but instead I was brought down with him.' In the same interview he was asked who might be responsible for the killing of the King of Pop. Murray was adamant in his answer: 'I did not kill Michael Jackson. He was a drug addict. Michael Jackson accidentally killed Michael Jackson.'[3]

In another interview, this time with CNN's Don Lemon on 26 June 2014, the day after the fifth anniversary of the singer's death, Murray continued to suggest that Jackson administered the drugs himself:[4]

Don Lemon: You said that he gave himself the drugs. You believe he gave himself the final dose?

Dr Murray: The premises cannot be breached. It was not breached. There was no one else in the house, in the upper chambers but Michael and myself. I was away from him. The phone records show that.

After serving time in jail, Murray had his story and was sticking to it. This was despite the fact that his only official account of the night in question, the one he had given to the LAPD in his only judicial interview just two days after Jackson's death, had been taken apart piece by piece during his trial by the prosecution and by witnesses who seemed to contradict virtually everything Murray had told the detectives. Constantly and consistently, so many things that Murray had said just simply didn't add up.

So what did really happen when Dr Conrad Murray left Michael Jackson's bedroom on that fateful night of 24/25 June 2009? What were the actual circumstances that led to Murray coming back into the room shortly after 11:51am while on the phone to one of his girlfriends, Sade Anding to find the singer unresponsive, so setting off an 83-minute chain of events that would result in Jackson's lifeless body being rushed into the ER at UCLA Medical Center? And how did everything conspire that night to cause the death of Michael Jackson, the superstar King of Pop?

To understand, we first have to consider some other scenarios – consider them in order to eliminate them.

Before that though, let's imagine that Michael Jackson never actually died on the night of 24/25 June 2009. Let's imagine an alternative timeline that begins as the singer, as happened, arrived back home from rehearsals at the Staples Center to his rented Carolwood home shortly after midnight. As he always did, Jackson met the scattering of fans waiting outside his house, even at this hour, signed autographs and posed for photos, before heading into the mansion. Once inside, he climbed the stairs and entered his bedroom to be greeted by Dr Murray. They would have their usual brief conversation about how rehearsals went before the singer would have a shower, after which Dr Murray would go through his standard routine of applying lotion to Jackson's back before the King of Pop would settle down to sleep. All is just as it had been each night for the last two months.

But then our alternative timeline kicks in: there would be no Propofol administered by Murray that night; a few days before, he had started a programme to wean Jackson off the drug and now the singer finds he can sleep without Propofol. In fact, this is the fourth consecutive night Jackson has been able to sleep without the drug after two months of nightly infusions. Murray diligently continues to monitor Jackson, spending the night observing him with all the correct equipment he has purchased for the job or had ordered for him by AEG Live – after all, he is fully aware of the duty of care to his patient. He never leaves Jackson's bedside, doesn't go into another room to talk on the phone to one of his many mistresses or conduct his business affairs, and, consequently, the singer never has a cardiac arrest.

In this imaginary timeline, Jackson wakes in the morning after another good night's sleep and is reminded by Dr Murray that he has to grant AEG Live access to his medical records for the past five years and also to agree to a medical in London. Jackson, fully rested and looking forward to his concerts in London, not only gives his permission to Dr Murray to sanction a medical in London as well as allowing him access to all his medical records, but he also signs Murray's contract of engagement. In turn, Dr Murray sends an email to Bob Taylor at the insurance company in London informing him Jackson has agreed to all of the demands laid out by them and, consequently, the wheels are set in motion for the forthcoming trip to London. Everyone is happy: Jackson, Murray, the insurers and AEG Live.

Over the next few days an invigorated Jackson storms through rehearsals at the Staples Center in Los Angeles; everyone who witnesses his performances is encouraged by what they see. The magic has returned, if it ever went away, and the show promises to be a spectacular pop extravaganza. With everything in place, the whole production then moves to London for the final technical rehearsals. While in England, Jackson and his children live in the splendour of an estate in the Kent countryside with Dr Murray living close by and continuing to care for the singer. After a number of weeks of considered treatment, Dr Murray has gradually, and then totally, weaned Jackson off Propofol and, with the singer thousands of miles away from Los Angeles and the clinic of Dr Klein, his apparent supply of Demerol has also been cut off. Slowly but surely, Jackson has become less reliant on medication and, when a sympathetic doctor is found in London, he undergoes the medical to satisfy the insurance company that he can, indeed, be insured for the remaining concerts that were, up to that point, uninsured, and that he is fit and able to perform all the concerts at the O2.

Beginning in July 2009, Michael Jackson fulfils his contract and performs all 50 shows at the O2. They prove to be a massive critical and commercial success, leading to phenomenal demand from fans to add extra shows, and reviewers to state universally that the King of Pop is back on his throne. Jackson then embarks on a major world tour. Starting in Europe, the singer sells out arenas and stadiums across the continent before heading to Japan where his adoring fans ensure shows are sold out within minutes. Finally, in the autumn of the year, Jackson heads back to the USA for a triumphant homecoming tour.

Such has been the success of the tour and revival in his music that his financial worries are well and truly behind him[5] and he is now free to concentrate his efforts on forays into the world of films, in particular his over-riding passion for a film project about Egypt's King Tut.

At last, with his legacy secure, Michael Jackson is clean of drugs, free from financial woes and has finally found serenity in his life.

When he met Randy Phillips of AEG Live some years earlier, Jackson had said to Phillips that, 'I'm tired of being a vagabond. I just want a home for me and my kids'.[6] At last, Jackson's wishes have become a reality.

What of Dr Conrad Murray in this imaginary timeline?

He accompanies Jackson on all legs of the tour, forming a lifelong friendship and having experiences that would remain with him forever. Murray returns with Jackson to the USA and sees out the remainder of the tour as his personal physician. The money he makes from working on the tour ends up amounting to over $2 million and, by remaining as Jackson's personal physician after the tour finishes, his financial security is safe for some time to come. So much so, that Murray eventually realises his dream of setting up his own clinic, named after his father, on his home island of Trinidad. Here, Murray devotes himself to treating those unable to afford medical services and, in doing so, his own legacy is written.

This would have been the dream scenario for both of them. In fact, not only for Murray and Jackson, but for all the performers, fans and, of course, AEG Live who stood to make a fortune from the tour. But Jackson was experienced enough to know that the scale of the challenge ahead was totally unrealistic, yet the alternative probably meant utter and complete ruination for him. The whole entire enterprise was delusional. Michael surely knew it, but likely hoped that at some point an exit strategy would magically appear. He was a frail, deeply insecure, vulnerable, unfit, 50-year-old with a chronic addiction to a wide variety of prescription medicines, and the whole tour would have seemed just what it was: an impossible mountain for him to climb.

***

As the world knows, this imaginary timeline never happened. Not only did Jackson's comeback and his financial salvation never materialise, but Murray and AEG Live lost out too, not to mention the hundreds of thousands of fans whose dreams of seeing their idol perform one last time never materialised, in the most tragic of circumstances. From the outset many fans may have had the premonition that, realistically, the shows were never actually going to happen; too many had been here before. Upon hearing of Jackson's death, even some members of his family initially assumed that it was a hoax created by Jackson in order to pull out of the tour. Such was even their cynicism. After all, they too had heard similar rumours before.[7]

So if our previous imaginary timeline was, indeed, preposterous, we should consider two other different timelines and scenarios, and unlike the first imaginary scenario, one, if not both of these, must have been considered very seriously by all at AEG Live as the deadline to London loomed.

What if Michael Jackson had somehow, against the odds, made it to London? Maybe he was cajoled, encouraged or ordered to cross the Atlantic, but nevertheless, he had arrived in the UK. Suddenly, all about him, a press-frenzy was manifesting itself as the opening night at the O2 grew ever nearer. Across London, huge advertising and publicity campaigns were alerting everyone to Jackson's impending comeback. Tickets for the shows were changing hands on eBay for extortionate prices and exclusive VIP packages for the O2 concerts had long been snapped up. Behind the scenes, AEG Live had nervously shipped the entire production over at enormous expense and an army of workers were tirelessly preparing for the shows.

However, behind the scenes Michael Jackson fails the required medical in Harley Street; it's much tougher than the one he had gone through in the USA, and AEG Live's attempts to get Jackson's insurance policy to cover the full 50-show run are scuppered, meaning that the final 20 shows can't be insured. What happens now with Jackson having failed the medical? While discussions are held behind the scenes and plans made, AEG Live continue to prepare for the first 30 shows they are definitely covered for and frantically consider contingencies. It is an impending nightmare scenario for them.

Or here's the second scenario. Even if Jackson passes the medical and the concerts actually begin, even if he manages against the odds to complete, let's be generous, the first nine shows, then returns without warning to the USA, or even the Middle East perhaps, and cancels with immediate effect the other 41 shows. What would happen then? Hundreds of thousands of fans would be desperately disappointed and the press would have a field day, saying the singer had lived up to his 'Wacko Jacko' moniker and proclaiming that such a cancellation shouldn't come as a surprise. But most of all in this scenario, a great deal of people would be out of pocket.

Amongst them would be AEG Live. They would have to reimburse over 80 per cent of the $85 million they had taken in ticket sales to disappointed fans, except for the fortunate few who had seen the first nine shows. And they would have to write off the $35 million they had apparently spent so far in setting up the tour. The prospect of Jackson beginning the concerts but not completing the tour was the worst possible scenario for AEG Live, particularly as 20 of the later shows appeared not to be insured for cancellation.

But right at the outset, AEG Live had been resourceful and put into place a caveat to protect themselves, at least with regard to the show's production costs.

A clause in the contract between AEG Live and Michael Jackson (a contract which as we have seen has many discrepancies and may not be a contract at all but simply a Letter of Intent) stated that the singer would not only be responsible for all production costs but he would also forego to AEG Live every asset he owned if the concerts were cancelled.

And, of course, these assets included the prized Sony/ATV catalogue. With this in mind, it suddenly appears that the only way AEG Live might get away with minimum damage from this fiasco was if Jackson did not perform *any* concerts in London. This vaguely attractive option, which became increasingly closer to a reality for AEG Live as Jackson's rehearsals stalled and his drug use became more evident, not to mention his unwillingness to fulfil the insurance demands, meant that the best outcome in June 2009 for AEG Live was for Jackson not to turn up in London at all. Certainly, for him to begin the shows and then pull out would be an utter disaster. Sure, they could sue Jackson, but what could they expect to receive in damages from a singer half a billion dollars in debt? And, even if they did sue Jackson, AEG Live would find themselves at the back of a very long queue of creditors wanting payments for aged debts from the deals Jackson had previously reneged upon.

It's inconceivable that these scenarios weren't being played out in other people's minds, too; the 'what ifs' connected with any tragedy or mystery that cannot be comprehensively explained in fact.

The tragedy of Michael Jackson's death is that, like most addicts, it was wrought from the tragedy of his own life, a tragedy in which he was plainly the central character, but a central character ill-equipped to cope with such a leading role in such a long-running production. The surrounding and supporting cast in Jackson's life was made up of conspiring relatives and fly-by-night friends, charlatans and thieves, snake-oil salesmen and willing opportunists. And the themes that connected and consumed them all, including Jackson himself, were ambition, fate, deception and avarice. With hindsight, it now seems inevitable that Michael Jackson's life would end in tragedy. Throughout, he was fighting superior forces as well as his own demons, and his life was bound to end in a sorrowful and disastrous final denouement.

***

So, what really happened on the night and morning of 25 June 2009 in the second floor bedroom of Michael Jackson's Carolwood mansion? The likeliest explanation, of course, is that, in the end, Dr Conrad Murray unwittingly gave Michael Jackson a lethal dose of Propofol that was administered first by an injection and then continued over a course of hours via his uniquely adapted delivery system. The Propofol alongside the other cocktail of drugs already in Jackson's system, a cocktail prescribed and administered by Murray, combined to create a lethal mixture that could only have been avoided if Murray had been monitoring his patient constantly. As we know, Murray was not only on the phone, but was in a completely different room. And he was able to spend so much time on the phone because Jackson was dying. Or, more likely, already dead.

This scenario is based on the evidence provided for the trial by the autopsy, the toxicology analysis and the witness statements: the amount of Propofol and other drugs in Jackson's body when he died; the fact that a saline bag was found with a cut in it with a vial of Propofol sitting at the bottom of the bag (and the only fingerprint found on this system of administration was the fingerprint of Murray[8]); the fact that Alberto Alvarez saw this system of administration in operation on Jackson and was ordered to hide the administration contraption, as well as countless other vials and bottles of medication before the paramedics arrived on the scene; and the fact that, during the trial, every one of the witnesses had similar testimonies and none of them corresponded with Murray's one police interview, upon which he based his entire defence.

On going back to the morning in question, Murray's call at 11:51am on 25 June to one of his girlfriends, Sade Anding, raises many questions. She testified that she heard voices in the background at the exact time Murray stopped talking to her and dropped the phone or put it in his pocket without turning it off. Why did Murray do this? What was happening? Was Jackson calling out for help? Did he gasp? Did he choke? Just what was it that Sade Anding was hearing? Maybe what she heard, and what she thought she heard, were not the same thing.

What if Conrad Murray deliberately gave Jackson a lethal dosage of Propofol? This has to be considered, albeit briefly, even though it is unlikely, as surely even Murray would have made better preparations to dispose of the incriminating evidence and concoct a story that would at least tally with other witnesses. In fact, Murray, perhaps more than anyone, had much to gain by Jackson going to London and undertaking the series of concerts. Like Jackson, Murray was financially stricken, on the verge of bankruptcy, facing the loss of his house, and with no end in sight to the monetary liabilities incumbent on him with seven children to provide for. The $150,000 a month he was getting paid for his role as Jackson's personal physician was a financial lifeline for Murray,[9] and the prospect of a 'This Is It' world tour following on from the UK dates would increase not only Murray's bank balance, but also his standing within the world of celebrity doctors. Who knows, regular television appearances could follow and perhaps even a major publishing contract. The world, for Murray, was there for the taking, so it seems highly unlikely, almost implausible, that he had anything to gain by deliberately killing Michael Jackson, whatever conspiracy theorists might think.

However, the fact that Murray hadn't been paid for his work up to the time of Jackson's death (and, in fact, has never received any payment for his role as the singer's personal physician) raises another question: just who was employing Dr Conrad Murray? Was it Jackson himself or was it AEG Live? The contract that Jackson had with AEG Live was extremely unfavourable to the singer. It demanded that all production costs were at his expense, and this would have included the provision of a personal physician. However, the contract that AEG Live presented to Dr Murray stated that:

4. RESPONSIBILITIES OF GCS/DR MURRAY. Without in any way limiting any other term or provision of this Agreement or any obligation of GCA or Dr Murray hereunder, GCA and Dr Murray shall:
4.1 Perform the Services reasonably requested by Producer.

The Producer was none other than AEG Live. So, while it would appear that Jackson would ultimately meet the financial payments to Murray (although there is some debate as to whether Jackson or AEG Live would be paying him[10]), the doctor was at the beck and call of AEG Live. Might this explain the frantic exchanges of emails on the night of 24 June and morning of 25 June, as Murray was encouraged by AEG Live representatives to try to persuade Jackson to release his medical records and agree to a second medical in London? Without this, there would be no insurance policy for the final 20 concerts. And no insurance policy would directly affect AEG Live.

As the concerts grew nearer, AEG Live would have been growing increasingly nervous about Jackson not agreeing to the requests of the insurers. Might this be a contributing reason they postponed the start of the tour,[11] as well as the fact that the singer was appearing to be struggling in rehearsals? They appear to have been putting pressure on Murray to attempt to persuade the singer to accede to the insurance company's demands. Therefore, if the singer was flatly refusing to release his medical records and undertake a second medical, did AEG Live, or anybody come to that, have a contingency plan in place? And, if so, was Murray part of a grander scheme?

Michael Jackson had long been surrounded by the enablers who had given him access to the prescription drugs he was so addicted to.[12] The Jackson family lawyer said, shortly after Michael died, that, 'The people that have surrounded him have been enabling him... If you think that the case of Anna Nicole Smith was an abuse, it was nothing to what we have seen in Michael Jackson's life.'[13] Dr Murray was simply the latest potential enabler. But what made Murray different was that he was desperate for any form of financial salvation given the scale of the debts he was in. The initial contract, whenever it would be duly signed, promised him $150,000 per month plus expenses. It was a lifeline to him. However, as it hadn't been signed, none of the money he was expecting, and desperately needed, had arrived, nor would any arrive until the contract *was* signed. Consequently, Murray was, himself, in a weak position on many fronts and, as such, was vulnerable to approaches from superior forces. If somebody, or some organisation, wanted to dispose of Michael Jackson, then Dr Conrad Murray was, if required, in the perfect place to enable them to do so.

Murray's flimsy defence in court was based on the theory that

Michael Jackson gave himself an overdose of drugs during the time – two minutes according to Murray – that he had left the room to visit the bathroom. He told the LAPD detectives that he had given Jackson 25mg of Propofol at some point between 10:40am and 10:50am, watched the singer go to sleep, and then at 11am he had left Jackson's room to go to the toilet for two minutes.

Could it really be possible, therefore, that Dr Murray might have been persuaded, perhaps for money, by a superior force to leave a lethal dose of Propofol within reach of Jackson, and then conveniently leave the room? It's virtually inconceivable given the timescale as revealed to the court throughout the trial, especially if we take Murray's word that he introduced Propofol at 10:50am. This is the timescale that Dr Rogers, the Chief of Forensic Medicine at the Los Angeles County Coroner, was working to when he reached his conclusion that Jackson couldn't have possibly self-administered.

But we have to consider another possible theory, one that might be just as unlikely but one that has to be considered nonetheless: what if Murray had left the room *earlier* having placed a lethal dose of Propofol tantalisingly close to Jackson, a confirmed drug addict desperate for his next fix? This was more likely to take the form of a conveniently loaded IV drip, full of Propofol, which could be self-administered by simply opening the roller clamp[14] that controlled the flow of drugs through the IV into the body. This could, therefore, allow the drug to free-flow into the singer's body if desired. Murray told the LAPD that Jackson had done this in the past. In his interview on 27 June 2009, Murray said to the detectives, 'He never told me that he administered it himself, but he said to me that the doctors allowed him to infuse it himself.' According to Murray, Jackson went on to say after Murray had refused to allow him to self-administer Propofol, 'Why don't you want me to push it? I love to push it.'

As we know, there are two major time periods when no phone calls were made to, or from, Murray's phones. One was from 8:49am until 9:23am on 25 June, a 34-minute window when Murray could have left Jackson, enabling him time to self-administer. Then from 10:24am to 11:17am, a 53-minute window, and the one which seems to fit the timeframe much more conveniently, not least because Murray uses this time to call Stacey Ruggles in his office for almost nine minutes from 10:34am to 10:43am. What better alibi, if we consider this as a potential scenario, than a call to his office which, more than likely, took place outside of Jackson's bedroom?

At 10:43am, Murray may have re-entered Jackson's bedroom to check whether the singer had self-administered. Finding him not breathing, Murray does nothing to revive him but, instead, may have turned up the heating in the house even though it was a balmy day in June. In her book, *Starting Over*, La Toya Jackson recalls going into Jackson's Carolwood bedroom on the evening of his death and noticing immediately, and to her surprise, that the room was excessively hot. She was told that Michael always kept the heating on because he was generally freezing but wondered whether the truth might be that the heating was really kept on to keep Jackson's body warm following his death in an attempt to make it look like he had died closer to the actual 911 call, which was placed at 12:21pm.[15]

At 11:07am Dr Murray receives another phone call from his office. It's a brief call, perhaps Murray makes his excuses for not being able to chat. Could something else have been pre-occupying him? From 11:18am, Murray begins a series of emails and phone calls that occupy him right up to the moment he re-enters the bedroom while he is on the phone with one of his girlfriends to find Jackson not breathing. Did Murray use these phone calls to give himself a convenient alibi, the most convenient of all being the one to Sade Anding at some time after 11:51am when he re-entered the bedroom to 'find' Jackson not breathing? All these phone calls would certainly allow Jackson the opportunity to inadvertently self-administer a fatal dose of Propofol but if so, did Murray facilitate these actions at the behest of a superior force? Did Jackson really self-administer the drugs? Or was, as is most likely, Murray simply neglecting his duties and not monitoring his patient, with no trace of deliberate foul play involved?

The truth is that Michael died, unquestionably, from a much larger dosage of drugs than Murray claimed to have administered. It was proven indisputably by the toxicology report. The question is, how did the drugs that killed Michael Jackson get into his body?

In an interview with *The Mail on Sunday* on 24 November 2013, following his release from jail, Murray said, 'I received a phone call at 11:07am, and when I left Michael at 11:20am, he had a normal heartbeat, his vital signs were good. I left the room because I didn't want to disturb him. I believe he woke up, got hold of his own stash of Propofol and injected himself. He did it too quickly and went into cardiac arrest.'

This account by Murray is riddled with contradictions when compared to his interview with the LAPD on 27 June 2009, two days after Jackson's death. In this one interview with the LAPD, the only time Murray spoke to any form of judicial authorities about the death of Michael Jackson, he said he administered Propofol to Jackson between 10:40am and 10:50am, monitored the singer as he went to sleep, and then left the bedroom at 11am to go to the toilet, a break lasting no more than two minutes, after which he re-entered the bedroom to find the singer lifeless. Remember, these versions of events were given by Murray on 27 June 2009, just two days after Jackson's death, so should have been fresh in his mind.

However, in *The Mail on Sunday* interview, some four years after Jackson's death, Dr Murray claims that he received a brief phone call at 11:07am. The phone records verify this call took place. It was from Stacey Ruggles who was his office assistant. If Murray had come back into the room at 11:02am, as he told the LAPD detectives, and found Michael not breathing, would he really have answered a call at 11:07am? And, if he did, surely he would have instructed Stacey Ruggles to call an ambulance. At the very least, she would have noticed something unusual about his demeanor if he had just discovered his patient was not breathing. But she did not.

It appears from his interview with *The Mail on Sunday* that Murray is suggesting he didn't leave the room during the duration of the phone call to Ruggles as he goes on to say he only actually left the room, and therefore Michael, at 11:20am because, '…I didn't want to disturb him'.

Why would Murray not want to disturb Jackson at 11:20am but found it okay to answer a call in his presence at 11:07am? And how does this fit when he claims earlier that he found Jackson not breathing at 11:02am? Again, phone records verify that Murray did, in fact, make a phone call, but it was at 11:18am and not 11:20am. It was a call that lasted for 32 minutes to his Las Vegas practice. Once again, this contradicts his claim that he found Jackson not breathing at 11:02am.

If Jackson did self-administer a lethal dose of Propofol inadvertently, then according to *The Mail on Sunday* interview, Murray is suggesting that it must have been somewhere between 11:18am and 11:51am when Jackson woke up, got hold of some Propofol and self-administered. Throughout this period, Murray says he was, conveniently, out of the room.

So we can conclude, without doubt, that Murray never re-entered the room to find Jackson lifeless at 11:02am. It also seems highly unlikely Jackson could have injected himself, as Murray claims. Remember, Michael Jackson was phobic about needles. Not only that, it takes multiple draws, and therefore time, to actually get Propofol from vial to syringe, and Propofol causes pain upon injection, hence the need for Lidocaine to be administered to the injection site first. Drug addict or not, this method of self-administration by Jackson is inconceivable.

And this looks even more unlikely when we consider the amount of Propofol supposedly taken by Jackson. In his LAPD interview, Murray stated that he had only given Jackson 25mg of Propofol. So how does this compare to the levels of the drug that were actually found in Jackson's body?

The toxicology report found Propofol riddling Jackson's system – in his heart blood, his hospital blood, his femoral blood, his liver, his stomach contents and his urine. At the trial, Dr Steven Shafer, a Professor of Anaesthesiology at Columbia University gave his verdict based upon the toxicology report. He explained that the Propofol concentration found in Jackson's femoral blood was 2.6mg/ml. In a study showing what concentration of Propofol is needed for a person to stop breathing, it was found that at 2.3mg/ml around 50 per cent of patients would be expected to stop breathing. At 3.3mg/mg, 95 per cent of patients stop breathing. He continued by suggesting that if Jackson was given 2.5mg of Propofol, as Murray suggested, he would have stopped breathing for anywhere between 60 and 150 seconds. After three minutes, every patient would be expected to breathe again. [16]

But Shafer suggested this was not what happened.

The levels of Propofol found in Jackson's body were 82.5mg of residual Propofol. Dr Shafer showed the trial a table that illustrated how much Propofol goes into a patient's urine depending on the quantities they produce during surgery. A typical patient given 200mg of Propofol would have a reading of 70.71mg within four hours of administration. Jackson's was considerably higher, indicating that he must have received more Propofol than 200mg, way above the 25mg that Murray insisted he administered.[17] Going back to Murray's claim that Jackson administered Propofol to himself in the two minutes he was out of the room (though no one is entirely clear when these two minutes occurred), this would mean that he would have had to use at least two 100mg vials in two separate injections, and there's simply no way this can be done in two minutes, particularly when the first injection would knock the patient out.

So where does that leave us. With Conan Doyle's most famous of quotes: 'Once you eliminate the impossible, whatever remains, no matter how improbable, must be the truth.'[18]

The most probable scenario was that a Propofol infusion was started at approximately 9am, using Murray's unique and haphazard delivery system. But before that there was a bolus Propofol injection, given by Murray. As the levels of Propofol in Jackson increased, flowing freely into him from the infusion drip, so his breathing slowed down and his carbon dioxide levels would have gone up. At 10am Jackson was still breathing but more erratically. But there was no discernable problem to the naked eye and as he's not using the correct monitoring equipment, Murray doesn't see or recognise that there are problems. He may even be moving in and out of the room, distracted by his personal concerns. At around 11:30am to 11:45am Jackson stopped breathing, as there was no oxygen in his lungs. Some time before noon, Jackson died with the infusion still running.

So how does this scenario correspond with Murray's movements on the morning of 25 June? Murray made no phone calls between 8:49am and 9:23am, although two texts were evident on his phone records. So, in these 34 minutes, Murray could have begun administering Propofol and sat by the bed to monitor Jackson. Perhaps the texts were sent or received and checked in moments of boredom during this period while Murray was at the bedside. But, remember, at no point during his administration of Propofol did Murray place the pulse oximeter (cheap version though it was) on Jackson.[19] So Murray had no effective way of monitoring the singer.

At around 10:07am, when Jackson's breathing would have been slowing down, what was Murray doing? Completing a lengthy 22-minute phone call with Marissa Boni[20] that had started at 9:45am, so he could well have returned to the room after this call. If he had done so he would still have found Jackson breathing and would have detected a pulse. However, as we now know, he was not monitoring Jackson as rigorously as he should have been. Jackson's breathing would, by now, have been slowing and his carbon dioxide levels would be beginning to reach a critical level. When, we believe, Jackson finally stopped breathing sometime between 11:30am and 11:45am, where was Murray? Making a 32-minute call on his iPhone to his Nevada practice. This call began at 11:18am and ended at around 11:49am. He then called Bob Russell until approximately 11:51am, and finally he called Sade Anding.

So, we can see that the only truth that Dr Murray told the LAPD was that he went for a toilet break. And we are not even sure of what time that was.

The rest is mostly lies.

When Murray was supposedly finally alerted to Jackson's condition, he was talking on the phone to the cocktail waitress Sadie Anding. Earlier in the morning he had emailed an insurance agent for the 'This Is It' tour in London and said press reports that Jackson had health problems were entirely fallacious, but that Jackson was unwilling to undergo another medical in London and was not willing to release his medical records to the insurers. So at some point throughout the night he must have broached the subject of the insurer's requests with Jackson who had resolutely said no. This weighed heavily on Murray, as he had been tasked by AEG Live to persuade Jackson to do as the insurers demanded.

Perhaps it was then, and only then, that he had realised this would mean the tour was, in all likelihood, not going to happen.

Murray sends this email and takes all these calls for much of the time, we can assume, in an adjacent room. He certainly makes the final call to the cocktail waitress Sade Anding from another room because it's during this call that she claims Murray stops talking to her upon his return to Jackson's bedroom. This seems to be the moment that Murray first sees the stricken Jackson. He suggests, in his LAPD interview, that it's 11:02am, but we know that is not true, that it has to be between 11:51am and 12:02pm, because that's when phone records state he was calling Sade Anding, and that's when she says the conversation between them stopped and that the line between them eventually went dead. Part-way through this call the phone is either dropped by Murray or put in his pocket without being disconnected, and Sade Anding can hear 'coughing, mumbling, and sounds of panic' down the line.

What exactly is it that Dr Murray sees that makes him stop talking and either drop the phone or forget to turn it off in his panic and place it in his pocket? What makes someone actually drop a phone to the floor as opposed to saying, 'hold on, I'll call you right back'? What makes them put it into their pocket without turning it off?

From across the room as Murray re-entered, it wouldn't be clear to him that Jackson was not breathing. Surely in such circumstances the caller would likely say, 'Call you back', and then hang up and investigate? Unless, of course, Jackson had fallen out of bed and Murray panicked. But Jackson couldn't have fallen out of bed because he would have still been on the floor when Alberto Alvarez entered the room, and he said he saw Jackson on the bed. Murray told the LAPD detectives he couldn't lift Jackson *off* the bed (to do CPR later), so how could he lift him back *on* the bed in the first place?

So what exactly was it that the cocktail waitress heard? What, or who, was 'coughing, mumbling' and what were the 'sounds of panic'? Is Sade Anding even a reliable witness? A few days after Jackson's death, according to her court testimony, Murray spoke with Anding again and when she told him that she had been questioned by police, Murray allegedly told her not to speak with them again without his lawyer. He supposedly told her, 'I'm going to give you my lawyer's number and make sure before you speak to LAPD you have my lawyer present.'

This is perhaps a good point to ask the question: when Sadie Anding said she heard 'coughing and mumbling', is there an implication that somebody else, other than Murray or Jackson, might have been present in the room? In 2010 Joe Jackson told reporters that 'Murray's the fall guy There's other people, I think, involved with this whole thing.' And, certainly, LaToya Jackson was convinced that her brother was murdered and that Dr Murray was innocent and that, in her opinion, other people were involved. Could these 'other people' possibly explain the 'mumbling and coughing' that Anding heard? In a 2011 interview with CNN Entertainment, Piers Morgan asked LaToya directly, 'Do you think it's murder?' She responded by saying, 'Absolutely. I said it in the beginning and I believe it to this day. You must remember Michael told me repeatedly that they were going to kill him, that he was going to die.' She wouldn't name specific names but simply said that the people behind his murder were, 'The people who were controlling him'. Until LaToya provides detailed evidence of murder or reveals specific identities of those who she believes murdered her brother instead of hiding behind nameless accusations and tawdry publicity stunts, the claim that Michael Jackson was murdered by other people within the room on the night of 25 June is without substance.

Throughout the trial neither side disputed that Conrad Murray was absent from Jackson's room when the singer died. Murray didn't appear overly concerned about Jackson's well-being or whether he was in any danger on that June night. After all, why should Murray be concerned? He'd given the singer a cocktail of drugs including Propofol almost every night for the last two months, apparently without any problems.

But something did not go well this night.

Once Michael Jackson stopped breathing his body switched to anaerobic metabolism, his lactic acid levels began to build, and his organs quickly failed. It is likely that, at some time between 11:37am and 11:45am, Jackson went into cardiac arrest and, because he was sedated by the free-flowing Propofol, there was no way his body could react, rendering him unable to wake himself. Arrested blood circulation prevented delivery of oxygen and glucose to his body. And when cardiac arrest goes untreated for more than three to four minutes, brain injury is inevitable. For the best chances of survival and neurological recovery, immediate treatment is vital. But where was Dr Murray, his personal physician? He was in another room, and on the phone.

Murray would have known immediately upon discovering Jackson, that 20 minutes of pulseless arrest means the victim has virtually no chance of being successfully resuscitated, and that even if his heart is miraculously restarted, his brain will likely be severely damaged to a vegetative state. Upon seeing Jackson lifeless, Murray became frantic, so frantic that he, a *cardiologist* of all people, panicked and forgot how to do proper CPR. So frantic, that he forgot there was an Ambu Bag present in the room. And so frantic that he didn't call 911.

Cardiologists are extensively educated in all manner of the anatomy, physiology, health and disease processes of the human heart. It's their primary business. So when the paramedics eventually arrived at Carolwood following the delayed emergency call, and hooked up the cardiac monitor to Jackson in the bedroom of the mansion to reveal asystole – a flatline – Murray knew his patient was dead. He would have known all about advanced cardiac life support, *he* of all the people at the scene would have known the likelihood of resuscitating Jackson was essentially zero. He would have known, when he saw the flatline, and a few errant bits of electrical activity, that the game was over. And he would have known, at that moment, that he had been out of the room on his mobile phone for too long.

But Dr Murray didn't want to be the one to both *cause* the cardiac arrest of Michael Jackson *and pronounce* the singer dead. Hence his efforts to persuade the paramedics to take Jackson to UCLA Medical Center, and the reasons why he continued to protest that he could feel a pulse in Jackson's body when, quite evidently, the singer was dead.

Dr Conrad Murray gave a flawed and inaccurate version of what happened on 25 June in his interview with the LAPD two days later, despite having time to formulate his evidence. He refused to take the witness stand during his trial. All the evidence points to the fact that Murray administered greater levels of Propofol than he suggested, lethal levels in fact, and then left Jackson alone for a crucial period, during which time the singer suffered a cardiac arrest and died. This is what happened that night. They are simply the facts of how Michael Jackson passed away.

Also beyond doubt, is the fact that Michael Jackson was worth far more dead than he was alive. Everybody knew that, even Michael Jackson knew it. He actually said it.[21] So who really stood to gain the most from Jackson's death?

There are essentially three candidates: the Jackson family themselves, John Branca (his ex-attorney who had somehow managed to return to the fold) and AEG Live.

The Jackson family had been estranged from Michael for some time, with the exception of his mother, Katherine. Michael would even forbid his siblings entry to his Carolwood home without advance notice,[22] and his relationship with his father had been severely strained for many years. Michael had caused the collapse of The Jacksons' reunion concert by refusing to take part in it and, as a consequence, his siblings had all suffered financially. In fact, Michael even owed his brother, Randy, in excess of $1.6 million.[23]

But it went deeper than that. Michael had been a superstar and had scaled the heights of the music and entertainment industry. His brothers had been left in his wake. Jermaine, despite marrying the boss's daughter, had had an unsuccessful career at Motown, with only one hit single and when Michael was arrested on new child molestation charges in 2003, Jermaine went to publishers in New York offering a 'tell-all' book proposal.[24] At the time of Michael's death, Tito was performing as a guitarist in a jazz band in low-key gigs around LA, Jackie was running the Jesco record company, and Marlon was stacking shelves in San Diego. Within a year, the three of them attempted to cash in on the Jackson name in an ill-fated reality show that lasted just six episodes. La Toya continued her job as a reserve policewoman and Janet, the most successful of all Jackson's siblings, prospered as an actress and singer. But they all depended on Michael's earnings, usually distributed to them through their mother, Katherine. The LA attorney and radio host, Leo Terrell, said of the Jackson family, 'They all looked to Michael as an ATM machine.'[25] But despite helping to alleviate Michael of his money, the family all knew that Michael's spending was out of control and that he had a serious and chronic addiction to painkillers. And his trials and tribulations in the press, especially surrounding the accusations of child molestation, severely embarrassed the Jackson family.

But he was blood; Katherine loved her son and La Toya

claimed to love her brother. Throughout the years they had tried, at various intervals, to intervene and help him overcome his drug abuse. But each time they had failed. So could the Jackson family really consider the death of their son? He was the main earner within the family, but none of the other members of his family ever saw any of the massive financial rewards that he saw, only a drip-fed allowance from Katherine.[26] He was the source, they believed, of their financial woes, especially by refusing to perform with them any more, and they were undeniably jealous. To most of his brothers he had sabotaged their careers for his own selfish means. If Michael Jackson was dead, *and* there was no will, in all likelihood Katherine would immediately assume control of his estate, and that would include the lucrative Sony/ATV music catalogue. She would have known this, as would all of the family. Indeed, all the members of the Jackson family would have known that the death of any superstar was a lynchpin for creating an enormously profitable empire. Just look at the Elvis estate following his death.

But the moment John Branca emerged from the shadows with a copy of the 2002 will, of which he was an executor, the Jackson family realised that they had no control over the estate.

In fact, Jackson had made four wills; the first was in 1995 (with Branca as an executor then), the second in 1997 and then two in 2002. All the wills were remarkably similar and all provided for a consistent distribution of the estate. His three children, his mother and charities would benefit. No other members of the Jackson family were entitled to receive anything. Consequently, Branca throwing the will into the mix was a nightmare for the Jacksons, and so the Jackson family would collectively spend several years, and many thousands of dollars, unsuccessfully contesting the validity of the will. In their ignorance, the Jackson family could have had a financial motive to be part of Jackson's death, but if their aim was to control the estate after his demise, then it seriously backfired on them.

What of John Branca, the man fired by Jackson who suddenly re-emerged as part of Jackson's key team only days before the singer died? The man who remained as executor of the will for years after Jackson had instructed him to hand over all documents and all financial controls to other lawyers. It's fair to say that Branca has done extremely well out of his administration of the Jackson estate since the singer's death, as both Branca and co-executor John McClain receive a 10 per cent cut of all profits they secure for the King of Pop's estate.[27] Since Jackson died, Branca has overseen deals for the Cirque du Soleil show in Las Vegas; a Spike Lee documentary on Jackson; the 'Immortal' tour celebrating Jackson's legacy, which has grossed over $300 million; the 'This Is It' concert film with combined revenues exceeding $250 million; a new Sony recording deal in 2010 credited as the largest record deal in history; and the licensing of Jackson's music for use in video games, films and theatrical performances. A 10 per cent cut of all profits generated on these projects, and more, will prove extraordinarily lucrative for John Branca and his fellow executor, John McClain.

But Branca wasn't to know that no other wills existed and, upon his firing in 2003, may simply have held on to the 2002 will for insurance purposes. After all, as far as Branca might have been concerned, he was the man responsible for boosting Jackson's earnings earlier in the singer's career. He was pivotal in the production and release of Jackson's 'Thriller' video, he helped Jackson purchase ATV Music Publishing in 1985 and he brokered the purchase of Neverland. Branca was, without doubt, a critical driving force in Jackson's career and may have felt he was entitled to some sort of insurance based on his dealings and negotiations on Jackson's behalf over a number of decades.

The controversy over the validity and authenticity of this 2002 will (remember that Michael Jackson was apparently in New York on the day that the will was supposedly signed by him in Los Angeles), continues to rumble on in internet forums. There appears to be little indication as to why Barry Seigel resigned as a co-executor of Jackson's will but if it was genuine, why did Seigel want nothing to do with it and withdraw his name as an executor in 2003? Was he aware of something going on behind the scenes? Or was he simply unable to fulfil the duties requested of him? Like so many things in Jackson's life and death, these remain unanswered questions.

Whether this will was authentic or not, and it has never been proven to be fake, Branca was already a wealthy man and a respected lawyer. It is inconceivable that he had any part in the death of Michael Jackson. Why would he? Branca wasn't just a business associate of Jackson, but a close friend too.[28] Despite coming back into the Jackson fold in the week before the singer died, Branca really came into his own following Jackson's death and much of the financial success of the estate in the years since could only have happened with Branca's expertise and dedication. He simply saw an opportunity, being in possession of the will, and exploited it profitably. And he was totally within his rights, legally, to do so.

So that brings us to AEG Live.

AEG Live had a lot to lose. They had a significant stake in the 'This Is It' tour and, if Jackson reneged on the deal prior to leaving for London, suing him would be pointless as there was no way he could pay given his dire financial straits. AEG Live had taken $85 million in ticket sales, but this would have to be returned if and when Jackson cancelled. The large insurance policy that covered every one of the 50 shows[29] was invalid as Jackson hadn't released his medical records or agreed to another medical, and AEG Live even eventually dropped their $17.5 million insurance claim that they did have in place for the cancelled comeback concerts with Lloyd's of London.[30]

But the biggest blow for AEG Live would surely come on Wall Street, home to the world's two largest stock exchanges, the New York Stock Exchange and NASDAQ. AEG Live, a subsidiary of AEG, were not a publicly traded company in 2009 and therefore not listed on the New York Stock Exchange, but were determined to overtake Live Nation as the world's premier promoters.[31] If AEG Live could overtake Live Nation and become the largest concert promoters in the world, then they would be an attractive option if the company was listed for sale and eventually become a publicly traded company. In 2012, three years after the cancelled Jackson shows, AEG *was* put up for sale for $8 billion.[32] One can only imagine how much the sale value of the company might have been if the Jackson tour had gone ahead and been a huge commercial success. Such a tour might have catapulted AEG Live above Live Nation and, in these circumstances, the sale price of AEG would have increased correspondingly, making billionaire Philip Anschutz even wealthier.

But in order for these longer term plans to happen, first Jackson had to complete his 50 shows at the O2. In promising to bring Jackson to the O2, AEG Live had taken a major gamble, but if it backfired, and it appeared by 24 June it absolutely would, and Jackson failed to turn up or cancelled after just a handful of concerts, then it could be potentially disastrous for AEG, both in the short term with regards to initial financial losses, but also in the long term with their possible vision of selling the company for a vast sum on the world's financial markets.

In addition, if Jackson started the shows and then pulled out, AEG may also have been branded irresponsible and unprofessional for taking such a risk and not putting all the necessary processes in place, such as conducting due diligence in their checks on Conrad Murray or not being able to secure insurance for all 50 of the concerts. AEG Live would be threatened with a tarnished image within the world of concert promotion. Add to this the evidence, which would surely come out, of the debacle of Jackson's London press conference when the singer was drunk, his no-shows at rehearsals and his drug dependency, then AEG Live's professional judgement would have been exposed and seriously called into question. As far as AEG Live was concerned, Jackson either did the whole tour or did no tour at all, meaning he never left Los Angeles. Nothing, absolutely nothing, in between would work financially.

So, what would happen if Jackson didn't make it to London? Damage limitation would be managed and spun. AEG Live would have to reimburse ticket holders, but as we've seen, they rapidly devised an ingenious plan to make millions of dollars, possibly as much as $42.5 million from sending those ticket holders who requested their exclusive 3D tickets as a souvenir. They would also have to write off their $35 million investment. But, again they were shrewd; out of nowhere they began filming rehearsals two days before Jackson died. In addition, incredibly, almost to the hour of Jackson's death, they locked down the Staples Center and seized all footage from members of the cast, crew and production staff and, as Randy Phillips said, 'put all of our intellectual property into the vault at Staples Center so nobody could get near it or leave with it'.[33] There was no contract with Jackson establishing film rights for this footage, but AEG Live edited it into the *This Is It* film following Jackson's death and it has since become the most successful music film of all time, guaranteeing AEG Live, and the Jackson estate, enormous profits.[34] They certainly seemed to maximise their returns from what appeared to be a tragic end to Jackson's life.

Conspiracy theorists will always attempt to prove that Michael Jackson was murdered. As we have done, they will show that there are a number of parties who had much to gain from Jackson's death. True, there are many coincidences and many questions still left unanswered. For example, there is one other figure that comes into the equation with AEG Live. Tom Barrack was the man who put Jackson in touch with AEG Live in the first place, but only after he had helped Jackson out in the ongoing saga of Neverland. Barrack helped Jackson save Neverland from foreclosure in 2008 with $22.5 million of his own money from his firm Colony Capital, the same firm that, by chance perhaps, owned the mortgage on Conrad Murray's $1.6 million house. Under the terms of the agreement struck up between Jackson and Colony Capital in 2008 it said that, '…when Neverland is eventually sold, Colony will recoup its investment in the note plus the accrued interest, its management and upkeep expenses, and around 12 per cent of above that as a success fee. The rest will go to the estate.'

On 29 May 2015, it was announced that Neverland was up for sale. Now known by its original name of Sycamore Valley Ranch, the property was put on the market for an astonishing $100 million, $77.5 million more than Tom Barrack provided to Michael Jackson to save it from foreclosure in 2008. The property agent, Suzanne Perkins, confirmed when contacted that, 'Tom Barrack is the full owner of Neverland through a subsidiary'. The subsidiary is Colony Capital and in a statement a spokesperson for Michael Jackson's estate said, 'We are saddened at the prospect of the sale of Neverland which, under the agreement negotiated during Michael's lifetime, Colony has the right to sell.'[35]

Not a bad return for a property. Interestingly, Colony Capital also formed a partnership with the Saudi Prince Alwaleed to create the Raffles and Fairmont hotel chains. Prince Alwaleed was a good friend of Michael Jackson and partnered with the singer and Sony to form MJJ Productions, among other things. So this connection may have given Colony Capital, and Tom Barrack, a potential way into the Sony/ATV music catalogue, the most lucrative element of Jackson's business affairs.

But back to AEG Live, would they really push a fading and unfit pop star, in dire financial problems and with a chronic dependency on drugs to the limit?

The Jacksons took AEG Live to court and lost. And it appears that the shocking death of Michael Jackson has its likely true explanation in the testimony by Dr Chris Rogers and Professor Steven Shafer. That is, that Dr Conrad Murray administered a cocktail of drugs throughout the night, which then interacted with a large dosage of Propofol given to Jackson at some point on the morning of 25 June. While Dr Murray was on the phone and out of the room, the singer suffered a catastrophic cardiac arrest and, when Murray returned to the room, it was simply too late. AEG Live, John Branca and the Jackson family themselves, despite having their fingerprints somewhere on the periphery, were merely bystanders in this final tragic episode.

So, finally, what were the real circumstances that led to this tragic event?

On 24 June, Dr Murray was being pestered by AEG Live to persuade Michael Jackson to agree to release his medical records and undergo a further medical in London to get insurance for the final twenty shows. But Jackson had refused, and with such a refusal, the whole tour was in jeopardy. And with no tour, nobody would get paid – disaster for Murray and disaster for AEG Live.

Further up in the AEG Live hierarchy, whispers had probably already been heard that there were problems with the tour and the prospect that Jackson might back out after a few concerts. When those rumours reached the very top and the ears of

Philip Anschutz, the owner of AEG Live, something had to be done. Anschutz is an astute businessman who, despite never using a mobile phone or email, has amassed an estimated personal fortune of $7 billion. Avoiding the public spotlight, he made his fortune in oil and gas, as well as in real estate, railroads, telecommunications and sports and entertainment. Despite his wealth, he would have discovered the staggering financial outlay that had already left AEG Live's coffers in bringing Jackson to the O2. The original budget had more than quadrupled, and there was no end in sight to the potential over-spend. Anschutz may have been told that Jackson was proving unreliable, that he was refusing to submit his medical records and unwilling to undertake a second medical. Not only that, there was also a history of unreliability. So Anschutz may have made the decision to cut AEG's losses and pull out of the tour. It simply wasn't worth the effort any more and the potential harm to his company could be devastating. Especially as there may have been plans to sell the company in the future.

His decision may have filtered back down to the team close to Jackson. This team would have included Randy Phillips and Paul Gongaware. Dr Murray may have known too, or at least sensed what was in the offing, hence his desperation to convince Jackson to accept what the insurers in London wanted. At that point Murray realised it might be a good opportunity to get his contract signed, which he did at the last moment on 24 June. But it was too late.

When the news came through that Jackson was not going to agree to the requests of the insurance company, Anschutz may have decided that was the final straw, enough was enough, and he put into motion the chain of events that would have eventually led to the cancellation of the 'This Is It' tour. Murray may have found this out and, with the end of the tour, his hopes of financial salvation disappeared, hence his futile attempt at getting his

306

contract signed might somehow transpire to be his one and only opportunity to be paid.

On the night of 24 June, Murray's dreams had likely died minutes before his patient did. His email to Bob Taylor at 11:17am confirming that Jackson was not going to release his medical records and undertake a second medical simply confirmed that. But by then, Murray had unwittingly given Jackson the fatal dose of Propofol. With his mind on other things, Murray left the room to make a number of phone calls. It was during one of these phone calls that Sade Anding noticed that Murray wasn't sounding his usual self. It is more than likely that he was downbeat and distracted as it had just hit home that the tour was not going to happen and, consequently, he would not see any money. In the end it was perhaps the distraction of the tour ending that ironically contributed to his dereliction of duty. And this dereliction of duty ultimately caused the death of Michael Jackson.

Jackson's death simply saved AEG Live from officially cancelling the concerts. Through a series of circumstances and medical negligence, Dr Murray was in the wrong place at the wrong time and gave Michael Jackson the drugs that killed him. With the death of Michael Jackson, it was AEG Live, John Branca and, to a lesser extent, Tom Barrack who appear to be the major winners. Their financial gains were enormous, and between them they continue to accrue astonishing profits, and will do for the foreseeable future.

Dr Conrad Murray was jailed for four years for the involuntary manslaughter of Michael Jackson, but does the responsibility of his death actually lie with whoever allowed Dr Conrad Murray to care for the singer? After all, nobody performed any due diligence on his background. Nobody found out that he was not licensed to administer strong drugs in California.[36] And nobody bothered to even check his financial and criminal background. Katherine Jackson lodged a billion-dollar lawsuit against AEG Live in 2013 blaming them for the King of Pop's death, claiming that AEG Live employed, in Murray, an unfit doctor whose negligence led to Michael Jackson's overdose on sedatives and Propofol. However, the jury ruled in favour of AEG Live, saying that Murray was competent to serve as the singer's physician and that Jackson orchestrated his death with bad behaviour and poor choices. It appears that if the deviations from the standard of care had not happened, Michael Jackson would almost certainly be alive today, or at least have survived that particular night and morning.

But we have to remember that, long before these deviations from the standard of care, the relationship between Murray and Jackson was spiralling into disaster. The nature of their relationship, how it was set up, the amounts of money involved, and how badly adulterated it was, meant there was no way it could go well for the patient.

Having a personal physician can be a terrible idea for any celebrity, especially a celebrity who is also an addict with psychiatric problems. Systems have evolved and been put in place throughout the medical world to take care of patients, whatever their problems, and a personal physician in the employment of any celebrity can be vulnerable to deviations from normal standards of care. As we have seen, and as the world found out, Dr Conrad Murray was not, nor ever would have been, suited to be the caretaker of a complicated patient like Michael Jackson.

And from the moment they met, their fate was sealed.

13

All children, except one, grow up.
J.M. Barrie, *Peter Pan*

Throughout his life, and what a life it was, Jackson never grew up. In his childhood he was prevented from doing so and then, when older, he chose not to. Beginning as a child star, he was alienated from a normal life and, therefore, throughout his later years, was perhaps seeking to reclaim the childhood that was stunted as a result of arrested development.

Jackson was a consummate professional in the recording studio, indisputably the greatest showman of all time and a visionary in the way he adapted to shifting musical tastes and the new world of video in the 1980s. But he was, essentially, the boy who never grew up. His Neverland ranch was populated with a zoo, a railway track, a funfair, and inside were collections of toys and of Peter Pan paraphernalia. Jackson even had a secret vault at Neverland. When the ranch was raided in November 2003, this secret vault was almost overlooked by the officers. At the back of a wardrobe was a door that opened into a narrow stairwell, which descended to a tiny windowless room – approximately 8 ft by 7 ft. There were shelves with toys stacked on them. The walls were lined with images of children, some in nappies, all smiling broadly. One of the images is of the face of the tragic child star and Peter Pan's voice in the Disney animation, Bobby Driscoll.[1] It was Michael's private place. Whatever purpose it truly served, only he knew. There were three deadbolt locks on the inside of the door to ensure privacy. Very few had been in this special place with him. All those who alleged he abused them, without exception, didn't even know of its existence.

As a man, Jackson had no idea of responsibility, particularly with his finances, and his relationship with children was never one with the classic paedophilic undertones of overt sexual interest in children. He was described as a classic paedophile in the Gavin Arvizo[2] court case, a predator who groomed and then sexually abused boys. But if this was actually true, then where were these other boys he abused? Aside from Gavin Arvizo, whose accusations were entirely discredited, only four other alleged victims have come forward.[3] None of these alleged victims have been able to provide irrefutable evidence that has resulted in a clear judgement being passed on Jackson. One of Jackson's problems was by reaching financial agreements with any or all of his accusers it was perceived by the general public that he was guilty. Throughout his trials, there was never any conclusive, credible or direct evidence to confirm that Jackson abused any boys. He was deemed to have a pattern 'of questionable and abnormal behaviour with boys', but it is almost certain that Jackson's sexuality – or in reality – lack of it, was simply a part of his arrested development and was uniquely combined with who he was and how dysfunctional his life had become. What was normal to Michael Jackson would have been incomprehensible to most people. In the end Jackson admitted he just enjoyed the company of children, he could relate to them and he felt secure with them, although, on occasion, his behaviour was likely entirely inappropriate.

It's hardly surprising though that he had such an affinity with children when the other people who surrounded him were all adults who were, generally, unscrupulous 'yes' men, enablers, criminals and opportunists. From his father, Joe, to AEG Live and a catalogue of names in between, they guided Jackson only for their own benefit, and while Jackson made astronomical amounts of money, so did those around him. The authoritative figures that truly helped Michael Jackson forge his career were, in turn, rejected, most likely because they reminded him of the abusive authority of his father Joe. In turn he would be alone again, vulnerable, and so the cycle continued.

This pattern was part of his addiction, an addiction that was characterised by compulsive drug seeking and use, despite the knowledge of the harmful and inevitable consequences. A few who cared about him tried to help (over the last two decades there had been at least three failed attempts at intervention and stints in rehab for Jackson), but the majority fed his addiction. As enablers do.

Michael Jackson's addiction to drugs most probably began in 1984 following his accident on the Pepsi commercial shoot, a venture he didn't even want anything to do with and he was only there after much persuasion from his brothers. From then on, his desire for prescription medicine became, over the years, a chronic addiction so severe that he, an intelligent, gifted and rational person, would risk death on a regular basis.

Only an addict really knows what that means, truly knows what addiction is, and only their family and loved ones know how utterly destructive it can be. Perhaps, as soon as he took that first painkilling medicine in 1984, Jackson's fate was inevitably sealed. And the progressive chronic disease that is addiction will only ever end in one of three ways if left untreated: jail, institution or death.

Jackson narrowly escaped jail. His status prevented him from being institutionalised, although at times his behaviour warranted it. There was always only going to be one outcome for Michael Jackson. In the end it was an early death. It was always destined to be.

Like Peter Pan, Michael Jackson was never going to grow old. He was one of the few true superstars that you could never imagine as an old man, playing with his grandchildren, counting shooting stars, sipping lemonade and laughing about who he used to be.

But for his loving audience, the legacy of Michael Jackson as one of the greatest entertainers to have ever lived will remain forever. After all, the dead are never dead to us, until we have forgotten them.

* * *

Founded by a group of businessmen from San Francisco in 1906, the Great Mausoleum at the Forest Lawn Memorial Park in Glendale, California,[4] is the final resting place of Michael Jackson. The founder of the cemetery was Dr Hubert Eaton who was an extremely close friend of none other than Walt Disney.[5] Eaton firmly believed that life after death would be a joyous experience and that most cemeteries were simply grey and depressing monuments to death. He wanted to create something that was the complete opposite of this. He wanted to create a cemetery that was filled with towering trees, sweeping lawns and splashing fountains with beautiful memorial architecture instead of drab, stone monuments. What he created wasn't so much a cemetery but a memorial park, art gallery, museum and architectural showcase, not to mention a Hollywood tourist attraction. Within the grounds there are more Hollywood superstars buried than in any other cemetery in the world.

For decades, Forest Lawn refused entrance to blacks, Jews and

Chinese. Now, however, it welcomes everyone and attracts over 1 million visitors per year – as long as they pay.

However, not one of them has been allowed to visit Michael Jackson's gravesite.

The singer's grave lies somewhere in the massive marble and concrete building known as the Great Mausoleum, a building that is strictly off limits to visitors[6] and one in which the precise location of Michael Jackson's golden casket might remain a mystery forever.[7]

For the 30 days immediately after his funeral, security guarded the site 24 hours a day, seven days a week and, to this day, fans are only able to leave flowers outside the crypt while pressing their noses against the impenetrable double-paned and tinted glass window in an attempt to glimpse inside the building to try to spot Jackson's grave.[8]

Michael Jackson was finally buried on 3 September 2009, 10 weeks to the day since his death. His family and 200 of their closest friends gathered to bid farewell to the King of Pop.

It was 90 minutes after the scheduled start of the service before the 26 cars carrying the Jackson family arrived at Forest Lawn Cemetery. His five brothers, each wearing one sequined glove, carried the singer's casket, adorned with flowers, onto the outdoor stage where his three children placed a crown on top of their father's coffin. After the opening prayer, Gladys Knight sang 'His Eye Is On The Sparrow' and then Clifton David sang 'Never Can Say Goodbye'. Following this, out of the glare of the media spotlight, friends and family took to the lectern to spontaneously celebrate Michael's life. When the service finished after one hour, his brothers carried Jackson's casket into the Great Mausoleum where he was placed in his crypt at 9:43pm.

It seems deeply ironic that Michael Jackson, a man who craved and revelled in the adulation and adoration of his fans is now buried in relative obscurity, out of touch and out of sight of the fans for whom he cared so much.

It's not known if the security surrounding Jackson's final resting place at Forest Lawn will ever be lifted, but even if it is, one man who will never visit the grave is Conrad Murray. Despite being released from jail in 2013, a source told HollywoodLife.com that Murray would not be visiting the grave. 'Out of respect for Katherine and the family, he will grieve, just like they are, but from a distance. He loved Michael – and he too can't believe his dear friend is gone,' the source said.[9]

Michael Jackson and Dr Conrad Murray had a relationship that was intense but brief. It ended with Jackson losing his life, and with Murray's life being all but destroyed.

In a grim forewarning of what was to come, Michael Jackson supposedly once said to Conrad Murray, 'You know, for the rest of your life and my life our names will become inseparable.' When the doctor asked Jackson what he meant, the singer replied, 'I am a clairvoyant.'

***

Michael Joseph Jackson, singer, died on 25 June 2009. He is survived by his three children.

ACKNOWLEDGEMENTS

MATT: My thanks go to the many people who have helped to bring this book to fruition. To list them all would be an impossible task, but there are a few that deserve a special mention. Throughout the writing, two books in particular have been a great source of reference and inspiration: the works by Randall Sullivan and J. Randy Taraborrelli are, without doubt, the definitive Michael Jackson biographies and exhibit a level of research and writing that one can only aspire to. Without these two books, writing this book would have been a much more formidable task. In addition, Lynton Guest's book about the trials and tribulations of the singer in his later life was also invaluable. The advice given by Yolanda Pascual regarding the medical and clinical information has proved indispensable and the constant doubt from my wonderful son, Thomas Richards, that this book would ever be completed proved to be an unwitting source of encouragement. Many thanks to all at Blink Publishing, especially Perminder Mann and our editor, Emily Thomas, who have been guiding lights throughout. But, above all, there are two people without whom this book would never have happened. Firstly, my co-writer Mark Langthorne has been the best writing partner any author could wish for. He has been a constant source of enthusiasm, information, encouragement and creativity, and he has ensured every obstacle we have faced has been overcome with a mixture of determination, Yorkshire grit and northern humour. Every meeting, phone call and email has proved inspirational, and perhaps the best compliment I can give him is that not only is he the best writing partner any author could wish for, but he's also one of the best friends anyone could hope to find. And finally, the other person without whom I couldn't have written this book is my partner, Lucy Abbott. Without fail and without complaint, she has sustained me during the many months of research and writing and, as well as providing me with untold cups of tea, has offered reassurance, confidence, encouragement, inspiration and, more than anything, all the love in the world. Thank you Lucy for all your support and for making my world an infinitely better place with you in it.

MARK: Aside from all the thanks Matt has mentioned already, I want to reiterate that no biography exists in isolation. With that in mind I want to thank all the fans who assisted us in the writing of this book, through their dedication and commitment to Michael Jackson, and we hope in some way we have tried to give them some answers.

I want to thank above everyone else my co-writer Matt who is an incredible source of inspiration and a brilliant writer. His level of detail, dedication and commitment is formidable, but above all he is a warm, genuine and caring person who I am really proud to call my writing partner, and without whom this book certainly would not have happened.

I have to also thank Marc, who never falters in his encouragement and enthusiasm; he amazes and surprises me everyday. And thanks to Roland for his consideration and honesty.

Thanks too from me to Emily, Perminder and all the team at Blink for their support.

And a final thanks must go to Michael Jackson himself. Without him the world is a less colourful place.

SELECT BIBLIOGRAPHY

Books

Barrie, J.M., *Peter Pan* (Puffin Books, 1911)

Borsboom, Jos, *Michael Jackson – The Icon* (self-published, Lulu. com, 2011)

Cascio, Frank, *My Friend Michael* (HarperCollins, 2011)

Dimond, Diane, *Be Careful Who You Love – Inside The Michael Jackson Case* (Atria Books, 2005)

Greenburg, Zach O'Malley, *Michael Jackson, Inc. – The Rise, Fall & Rebirth of a Billion-Dollar Empire* (Atria Books, 2014)

Guest, Lynton, *The Trials of Michael Jackson* (Aureus Publishing, 2006)

Halperin, Ian, *Unmasked – The Final Years of Michael Jackson* (Pocket Books, 2009)

Hughes, Geraldine, *Redemption – The Truth Behind The Michael Jackson Child Molestation Allegations* (Branch & Vine, 1994)

Jackson, La Toya, *Starting Over* (Gallery Books, 2011)

319

Jackson, Michael, *Moonwalk* (Arrow Books, 1988)

Jager, Phyllis, *Michael Jackson – The Autopsy Is In… It Was Homicide* (Script To Screen Productions Inc., 2009)

Moriarty, Karen Dr, *Defending A King – His Life & Legacy* (Outskirts Press, 2012)

Roberts, Chris, *Michael Jackson – The King of Pop* (Carlton Books, 2009)

Rowe, Leonard, *What Really Happened To Michael Jackson – The Evil Side of the Entertainment Industry* (Linell-Diamond Enterprises, 2010)

Sullivan, Randall, *Untouchable: The Strange Life & Tragic Death of Michael Jackson* (Grove/Atlantic, 2012)

Taraborrelli, J. Randy, *Michael Jackson – The Magic & The Madness* (Sidgwick & Jackson, 2003)

Vogel, Joseph, *Man In The Music – The Creative Life & Work of Michael Jackson* (Sterling, 2011)

Whitfield, Bill and Javon Beard, *Remember The Time – Protecting Michael Jackson In His Final Days* (Scribe, 2014)

Websites
www.abcnews.com
www.bbc.co.uk
www.billboard.com
www.bloomberg.com
www.cnn.com
www.dailymail.co.uk
www.dailymichael.com
www.essentialdrugs.org
www.forbes.com
www.essentialdrugs.org
www.health.harvard.edu
www.hollywoodreporter.com

www.huffingtonpost.com

www.ibtimes.com

www.independent.co.uk

www.latimes.com

www.metnews.com

www.michaeljacksoneurope.mjjcommunity.com

www.michaeljacksonallegations.com

www.mirror.co.uk

www.mjfancommunity.com

www.mtv.com

www.muzikfactory.co.uk

www.nbcnews.com

www.nydailynews.com

www.nytimes.com

www.people.com

www.radaronline.com

www.rollingstone.com

www.scientificamerican.com

www.standard.co.uk

www.teammichaeljackson.com

www.telegraph.co.uk

www.theguardian.com

www.the poisonreview.com

www.time.com

www.tmz.com

www.trialsandheirs.com

www.vindicatemj.wordpress.com

ENDNOTES

1

[1] Transcript of 911 call released by Los Angeles Fire Department, 27 June 2009.

[2] Official court transcript: People v. Conrad Murray.

[3] Official transcript of Los Angeles Police Department: 'Recorded Interview of Conrad Murray', 27 June 2009.

[4] TMZ.com, 'Starline Tourists See Jackson Drama Unfold', 26 June 2009, www.tmz.com.

[5] Emergency Medical Services.

[6] Official court transcript: People v. Conrad Murray.

[7] Official court transcript: People v. Conrad Murray.

[8] Official court transcript: People v. Conrad Murray.

[9] Spontaneous circulation is a palpable pulse.

[10] Official court transcript: People v. Conrad Murray.

[11] Official court transcript: People v. Conrad Murray.

[12] Frank Dileo interview with Raffles van Exel, 4 November 2009.

[13] Official court transcript: People v. Conrad Murray.

[14] Official court transcript: People v. Conrad Murray.

2

[1] It was built by the eccentric theatre developer Horst Schmidt and had 1.7 acres of lush grounds graced by Spanish Mediterranean Revival architectural features.

[2] At the time of his death, the collection had vanished. Valued now in excess of $1 billion by some, its whereabouts and ownership remain unknown. (Rapti Gupta, 'Michael Jackson's Vegas Rental Up for Grabs at $19.5 million', *Realty Today*, 5 August 2014, www.realtytoday.com).

[3] When Sony and ATV merged in 1995 they became the second largest music publisher in the world. As well as owning The Beatles' catalogue and many Elvis Presley hits written by Jerry Leiber and Mike Stoller, they also owned publishing rights to hits by The Searchers, The Kings, Donovan, The Moody Blues, Roy

Orbison and over 55,000 country hits, as well as 125,000 songs owned by Famous Music, including 'Footloose' and 'Moon River'. In 2012 Sony/ATV acquired EMI's catalogue to become the largest music catalogue in the world with the copyright to over 2 million songs and annual revenues in excess of $1.26 billion.

[4] Released in August 1979, *Off The Wall* sold in excess of 20 million copies worldwide and Michael Jackson received a Grammy Award for Best Male R&B Vocal Performance. In his book *Michael Jackson: The Magic & The Madness*, J. Randy Taraborrelli writes: 'The album showcased an adult Michael Jackson, for the first time a real artist, not just someone's vocal stylist. Michael Jackson had officially arrived.'

[5] The video for 'Thriller' was directed by Hollywood director John Landis, who had recently seen success with his horror film, *An American Werewolf in London.*

[6] rsiwebadmin, 'Triumph & Tragedy: The Life of Michael Jackson', *Rolling Stone India*, 25 August 2009, www.rollingstoneindia.com.

[7] J. Randy Taraborrelli, *Michael Jackson, The Magic & the Madness* (Sidgwick & Jackson, 2003).

[8] 'Billie Jean' alone sold 5.25 million copies worldwide and Jackson received sole writing credit.

[9] Jim Miller, 'Is Rock On The Rocks?', *Newsweek*, 19 April 1982.

[10] Mark Ellen, 'Are the Stars Out Tonight…', *Smash Hits*, 6 January 1983.

[11] This was the last British interview that Michael Jackson ever gave.

[12] When the Los Angeles Police Department searched the property in November 1993 in relation to the Jordan Chandler case, they found that Michael's private two-level suite, the only bedroom in the house with a private entrance, was full of his trademark clutter including framed pictures of toddlers that decorated the walls and a hanging poster of Peter Pan.

[13] Katherine Esther Scruse was born in 1930 in Russell County, Alabama to Prince Scruse and Martha Upshaw.

[14] The children were Maureen, Sigmund, Tariano, Jermaine, La Toya, Marlon, Michael, Stephen and Janet. Another child, Brandon, died within hours of birth (he was one of a set of premature twins with Marlon).

[15] Randall Sullivan, *Untouchable: The Strange Life & Tragic Death of Michael Jackson* (Grove/Atlantic, 2012).

[16] It was at The Regal Theatre in Chicago that The Jackson Five would open for established Motown acts Gladys Knight & The Pips and Bobby Taylor & The Vancouvers in August 1968.

[17] They actually recorded four songs that were released on two 45rpm discs: 'Big Boy' was released with 'You've Changed' as the B-side and this was followed up with 'We Don't Have To Be Over 21' with 'Jam Session' as the B-side.

[18] At this point, Motown were already overseeing such talent as Stevie Wonder, The Supremes, Smokey Robinson, The Temptations and Diana Ross.

[19] Berry Gordy had wanted Joe Jackson to sign a standard
Motown contract, which would have tied The Jackson Five
to the label for a minimum of seven years. Joe managed to
convince Gordy to adjust the contract to a one-year obligation,
which he signed but failed to read that The Jackson Five were
prevented from recording for another label for five years
from the expiration of the deal, that Motown were under no
obligation to record or promote the group for five years, that
they would only be paid upon release of a record – not simply
the recording of a record – and, as it turned out, each member
of The Jackson Five would only earn one per cent for every
record actually sold. One year or seven, Gordy was going to be
the major winner in this deal.

[20] Michael Jackson was born on 29 August 1958 so he was actually
only days away from his tenth birthday.

[21] The new name was decided during a discussion between Berry
Gordy and Motown producer/composer Deke Richards. Richards
was also a co-writer and co-producer of 'I Want You Back'.

[22] '500 Greatest Songs of All Time', *Rolling Stone*, 7 April 2011.

[23] For the first time Michael's mother, Katherine, and his other
siblings, La Toya, Janet and Randy, joined them. Katherine would
later recall that she thought the size of the house was twice as
large as the one they had left in Gary, Indiana.

[24] During their touring, the boys would be accompanied by a
tutor, Rose Fine, who ensured that they continued their schooling
whilst travelling.

[25] Michael performed the song at the Oscar ceremony but the song lost out to 'The Morning After' from *The Poseidon Adventure*.

[26] It is not known exactly why Katherine Jackson didn't follow through with her divorce of Joe in 1973. There are rumours that representatives of the Jehovah's Witnesses intervened, although divorce is permitted amongst Jehovah's Witnesses if sexual relations outside marriage had taken place. Another theory is that Katherine feared bad press if she divorced Joe. In her 1990 autobiography, *My Family, the Jacksons*, Katherine wrote, 'I didn't think I could forgive him for what he'd done. I remained in this muddled state for longer than I'd care to admit: seven years. During this period I heard rumours of other affairs. But I still couldn't bring myself to file for divorce, even though a couple of times I came close.'

[27] 'Music & Me' only sold 2 million copies worldwide and reached a lowly 92 on the US *Billboard* 200 Album Chart while 'Forever Michael' only reached Number 101.

[28] Michael Jackson, *Moonwalk* (Arrow Books, 1988).

[29] 'Show You The Way To Go' reached Number 28 on the US *Billboard* Hot 100 and Number 1 in the UK charts.

[30] *Goin' Places* only sold 500,000 copies worldwide and is considered their lowest-selling album.

[31] Sidney Lumet was a respected Hollywood film director who had overseen a string of classic films from the 1950s onwards including *12 Angry Men*, *Serpico* and *Dog Day Afternoon*. Following Michael Jackson's death, Lumet was quoted: 'Michael

Jackson is the most gifted entertainer to come down the pike since, I guess, James Dean. He's a brilliant actor and dancer, probably one of the rarest entertainers I have ever worked with. His talent is awesome.'

[32] Astoria Studios was originally built in 1920 and opened by Adolph Zukor. Between 1920 and 28, New York was the centre of the fledgling film industry and all the greats of the silent era worked here from Valentino to Swanson to Gish. The first two Marx Brothers films were made at Astoria and Paramount Pictures based their studio filming there until they moved to California in 1932. From 1942 to 70 the US Army used the studio for their productions and it wasn't until 1971 that commercial film and TV production returned to the studio.

[33] The film only took $13.1 million at the box office and led to Hollywood steering away from all-black productions for a number of years. It did receive four Academy Award nominations, though, for Best Art Direction, Best Costume Design, Best Original Movie Score and Best Cinematography. It failed to win in any category.

[34] Legendary film critic Roger Ebert said that, 'Michael Jackson fills the role with humour and warmth'.

[35] They were overseen throughout the whole process by CBS executive producers Bobby Colomby and Mike Atkinson.

[36] 'Blame It On The Boogie' was actually written by English singer-songwriter Mick Jackson in 1977 with the hope of it being sold to Stevie Wonder. Mick Jackson had a minor hit with it himself, reaching Number 61 in the USA, but when The Jacksons

released their version it returned them to the USA charts after five flop singles.

[37] The song was edited from its eight-minute album version to a three-minute radio version, which was released as the single version.

[38] 'Shake Your Body…' was co-written with his brother, Randy.

[39] *The Pawnbroker* was directed by Sidney Lumet, who would also later work with Michael Jackson on *The Wiz*.

[40] Co-written with Louis Johnson.

[41] 'This Place Hotel' was originally called 'Heartbreak Hotel' but the record company changed the title to avoid confusion with the Elvis Presley song. Michael Jackson wasn't influenced by Presley in any way and in his 1988 autobiography *Moonwalk* Jackson wrote, 'People thought if I kept living in seclusion the way I was, I might die the way he did. The parallels aren't there as far as I'm concerned and I was never much for scare tactics. Still, the way Elvis destroyed himself interests me, because I don't ever want to walk those grounds myself.'

[42] La Toya contributed the scream to the beginning of 'This Place Hotel'.

[43] Michael had the original Hayvenhurst house demolished and rebuilt as a Tudor mansion, his family living in his apartment while the work was being completed. In the grounds Jackson assembled a collection of birds and animals, including a giraffe named Jabbar.

[44] 'Billie Jean' was almost called 'Not My Lover' as Quincy Jones felt listeners might immediately think of the tennis player, Billie Jean King.

[45] Rod Temperton's third song on the album was provisionally titled 'Starlight' also.

[46] The two Number 1 songs from the album were 'Billie Jean' and 'Beat It'.

[47] He had recorded only one Top 10 record in his time at Motown: 'Let's Get Serious', produced by Stevie Wonder.

[48] Co-written with Marlon Jackson.

[49] Co-written with Randy Hansen.

[50] The song was originally intended for the *Thriller* album, and was planned to be a duet with Freddie Mercury.

[51] The tour was going to be called 'The Final Curtain' as it was considered to be the last tour the brothers would undertake together.

[52] The original tour was set to run for 40 shows and the projected gross revenue was $30 million. After expenses the group would receive 85 per cent, roughly $3.4 million for each Jackson group member.

[53] Darvocet was a narcotic pain reliever that was withdrawn from the USA market in November 2010 as it was proved that the drug resulted in adverse heart side effects. Prior to these findings,

it was known that the drug was habit-forming. Percocet was used to relieve moderate to severe pain and is also known to be habit-forming.

3

---

[1] Jackson donated the $1.5 million to the Brotman Medical Center in Culver City, California where he received treatment for his burns. The Center was subsequently renamed the Michael Jackson Burn Center.

[2] Australian billionaire, Robert Holmes à Court owned the catalogue.

[3] 'We Are The World' sold over 20 million copies worldwide and made over $10 million for the USA for Africa charity.

[4] Directed by Oscar winner Francis Ford Coppola, this film was, at the time, the most expensive film ever produced on a per-minute basis. The 17-minute film cost $30 million, which averaged out at $1.76 million per minute.

[5] Part of the publicity for this film included Jackson deciding to be photographed inside a hyperbaric chamber under the premise that he sleeps there every night in order to extend his life to 150 years. The fictional story made headlines around the world, which created ideal publicity for his upcoming sci-film.

[6] Michael was credited as co-producer.

[7] Michael wanted to release a three-disc album.

[8] There was an additional 'bonus track' on the CD and digital download editions, 'Leave Me Alone', composed by Jackson.

[9] The two tracks he had no part in composing were 'Just Good Friends', written by Terry Britten and Graham Lyle, and 'Man In The Mirror', composed by Glen Ballard and Siedah Garrett.

[10] It entered the chart at Number 1.

[11] The five singles were 'I Just Can't Stop Loving You', 'Bad', 'The Way You Make Me Feel', 'Man In The Mirror' and 'Dirty Diana'. By contrast, 'I Just Can't Stop Loving You' was the only single that reached Number 1 in the UK.

[12] The *Los Angeles Times* review called *Bad* '…a respectable successor to *Thriller*', while *Rolling Stone* magazine stated, 'Comparisons with *Thriller* are unimportant, except this one: even without a milestone recording like 'Billie Jean', *Bad* is a better record.'

[13] Lisa D. Campbell, *Michael Jackson: The King of Pop* (Branden Publishing, 1993).

[14] *Bad* won the Grammy for Best Engineered Recording – Non-Classical.

[15] The tour was sponsored by Pepsi and began in Tokyo at the Korakuen Stadium on 12 September 1987 and ended on 27 January 1989 at the Memorial Sports Arena in Los Angeles. In between there were 127 concerts across 15 countries and the tour was seen by almost 4.5 million fans.

[16] Named after the fantasy island in J.M. Barrie's *Peter Pan*.

[17] Sycamore Ranch had been on the market for $35 million.

[18] Neverland would also cost Jackson a reported $4 million annually in operating costs.

[19] According to Diane Dimond's book, *Be Careful Who You Love* (Atria Books, 2005), Jordan Chandler had already met Michael Jackson. Once they met by chance at the Golden Temple Restaurant in Los Angeles when Jordan was five years old, and following Jackson's accident filming the Pepsi commercial, Jordan wrote Michael a 'Get Well' note and sent it to the hospital with a picture and his phone number. Michael apparently called Jordan that same day to thank him.

[20] *Dangerous* entered the UK album charts at Number 1 and also peaked in seven other territories. It eventually sold over 35 million copies worldwide.

[21] In the UK, seven singles from the album broke into the Top 10 which equalled Jackson's record set previously by *Bad*. This record was broken by Calvin Harris in 2013 who had eight Top 10 singles from his album *18 Months*.

[22] In her book, *Be Careful Who You Love*, Diane Dimond states that Jackson had been phoning Chandler regularly throughout the tour, calling him for two or three hours at a time from wherever in the world his tour schedule had taken him.

[23] Released in 1973, *The Exorcist* was directed by William Friedkin and was named the scariest film of all time by *Entertainment Weekly*.

[24] Studies of sexual offenders have found that deliberate tactics are often used to select victims and engage them in sexual abuse. One such tactic is to charm, to be likeable, to radiate sincerity and truthfulness. This is all crucial in gaining access to children. Some offenders will attempt to establish peer relationships with people much younger than themselves, as they prefer the company of children to adults, rather than looking for age-appropriate relationships. They will also attempt to establish a trusting relationship by spending time with children and listening to them. They give the child presents and compliments, and use these gifts and trickery to manipulate the child and silence them into keeping any assault a secret. Was this a pattern that Jackson was following in his relationship with Jordan Chandler?

[25] Jordan Chandler's father, Evan, kept a diary that noted this chronology. His 29 March entry reads: 'That night Michael and Jordie watched *The Exorcist* and Jordie got scared. Michael asked Jordie if he wanted to stay with him so he wouldn't feel frightened. Jordie said yes and they slept together. This was the first time Jordie slept in the same bed with Michael. There was no sexual contact.' The following day's entry, 30 March, reads 'When June woke up she went into Jordie's room and noticed his bed was made. When she asked Jordie where he had slept last night, he told her he slept in bed with Michael. June was upset and told Jordie not to do it again.' – *Be Careful Who You Love* by Diane Dimond.

[26] The LAPD claimed to have found a youngster who had stated Jackson had molested him/her. The sex of this child wasn't revealed, but there doesn't ever seem to have been any allegations against Jackson made by girls and there are no photographs of Jackson with young girls. He is only ever photographed with young boys.

[27] Actress Carrie Fisher was amongst his patients and in her book *Shockaholic*, she claims that he was known as the 'dentist to the stars'.

[28] Jackson's team suggested a counter offer of $1.05 million, which consisted of a proposed deal for the Fox Network to 'buy' three screenplays written by Evan Chandler for $350,000 over a three-year period. Chandler rejected this, and also a second offer, which had reduced to just $350,000 – *Be Careful Who You Love* by Diane Dimond.

[29] J.Randy Taraborrelli, *Michael Jackson: The Magic and the Madness* (Sidgwick & Jackson, 1991)

[30] At a personal cost to him of $10 million.

[31] Upon entry into the UK, 18 vials of medicine were found in Jackson's suitcase.

[32] Neverland had already been subjected to a police search in August 1993, and publicity surrounding the search became major news, sparking headlines around the world.

[33] This involved examining, photographing and videotaping his entire body when naked, including his genitalia and buttocks. Authorities wanted to use this photographic evidence to compare them with the descriptions his accuser, Jordan Chandler, had previously given to the police in order to prove or disprove the alleged child molestation by Jackson. Initial media reports citing law enforcement agencies suggested that Chandler's description of Jackson's genitalia did not match the photographic evidence, although later a story emerged following an interview given to *Vanity Fair* by District Attorney Thomas Sneddon, that

the photos did match Chandler's description, which, actually, appeared to be no more than an educated guess.

[34] Jim Newton, 'Jackson's Sister Says She Believes he is a Molester', *Los Angeles Times*, 9 December 1993.

[35] J. Randy Taraborrelli, *Michael Jackson: The Magic & The Madness* (Sidgwick & Jackson, 2003).

[36] J. Randy Taraborrelli, *Michael Jackson: The Magic & The Madness* (Sidgwick & Jackson, 2003).

[37] Evan Chandler committed suicide on 5 November 2009. He was found dead in his New Jersey apartment after shooting himself in the head. There was no suicide note. He was 65 years old. His son, Jordan Chandler, now lives under an assumed name in Long Island, New York.

[38] Lynton Guest, *The Trials of Michael Jackson* (Aureus Publishing, 2006).

[39] J. Randy Taraborrelli, *Michael Jackson: The Magic & The Madness* (Sidgwick & Jackson, 2003).

[40] J. Randy Taraborrelli, *Michael Jackson: The Magic & The Madness* (Sidgwick & Jackson, 2003).

[41] J. Randy Taraborrelli, *Michael Jackson: The Magic & The Madness* (Sidgwick & Jackson, 2003).

[42] J. Randy Taraborrelli, *Michael Jackson: The Magic & The Madness* (Sidgwick & Jackson, 2003).

[43] Others had advised Michael that John Branca's influence in his affairs had grown too large and they remained apart for three years, but Branca was to be rehired, fired and rehired again by Jackson at a various stages throughout his career.

[44] The first disc was a compilation of greatest hits while the second disc was entirely new material or cover versions.

[45] The debut single from the album, 'Scream/Childhood' entered the *Billboard* Hot 100 at Number 5 but failed to go any higher. After 'You Are Not Alone' topped the *Billboard* Hot 100, the other singles released fared poorly. 'Earth Song' didn't even chart on the Hot 100, 'They Don't Care About Us' stalled at Number 30 and 'Stranger In Moscow' could only reach Number 91 in the US *Billboard* Hot 100.

[46] Interestingly, the only concerts of the tour to be in the USA were two concerts held in Hawaii, and the whole tour began with a free concert in Brunei in celebration of the fiftieth birthday of the Sultan of Brunei.

[47] Jackson collapsed while rehearsing for an HBO special, which they hoped would be watched by 250 million people worldwide. He collapsed at the Beacon Theater at 5pm and was rushed to Beth Israel Medical Center North on New York's Upper East Side. He was given oxygen and was said to be suffering from low blood pressure. It later emerged he was suffering from a viral infection that brought on an irregular heartbeat.

[48] The Associated Press, 19 January 1996.

[49] Randall Sullivan, *Untouchable: The Strange Life & Tragic Death of Michael Jackson* (Grove/Atlantic, 2012).

[50] J. Randy Taraborrelli, *Michael Jackson: The Magic & The Madness* (Sidgwick & Jackson, 2003).

[51] J. Randy Taraborrelli, *Michael Jackson: The Magic & The Madness* (Sidgwick & Jackson, 2003).

[52] Apparently, on their wedding night, Michael did not sleep with Debbie, but stayed in another room at the Sheraton on the Park Hotel in Sydney with an 'assistant', in order to get some rest.

[53] Debbie Rowe would receive a reported $8 million divorce settlement in exchange for giving Jackson full custody rights of the two children. This consisted of $6 million plus ownership of the couple's Beverly Hills mansion.

[54] In documents filed in a California court in 2005 for a custody hearing, Debbie Rowe claimed she was artificially inseminated by an anonymous sperm donor before giving birth to both children.

[55] The 'Dunkirk Clause' enabled artists to gain ownership of the mechanical copyright of their recordings when their contract expired. This was significantly different from the 1960s, when artist deals gave recording companies the mechanical copyright for eternity.

[56] J. Randy Taraborrelli, *Michael Jackson: The Magic & The Madness* (Sidgwick & Jackson, 2003).

[57] J. Randy Taraborrelli, *Michael Jackson: The Magic & The Madness* (Sidgwick & Jackson, 2003).

[58] 'Speechless' was only released in Korea, 'You Rock My World' reached Number 10 in the US *Billboard* Hot 100 and Number 2 in the UK, 'Cry' was not released in the USA and only reached the Top 10 in Spain, and 'Butterflies' was only released in the USA where it peaked at Number 14.

[59] The only songs he performed by himself were 'Billie Jean' and 'Rock My World' on the first night and 'The Way You Make Me Feel' and 'Billie Jean' on the second night.

[60] $150,000 per minute on stage.

[61] Jennifer Vineyard, 'Michael Jackson Shocks Al Sharpton By Calling Tommy Mottola A Racist', MTV News, 7 August 2002.

[62] Jackson later produced a documentary special for Fox, which used the footage his own camera crew had shot during the making of Bashir's film. *The Michael Jackson Interview: The Footage You Were Never Meant To See* used identical footage shot by Bashir, except Jackson's own crew shot it. When shown together, it illustrated how the editing of Bashir's film manipulated the footage to create a very different picture of Jackson for the audience. Jackson was paid $5 million for this footage.

[63] *The Daily Telegraph*, 'Former Manager Unveils Scale of Michael Jackson's Drug Use', 1 July 2009.

[64] The child in question was Gavin Arvizo, and amongst the charges laid against Jackson were false imprisonment and administering an intoxicating agent to a minor.

[65] During the trial, Jackson's defence team sought to portray both Gavin Arvizo and his family as 'dishonest gold diggers' (BBC News, 13 June 2005). As the trial progressed, Jackson's defence lawyers were able to damage Gavin Arvizo's credibility by revealing that he had taken acting lessons ahead of a previous lawsuit against the US retailer, JC Penney. They discovered that, in separate interviews with a social worker and a teacher, Gavin had denied being molested by Jackson. Gavin's mother, Janet, was one of the most explosive witnesses who drew laughter from the courtroom and the defence said she had concealed sources of income while receiving welfare cheques. (Matthew Davis, *BBC News: The Arvizo Family*, 13 June 2005.) In August 2005, Los Angeles County prosecutors filed fraud and perjury charges against Janet Arvizo for fraudulently receiving more than $18,000 in government benefits. (*Los Angeles Times*, 24 August 2005.)

[66] While Michael Jackson was on trial, the Bank of America, an established US institution, grew nervous as Jackson was in debt to them for a considerable amount of money. They held security in the form of Jackson's shares in Sony/ATV and Mijac (Jackson's catalogue), but knew that once the child molestation charges had been laid to rest, anything could happen. They needed to offload the Jackson debt as soon as possible, while ensuring they managed to keep their whole relationship with Jackson off the radar. So, secretly, the Bank of America sold Jackson's mortgage to a New York investment group called Fortress, a company specialising in high-risk debts. All Sony had to do now, having been in talks with Fortress for some time, was to wait for Jackson

to default on the loan, as Sony were entitled to first refusal on the Sony/ATV shares should Jackson be forced into selling any or all of them. Biding their time, it wasn't until 2005 that Sony was able to take another 25 per cent of the catalogue off Jackson, leaving them in complete control of it.

[67] Michael's brother, Jermaine, had formed a close friendship with Sheikh Abdullah in 2001 following his conversion to Islam in Saudi Arabia.

[68] Ryan Kisiel, 'Michael Jackson Failed To Keep £4.6 Million Music Deal' *The Daily Mail*, 18 November 2008.

[69] In an interview with *The Daily Telegraph* in 2011, Jermaine Jackson stated that a private jet, financed by a friend, was on standby to whisk the King of Pop to Bahrain if Michael had been convicted at the end of the 2005 trial. Bahrain does not have an extradition treaty with the USA.

[70] William Lee Adams, 'Michael Jackson Settles Out of Court with Sheik' *Time*, 24 November 2008.

[71] Ugandan born Grace Rwaramba began working for Michael Jackson in 1991 as his secretary before working as a nanny once the children arrived.

[72] Al Arabiya News, 'Bahraini Prince Sues Michael Jackson in UK', 17 November 2008.

[73] *Billboard*, 'Michael Jackson Sued Over Album Advance', 17 November 2008.

[74] Jackson was also paying $4.5 million per month on interest payments to service this debt.

[75] Jeff Leeds and Andrew Ross Sorkin, Michael Jackson Bailout Said To Be Close', *The New York Times*, 13 April 2006.

[76] *The Guardian*, 'Michael Jackson Sued by King of Bahrain's Son', 17 November 2008.

[77] By the time Michael returned to Las Vegas in 2006, the rest of the Jackson family was suffering their own financial hardships. The millions they had made from the 'Victory' tour had evaporated: Marlon was stacking shelves, Randy fixed cars at a garage and Jackie was managing his son to make ends meet. Jermaine had charges on file against him totalling $5 million and Tito was playing in a band, which charged $1,000 per performance. Even Joe and Katherine had been declared insolvent.

[78] Anyone who came to the house had to sign confidentiality agreements that carried a $10 million penalty for disclosing any details about Jackson.

[79] Randall Sullivan, 'The Billion Dollar Shopping Spree That Killed Michael Jackson', *Daily Mail*, 17 November 2012.

[80] *Untouchable: The Strange Life & Tragic Death of Michael Jackson* by Randall Sullivan (Grove/Atlantic, 2012).

[81] The contract Jackson had signed with Sheikh Abdullah gave the Sheikh rights to all future or live-recording performances Jackson might undertake. In effect, the career of Jackson was frozen until

this lawsuit was settled. Jackson and Sheikh Abdullah reached an undisclosed out of court settlement in November 2008.

[82] Bill Whitfield and Javon Beard, with Tanner Colby, *Remember The Time: Protecting Michael Jackson in His Final Days* (Scribe Publications, 2014).

[83] Jackson would cover up all of the nude pictures within the suite, as he didn't want his children looking at them.

[84] *Thriller 25* would include guest artists such as will.i.am, Kanye West, Akon and Fergie.

[85] Dr Tohme Tohme assumed the role of Jackson's business manager in 2008, arranging for Jackson to pay him $35,000 a month plus expenses to act as manager plus $100,000 a month, later, to act as producer for Jackson's forthcoming London engagements.

[86] The Associated Press, 'Jackson's Mysterious Advisor Opens Up', 4 July 2009.

[87] He had called Barrack previously to suggest he meet with Jackson but Barrack had declined.

[88] Benjamin Wallace, 'Monetizing The Celebrity Meltdown' *New York* magazine, 28 November 2010.

[89] Mijac was Jackson's own music catalogue, which contained his own songs, as well as titles by Sly & The Family Stone, Ray Charles, Elvis Presley and Aretha Franklin.

[90] Zack O'Malley Greenburg, *Michael Jackson, Inc. – The Rise, Fall & Rebirth of a Billion-Dollar Empire* (Atria Books, 2014).

[91] Josh Gittelsohn and Nadja Brandt, 'Jackson Neverland Ranch Being Readied For Sale by Colony', *Bloomberg*, 31 July 2014.

[92] Benjamin Wallace, 'Monetizing The Celebrity Meltdown' *New York* magazine, 28 November 2010.

[93] Chris Lee and Harriet Ryan, 'Others Have Tried To Revive The Onetime Pop Star's Performing Career. Tom Barrack Is Convinced He's The "Caretaker" To Do It', *Los Angeles Times*, 30 May 2009.

[94] Randall Sullivan, 'The Billion Dollar Shopping Spree That Killed Michael Jackson', *Daily Mail*, 17 November 2012.

4

[1] Fan voting was employed in each country to determine the tracks on the album, ensuring each country had a different version on sale. 'Billie Jean' was the only song to appear on all versions of the album. In total, the album sold over 2 million copies but was, curiously, never released in the USA.

[2] Curiously, in the contract AEG Live are referred to in the first line of the contract as 'AEG Live, LLC dba Concerts West'. 'dba' can mean 'doing business as', so, in this instance, AEG Live LLC dba can work under any other name than its legal name.

[3] This $15 million would be used as a down payment on the Sultan of Brunei's property in Durango which was valued at $55 million and which Michael had set his sights on for some time. The lure of using this as a down payment was another tool Tohme Tohme used to persuade Jackson to sign the contract.

[4] The Michael Jackson Company, LLC.

[5] Agreement between AEG Live, LLC dba Concerts West and The Michael Jackson Company, LLC, 26 January 2009.

[6] Randall Sullivan, 'The Billion Dollar Shopping Spree That Killed Michael Jackson', *Daily Mail*, 17 November 2012.

[7] Bill Werde, 'Michael Jackson May Play 25 London Shows', *Billboard*, 5 March 2009.

[8] Leonard Rowe, *What Really Happened To Michael Jackson – The Evil Side of the Entertainment Industry* (Linell-Diamond Enterprises, 2010).

[9] Aka Randy Phillips.

[10] Agreement between AEG Live, LLC dba Concerts West and The Michael Jackson Company, LLC, 26 January 2009.

[11] Agreement between AEG Live, LLC dba Concerts West and The Michael Jackson Company, LLC, 26 January 2009.

[12] Legally, facsimile or photocopied documents are not considered legal or binding, thereby meaning any documents signed in such a way are invalid and void.

[13] Agreement between AEG Live, LLC dba Concerts West and The Michael Jackson Company, LLC, 26 January 2009.

[14] Clause 13.1 Cancellation Insurance, agreement between AEG Live, LLC dba Concerts West and The Michael Jackson Company LLC, 26 January 2009.

[15] Agreement between AEG Live, LLC dba Concerts West and The Michael Jackson Company, LLC, 26 January 2009.

[16] Ian Halperin, *Unmasked: The Final Years of Michael Jackson* (Pocket Books, 2009).

[17] Daphne Barak, 'I Love My Babies And I Miss Them…When Michael Jackson Was Around They Froze', *Daily Mail*, 28 June 2009.

[18] A huge auction of Jackson memorabilia had been planned in Los Angeles in April 2009. The auctioneer, Darren Julien, had signed an agreement with Tohme Tohme and removed hundreds of items from Neverland for the sale, which it was hoped would fetch around $10 million. Despite Julien spending roughly $2 million preparing the sale and exhibit (which included Jackson's red, gilded throne, sequined costumes and his Rolls-Royce stretch limo), Jackson's production company filed a lawsuit in Los Angeles on 4 March demanding the return of specific items. (*Reuters*, 'Michael Jackson Auction Cancelled' by Jill Serjeant, 14 April 2009.) The lawsuit claimed the singer had never signed the auction contract. The *Los Angeles Times* tried to contact Tohme Tohme for a comment but he could not be reached. An agreement was apparently reached between Michael Jackson and Julien's Auctions. (*Los Angeles Times*, 'Michael Jackson Auction Cancelled' by Yvonne Villarreal, 15 April 2009.)

[19] Phillips later stated in an email to his boss, Tim Leiweke, that Jackson '…is an emotionally paralysed mess riddled with self-loathing and doubt now that it is show time.'

[20] Alan Duke, '"Miracle' of Michael Jackson's Concert Announcement Described', *CNN*, 13 June 2013

[21] Official court transcript: Jackson v. AEG: deposition of Randy Phillips.

[22] Alan Duke, 'Promoter: I Slapped "Despondent" Michael Jackson', CNN, 10 June 2013.

[23] A story appeared in the *Plymouth Herald* on 29 May 2015 under the headline, 'Famous 1999 Michael Jackson Concert Was "Performed By A Lookalike" in Stunt Orchestrated by Plymouth Man'. In the article, professional dancer Anthony King from Plymouth, claimed that the whole concert was a stunt arranged by one-time Jackson bodyguard, Matt Fiddes. King claimed that his brother played Michael Jackson on that day. 'We, my brother and the team went down to Devon and we performed the show. Now, nobody said that Michael Jackson was performing. What happened was that we turned up to the theatre in a very extravagant way,' said King. He continued, 'The next day the media went crazy, Michael Jackson had performed in Devon. I thought it was fun, I thought my brother looked amazing… The dancers, Frazier, Solomon, Ron and myself. I thought that it was okay but I did not think that it would convince people but it obviously did and the word really did get out across the whole world and even when Michael Jackson's record company put out a statement saying that it wasn't Michael Jackson, people STILL didn't believe it.'

[24] Mark Lester, now an osteopath in Gloucester, was eight years old when he starred in the Oscar-winning film *Oliver!* in 1968. Receiving £180,000 for the film from a trust fund that matured when he was 18, Lester squandered the money on cars and cocaine. Retiring from acting aged 22, Jackson contacted Lester in 1980 who had loved his performance as Oliver. They formed a close and bizarre friendship, which resulted in Lester donating sperm at a Harley Street clinic in 1996 at the request of Jackson. One year later, Prince Michael was born. Lester also suggests that Paris bears a striking resemblance to his own daughter, Olivia. (Alison Boshoff, 'Is My Ex-Husband Mark Lester the Father of Jacko's Children? No, He's Completely Nuts', *Daily Mail*, 16 August 2009.)

[25] Randall Sullivan, *Untouchable: The Strange Life & Tragic Death of Michael Jackson* (Grove/Atlantic, 2012).

[26] Randall Sullivan, *Untouchable: The Strange Life & Tragic Death of Michael Jackson* (Grove/Atlantic, 2012).

[27] Jackson never went on record as disliking Prince, but the two were considerable rivals in the 1980s. Prince wrote a lyric for his 2004 album *Musicology* that went, 'My voice is getting higher/ And I ain't never had my nose done/That's the other guy'.

[28] Randall Sullivan, *Untouchable: The Strange Life & Tragic Death of Michael Jackson* (Grove/Atlantic, 2012).

[29] Jeff Gottlieb, 'Michael Jackson Could Have Earned $1.5 Billion, Accountant Says', *Los Angeles Times*, 15 July 2013. In this same article, it reports that Erk's projections were that '...the often-extravagant Jackson would have probably spent $134 million in the [15] years leading up to his sixty-fifth birthday.'

[30] United States District Court Southern District of New York: AllGood Entertainment Inc. et al. v. Jackson et al., No 1:2009cv05377 – Document 86, signed Judge Harold Baer, 19 August 2010.)

[31] Interview with Patrick Allocco conducted by MJJCommunity, 5 December 2009, www.mjjcommunity.com.

[32] Randall Sullivan, *Untouchable: The Strange Life & Tragic Death of Michael Jackson* (Grove/Atlantic, 2012).

[33] There was considerable confusion towards the end of 2008 and the beginning of 2009, as to who Michael Jackson's manager actually was. In *Remember The Time* by Bill Whitfield, Javon Beard and Tanner Colby, they refer to the confusion: 'By the end of March [2009], Tohme Tohme, Frank Dileo and Leonard Rowe were all moving independently about Los Angeles, each claiming to be Michael Jackson's manager. Underlining the confusion, on April 2nd [2009], an industry news site published an article entitled, "Will Michael Jackson's Real Manager Please Stand Up?"'

[34] In the 2010 court case relating to the AllGood Entertainment Inc. agreement it was recorded that, 'Dileo Defendants dispute the characterization of Frank Dileo's relationship with Lamicka, and contend that they were never business partners or associated in any relevant way.' (United States District Court Southern District of New York: AllGood Entertainment Inc. et al. v. Jackson et al., No 1:2009cv05377 – Document 86, signed Judge Harold Baer, 19 August 2010.)

[35] The agreement was signed by Allocco, Dileo and other associates of the two men: Terry Harvey, Mark Lamicka, Ladd

Biro and James McGale. (United States District Court Southern District of New York: AllGood Entertainment Inc. et al. v. Jackson et al., No 1:2009cv05377 – Document 86, signed Judge Harold Baer, 19 August 2010.)

[36] *Daily Mail*, 'Michael Jackson's Comeback Gigs in London Could Face Legal Challenge', 12 May 2009.

[37] Interview with Patrick Allocco conducted by MJJCommunity, 5 December 2009, www.mjjcommunity.com.

[38] Natalie Finn, 'Michael Kills Jackson 5 Reunion Rumour', Eonline.com News, 30 October 2008, www.eonline.com.

[39] Interview with Patrick Allocco conducted by MJJCommunity, 5 December 2009, www.mjjcommunity.com.

[40] Randall Sullivan, *Untouchable: The Strange Life & Tragic Death of Michael Jackson* (Grove/Atlantic, 2012).

[41] Randall Sullivan, *Untouchable: The Strange Life & Tragic Death of Michael Jackson* (Grove/Atlantic, 2012).

[42] Roger Friedman, 'Joe Jackson's Partner: Jail Sentences and Lawsuits on Resume', Roger Friedman's Showbiz411.com, 22 July 2009, www.showbiz411.com.

[43] BBC News, 'Singer R. Kelly Seeks Unpaid Fees', 7 October 2008.

[44] Leonard Rowe, *What Really Happened To Michael Jackson – The Evil Side of the Entertainment Industry* (Linell-Diamond Enterprises, 2010).

[45] Leonard Rowe, *What Really Happened To Michael Jackson – The Evil Side of the Entertainment Industry* (Linell-Diamond Enterprises, 2010).

[46] Leonard Rowe, *What Really Happened To Michael Jackson – The Evil Side of the Entertainment Industry* (Linell-Diamond Enterprises, 2010).

[47] Leonard Rowe, *What Really Happened To Michael Jackson – The Evil Side of the Entertainment Industry* (Linell-Diamond Enterprises, 2010).

[48] Leonard Rowe, *What Really Happened To Michael Jackson – The Evil Side of the Entertainment Industry* (Linell-Diamond Enterprises, 2010).

[49] Leonard Rowe, *What Really Happened To Michael Jackson – The Evil Side of the Entertainment Industry* (Linell-Diamond Enterprises, 2010).

[50] Interview with Patrick Allocco conducted by MJJCommunity, 5 December 2009, www.mjjcommunity.com.

[51] Randall Sullivan, *Untouchable: The Strange Life & Tragic death of Michael Jackson* (Grove/Atlantic, 2012).

[52] Interview with Patrick Allocco conducted by MJJCommunity, 5 December 2009, www.mjjcommunity.com.

[53] Interview with Patrick Allocco conducted by MUZIKfactorytwo in 2010, 24 May 2011, http://muzikfactorytwo.blogspot.co.uk/2011/05/interview-with-patrick-allocco.html

[54] By this point, Jackson had already signed the document with AEG Live.

[55] The plan was for a one-off concert on 3 July 2010 at Texas Stadium in Irving, Texas. (Alex Dobuzinskis, 'Michael Jackson Concerts May Face Legal Challenge', Reuters, 11 May 2009.)

[56] Bill Whitfield and Javon Beard with Tanner Colby, *Remember The Time* (Scribe, 2014).

[57] *Remember The Time.*

[58] Leonard Rowe, *What Really Happened To Michael Jackson – The Evil Side of the Entertainment Industry* (Linell-Diamond Enterprises, 2010).

[59] Leonard Rowe, *What Really Happened To Michael Jackson – The Evil Side of the Entertainment Industry* (Linell-Diamond Enterprises, 2010).

[60] Randall Sullivan, *Untouchable: The Strange Life & Tragic Death of Michael Jackson* (Grove/Atlantic, 2012).

[61] CNN, 'Larry King Live': interview between Larry King, Joe Jackson & Leonard Rowe, 20 July 2009.

[62] Randall Sullivan, *Untouchable: The Strange Life & Tragic Death of Michael Jackson* (Grove/Atlantic, 2012).

[63] Official press release issued by Champion Management, www.MUZIKfactory2.com

[64] *Remember The Time.*

[65] 25 March 2009.

[66] Leonard Rowe, *What Really Happened To Michael Jackson – The Evil Side of the Entertainment Industry* (Linell-Diamond Enterprises, 2010).

[67] *Remember The Time.*

[68] *Remember The Time.*

[69] *Remember The Time.*

[70] BBC News, 'Jackson Sued Over Reunion Concert', 11 June 2009.

[71] In the book, *Remember The Time*, co-author Bill Whitfield writes, 'Even after Tohme Tohme was fired, he was still going around, claiming to be Michael Jackson's manager. Somehow this Frank Dileo character had leveraged his way in and gotten himself hired by AEG in some capacity, and now he was claiming to represent Mr. Jackson too. It was chaos. Total confusion. These people were all out signing deals, saying they were Michael Jackson's manager. And because Mr. Jackson would sign whatever was put in front of him, there were all these conflicting contracts and letters of agreement going around, and everyone was threatening to sue everybody else for violating this deal or that deal.'

[72] Official medical records from Brotman Medical Center, 27 January 1984.

[73] Andrew Zajac, 'Painkillers Darvon, Darvocet Withdrawn at FDA Request', *Los Angeles Times*, 20 November 2010.

[74] The medical records state that Jackson is single, a Jehovah's Witness and a vegetarian. They also state he was known to be a well-developed, well-nourished male with no allergies.

[75] Percocet is a narcotic pain medication that is also habit-forming and should never be given to anyone with a history of drug addiction.

[76] Jackson had known Dr Klein since 1983 when David Geffen introduced the two of them to each other. Dr Klein immediately noticed a 'butterfly rash' on Jackson's face and crusting of the scalp, and diagnosed Lupus.

[77] Mark Seal, 'The Doctor Will Sue You Now', *Vanity Fair*, March 2012.

[78] Mark Seal, 'The Doctor Will Sue You Now', *Vanity Fair*, March 2012.

[79] Susan Donaldson James, 'Friend Says Michael Jackson Battled Demerol Addiction' ABC News, 26 June 2009.

[80] Mark Seal, 'The Doctor Will Sue You Now', *Vanity Fair*, March 2012.

[81] On 11 April 2014, ABC News reported that Marc Shaffel and Debbie Rowe, the mother of Michael Jackson's two oldest children, were engaged and set to marry.

[82] Susan Donaldson James, 'Friend Says Michael Jackson Battled Demerol Addiction' ABC News, 26 June 2009.

[83] Jeff Gottlieb and Matt Hamilton, 'Debbie Rowe: Michael Jackson Used Propofol to Sleep in the 1990s', *Los Angeles Times*, 15 August 2013.

[84] In his book *My Friend Michael*, author Frank Cascio recalls that the journey to the hospital wasn't in an ambulance but instead in the black van they'd arrived at the stadium in. Despite having a German driver, Cascio recalls how they kept getting lost on the way to the hospital and it took them 45 minutes to find a clinic.

[85] Frank Cascio, *My Friend Michael*, (HarperCollins, 2011).

[86] Frank Cascio, *My Friend Michael*, (HarperCollins, 2011).

[87] Debbie Rowe testified this to the Jackson trial on 13 August 2013.

[88] Ann Pride, 'New Book Reveals Prankster Michael Jackson's Playful Side and Love of Nerdy Women', *Daily Mail*, 20 November 2011.

[89] Frank Cascio, *My Friend Michael*, (HarperCollins, 2011).

[90] Debbie Rowe, Jackson's second wife, was also an employee of Dr Klein.

[91] Alan Duke, 'Michael Jackson's Drug Use Explored In Trial', CNN, 26 July 2013.

[92] Dr Klein recalled, in an interview with Harvey Levin of TMZ, going to Jackson's house and finding Dilaudid he had got from his other plastic surgeon. Dilaudid is 10 times stronger than Morphine and Klein flushed it down the toilet. (Interview with Dr Arnold Klein by Harvey Levin of TMZ on 5 November 2009.)

[93] Dr Klein had professed that he had twice intervened to get Jackson off his drug addiction. (Interview with Dr Arnold Klein by Harvey Levin of TMZ on 5 November 2009.)

[94] Tylenol is a pain reliever and fever reducer used to treat many conditions such as headache, muscle aches, arthritis, colds and fevers.

[95] In Dr Metzger's entry regarding this call, he notes the name Omar Arnold into his log as well as Michael Jackson. They discuss Jackson (or Arnold) taking Tylenol for sleep but, during the trial, Metzger said he couldn't recall if Jackson had phoned to ask for a prescription.

[96] Official court records, Katherine Jackson v. AEG, testimony of Dr Allan Metzger.

[97] The usual dosage of Demerol in adults is 50mg to 150mg for relief of pain.

[98] Traces of Prednisone were found in Jackson's autopsy and a bottle of the pills, prescribed by Klein on 25 April, were found amongst Jackson's belongings.

[99] Alan Duke, 'Nurse Details Michael Jackson's Fatal Search for Sleep', *CNN*, 29 August 2013.

5

[1] Conrad Murray never saw his father until he was 25 years old and so took the surname of his mother.

[2] David Jones, 'Born In The Ghetto, He Has Seven Children By Different Women And A Mountain Of Debts', *Daily Mail*, 5 February 2010.

[3] He was also licensed in Hawaii in 2001.

[4] Dr Murray kept an office at this clinic, which was owned by Dr Davill Armstrong who, between 2006 and 2009, had his licence suspended by the state medical board for improperly treating 15 patients. In 2008 he was also fined $2,000 for allowing his wife to prescribe medicine to a patient without any physician being present.

[5] Conrad Murray actually met his father for the first time in 1978.

[6] Nick Allen, 'Dr. Conrad Murray: Profile', *The Telegraph*, 7 November 2011.

[7] Nick Allen, 'Dr. Conrad Murray: Profile', *The Telegraph*, 7 November 2011.

[8] Harriet Ryan, 'Dr. Conrad Murray Deep In Debt, Records Show', *Los Angeles Times*, 8 February 2010.

[9] David Gardner, 'Revealed: Conrad Murray's Secret Double Life as a Deadbeat Dad and a Compulsive Womaniser Turned Doctor to the Stars', *Daily Mail*, 8 November 2011.

[10] Jim Avila, Luchina Fisher and Sheila Marikar, 'Investigating Michael Jackson's Personal Doctor', ABC News, 30 July 2009.

[11] The Associated Press, 'Michael Jackson's Doc Conrad Murray in Deep Financial Straits', 1 August 2009.

[12] Nenita Malibiran was already married when she began her affair with Murray who, himself, was married. They had a son together but Murray made little effort to visit him. Even though Malibiran won the case against Murray for child support, she had to sue him on a number of occasions to try and get payments.

[13] They were married in 1989 and were medical classmates at Meharry School of Medicine together.

[14] Her IMDb profile lists just three credits between 2003 and 13. She played 'Courtney' in the 2003 short *Her Knight*, she was 'Hot Chick' (uncredited) in the 2008, $10 million film *Days of Wrath* and she was 'Katrina' in one episode of *Justified* in 2010.

[15] The child, Che Giovanni Murray, was born on 2 March 2009.

[16] Stadol is a powerful pain reliever with some similarities to Demerol.

[17] Nubain is a powerful pain reliever administered through IV. It's similar to Morphine and used as a supplement to anaesthesia.

[18] Phenergan is a moderate painkiller, which is also used as an antihistamine.

[19] Talwin is a pain reliever/narcotic used before surgery and as an anaesthetic.

[20] Luchina Fisher, 'Like Father, Like Son? Conrad Murray's Dad Once Cited for Medical Misconduct', ABC News, 23 July 2009.

[21] James C. McKinley, 'Differing Sides of Physician Who Tended to Jackson', *New York Times*, 26 September 2009.

[22] Dr David Slavit graduated from Cornell University in 1982 before attending the Mount Sinai School of Medicine of the City of New York.

[23] Bob Taylor of Robertson Taylor, the London-based insurance brokers, requested the physical.

[24] Dr Slavit charged $6,000 for the physical examination including time away from office, $3,000 for medical supplies, lab specimen collection and processing, preparation of reports, completion of insurance forms and review of confidentiality agreement, as well as $5,849 for travel expenses, hotel and so forth.

[25] Interview with *Access Hollywood*, 25 August 2009.

[26] According to testimony in court by Dr Slavit the whole visit took no more than three hours.

[27] The report erroneously dated the examination as taking place on 4 February 2008 rather than 2009, which Dr Slavit attributed to a typographical error.

[28] Los Angeles Police Department, recorded interview of Conrad Murray, 27 June 2009.

[29] During the People v. Conrad Murray trial, Faheem Muhammad, Jackson's Head of Security, said he first met Murray in March 2009. Alberto Alvarez, Jackson's Director of Logistics, said he first met Murray in January 2009, but only saw him regularly between April/May to 25 June.

[30] People v. Conrad Murray trial.

[31] *Access Hollywood*, 'Michael Jackson Death Investigation: Who is Doctor David Slavit?', 25 August 2009.

[32] Eriq Gardner, 'Michael Jackson Company: Singer Fit to Perform Before Death', *Hollywood Reporter*, 2 January 2014.

[33] Official court records, Katherine Jackson v. AEG, testimony of Dr David Slavit, 15 August 2013.

[34] Remarkably, as early as June 2008, Murray had been calling himself Jackson's personal physician to his mistress, Nicole Alvarez.

[35] One of Michael Jackson's aliases.

[36] Harriet Ryan, 'Southern California – This Just In', *Los Angeles Times*, 5 October 2011.

[37] Mary Manning and Jeremy Twitchell, 'DEA Searches Vegas Pharmacy in Probe of Doctor', *Las Vegas Sun*, 11 August 2009.

[38] Paul Harasim, 'Is Anyone Watching The Pharmacy Industry?', *Las Vegas Review Journal*, 14 October 2012.

[39] The Enterprise Report, 'Autopsy of Dr Conrad Murray Vegas Pharmacy' by TER Staff, 1 October 2009.

[40] It was confirmed during his autopsy.

[41] Official court records, People v. Conrad Murray, testimony of Tim Lopez, 10 January 2011.

[42] Jackson was photographed leaving Klein's clinic on this date looking fine and wearing dark sunglasses.

[43] Official court records, People v. Conrad Murray, testimony of Tim Lopez, 10 January 2011.

[44] Official court records, People v. Conrad Murray, testimony of Tim Lopez, 10 January 2011.

[45] Official court records, People v. Conrad Murray, testimony of Tim Lopez, 10 January 2011.

[46] Benjamin C. Wedro, MD, FACEP, FAAEM, 'Michael Jackson's Death: Propofol FAQ', 8 November 2011, www. MedicineNet. com.

[47] Official court records, People v. Conrad Murray, testimony of Tim Lopez, 10 January 2011.

[48] The Associated Press, 'Doctor's Girlfriend Discusses Medical Shipments', *The Guardian*, 4 October 2011.

[49] Official court recording, People v. Conrad Murray, Sally Hirschberg testimony, 5 October 2011.

[50] Official court recording, People v. Conrad Murray, testimony of Sally Hirschberg, 5 October 2011.

[51] Official court transcript, People v. Conrad Murray, testimony of Kenny Ortega, 4 January 2011.

[52] Official court records, People v. Conrad Murray, testimony of Tim Lopez, 10 January 2011.

[53] Shortly after testifying that he had shipped a large amount of Propofol to Murray, Tim Lopez apparently vanished after leaving the USA and could not be located for the September 2011 trial. He was finally found after a 'mysterious' trip to Thailand and relocated to the USA just in time for the trial. (TMZ.com, 'Pharmacist Tim Lopez Testifies', 4 October 2011, www.tmz.com.)

6

[1] Intralesnl+7 is actually Intralesional Steroid therapy, which is used to treat, amongst other things, scar tissue, discoid lupus and alopea areata, a form of hair loss. These steroids can cause pain and potential infection and, coupled with the other injections Jackson was having from Klein during the last week of April, it is no surprise he was photographed wearing a mask, hat and veil on a trip out of the clinic on 27 April.

[2] Bearden is one of the world's top celebrity musical directors and has performed with acts such as Sting, Whitney Houston, Lenny

Kravitz, Luther Vandross, Stevie Wonder, Liza Minelli, Elton John and Aretha Franklin, amongst others.

[3] Kenny Ortega had signed a contract with AEG Live on 26 April 2009 through his own company, KO, and received his first payment for his services on 11 May, although he had been working in good faith on the concerts for a number of weeks beforehand.

[4] Work on the show took place at Center Stages in Burbank from 28 March until 27 May 2009 then moved to the Forum in Los Angeles from 27 May until 23 June, upon which it moved to the Staples Center until Jackson's death.

[5] Payne acknowledged that, during the *Dangerous* tour, it was generally known that pain was an ongoing issue for Jackson following the Pepsi commercial accident. (Official court transcript, Jackson v. AEG Live, testimony of Travis Payne, 13/14 May 2013.)

[6] Stacy Walker began working with Jackson in 1996 on the short film, *Ghosts*, and then worked with him on the *HIStory* tour. In addition she has worked with artists such as Britney Spears, Lady Gaga, Justin Timberlake and Usher.

[7] Jackson never brought any of his children to see the rehearsals, as he wanted them to focus on their schooling in the first instance, and then see the finished production once they all travelled to London.

[8] When Payne was asked the question, 'Do you know who was setting the rehearsal schedule?' during the Jackson v. AEG Live

case, he answered, 'I would assume the higher up in production, with Michael's approval.'

⁹ Unless, of course, Jackson's appointments with Klein were scheduled after rehearsals. However, rehearsals often didn't begin, at least with Jackson's input, until the evenings meaning any appointments with Klein would have to be in the early hours of the morning, which was unlikely.

¹⁰ Jackson v. AEG Live, Superior Court of the State of California, County of Los Angeles, Central District, Case BC445597.

¹¹ Jackson v. AEG Live, Superior Court of the State of California, County of Los Angeles, Central District, Case BC445597.

¹² David Gardner, 'Michael Jackson Was Hooked on Painkillers', *Daily Mail*, 27 October 2011.

¹³ People v. Conrad Murray, official court records, testimony of Dr Robert Waldman, 27 October 2011.

¹⁴ AEG Live bought the assets of Concerts West, which included Paul Gongaware.

¹⁵ Dr Nichopoulos (Dr Nick) had been writing prescriptions for Elvis Presley since January 1975. In fact, they were so close that Presley had given him a green Mercedes-Benz. Between 1 January 1977 and 16 August 1977, Dr Nick had written Elvis prescriptions for an astonishing 8,805 prescription drugs, varying from pills to injectables, including Percodan, cocaine and Demerol. The quantities of these prescriptions were so large that they were more in keeping for patients terminally ill with cancer. Dr Nick

was preparing to prescribe Elvis more doses of Dilaudid (an opiate that was Presley's favourite drug) at 2am on the morning of Presley's death after the singer had phoned him to get the drugs. At 2:33pm on 16 August 1977, Memphis Fire Station received a call indicating that someone at 3754 Elvis Presley Boulevard was having problems breathing. When the two medics arrived at the address, they were sent upstairs to the bedroom where, passing through to the enormous bathroom, they discovered Elvis Presley stretched out on his back on the floor with a dozen people huddled over his lifeless body, attempting mouth-to-mouth resuscitation. The medics found no pulse and decided that emergency treatment in a hospital offered the only chance to save Elvis. Five men were needed to lift his body onto the stretcher, as Elvis, by now, weighed around 250lbs. They had just managed to get the stretcher into the ambulance when a green Mercedes pulled up and Dr Nick leapt from it into the ambulance. When Elvis arrived at hospital the medical team waiting there were astonished that they were expected to work on the already-dead body, with Dr Nick remaining in the room. After 20 minutes, they gave up on their futile task, after which Dr Nick left the hospital without giving cause of death, but not before securing the signature of Elvis's father, Vernon Presley, on a document authorising the hospital autopsy to be paid for by the Presley estate, ensuring the report could, in theory, keep the cause of Elvis's death a secret and Dr Nick's involvement in it unconnected. Meanwhile, before the authorities could investigate Presley's home, it had been cleaned up, although the scrupulous investigators found two syringes. It was announced that Presley had died from heart failure. Dr Nick announced he had been Elvis's private physician for 10 years and knew for a fact that Elvis had not been taking hard drugs. He concluded, 'Elvis's death was simply a bolt out of the blue, a tragedy no-one could have prevented.'

[16] Official court records, Jackson v. Conrad Murray, testimony of Paul Gongaware, 30 May 2013.

[17] Alan Duke, 'AEG Expert: Michael Jackson Was A Drug Addict', CNN, 28 August 2013.

[18] The 'B' party consisted of band and administration. The 'A' party was the artist party, the 'C' party was crew and the 'D' party was documentary.

[19] In 2011, Live Nation sold 22 million tickets to its events compared to 12.2 million sold by AEG Live.

[20] Richard Johnson, 'Concert Promoters Pulled Fast One on Jackson, E-mails Imply', *New York Post*, 29 May 2013.

[21] Richard Johnson, 'Concert Promoters Pulled Fast One on Jackson, E-mails Imply', *New York Post*, 29 May 2013.

[22] David Campbell ran the O2 complex in 2009, including the O2 Arena.

[23] Jessica Koravos ran AEG Live London in 2009.

[24] Randy Phillips was also cc'd into this email.

[25] Randall Sullivan, *Untouchable: The Strange Life & Tragic death of Michael Jackson* (Grove/Atlantic, 2012).

[26] Richard Johnson, 'Concert Promoters Pulled Fast One on Jackson, E-mails Imply', *New York Post*, 29 May 2013.

[27] She had known him for 27 years, so could be expected to provide a reliable character assessment.

[28] This was signed on 26 January 2009.

[29] Randall Sullivan, *Untouchable: The Strange Life & Tragic death of Michael Jackson* (Grove/Atlantic 2012).

[30] Superior Court of California, County of Los Angeles, Joseph Jackson v. Conrad Murray et al., Case No. BC450393, 6 September 2011.

[31] Randall Sullivan, *Untouchable: The Strange Life & Tragic death of Michael Jackson* (Grove/Atlantic 2012).

[32] Murray said he had clinics in Houston, Las Vegas, San Diego and Hawaii.

[33] Between the phone calls, Gongaware had called Dr Finkelstein to enquire how much he might charge for such a role. Dr Finkelstein responded by saying he would charge $10,000 per week.

[34] Jeff Gottlieb, 'Murray Wanted $5 million to Treat Jackson, AEG Chief Testifies', *Los Angeles Times*, 3 June 2013.

[35] In a financial declaration submitted on 8 April 2008 in one of his child support cases, Murray stated under penalty of perjury that his gross monthly income was $3,300. It is easy to see why Murray so readily accepted the offer of $150,000 per month, despite it being a massive drop from his initial request of $5 million, as, combined with the additional costs covered by AEG

of $39,045 each month, the package of $189,045 a month was a big enough inducement for him to give up his current clinics which were providing him with a gross monthly income of just $3,300 some $185,745 per month less than what he was being offered by the concerts.

[36] CNN, 'Manslaughter Trial of Conrad Murray Begins', 27 September 2011.

[37] Conrad Murray was listed as a production expense in April, May, June and July at $150,000 per month in the approved tour budget, dated 16 May 2009, despite formal negotiations not taking place before May 2009.

[38] It was these consecutive visits to Klein that resulted in Dr Waldman stating that, by this point, Jackson was having an increasing tolerance to Demerol and was probably addicted to opioids.

[39] In *The Telegraph* on 29 November 2011, Nick Allen wrote following the sentencing of Murray that, 'The judge said the most disturbing aspect of the six week trial had been a tape recording Murray made of his vulnerable patient slurring his words under the influence of drugs. He said his belief was that Murray had made the surreptitious recording as an "insurance policy".

[40] Superior Court of California, County of Los Angeles, Joseph Jackson v. Conrad Murray et al., Case No. BC450393, 6 September 2011.

[41] Upon hearing the recording, Michael Amir Williams testified that, 'Not that extreme, but I have heard him talk slow before.'

Faheem Muhammad, who would drive Jackson to Klein's office said he would go '…almost every day', and that he appeared intoxicated when he left and even Paul Gongaware himself said he noticed Jackson had '…a little bit of a slower speech pattern, just a slight slur in the speech' following a visit to Klein.

[42] Forensic computer investigator, Stephen Marx, retrieved the message from Murray's iPhone three months after the singer's death.

[43] Although, for practical purposes, traces of Demerol can still be detected through drug testing up to 20 hours after administration and some drug tests can detect Normeperidine, a metabolite of Demerol, up to 30 hours after administration.

[44] CNN, 'Conrad Murray: "I'm Remorseful"', 26 June 2014.

[45] The Associated Press, 'Michael Jackson Death Trial: Doctor's Girlfriend Discusses Medical Shipments', *The Guardian*, 4 October 2011.

[46] Official court transcript, People v. Conrad Murray, testimony of Tim Lopez, 10 January 2011.

[47] Official court transcript, People v. Conrad Murray, testimony of Tim Lopez, 10 January 2011.

[48] Alison Boshoff, 'Comeback King? Michael Jackson Has Managed Two of 45 Rehearsals For His £65m Concerts', *Daily Mail*, 22 May 2009.

[49] In fact, there is a photograph of Michael Jackson apparently attending rehearsals on 6 May 2009. The photograph shows no evidence of any rehearsals actually taking place, and is simply a photo of Michael Jackson in a circle of people (Kenny Ortega and Travis Payne are standing close to the singer) in what could be a dance or rehearsal studio, with their arms all raised. Jackson is wearing his trademark sunglasses and appears to be cheering or yelling along with the others pictured. On 6 May 2009, Jackson had visited Dr Klein in Beverly Hills and received a 200mg injection of Demerol. Demerol in a person's blood system will drop by 50 per cent every 2.5 to 4 hours so, it is possible Jackson did attend rehearsals on 6 May if he had had injections of Demerol early in the day and arrived at the rehearsal studios in Burbank much later in the day. This photograph was released courtesy of Michael Jackson's estate on 8 September 2012, so there is no way of knowing if it was actually taken on 6 May.

[50] Los Angeles Police Department, recorded interview of Conrad Murray, 27 June 2009.

[51] Ian Halperin, *Unmasked – The Final Years of Michael Jackson* (Pocket Books, 2009).

[52] Alison Boshoff, 'Comeback King? Michael Jackson Has Managed Two of 45 Rehearsals For His £65m Concerts', *Daily Mail*, 22 May 2009.

[53] The Associated Press, 'Jackson Chef: I Thought Singer Was Sleeping Late', *The Guardian*, 30 July 2009.

[54] It is common in medicine, for oxygen to be used and mixed with anaesthetics during surgery.

7

<hr>

[1] In the interview, Dr Klein stated that Michael Jackson didn't visit his clinic in the two months prior to his death, saying, 'We didn't see him in May, we didn't see him in June. Remember that. We had a two month period where we didn't see him.'

[2] Randall Sullivan, *Untouchable: The Strange Life & Tragic Death of Michael Jackson* (Grove/Atlantic, 2012).

[3] In the same interview with TMZ, Klein admitted it was a mistake to send the final invoice to Jackson's creditors but revealed he felt he deserved the money: 'My lawyers were silly, they should have hid the bill and secondly, I'll donate the money to charity. But you know what, he's made $100 million worth of records, Michael's not here anymore and I think I have a right to that money and I'll donate to a charity in his name. But I have a right to the money for the work I did because I would take my whole weekends off. Do you know how many weekends I spent with him doing this, and just working on his face, trying to rebuild his face? It's not easy. And, you know, I had to rent helicopters because he decided that he wanted to do it that day and I was 200, 300 miles away.'

[4] Equivalent to $116 million in 2015.

[5] A board meeting was held by AEG Live on 26 May 2009 to discuss, amongst other business, this overspend.

[6] CNN, 'Michael Jackson: The Final Days', 5 April 2013.

[7] Withdrawal symptoms of Demerol include the patient/addict suffering from chills, fever and anxiety amongst other symptoms within, typically, 6–36 hours after the last use of the drug.

[8] Official court transcript, Katherine Jackson v. Conrad Murray, testimony of Kai Chase, 19 June 2013.

[9] This would be one of a number of the short films used as a backdrop, on giant screens, to the stage performance at the O2. 'The Drill' was a military-style dance sequence, which featured samples of 'Bad', 'Dangerous' and 'Mind Is The Magic'.

[10] Jackson visited Dr Klein on 4 June, but no treatment or injections of Demerol were administered.

[11] Jackson also visited Dr Klein on 10 June and received an injection of 200mg of Demerol.

[12] In a response to a query from the *Sunday Mirror* about Jackson's rehearsal schedule and whether or not he was attending, Paul Gongaware said, 'We can only make this work, of course, if MJ puts on the best show of his life. I'm here to tell you that he will. I have seen it for myself, Last night [4 June] he ran nine songs with full band, singers and dancers.'

[13] Travis Payne had a contract with AEG Live dated 1 April 2009. He was to be paid a minimum of $160,000 to secure his availability throughout the pre-tour rehearsal period. In addition he would be paid $1,500 for each day his services were actually performed at rehearsals or on tour from 15 July 2009, as well as a fixed fee of $25,000 for any modifications or dance moves used in additional media. Finally, Payne was entitled to $100 per day.

[14] Corina Knoll, 'Jackson Trying To Get "Down To My Fighting Weight," Witness Says', *Los Angeles Times*, 14 May 2013.

[15] Karen Faye was also a patient of Dr Arnold Klein.

[16] The dosage used for general anaesthesia in a surgical procedure is between 100mg and 200mg. This will put a patient under and will be followed by a continuous infusion of much smaller amounts, with the patient's physical weight determining how many mg/min will be used. So the daily dose available to Jackson was the equivalent of what is used in a hospital for approximately 10 operations per day.

[17] Kenny Ortega sent an email to Paul Gongaware saying, 'MJ didn't have a good day Friday, didn't show up Saturday.'

[18] Alan Duke, '"I Kind of Knew What Was Going To Happen" to Michael Jackson', CNN, 28 May 2013.

[19] Jackson had visited Dr Klein again on 16 June and had some work done on his acne scars and hollows under the eyes, which was accompanied by a 100mg injection of Demerol. Karen Faye recalled the singer looking frightened but stoic when he turned up to rehearsals on the 16th.

[20] Michael Jackson wore a condom catheter and these bags would have been essential.

[21] A week later, on 22 June, Murray's Las Vegas office places an order for catheters, urine bags and leg bags for catheters. These were never shipped as on 26 June, Ng called to cancel the order at 9:26am.

[22] Raymone Bain had originally reached a financial settlement with Jackson for $488,820 upon her dismissal in 2007.

[23] In the book *Remember The Time*, co-author Bill Whitfield wrote, 'At any given time there were hundreds of lawsuits pending against him, literally.'

[24] After Jackson died, there were an estimated 100 lawsuits pending against him.

[25] Jeff Gottlieb, 'Tour director in tears as he recalls Michael Jackson's decline', *Los Angeles Times*, 10 July 2013.

[26] Claire Hoffman, 'The Last Days of Michael Jackson', *Rolling Stone*, 6 August 2009.

[27] Stan Wilson, 'Father of Michael Jackson Accuses AEG of Singer's Death', CNN, 18 June 2010.

[28] Christopher Morris, 'Michael Jackson's Mother Sues AEG', *Variety*, 16 September 2010.

[29] Superior Court of the State of California, County of Los Angeles, Central District, Katherine Jackson v. AEG Live, Case No. BC445597, 15 September 2010.

[30] Alan Duke, 'Choreographer: AEG Considered "Pulling The Plug" on Michael Jackson's Comeback', CNN, 15 May 2013.

[31] At this point, Dr Murray was creating the daily schedule for Jackson in order that he could be guaranteed to attend rehearsals.

[32] Karen Faye's capitals.

[33] This new contract continued to have 1 May 2009 as Murray's commencement of services.

[34] A simple check of drug interactions shows that Ativan used with Propofol may have increased effects on breathing, heart rate, blood pressure and sedation, and that administration has to be closely monitored by the surgical team. Valium has similar effects, as does Versed.

[35] Ortega testified as such.

[36] Kenny Ortega asked Randy Phillips to assign someone to be stationed near Jackson's dressing room on 23 and 24 June to see if he needed tea, water, food, etc. The person who was going to fulfil this role on tour was Brigitte Segal, but she was, at this point in time, in London scouting houses for Jackson and Murray (she sent an email to Paul Gongaware on 24 June to confirm she had secured Chislehurst House in Kent for Jackson). Jackson had four bodyguards and an assistant at the rehearsals at the Staples Center but, in the words of Randy Phillips, '…no one seemed to care about what his needs were'.

[37] Jeff Gottlieb, 'Michael Jackson "A Lost Boy" Concert Director Said In Email', *Los Angeles Times*, 10 July 2013.

[38] Jim Avila, Kaitlyn Folmer and Jessica Hopper, 'Michael Jackson Audio Mumbles About "Lost Childhood"', ABC News, 5 October 2011.

[39] Jim Avila, Kaitlyn Folmer, Bryan Lavietes and Jessica Hopper, 'Michael Jackson Tour Director Alarmed by "Incoherent Star" Days Before Death', ABC News, 27 September 2011.

[40] Ryan Parry, 'Michael Jackson's Doctor Conrad Murray Goes On Trial For King of Pop's Death', *Daily Mirror*, 28 September 2011.

[41] *Michael Jackson & The Doctor: A Fatal Friendship*, October Films, 2009.

[42] *Michael Jackson & The Doctor: A Fatal Friendship*, October Films, 2009.

[43] Jackson's weight issues were obvious to the crew. On one occasion when Jackson was sweating profusely, one of his assistants, Michael Bush, took him to the bathroom to give him dry clothing. When he came out, Bush went to Faye and said to her: 'Oh my God Turkle, I can see Michael's heart beating through the skin on his chest'.

[44] Official court records, Jackson v. Conrad Murray, testimony of Karen Faye.

[45] Jeff Gottlieb, 'Jackson Friend Told AEG Executive of Fears Singer Might Die', *Los Angeles Times*, 9 May 2013.

[46] CBS News, 'Jackson Begged For Sedative, Nurse Says', 30 June 2009.

[47] *The Telegraph*, 'Clinic Worker Claims To Have Had Homosexual Love Affair With Michael Jackson', 21 August 2009.

[48] RadarOnline.com, 16 April 2013.

[49] RadarOnline.com, 16 April 2013.

[50] Official court records, Jackson v. AEG Live, testimony of Karen Faye.

[51] Matilda Battersby, *The Independent*, 27 June 2013.

[52] Nancy Dillon, *New York Daily News*, 30 May 2013.

[53] Although Karen Faye testified that Jackson was still cold on the 23rd and continuing to repeat speech patterns, and in the 2011 Joseph Jackson v. Conrad Murray Trial, Michael Jackson was reported to be, '…disoriented and freezing cold,' at rehearsals with his assistants having to '…give him several shirts to wear under his long heavy coat because he was so cold'.

[54] Walker referred to Jackson, at this rehearsal, being '…great, sassy and bratty, like he normally is'.

[55] Jackson was using his familiar alias of Omar Arnold.

[56] Alan Duke, 'Lawsuit Evidence: Michael Jackson Lost Dance Moves In Last Days', CNN, 16 June 2013.

8

[1] Michael Amir Williams had worked for Jackson for a little over two years after originally being hired to archive his DVD collection. Now, as his personal assistant, his duties involved

answering calls, arranging day-to-day operations, hiring staff or anything Jackson needed, even '…sending me to pick up popcorn'.

[2] In the March 2010 legal case of Joe Jackson v. Conrad Murray, Joe Jackson claimed that, 'On 25 June 2009, prior to treating Michael Jackson, the defendant was at a "strip club" called Sam's Hofbrau in Los Angeles where he had been "drinking". It was reckless for him to "drink" prior to administering anaesthesia to Michael Jackson. He concealed his conduct from Michael Jackson.' A member of Murray's defence team told celebrity website TMZ.com that the allegations were false and that Murray doesn't drink.

[3] Steven Echols' firm, Security Measures, would later sue Jackson's creditors for $261,169 in unpaid security costs following the singer's death. According to legal documents, the firm supplied Jackson with three guards around the clock at $25 per hour.

[4] Michael Jackson fired Leonard Muhammad in the spring of 2004, in a move orchestrated by Randy Jackson who had his own ideas for Jackson's future.

[5] Matthew Moore, 'Michael Jackson: Was He Influenced by the Nation of Islam?', *The Telegraph*, 29 June 2009.

[6] Louis Farrakhan had been banned by successive home secretaries from entering Britain since 1986, on the grounds he expressed racist and anti-Semitic views, and that he could threaten public order if he entered Britain.

[7] *People* magazine, 29 November 1984.

[8] Quote from an interview on *The Arsenio Hall Show*.

[9] Jennifer Vineyard, 'Is The Nation of Islam Taking Control of Jackson's Affairs?', MTV News, 31 December 2003.

[10] Wallace D. Fard Muhammad arrived in Detroit in 1930 with an obscure background and a number of aliases: the FBI suggest as many as 58. He had an Indian appearance, had a Russian Jewish mother, was a dapper dresser, and told his followers he was born in the holy city of Mecca. However, the general consensus is that Fard was born in New Zealand in 1893. Within three years of his arrival in Detroit, the followers of his Allah Temple of Islam had risen to 8,000 as he sought to liberate the African Americans from their 'half-slave and half-free' condition, although conflicts arose between this community and the police when his followers started to refuse to send their children to school, and there were even allegations that one of the group, Robert Harris, who renamed himself Robert Karriem, had participated in human sacrifice to bring himself closer to Allah. Karriem was found to be insane but Fard was facing possible charges in connection with the murder, so he renounced the ATI and said he would use his influence to disband the organisation, as ordered in 1932 and agree to leave Detroit immediately to receive immunity. This he did, only to reappear in January 1933 in the city. The ATI had now become the Nation of Islam and Fard's activities in the city once again alerted the authorities, who ordered him to leave Detroit again in May 1933. Following a brief spell in Chicago, where he was arrested for disturbing the peace, Fard returned to Detroit again. Following another brush with the law he left Detroit for good in April 1934 with Elijah Muhammad assuming control of the Nation of Islam until 1975 after a short leadership struggle. Fard disappeared into history. There were rumours of

him becoming a Nazi spy during the Second World War, but nobody can positively pinpoint what happened to him. However there were reports that a Wallace D. Fard died in Chicago in 1971. Jay-Z, Ice Cube and Wu Tang Clan, amongst others, have since made references to Fard's teachings in their music.

[11] *New York Times*, 30 December 2003, *"Dispute in Michael Jackson Camp Over Role of Nation of Islam"*, Sharon Waxman

[12] *The Telegraph*, 'Michael Jackson's Aide "Quit Due to Nation of Islam"', 7 July 2009.

[13] Sharon Waxman, 'Dispute In Michael Jackson Camp Over Role of Nation of Islam', *New York Times*, 30 December 2003.

[14] Jermaine Jackson is not a member of the Nation of Islam, but Rwaramba is.

[15] Bob Jones and Stacy Brown, *Michael Jackson, the Man Behind The Mask: An Insider's Story of the King of Pop* (SelectBooks, 2009).

[16] In an interview with Fox News, Leonard Muhammad said, 'We have not tried to recruit Michael, nor has he expressed any interest in becoming a member of the Nation of Islam.'

[17] Neil Syson 'The Way You Mecca me Feel', *The Sun*, 21 November 2008.

[18] In an interview on 22 January 2010, Jermaine Jackson gave an hour-long interview to Al-Arabiya television. During the interview he confirmed that Michael Jackson had not converted

to Islam, but stated that he was on the verge of converting at the time of his death. He acknowledged that Jackson hired a team that was all Muslim and revealed that the King of Pop was drawn by Islam, that he loved hearing the Muslim call to prayer and eagerly read books on Islam.

[19] Caroline Graham, 'No, I Didn't Kill Michael. He Did It Himself… With A Massive Overdose Using His Own Stash', *The Mail on Sunday*, 24 November 2013.

[20] Part of the bedtime routine was for Dr Murray to sit by Jackson's bed and read travel magazines or medical journals to him. In an interview with *The Mail on Sunday* in 2013, Murray said, 'In the beginning we talked a lot about medicine. He was fascinated by human anomalies and congenital malformations. He was obsessed by the Elephant Man'. (A rumour in 1987 suggested Jackson had tried to buy the skeleton of John Merrick, the Elephant Man, from the Royal London Hospital.)

[21] Dr Murray described Jackson's veins as being 'sclerotic'. This means his veins, particularly around normal IV sites, such as arms and hands, had become hardened through excessive injections and, consequently, it was becoming increasingly difficult to administer further injections in these sites.

[22] Timm Woolley and Randy Phillips of AEG Live had been cc'd throughout this email exchange, as had Dr Murray. Another recipient was Shawn Trell, AEG Live's Senior Vice President. Trell had been active in the issuing of the contract to Jackson since January. One earlier email exchange between Trell and Ted Firke, the General Counsel for AEG, seems to illustrate the lack of respect AEG representatives had towards Michael Jackson.

In January 2009, Trell revealed to Firke that he was going to Jackson's home to sign the contracts. 'Does this mean you get to meet the freak?' Firke emailed back to Trell, who replied, 'Apparently. Not sure how I feel about that. Interesting for sure, but kind of creepy.'

[23] Matilda Battersby, 'Prince Jackson Claims Late Father Michael Thought "This Is It" Rehearsals Were Going To Kill Him', *The Independent*, 27 June 2013.

[24] Alan Duke, '"They're Going To Kill Me", Michael Jackson Told Son', CNN, 27 June 2013.

[25] Dr Murray had two phones: one was an iPhone under a contract from AT&T, the other was a Sprint phone.

[26] In an interview with Caroline Graham of *The Mail on Sunday* on 24 November 2013 Murray revealed that Jackson always wore dark trousers because, '...after he went to the toilet he would drip for hours'. He continued, 'I held his penis every night. I had to put a condom catheter on him because Michael dripped urine. He had a loss of sensation and was incontinent'. However, in his interview with the LAPD on 27 June 2009, following Michael Jackson's death, Dr Murray said, 'Mr Jackson had trouble urinating...In the course of the last three months, he explained to me that when he went to the bathroom, it would take him hours to urinate'. Murray had prescribed the singer Flomax as he thought Jackson had benign prostatic hypertrophy and this medication would shrink Jackson's prostate and allow him to urinate properly.

[27] Kai Chase had been a professional chef for 17 years, having studied in Paris at the prestigious Le Cordon Bleu. Upon returning to the USA she started her own catering company and had since cooked for clients such as Bernie Mac, Macy Gray and President Barack Obama. Her catering company closed down in 2001, following 9/11, and she entered the private chef world. She had started work for Jackson at the end of March, following a meeting with Michael Amir Williams and a second interview at Carolwood held solely by Jackson's three children. She would cook Jackson lots of lean proteins, such as chicken, fish and turkey, but never pork or beef, and lots of vegetables as well as juices, especially beet juice. But Jackson's favourite meal she cooked him was tacos made out of blue corn tortilla shells, vegan ground beef and guacamole salsa. In the first week of May, Chase was let go by Michael Amir Williams owing to a change of management in Jackson's hierarchy who were trying to get different employees to join Jackson in London, but Chase was re-hired on 2 June when Jackson's children requested her back. When she retuned, Chase noticed that Jackson '…looked very different. He appeared very weak. He looked much thinner, he looked undernourished, and he didn't look as well as I had seen him in April.' In June, Chase also witnessed Jackson's son, Prince, having to help his father up the stairs, as the singer was weak from the toll his rehearsals and schedule was having on him.

[28] The children were home-schooled from Monday to Friday with a teacher coming in every morning and leaving in the afternoon, after which they were allowed to do activities, such as all go to the theatre, and were encouraged to write about their experiences creatively when they returned home.

[29] Propofol has been referred to as 'milk of amnesia', a play on the term 'milk of magnesia', owing to its milk-like appearance and use as an anaesthetic.

[30] At this point in time, Murray hadn't received any money at all from AEG Live, despite his contract and oral agreements stating that he should have been paid his first instalment on 15 May and his second on 15 June.

[31] A pulse oximeter is a sensor device that is placed on a patient's fingertip to monitor the percentage of haemoglobin that is oxygen-saturated within a patient. Oxygen saturation should always be above 95 per cent.

[32] In his book, *My Friend Michael*, Frank Cascio wrote, 'Over the years I had grown accustomed to seeing doctors coming and going, particularly during tours, when Michael was under great stress and needed help falling asleep. I thought he was simply someone who had serious medical problems and used drugs to treat them.'

[33] Los Angeles Police Department, recorded interview of Conrad Murry, 27 June 2009.

[34] While he was on the phone, Murray also received a text at 10:36am from Texas.

[35] Bob Russell had been treated by Dr Murray following a heart attack in Las Vegas. Russell was convinced that Murray had saved his life and felt that initially, he was getting the best care in the world from Dr Murray. But all this changed after Murray sent out the letter to his patients telling them that he would be leaving his practice to follow a once-in-a-lifetime opportunity. From then

on, Russell felt abandoned by Murray at a critical point in his recovery and even threatened Murray with legal action to get the recovery care he felt he was entitled to from the doctor.

9

---

[1] Alvarez also happened to have recently given birth to Murray's seventh child, but his first by her.

[2] David Gardner, 'Revealed: Conrad Murray's Secret Double Life As A Deadbeat Dad And Compulsive Womaniser To The Stars', *Daily Mail*, 8 November 2011.

[3] Christina Caron, 'Conrad Murray's Girlfriends Testify', ABC News, 4 October 2011.

[4] Pete Samson, 'Jacko Might Still Be Alive if Randy Doc Hadn't Been On Phone To Me', *The Sun*, 2011.

[5] Pete Samson, 'Jacko Might Still Be Alive if Randy Doc Hadn't Been On Phone To Me', *The Sun*, 2011.

[6] Official court records, People v. Conrad Murray, testimony of Sade Anding, 7 January 2011.

[7] *Michael Jackson & The Doctor: A Fatal Friendship*, October Films, 2009.

[8] CPR is a first-aid technique that is used to keep blood and oxygen circulating within the body of a patient who is not breathing properly or whose heart has stopped by using chest compressions with rescue breaths.

[9] His waist measurement at this point was only 27 inches.

[10] Grace Rwaramba had been sacked in December 2008 for a second and final time after she had previously been sacked for supposedly calling in Jackson's mother, Katherine, and his sister, Janet, in an effort to get the singer to address his drug addiction. Michael Jackson accused her of betraying his trust after she had worked for him for ten years. Rwaramba claimed that Jackson had such a reliance on drugs that she had to frequently pump his stomach.

[11] Alberto Alvarez and Faheem Muhammad were the only security detail within the grounds of Carolwood on 25 June. Additional security guards were detailed to 'outside security'. These included, Derrick Cleveland, Eric and Isaac Muhammad, and Larry and Lewis Muhammad. They assumed security duty at the gates of the mansion and in the grounds.

[12] Faheem Muhammad was the driver who would take Michael Jackson on his visits to the clinic of Dr Klein in Beverly Hills. Jackson told Faheem that he had a skin condition which is why he had to see this doctor so often, but Faheem recalled Jackson being 'intoxicated' after his treatments by Klein and even said he saw the singer being brought downstairs by one of Klein's office staff, who turned out to be Jason Pfeiffer.

[13] In her testimony during the trial, Kai Chase said she didn't go to get security as instructed because Prince was in her eyesight and she felt the best thing to do was to get Prince instead of running outside to get security. In the Jackson v. AEG trial, Chase said, 'I went and got Prince because it was such a serious matter and he looked very panic-stricken. At that moment the fastest

thing I could think of is go get the person that's in my eyesight. I didn't think it would have made any sense for me to drop what I was doing to go out to the security booth and look for security that may or may not have even been there.'

[14] Propofol is not a benzodiazepine, but Lorazepam and Diazepam are.

[15] In medical terms, the phrase autotransfusion is strictly used to describe a procedure where blood is collected from an active bleeding site and blood is reinfused into the same patient for maintenance of blood volume.

[16] Official court records, People vs. Conrad Murry, testimony of Michael Amir Williams.

[17] Faheem Muhammad had only been upstairs at Carolwood once or twice before and only then when asked.

[18] In his book, *Untouchable*, author Randall Sullivan suggests this language could be 'Patois Trinidad', an uncommon foreign language spoken by many residents of Dr Murray's home country.

[19] The engine would remain parked outside the property on the road with one crew member staying with it at all times.

[20] Highly experienced, Richard Senneff is no longer assigned as a firefighter-paramedic but has been promoted to an instructor at the LAFD Academy where he teaches emergency medical treatment to experienced firefighters over three-day courses.

[21] Known within the fire department by the slang term of 'run sheets'.

[22] This referral to removing an IV needle from Jackson's leg contradicts with the testimony of the paramedics who say they found an IV with a needle connected to Jackson, although it wasn't working correctly.

[23] Alberto Alvarez testified that this was not the first time that he had seen Murray with this device. He had seen Murray with it a few days earlier when the doctor had come into the security trailer asking for some batteries, which Isaac Muhammad provided him with.

[24] Prince Jackson recalled at the 2013 Katherine Jackson v. AEG Live trial, 'My sister was screaming the whole time saying she wants her daddy'. NBC News, 'Michael Jackson's Son Tears Up In Court As He Recalls Dad's Death' by Maria Elena Fernandez, 26 June 2013.

[25] Senneff testified that one of the security detail said to him, 'Somebody should do CPR'. If this was the case, how did the security guards outside know what was going on in Jackson's room?

[26] At the trial in 2013 of Katherine Jackson v. AEG Live, Prince Jackson, by now 16 years old, took the witness stand and described what he saw when he entered the bedroom: 'My dad was hanging halfway off the bed and his eyes were rolling back in his head. Murray was doing CPR'. NBC News, 'Michael Jackson's Son Tears Up In Court As He Recalls Dad's Death' by Maria Elena Fernandez, 26 June 2013.

[27] Dr Murray failed to notify the paramedics that he was a cardiologist.

[28] Murray appeared specific in the bottles and vials that he instructed Alvarez to earlier put in bags and had not made any effort to conceal the vials and bottles scattered elsewhere around the room.

[29] Martin Blount testified that Dr Murray told him that '…the patient has gone to his private physician probably like a week prior to this episode.' Who was Murray referring to? He had considered himself as Jackson's private physician for some weeks now, so whom was he suggesting? It could possibly be Dr Klein. If so, was it an attempt by Dr Murray to plant the seed of another physician being responsible, in some way, for Jackson's death?

[30] Dr Murray had previously purchased an Ambu Bag. It was noted in one of his earlier medical equipment orders, but it appears he never used it at this critical time.

[31] Martin Blount recalled overhearing Murray tell Senneff that Jackson had been down '…about a minute' before calling 911.

[32] To estimate the time of death, the temperature of the body is used to make approximations. Following the moment of death, the body does not begin cooling immediately as some heat production occurs after death. The time before the body begins to cool is known as the 'temperature plateau'. This can last from one to six hours after death. In order to accurately determine the length of time that has elapsed since death the investigator would need to know the temperature at death and the length of the temperature plateau. Drugs can cause the temperature of

a living person to be higher than normal. Consequently, if the person dies while under the influence of drugs, it is likely that their body temperature will have started out significantly higher than normal. For Senneff to have noticed that Jackson was cool to the touch, taking into account Jackson's physiological and chemical state, it is not unreasonable to assume that Jackson had been dead for at least 90 minutes, and that is a conservative estimate. He could have been dead even longer as the room he was in was unusually hot. In her book, *Starting Over*, LaToya Jackson commented that, when she visited Carolwood on the evening following her brother's passing, the room was excessively hot posing the question – was the room kept hotter than normal in order to keep Jackson's body warm and so hide the actual time of death?

[33] Jackson's blood had become depleted of oxygen, signalling heart failure.

[34] An EKG machine tests for problems with the electrical activity of the heart. It translates the heart's electrical activity into line tracings on paper through a series of spikes and dips. No sign of activity will result in a flat line.

[35] A capnography reading measures the carbon dioxide levels from the body.

[36] They administered three rounds of starter drugs at 12:34pm, 12:36pm and 12:40pm.

[37] Veins are much more difficult to find in a patient when blood has not been circulating for some time.

[38] In his interview to LAPD, Dr Murray said he started CPR again and this was effective and, it was during this CPR, that he felt Jackson's femoral pulses with his compressions. He said, 'So I knew that his circulation was intact, was being kept going with my effort.' It was when Dr Murray checked for Jackson's femoral pulse in his groin area that Martin Blount first noticed the singer's condom catheter.

[39] Based on Los Angeles County EMS protocols, a patient found without a pulse, not breathing, pupils fixed and dilated, and having received attempted resuscitation for more than 20 minutes with no response to the resuscitation efforts can be pronounced dead in the field.

[40] Bicarbonate can be used to combat acidosis in a patient having a cardiac arrest. It works by mixing with lactic acid that forms in low perfusion states and in periods of inadequate oxygenation, such as cardiac arrest, converts into a form of carbonic acid that turns into carbon dioxide, which, in turn, is expelled through the lungs during ventilation. A central line is a long, thin flexible tube used to give medicines, fluids, nutrients or blood products through a catheter inserted into the arm or chest, through the skin and into a large vein. Magnesium has been investigated as a first line drug in cardiac arrest in addition to the standard interventions as per advanced life support guidelines but no benefit was found in either out of hospital or in hospital cardiac arrest according to a report by P. Kaye & I. O'Sullivan of Bristol Royal Infirmary published in the *Emergency Medical Journal*, Volume 19, Issue 4, 2002.

[41] Some of these treatments and routines were beyond the scope of a paramedic's training and they didn't carry the proper equipment with them.

10

---

[1] 2mg of Lorazepam would not typically cause a cardiac arrest in an adult male. It would typically cause respiratory depression to which the doctor would report that the patient is not breathing well.

[2] TMZ.com was a news site backed by Time Warner. It was launched in December 2005 as a joint venture between Telepictures Productions, a division of Warner Brothers, and AOL, which are both divisions of Time Warner. The name TMZ stands for 'thirty mile zone' – a 1960s Hollywood studio reference to location filming that has come to mean the area of Los Angeles most thickly populated with celebrities.

[3] Flomax is usually used for urinary problems in someone who has an enlarged prostate. The drug assists those who go to the toilet frequently as it relaxes the urinary muscle. During the autopsy on Jackson, it was revealed that he was suffering from an enlarged prostate that would have made it difficult for him to urinate. When treating Jackson, Murray used both a condom catheter on the singer's penis and incontinence sheets on his bed. Murray alluded to the singer suffering from incontinence, but an enlarged prostate would create the opposite of incontinence and make it harder for Jackson to urinate. Therefore, the condom catheter and incontinence sheets must have been used when the singer was sleeping under the influence of anaesthetic and unable to control his urinary movements.

[4] Doctors say that people can normally survive for up to four minutes after they stop breathing. After four minutes they are likely to suffer permanent brain damage even if they do survive.

If a person loses their pulse for more than six minutes and then requires more than 15 minutes of CPR to regain an adequate pulse, then there's very little chance of meaningful recovery according to Romergryko Geocadin, Director of the Neurosciences Critical Care Unit at John Hopkins Bayview. He says, 'By the time an ambulance arrives and paramedics use a defibrillator, most of those who are initially resuscitated will die in the hospital or remain in a vegetative state. Of the less than 20% of people who are successfully resuscitated, less than 10% recover their full cognitive abilities.' The odds were stacked against Jackson, even in hospital. *Hopkins Medicine*, Spring/ Summer 2009.

[5] Randy Phillips was actually in Westwood at the dry cleaners when he received the call from Frank Dileo.

[6] Vasopressin is an antidiuretic hormone, which is responsible for regulating plasma osmolality and volume. It has become increasingly important in the critical care environment in the management of, amongst other conditions, cardiac arrest. It acts as a neurotransmitter in the brain to control circadian rhythm, thermoregulation and adrenocorticotrophic hormone release.

[7] Dr Cooper confirmed that in her experience as a medical doctor, she had never been involved in, witnessed or been present in a situation where a medical doctor administered Propofol in a home setting.

[8] During the trial into Jackson's death, Dr Cooper revealed that she had been trained to give a certain amount of Propofol for procedural sedation. She described how she typically starts with a dose of 1mg per kg weight of the patient and that dose is usually

sufficient, so based on those calculations, someone weighing approximately 136lbs (60kg), as Jackson did at the time of his death, a 60mg dose would be sufficient for procedural sedation. Upon further questioning, Dr Cooper stated that, hypothetically, she would expect 60mg of Propofol in Jackson to sedate him for about 10–20 minutes. When pressed by DA Walgren as to whether a dose of 25mg of Propofol given to Jackson between 10:40am and 10:50am would or would not produce breathing problems in the singer at 12:00pm, she said, 'I wouldn't know why one would be using a medicine that is used to produce deep sedation and not give a dose that is sedating. 25mg, I wouldn't expect to have that effect.' She continued, 'If you give Propofol and you give an additional medicine that produces sedation, a benzodiazepine, or if you are giving narcotic medications, sometimes we do when we are doing procedural sedation, we commonly do that, you can have deeper levels of sedation than you anticipate.' She would later say that if she had known about the benzodiazepines and Propofol that Murray had given to Jackson it would have given her a clearer indication of what had occurred given her knowledge of the interactive effects of the drugs.

[9] ABC News, 'Conrad Murray Told Medics That He Was Treating MJ For Dehydration' by Jim Avila, Bryan Lavietes, Kaitlyn Folmer & Jessica Hopper, 30 September 2011.

[10] In the 27 March 2010 Joseph Jackson v. Conrad Murray legal proceedings, Joe Jackson claimed, 'At 13:21 hours or 1:21pm, the nurses and physicians at UCLA detected a weak femoral pulse and cardiac activity for Michael Jackson. At 13:22 hours he showed cardiac activity. At 13:33 he showed a weak ventricular rhythm (contracting of the lower heart chambers). Dr Cooper

reported that when Michael Jackson was intubated with an endotrachial tube he had good breath sounds and 'The initial cardiac rhythm appeared to be wide and slow in the 40s'. At 13:52 or 1:52pm he had a pulse of 53 beats per minute, with a MAE complex (major arrhythmic event).'

[11] Travis Payne recalled talking to Kenny Ortega on the phone as he was making his way down Sunset Boulevard on the afternoon of 25 June when news was beginning to emerge on the radio and Ortega said to Payne 'You know how that goes – you know how the media is'. MTV News, 'Michael Jackson's *This Is It* Crew On His Last Days' by Jocelyn Vena, 27 October 2009.

[12] MTV News, 'Michael Jackson's *This Is It* Crew On His Last Days' by Jocelyn Vena, 27 October 2009.

[13] Dr Adrian Kantrowitz introduced the intra-aortic balloon-pump in the late 1960s and it has since become the most widely used form of mechanical circulatory support. It consists of a polyethylene balloon mounted on a catheter, which is generally inserted into the aorta, the main artery in the human body originating from the left ventricle of the heart and extending down to the abdomen, through a femoral artery in the leg. The balloon inflates and deflates within the aorta to increase blood flow through a combination of a vacuum effect and retrograde flow. These actions combine to decrease myocardial oxygen demand and increase myocardial oxygen supply (*Texas Heart Institute*).

[14] A balloon-pump will not reverse the effects of the drugs, it will only help the heart to function better in these circumstances. Balloon-pumps are rarely used when there is no sign of a pulse.

Balloon-pumps do not make the heart beat but, instead, allow a beating heart to work less by giving it a break by assuming its workload briefly. Therefore, it appears there was no reason to use the balloon-pump in this instance, as there was no sign of a pulse, except to pacify Murray's request to 'not give up easily'.

[15] Michael Jackson's father, Joe, didn't attend the hospital at the time of his son's death as he was in another US State.

[16] Jocelyn Vena, 'Michael Jackson's "This Is It" Crew On His Last Days', MTV News, 27 October 2009.

[17] In his testimony at the People v. Conrad Murray trial, Amir Williams said, 'I knew we couldn't go back to the house. I'm not a detective, but I knew that is something we couldn't do.'

[18] Despite allegations that Joe Jackson beat Michael, the strained relationship between them and the papers running headlines such as 'Joe Jackson "No Longer a Part of the Family"', *New York Post*, 31 August 2014; Bill Whitfield, co-author of the book *Remember The Time* wrote about Joe Jackson, 'That was another thing Grace [Rwaramba] said that stuck with me. She said the only person who never stole from Michael Jackson was his father'.

[19] Jermaine's statement caused much speculation about Michael Jackson's religion at the time of his death with the inclusion of his phrase, 'May Allah be with you'. *The New York Times* published Jermaine's final statement as, 'May our love be with you always' on 26 June 2009. A day later it acknowledged that it had misreported the statement. Zahed Amanullah wrote in an obituary at altmuslim.com that, with those words, '…Michael's association with Islam and Muslims, wanted or not, was made eternal.'

[20] Perez Hilton is a showbiz gossip blogger whose real name is Mario Lavandeira. On 25 June, when reports of Jackson being rushed to hospital began to emerge, Hilton suggested it was a publicity stunt. 'Supposedly, the singer went into cardiac arrest. We are dubious! Either he's lying or making himself sick,' Hilton wrote on his blog before imploring ticket holders to, 'get your money back!' Reacting angrily to this, Jackson fans and other bloggers responded quickly on other websites with messages such as, 'That guy is seriously sick in the head. He does more harm than good and he needs to get off the Internet now.'

[21] Less than two hours after Madonna's statement was released, one of her business partners, Guy O'Seary released a claim of his own on Twitter stating Madonna intended to make an appearance at one of Jackson's O2 shows in London.

[22] *OK!* Magazine alone paid $500,000 for the photo.

[23] Anita Singh, 'Michael Jackson's Weird & Wonderful Life', *The Telegraph*, 26 June 2009.

[24] Susan Donaldson James, 'Friend Says Michael Jackson Battled Demerol Addiction', ABC News, 26 June 2009.

[25] Jessica Mulvihill Moran and Karlie Poulit, 'Demerol: Did It Cause Michael Jackson's Death?', Fox News, 26 June 2009.

11

[1] The 'other' Michael Jackson honoured in Hollywood was born in London on 16 April 1934. After the Second World War, his

family moved to South Africa and then to the USA in 1958. Jackson began hosting radio shows in San Francisco, playing chart music, before ending up in Los Angeles hosting a talk show on KABC for over three decades. In 2003 he was inducted into the Radio Hall of Fame. He is married to the daughter of the actor Alan Ladd. When he heard that people had been laying flowers on his Hollywood star rather than that of the singer he said on his website: 'I am willingly loan(ing) it to him and, if it would bring him back, he can have it. He was a real star.'

[2] Sky News, 'Grieving Jackson Fans "Commit Suicide"', 29 June 2009.

[3] In 2014, a French judge ruled that Dr Murray should pay five Michael Jackson fans one Euro in 'emotional damages' as they were distraught following the singer's death. Reuters said, 'The court ruling in the city of Orleans capped a two-year struggle by a group of 30 French, Swiss and Belgian fans of the pop star for legal recognition of their loss'. The lawyer for the fans, Emmanuel Ludot said the ruling would be communicated to Murray and commented that all parties in the proceedings in France had found the case amusing. 'I respected the suffering of the plaintiffs,' Ludot said, 'but the process wasn't easy because of all the sniggering.' Reuters, 'Michael Jackson Doctor Must Pay Grieving Fans 1 Euro: French Judge', 11 February 2014.

[4] Reuters, 'Michael Jackson Doctor Must Pay Grieving Fans 1 Euro: French Judge', 11 February 2014.

[5] Lakshmanan Sathyavagiswaran was a star witness at the 1995 O.J. Simpson murder trial.

[6] Based on these measurements, Jackson had a perfectly normal BMI (body mass index).

[7] Coronary artery atherosclerosis is the single largest killer of men and women in the USA and is the principal cause of coronary heart disease. It is a condition where the arteries become clogged up by fatty substances known as plaques or atheroma which cause the arteries to harden and narrow, restricting blood flow which can damage organs and stop them functioning properly. If the plaque ruptures it can cause a blood clot, which can block the blood supply to the heart, triggering a heart attack.

[8] A bandage was present on the tip of Jackson's nose during the autopsy.

[9] Andrew Blankstein, Rong-Gong Lin II, Harriet Ryand and Scott Gold, 'Michael Jackson's Doctor Interviewed by LAPD', *Los Angeles Times*, 28 June 2009.

[10] Paul Farhi, 'Investigators in Michael Jackson's Death Turn Attention to His Doctor', *The Washington Post*, 28 June 2009.

[11] TMZ.com, 'Second Autopsy For Michael Jackson', 27 June 2009.

[12] Alice Park 'What Killed Michael? What The Autopsy Could Reveal', *Time* magazine, 30 June 2009.

[13] Paul Thompson and David Harrison, 'Michael Jackson: Second Post Mortem Examination Taking Place', *The Telegraph*, 28 June 2009.

[14] Confused by the term 'milk', Detective Smith asked Murray if it was 'Hot milk or warm or just…' before he was advised by Murray that it was the term Jackson used for Propofol.

[15] Dr Murray refers in his interview to an instance in Las Vegas a few months previously when Michael Amir Williams had called Murray out of the blue saying Jackson wanted to speak with him urgently. When Dr Murray spoke with Jackson, it was clear the singer was in need of Diprivan (Propofol) to help him sleep. Murray told him he couldn't get any but, between them, they identified a Dr Adams in Las Vegas who, apparently, had given Jackson Propofol before and Murray allowed Dr Adams to use his office on a Sunday to give Jackson the Propofol he needed.

[16] Nancy Grace, 'DEA Joins Jackson Death Investigations', CNN, 2 July 2009.

[17] Over 1.2 million people worldwide entered the online lottery for the tickets to Jackson's memorial. Officials in Los Angeles released a statement asking fans who failed to get tickets to stay away from the city amid fears it would be swamped.

[18] Caroline Graham and Daniel Boffey, 'Jackson Family Fallout', *Daily Mail*, 5 July 2009.

[19] At this point, Katherine Jackson had temporary legal guardianship of Jackson's children.

[20] Michael Jackson's 2002 will stated that his entire estate be placed in a trust to be executed by three trusted advisors. This enabled Jackson to keep his wishes private rather than avoiding probate, a very public process; a trust is rarely made public while a will

generally is. Jackson's assets almost entirely consisted of assets that were non-cash and non-liquid, but totalled $567.6 million. These included his share of the Sony/ATV Music Publishing catalogue – valued at $390.6 million – his Neverland ranch and 'other entities'.

21 The provisions of the Michael Jackson Family Trust stated that the first 20 per cent of his estate is to be left to one or more children's charities, selected by a committee consisting of his mother and co-trustees. After deductions for estate taxes, medical bills, funeral expenses, attorney's fees and other costs incurred in settling Jackson's estate, the remaining estate was to be distributed 50 per cent equally amongst his three children and 50 per cent to his mother. Katherine's 50 per cent was to be held in a lifetime trust for her benefit with Branca and McClain serving as co-trustees. If Branca, McClain and Siegel were all not able to serve as trustees then Nations Bank, now known as Bank of America, would become trustee.

22 TMZ.com also verified this when they spoke with the Reverend Al Sharpton's representative, Rachel Noerdlinger, who confirmed Jackson was with Sharpton in New York on 6 and 9 July. So is it realistic to think he flew to Los Angeles and back over a weekend to sign a document?

23 Michael Jackson had hired corporate lawyer David LeGrand for a three-month period in 2003. His task was to sort out confusion over Jackson's business interests. BBC News, 'Jackson Trial: week 11', 13 May 2005.

24 Leonard Rowe, *What Really Happened To Michael Jackson: The Evil Side of the Entertainment Industry* (Linell-Diamond Enterprises, 2010).

[25] Mike Fleeman and Champ Clark, 'Debbie Rowe Won't Attend Michael Jackson Memorial' ,*The People*, 7 July 2009.

[26] P.J. Huffstutter and Richard Fausset, 'Around The World, A Shared Moment of Missing Michael', *Los Angeles Times*, 8 July 2009.

[27] Michael Jackson recorded 'Smile' for his 1995 double album, *HIStory: Past, Present and Future* and it was planned to be released as the eighth single from the album in 1998 but was withdrawn.

[28] As it happened, Jackson was eventually buried on 3 September 2009, 10 weeks to the day after his death. Two hundred family and close friends watched as Jackson's children placed a golden crown on his coffin at the beginning of a 75-minute service which ended with Jackson's brothers, all wearing suits with their brother's signature black armband and one sequined glove, carrying the casket into the Great Mausoleum.

[29] Also buried here is *Gunsmoke* actor, James Arness, sex-symbol Jean Harlow, comedian Red Skelton, the head of MGM Studios in its heyday – Irving Thalberg, acting superstars Clark Gable and Carole Lombard, as well as W.C. Fields, Lon Chaney and 'Hopalong Cassidy'. Jackson's great friend, Elizabeth Taylor was buried there following her death in 2011.

[30] Alan Duke, 'Lawyer: Manslaughter Evidence Sought At Jackson Doctor's Office', CNN, 23 July 2009

[31] Alan Duke, 'Jackson Family Aware Probe Could Be Criminal Case', CNN, 10 July 2009.

[32] Caroline Graham, '"Michael was Murdered… I Felt it From the Start"', *The Mail on Sunday*, 13 July 2009.

[33] J. Randy Taraborrelli, *Michael Jackson: The Magic and the Madness* (Sidgwick & Jackson, 1991).

[34] *The Poison Review*, 'Michael Jackson Toxicology Report Released', 13 February 2010.

[35] Joe and Katherine Jackson never officially divorced but have lived apart for several years.

[36] Stacy Brown, 'Joe Jackson "No Longer A Part of The Family"', *New York Post*, 31 August 2014.

[37] Stacy Brown, 'Joe Jackson "No Longer A Part of The Family"', *New York Post*, 31 August 2014.

[38] CBS News, 'Joe Jackson To Inherit Nothing From Son', 11 November 2009.

[39] *Extra*, 28 October 2009.

[40] Stacy Brown, 'Joe Jackson "No Longer A Part of The Family"', *New York Post*, 31 August 2014.

[41] In his book, 'Michael Jackson Inc.', Zack O'Malley Greenburg wrote, 'These ranged from petty to outrageous: the State of California sought $1,647.24 for its franchise tax board, a company called Intermedia Productions claimed an amount "not yet determined… in excess of $1 million", and a man named Erle Bonner insisted Michael Jackson had stolen his cure for herpes – and filed a suit for $1,109,000,503,600.00.'

[42] Mayer Nissim, '"This Is It" Has Unguarded Honesty', Digital Spy by, 22 October 2009.

[43] Mayer Nissim, '"This Is It" Has Unguarded Honesty', Digital Spy by, 22 October 2009.

[44] Ben Fritz, 'Sony Pictures To Produce Michael Jackson Film', *Los Angeles Times*, 11 August 2009.

[45] Lauren Streib, 'Michael Jackson's Money Machine', *Forbes*, 27 October 2009.

[46] *Box Office Mojo*, 'Opening weekend: $23,234,394 in 3,482 theatres'.

[47] In 2011, Justin Beiber's *Never Say Never* surpassed *This Is It* in terms of US lifetime gross in theatres with $73,013,910 compared to Jackson's $72,091,016. However, *Never Say Never* only made an additional $26,022,917 in foreign box office earnings while *This Is It* made an additional $189,092,572 at the foreign box office. (*Box Office Mojo*)

[48] Ben Sisario, 'Michael Jackson Estate Signs Deal With Sony', *New York Times*, 15 March 2010.

[49] Dorothy Pomerantz, 'Michael Jackson Leads Our List of The Top-Earning Dead Celebrities', *Forbes*, 23 October 2013.

[50] The breach of contract suit was eventually thrown out by a New York court who ruled that AllGood Entertainment Inc. only had an unenforceable letter of intent and not a firm agreement, and that there were '...no specific factual allegations' to support

AllGood's claim for tortuous interference and that there factual basis for fraud was '…at best, thin'.

[51] CBS's *60 Minutes*, 'Michael Jackson', produced by, 19 May 2013.

[52] The prosecutors were David Walgren and Deborah Brazil, both LA deputy district attorneys.

[53] Official court records, People v. Conrad Murray, testimony of Dr Christopher Rogers.

[54] On 12 October 2011, CNN reported that, 'Rogers bolstered the prosecution contention that Murray used a makeshift IV set-up to keep Jackson medicated and asleep, but that it malfunctioned while the doctor was not medicating the patient. The Propofol bottle that prosecutors contend Murray used for the IV drip had a slit in the rubber top that appeared to have been made with a medical spike, not a syringe needle. Murray could have pushed 'a spike into the rubber stopper and then the Propofol would flow out the end,' Rogers said. (CNN, 'Jurors View Michael Jackson Autopsy Photo' by Alan Duke, 12 October 2011.)

[55] Official court records, People v. Conrad Murray, testimony of Dr Alon Steinberg.

[56] The 17 deviations were: 1) The lack of the basic emergency airway equipment. 2) The lack of the advanced emergency airway equipment. 3) The lack of suction apparatus. 4) The lack of an IV infusion pump. 5) The lack of alarmed pulse oximetry. 6) The lack of, and failure to use, the blood pressure cuff.
7) The lack of electrocardiogram. 8) The lack of capnography.
9) The failure to maintain a doctor/patient relationship. 10)

The failure to continuously monitor the mental status of the patient. 11) The failure to continuously monitor the breathing of the patient. 12) The failure to continuously monitor and have available the blood pressure, pulse oximetry and heart monitors to maintain constant vigilant monitoring. 13) The failure to call 911 immediately. 14) The failure to document and chart at the outset of the procedure (egregious and unconscionable). 15) The failure to maintain written informed consent (egregious and unconscionable). 16) The failure to document throughout the course of sedation (egregious and unconscionable). 17) The failure to disclose to both the paramedics and UCLA the use of Propofol and the facts surrounding what Dr Murray witnessed at the arrest.

[57] Official court records, People v. Conrad Murray, testimony of Dr Steven Shafer.

[58] Initially, the Jackson family also sought $100 million in restitution payments to them from Dr Murray. But in January 2012, they withdrew their petition for restitution from Murray; it appears that the Jackson family realised there was simply no way that Murray could pay up. He had been sentenced to four years in jail, had his medical licence suspended and was bankrupt.

[59] The judge, Judge Pastor, also said he was particularly angered by a 'faux reality production', the television documentary called *Michael Jackson & The Doctor: A Fatal Friendship* that Murray had been secretly filming throughout the six-week trial. (*The Telegraph*, 'Michael Jackson's Doctor Conrad Murray Sentenced to Four Years for Involuntary Manslaughter' by Nick Allen, 29 November 2011.) The *Mail Online* also referred to this documentary, in particular how Murray might profit from it.

On 9 November 2009 an article appeared which said, 'Conrad Murray may be facing jail for the involuntary manslaughter of Michael Jackson – but he looks set to be a very rich man regardless of whether he goes to prison or how long he stays there. As the doctor awaits sentencing, it has emerged he took a starring role in a documentary about the King of Pop, which began filming almost immediately after his death in 2009. Entitled *Michael Jackson & The Doctor: A Fatal Friendship*, the film is set to be released this week and will reveal intimate details about the singer and his relationship with the disgraced doctor. While it is unclear exactly how much Murray will make from the film, worldwide interest in the trial suggests he will take a handsome cut of the profits.' The *Mail Online*, 'Murray The Millionaire? How Killer Doctor Is Set To Cash In On Michael Jackson's Death' by Sara Nelson and David Gardner, 9 November 2011.

[60] Miriam Hernandez, Subha Ravindhran, Carlos Granda, Elex Michaelson, Robert Holguin and Nannette Miranda, 'Conrad Murray Handed Maximum 4-Year Sentence', ABC, 29 November 2011.

[61] *Trinidad Daily Express*, 'Conrad Murray Not Hired By T&T Government', 12 March 2014.

[62] TMZ.com, 'Conrad Murray: I'm Back in the Medical Biz!', 12 March 2014.

[63] With the Jackson estate earning so much money since his death, it was only natural that before long, the USA tax authorities would want their share and in August 2013 reports emerged that the IRS were going to hit the estate with a $702 million bill which included $505 million in taxes and almost $197 million in

penalties. Attorney Howard Weitzman, on behalf of the estate, said that the estate had already paid over $100 million in taxes and was 'in full compliance with the tax laws'. Forbes commented that "Estate taxes are levied on the value of assets at the time of death, not at the time the tax bill is issued or announced. And as a result, it seems unlikely that the tax court will rule in favour of the IRS getting its $702 million". *Forbes*, 'Why The $702 Million IRS Tax Claim On Michael Jackson's Estate Won't Stand Up' by Zack O'Malley Greenburg, 23 August 2013.

[64] Cortney Harding, 'Michael Jackson, It's A Wonderful Afterlife', *Billboard*, 3 April 2010.

[65] Daisy Wyatt, 'Even In Death Jacko is Still Bigger Than Bieber', *The Independent*, 20 May 2013.

[66] Zach O'Malley Greenburg, 'Buying The Beatles: Inside Michael Jackson's Best Business Bet', *Forbes*, 2 June 2014.

12

[1] Owing to the increased overcrowding in USA state prisons, Murray had been allowed to serve his sentence in Los Angeles due to a new law aimed at easing overcrowding by placing non-violent offenders, such as Murray, to local facilities. Prior to his release, his lawyer Valerie Wass said, 'Dr Murray has not received any special treatment in jail and, in fact, has many less privileges than most inmates because of his notoriety.' She continued by saying that he '…is very much looking forward to his release and getting on with his life. However, the fact of his incarceration is increasingly difficult for him.'

[2] Caroline Graham, 'No, I Didn't Kill Michael. He Did It Himself', *The Mail on Sunday*, 24 November 2013.

[3] CNN, *Tonight*, 'Conrad Murray: "I'm Remorseful"', 26 June 2014.

[4] Bizarrely, Randy Phillips, the CEO of AEG Live, suggested that Michael *did* kill himself accidentally as Phillips' friend, Brenda Richie, the ex-wife of Lionel Richie, had spoken to a medium or had contacted Jackson's ghost herself and said that Michael had told her that it wasn't Dr Murray's fault and that he had accidentally killed himself. When Randy Phillips announced this evidence in the 2013 trial of Jackson's family seeking billions of dollars in damages against AEG Live, the LA County Superior Court Judge allowed his strange evidence to stand despite many in the courtroom bursting into laughter.

[5] At the AEG Live wrongful death trial, an entertainment industry expert suggested Jackson could have performed up to 260 shows globally as part of the 'This Is It' tour and would have earned himself $890 million.

[6] CNN, 'Conrad Murray Trial', 27 September 2011.

[7] In the book, *Remember The Time*, co-author and Jackson's former bodyguard, Bill Whitfield wrote: 'In my experience, nearly everything the media said about him was wrong pretty much all the time. I was actually with him when I heard that he died. The first time I heard that he died. We were in Virginia, driving. We'd just left Walmart and we were heading back to Chuck E. Cheese's to pick up the kids. Mr Jackson was sitting in the seat behind me when the radio announcer came on and interrupted the broadcast and said, "Hold on, we have an announcement… Hold

on just a minute, folks… Yes, we've just received breaking news that Michael Jackson, the King of Pop, has passed away." I turned around and said, "Mr. Jackson, did you hear that?" "No, what?" "On the radio. They're saying that you died." He just laughed. He said, "Yeah, I get that all the time."'

[8] *USA Today* reported that, 'A three-page document Walgren [the prosecutor] read aloud in court said that a print matching Murray's left index finger was found on a 100-milliliter bottle of Propofol. Los Angeles County Coroner's investigator, Elissa Fleak, testified Wednesday that she had found that bottle four days after Jackson's death within a saline IV bag. Both items were in a blue Costco Wholesale bag on the shelf of an armoire in the large walk-in closet adjoining the bedroom where Jackson was stricken, Fleak said.' *USA Today*, 'Fingerprint Mystery Surfaces In Jackson Doctor's Trial' by Martin Kasindorf, 6 October 2011.

[9] At the time of Jackson's death, Dr Murray hadn't been paid a dime. Despite having a contract made effective as of 1 May and expecting payments on the fifteenth of each month, not one of these payments had yet reached his bank account. Coincidentally or not, Dr Murray had only signed his contract of engagement on 24 June, less than 24 hours before the death of Jackson, and only after a series of amendments had been made to it. But, effectively, even this contract was not worth the paper it was written on, as Michael Jackson hadn't countersigned it. And unless he did so, there was no prospect of Dr Murray getting paid at all.

[10] AEG Live CEO Paul Gongaware had sent an email in which it said, 'We simply want to remind Murray that it's AEG, not MJ, who is paying his salary. We want to remind him what is expected of him.'

[11] On 20 May 2009, AEG Live announced that the opening four nights of the 'This Is It' tour had been delayed. The first show, scheduled for 8 July was pushed back by five nights and the three dates after that, on 10, 12, 14 July were rescheduled for March 2010.

[12] Jos Borsboom, *Michael Jackson: The Icon*(self-published, 2011).

[13] ABC News, 'Lawyer Points Finger At Jackson Drug "Enablers"', 26 June 2009.

[14] A roller-clamp is a small plastic roller that can be rolled counter-clockwise to close off primary IV tubing or clockwise to open it. It can also be manipulated to increase and decrease the flow of the IV solution and is easily moved with the thumb, making it a one-handed convenience in the administration of IV therapy.

[15] *Starting Over* by La Toya Jackson (Gallery Books, 2011).

[16] Official court records, People v. Conrad Murray, testimony of Dr Shafer, 20 October 2011.

[17] Official court records, People v. Conrad Murray, rebuttal testimony of Dr Shafer, 1 November 2011.

[18] Sir Arthur Conan Doyle, *The Sign of The Four* (1890).

[19] Alberto Alvarez recalled during the trial that he only saw Murray attach the pulse oximeter to Jackson when Alvarez had already reached the room after being called by Murray.

[20] A friend of Murray's daughter.

[21] Ian Halperin, 'How The King of Pop Made $1.5 billion… Over His Dead Body: Five Years On, Michael Jackson's Posthumous Fortune Has Broken All Records', *Mail Online*, 7 June 2014.

[22] In the book *Remember The Time*, co-author Bill Whitfield wrote, 'No one in his family was allowed past the front gate without advance notice, with the exception of Mrs Jackson, his mother.'

[23] Superior Court of the State of California, County of Los Angeles, Case No. YC052627, Ayscough & Marar v. Michael J. Jackson, 25 July 2006. In the same document it is revealed that Michael is 'generally not paying his debts as they become due' and lists a host of creditors including Attorney Zia Moddaber (owed $400,000), Attorney Brian Oxman (owed over $1,250,000), Attorney Michael Sydow (owed over $1,000,000), Criminal Defense Attorney Bob Sanger (owed over $1,200,00), Attorney Michael Abelson (owed over $100,00), Fortress (owed $325,000,000) and Attorneys Lavely & Singer (owed approximately $100,000). In addition claims of $48,000,000 and $64,000,000 were also pending and the document quotes that 'Mr Jackson was behind on paying his staff at Neverland'.

[24] Randall Sullivan, *Untouchable: The Strange Life & Tragic Death of Michael Jackson* (Grove/Atlantic, 2012).

[25] Randall Sullivan, 'Curse of Michael's Millions: How Michael Jackson's Family Preyed On his Wealth And Took It By The Vanload After His Death', *Daily Mail*, 10 November 2012.

[26] Katherine would apparently divide up the $25,000 cheque Michael sent to her every month among needy family members.

Daily Mail, 'Curse of Michael's Millions: How Michael Jackson's Family Preyed On his Wealth And Took It By The Vanload After His Death' by Randall Sullivan, 10 November 2012.

[27] John Patterson, 'Michael Jackson's Family: Where Did It All Go Wrong?', *The Guardian*, 14 August 2012.

[28] Jackson was the best man at Branca's first wedding. According to *The Hollywood Reporter*, Jackson brought, '…his chimp, Bubbles – clad in tuxedo – to the ceremony'. *The Hollywood Reporter*, 'Michael Jackson's Strange Final Days Revealed In Duelling Lawsuits' by Kim Masters, 19 July 2012.

[29] The insurance policy, with Lloyd's of London, covered '…the first 30 Concerts at the O2 Arena in London' and the artist covered in the document was Mark Jones, an alias of Michael Jackson.

[30] *Rolling Stone*, 'Michael Jackson Promoter Withdraws Insurance Claim Over Singer's Death', 12 September 2012.

[31] In 2010, Live Nation purchased Ticketmaster Entertainment for some $889 million to create a powerful live-music conglomerate.

[32] Philip Anschutz claimed he was selling the company as he was suffering from a debilitating back injury. But following corrective surgery, and a lack of bids that failed to reflect the 'uniqueness' of the company, he decided to abandon the auction. It is believed that Qatari Sports Investment and Colony Capital (the same company owned by Tom Barrack) made an all-cash offer of $7 billion, which was unsuccessful. (Bloomberg, 'Anschutz Says Luring NFL Team Is Priority After Ending AEG Sale' by Scott Soshnick, 15 March 2013.)

[33] Ray Waddell, '"This Is It" – The Inside Story of the Michael Jackson Movie', *Billboard*, 30 October 2009.

[34] In her book, *Starting Over*, La Toya Jackson writes how she is increasingly suspicious about the filming of rehearsals. She claims that, 'The sale of the rehearsal footage more than made up for any money lost on the shows, and that doesn't take into account distribution, ticket sales, or back-end participation for the film.' She goes on to write, 'Why would AEG film Michael's rehearsals when they had no agreement in place with him to make a concert film? And did they own the footage, or did Michael, as I suspect? If Michael owned it, how did AEG have the right to sell it, and would his children get a share of the profits from the sale that they deserved? When AEG found themselves in possession of the last footage of the legend performing on the nights before he passed, wasn't it a little heartless of them to immediately make plans to create a film that would allow them to profit from that material?'

[35] Chelsea White, 'This Is It! After Years of Teasing Michael Jackson's Neverland Ranch Is Up For Sale For An Astonishing $100m', *Daily Mail*, 29 May 2015.

[36] It transpired that Murray had DEA (Drug Enforcement Agency) numbers in Nevada and Texas, but didn't have one in California. He had to have registered with the DEA in any jurisdiction in which he would administer or prescribe controlled substances ranging from extra-strong cough syrup to powerful painkillers and, at the time of Jackson's death, he hadn't. (*Daily Telegraph*, 'Michael Jackson's Doctor Conrad Murray "Not Licensed To Adminster Strong Drugs"' by Tom Leonard, 7 July 2009.)

13

---

[1] Bobby Driscoll was discovered by chance at the age of five and a half in a barber shop in California. Over the next few years he had a golden career as a child actor. At the age of 13 he had his own star on the Hollywood Walk of Fame. But when he suffered severe acne at the age of 16, his film career stalled and shortly after voicing Peter Pan for Walt Disney in 1953, his contract was terminated. In the late 1950s and early 1960s he had numerous run-ins with the law, and was known to be a drug addict. In 1968, his body was found by two children in an abandoned tenement block in New York and, believed to be homeless and unclaimed, he was buried in a pauper's grave on Hart Island, New York.

[2] By bizarre coincidence, Gavin's mother Janet remarried. Her new husband is called Jay Jackson, so her married name is now Janet Jackson.

[3] The headlines in *The Mirror* on 5 April 2015 claimed that 'Michael Jackson Paid £134m Hush Money To Keep As Many As 20 Sex Abuse Victims Quiet, Layers Claim'. This story was related to the claims of abuse brought against Jackson's estate by Wade Robson and James Safechuck. On 28 May 2015, *The Guardian* reported that Wade Robson's May 2013 action, which saw him sue Jackson's estate over molestation, cannot be pursued as he had waited too long to file legal action. (*The Guardian*, 'Child Sex Abuse Claims Against Michael Jackson's Estate Ruled To be Too Late' by Associate Press, 28 May 2015.)

[4] Also known as the 'Country Club for the Dead'.

[5] Walt Disney, too ill to attend Eaton's funeral in 1966, was an honorary pallbearer at Eaton's funeral. Eaton was entombed in the Great Mausoleum and when Disney himself died a few weeks later, he was cremated and interred at Forest Lawn.

[6] Only family members are allowed inside the building.

[7] Following Jackson's death in June 2009, there were rumours that he was going to be buried at Neverland ranch in a resting place assigned to him there. The exact place where he would be buried at Neverland was going to be opposite the Neverland train station. It was a personal spot for the singer, as he would ride a train, named Katherine after his mother, from his house to the private zoo at Neverland. However, there were also concerns that Jackson's final resting place would be desecrated and vandalised or even his remains being exhumed, as there was still a campaign of hate against him following his child abuse charges. In addition, it is also a violation of Californian law to bury a body outside a cemetery, although Jermaine Jackson said that, 'The people who make the laws can change the laws'. Residents living near Neverland ranch would also be concerned, as a pilgrimage of fans would be anticipated, in excess of the 600,000 fans that visit Elvis Presley's tomb at Graceland.

[8] It is believed that Jackson's sarcophagus is located on Holly Terrace in the Sanctuary of Ascension at the end of the Corridor of Covenant.

[9] HollywoodLife.com, 'Why Conrad Murray Can't Visit The Grave' by Bonnie Fuller, 25 June 2014.

INDEX